Fodor's

THE BLACK HILLS
OF SOUTH DAKOTA

Welcome to the Black Hills

The Black Hills are a fascinating mix of Native American and Western history coupled with spectacular natural beauty. The region is known for Mount Rushmore, the iconic stone monument of four former U.S. presidents carved into the mountainside. You can also explore two national parks, Badlands and Wind Cave, and walk in the footsteps of Wild Bill Hickok and Calamity Jane in the old Western mining town of Deadwood. As you plan your upcoming travels, please confirm that places are still open and let us know when we need to make updates by writing to us at editors@fodors.com.

TOP REASONS TO GO

★ **Mount Rushmore.** This spectacular attraction is a must-visit.

★ **Outdoor Adventures.** Hiking, biking, ballooning, and horseback riding—the Black Hills has it all.

★ **Deadwood.** This historic Wild West mining town was and still is a party town.

★ **Badlands National Park.** Marvel at buttes, canyons, pinnacles, and spires in this 244,000-acre park.

★ **Needles Highway.** This 14-mile stretch in Custer State Park features stunning Black Hills scenery.

Contents

MAPS

Chapter 1

EXPERIENCE
THE BLACK HILLS
OF SOUTH DAKOTA

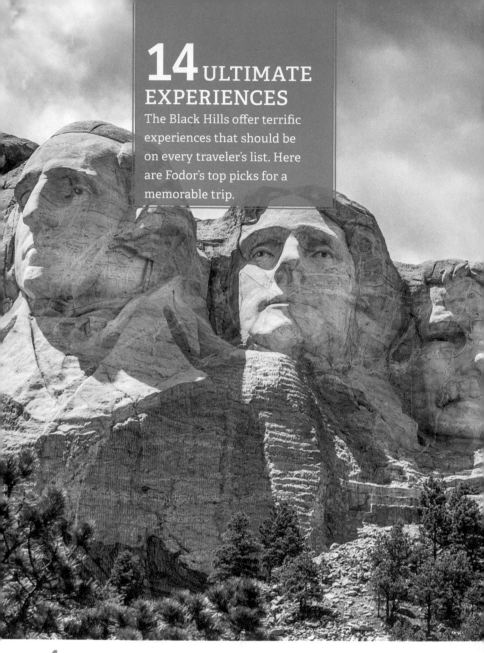

14 ULTIMATE EXPERIENCES

The Black Hills offer terrific experiences that should be on every traveler's list. Here are Fodor's top picks for a memorable trip.

1 Mount Rushmore

Recognized as America's Shrine of Democracy, Mount Rushmore National Memorial continues its role as the dominant visitor attraction. Carving the Presidential faces concluded in 1941. The iconic artistic and engineering tribute endures. *(Ch. 3)*

2 Visit Custer State Park

Explore more than 70,000 acres. Travel the 18-mile wildlife loop for the best view of 1,300 bison and other critters ranging from elk to prairie dogs. *(Ch. 5)*

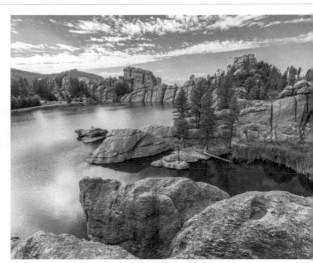

3 Hike the Black Hills

Hiking opportunities are everywhere; there are at least 450 miles of trails. The Mickelson and Centennial trails are more than 100 miles long. *(Ch. 3, 4, 5)*

4 Discover Deadwood

The gold rush was at full power by 1876, and rough-and-tumble Deadwood became the unofficial capital. Today, gambling, entertainment, and monthly festivals are reasons to visit. *(Ch. 4)*

5 Visit a gold mine

Miners pulled 40 million ounces of gold from the Homestake Mine in Lead (pronounced Leed). Digging stopped in 2001; scientists now operate a physics lab at the 4,800-foot level. *(Ch. 4)*

6 Sturgis Bike Rally

For 80 years, motorcycle enthusiasts from around the world have made the journey to Sturgis. What started as a weekend of flat track racing has grown into a 10-day, early-to-mid-August party. *(Ch. 4)*

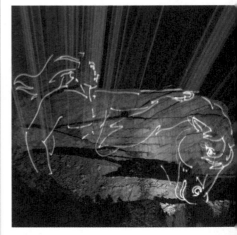

7 Crazy Horse Memorial

Sculptor Korczak Ziolkowski started the tribute to Lakota Chief Crazy Horse in 1947. Today, skilled carvers continue. See the carving and learn about Native American culture. *(Ch. 3)*

8 See a rodeo

In summer, there's a rodeo somewhere in the Black Hills—broncs, bulls, barrel racing, and more. The biggest are in Belle Fourche, Deadwood, and Rapid City. *(Ch. 3, 4, 5)*

9 Drive through Spearfish Canyon

In 19 miles see some of the best scenery in the Black Hills. The canyon is spectacular in the fall. There's trout fishing, hiking, rock climbing, and mining history. *(Ch. 4)*

10 Go fishing

There are 370 miles of streams plus seven lakes offering trout and 10 other game fish in this area. Some of the best and most accessible fishing is within the city limits of Rapid City and Spearfish. *(Ch. 3, 4, 5)*

11 Dinosaurs are still here

Get up close to ancient bones in the Black Hills at The Mammoth Site, Museum of Geology, Badlands Park's Visitor Center, and the Museum @ Black Hills Institute. *(Ch. 4, 5, 7)*

12 Reptile Gardens

Started by a tireless entrepreneur who really did hide a rattlesnake under his hat to surprise visitors, the Reptile Gardens now is the world's largest collection of reptiles. *(Ch. 3)*

13 See a show

Broadway standards and dramas are presented at the Black Hills Playhouse, Homestake Opera House, and Matthews Opera House. There are also chuckwagon supper venues. *(Ch. 3, 4, 5)*

14 Native American culture

More than 70,000 Native Americans live throughout South Dakota, so historic and
cultural connections are everywhere. *(Ch. 3, 5, 7)*

WHAT'S WHERE

1 Rapid City and the Central Black Hills. Rapid City is the de facto capital of the Black Hills. It's home to the commercial airport, multipurpose civic center, and regional hospital. With more than 80,000 residents, it's the hub for customary city services. Ellsworth Air Force Base is 12 miles east.

2 The Northern Black Hills. Hardrock gold mining was king for more than 125 years. The impact remains visible, especially in Deadwood and Lead (pronounced "Leed"). Visitors get to enjoy casino-style gambling, trendy dining, opera houses, museums, and hiking. The biggest event here is the Sturgis Rally.

3 The Southern Black Hills. Custer State Park is the jewel. Its 71,000 acres are home to 1,300 buffalo, deer, elk, bighorn sheep, prairie dogs, and even begging burros. Crazy Horse Memorial is near Custer, and farther south are Wind Cave National Park, Jewel Cave National Monument, and Hot Springs.

4 The Badlands. This region extends beyond the boundaries of the

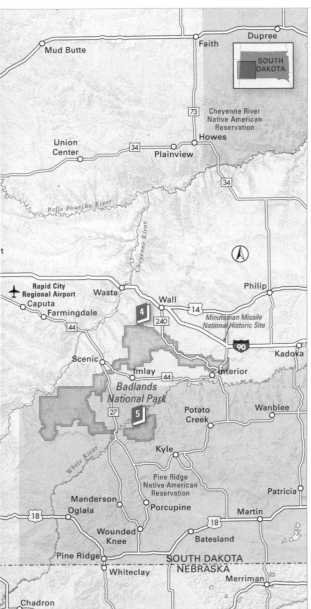

park with the same name and is rich with stories of Native American and settler history. The famed Wall Drug Store is along I–90, as is the Minuteman Missile National Historic Site that tells realities of the Cold War.

5 Badlands National Park. East of the Black Hills is a 250,000-acre national park you might mistake for a moonscape. The Badlands, a stretch of prairie where ancient sea beds have eroded into strange and colorful shapes, is a geologist's paradise.

6 Wind Cave National Park. The cave, located within a 28,000-acre park, is the world's sixth-longest. Rangers lead tours of its most interesting passageways. Wind Cave also offers more than 30 miles of hiking trails and chances to see buffalo, elk, deer, and other wildlife.

7 Cody, Sheridan, and Northern Wyoming. The wide-open plains of the Powder River Basin lie to the east of the Big Horn Mountains and to the west is the Big Horn Basin, nearly as arid as a desert. The storied town of Cody is located near Yellowstone National Park and Devils Tower is a must-see monument.

The Black Hills of South Dakota Today

The beauty of the Black Hills and symbolism of Mount Rushmore and the Crazy Horse Memorial are timeless. The visitor industry continues its competitive spirit to offer the best levels of quality and service possible. Businesses and government facilities, especially those emphasizing the outdoor experience for visitors, mostly remained open during the pandemic. Tourism numbers rebounded smartly in 2022, and held steady in 2023 despite weather and economic uncertainties.

MOUNT RUSHMORE UPGRADES

Contractors completed $9 million worth of infrastructure upgrades at Mount Rushmore National Memorial in 2021. The most noteworthy change involved widening and reconfiguring the popular and photogenic Avenue of Flags to enhance the sightline of the mountain sculpture. The colorful state and territorial flags remain part of the Rushmore experience, but now are on the sides of the pedestrian walkway that leads to the viewing terrace and amphitheater. Gutzon Borglum's studio, containing the artist's model of the monument, was remodeled three year prior.

LODGING LOWDOWN

Travelers should have no trouble finding a place to stay, especially if you favor corporate brand hotels with customary free breakfast. More than a dozen new or newish structures stand nearly parking lot-to-parking lot at Rapid City's I-90 exits 59 through 61. Lodging in Deadwood is very competitive, so you should see lots of attention paid to appearance and service. Similarly, popular names are in other Black Hills communities, just fewer in number. Cabin-style lodging remains popular, as are campsites for RVs, trailers, and tents—there are even glamping options. Expect rates to be seasonally high during the summer, with an added bump during the August Motorcycle Rally, including establishments outside of Sturgis as the Rally's impact extends throughout the Black Hills.

LIVE IN THE HILLS?

If you're interested in buying residential or investment property in the Black Hills, be ready to deal. The area continues to gain in popularity as a fresh and much less hectic locale for knowledge workers and those who have had their fill of big-city life. Home prices have soared, and availability is at a premium with an ongoing surge in population, estimated in 2023 to exceed 190,000 for the Black Hills region.

GET YOUR TICKETS

The Summit Arena at The Monument is a dazzling $130 million, 11,000-seat sports and entertainment arena in Rapid City that has become the region's new showpiece for top-tier concerts, tournaments, indoor rodeo, and other events that require up to 250,000 square feet of space. The expansive city-owned complex, formerly the smaller Rushmore Plaza Civic Center, also includes an adjacent theater, concert hall, exhibit rooms, and a 6,000-seat hockey rink.

TRAILS FOR EVERYONE

Mountain biking continues to gain in popularity, especially along the 109-mile Mickelson and 123-mile Centennial trails. Sharing of trails isn't contentious, but visitors should know that hikers, cyclists, and horseback riders are allowed on the long trails plus a network of others. The growing number of utility task vehicles and off-road motorcycles are restricted to gravel and paved roads, along with some designated off-road paths. Whether you're afoot or at the throttle, know and obey the rules so that everyone can enjoy. Also take note: E-bikes are out there in increasing numbers.

BET ON DEADWOOD

Deadwood holds its reign as party central for the Black Hills. Gambling revenues are on the increase after the lean pandemic years. The visitor and entertainment sectors work diligently to conduct at least one free, major event per month, usually centered on Main Street. The town's indoor Deadwood Grand concert venue maintains a full schedule of well-known acts. Voters in 2020 approved sports betting for Deadwood's brick-and-mortar casinos only (online wagering is not available), and those revenues have surged as well.

TAPROOMS ARE EASY TO FIND

Like the rest of the food and beverage sector, more than a dozen craft breweries in the Black Hills are finding their way. Rapid City has eight tap rooms, and the college town of Spearfish is home to three. One Spearfish brand, Crow Peak, is big enough to package several of its labels for sale on-site and elsewhere in the region. Sturgis Brewing Co. and Knuckle Brewing Co. (playing off the nickname of the famed Harley-Davidson V-Twin power plant) have the same capability in a pair of taproom-restaurants and in stores. Other taprooms are in Lead, Deadwood, Hill City, and Custer.

ART ALLEY

In Rapid City, the eclectic and recently renovated Art Alley sustains its popularity and quality of innovative street art. Electric and other infrastructure has been moved underground and the removal of utility poles has opened even more creative space for artists to add new work on the alley walls between 6th and 7th streets in the heart of downtown and its several upscale restaurants. The designs are provocative without being offensive and certainly catch the eye of visitors. Yes, it's spray-paint art, but done with

deliberation and permission of landlords who provide space for free expression.

DIGNITY: OF EARTH & SKY

If you are driving to the Black Hills westbound on I-90, when you reach the Missouri River, stop at the rest area between exits 263 and 265 to view the state's most prominent metal sculpture—*Dignity: of Earth & Sky*. The 50-foot-tall stainless-steel creation by artist-laureate Dale Lamphere of Sturgis pays tribute to the culture and strength of Lakota and Dakota people. In coming years, this creation and its site overlooking the river will grow in significance. Lamphere's creations can be found statewide, from the landmark Arc of Dreams spanning the Big Sioux River in Sioux Falls, to *The Hive*, centerpiece of a roundabout in Spearfish. The 20-foot tall *Hive* pays homage to Black Hills State University's mascot, the Yellow Jacket.

TO TOKE OR NOT TO TOKE

Recreational cannabis use remains a no-no in South Dakota, and all cannabis possession remains illegal under federal law. Residents and visitors with official, state-issued medical registration cards may possess up to three ounces of cannabis, and additional amounts of cannabis products, which may be purchased from nearly 100 licensed dispensaries across the state.

EXPANSION PROJECTS

Rapid City Regional Airport (RAP), a small air travel hub for western South Dakota, eastern Wyoming, and northwest Nebraska, is undertaking a 10-year, $200 million expansion to begin in 2024.

An $80 million project is transforming the 500 block of St. Joseph Street in downtown Rapid City. When completed in mid-2025, the 10-story building will include retail space, a Hyatt hotel, and a conference center.

What to Eat in the Black Hills

WALL DRUG DOUGHNUTS
A humble doughnut with a story: during the Cold War, when airmen maintaining Minuteman missiles traveled throughout western South Dakota they would take a break at Wall Drug: coffee and a doughnut were free. The missiles are gone. Doughnuts are still free to active or retired military.

NATIVE AMERICAN TACOS
A fusion of Native American and Mexican-style ingredients: fry bread topped with lettuce, chili, cheese, and sour cream. Find this local favorite at Cheyenne Crossing as you enter Spearfish Canyon or the Badlands National Park Visitor Center's café.

JEFFERSON'S ICE CREAM
From the historic kitchen at Monticello to Mount Rushmore, the ice-cream scoop shop that's part of the National Memorial's restaurant makes its vanilla from President Jefferson's original recipe. It's rich and the servings are generous, with toppings if you wish.

BUFFALO (BISON)
Don't worry about what name to use—"buffalo burger" in cafés or "bison" at an upscale evening place—the terms are interchangeable. To ship a box of the lean, flavorful delicacy home, visit the Wild Idea Buffalo shop in Rapid City.

TANKA BARS
Made in the region from a finely tuned recipe. Principal ingredients include bison and berries. Tanka is an energy bar that will really start your engine.

BEEF
Not many cattle are raised right in the Black Hills, but make no mistake, you're in the heart of High Plains ranch country. Beef, fixed any way you want, is on the menu of eateries everywhere, including Legends Steakhouse in Deadwood.

HOMESTEAD FAVORITES
The apple-centric German dessert *kuchen* is—by legislative decree—South Dakota's state dessert. The Czech pastry favorite *kolache* is not far behind. Hill City restaurants are the starting point for finding these humble reminders from what settlers called "the old country."

WALLEYE
Walleye is South Dakota's state fish, thriving in lakes across the state. Filets are tender, flaky, sweet, and buttery, with few bones. Many restaurant menus statewide feature savory batter-dipped and fried, grilled, or baked walleye dishes.

Chislic

CHOKEBERRIES

Try the jellies and syrups made from chokecherries that grow wild across the Dakotas. The small, deep-red-to-purple berries are tart, really tart, so generations of local cooks have learned how to soften the tang and sweeten the flavor. Locally grown chokecherries provide the distinctive, tangy sweet flavor to *wojapi* (pronounced "woe-jaw-pea"), which is the Lakota name for Native American berry sauce, most often spooned atop a freshly prepared piece of fry bread and served as a dessert treat.

CHISLIC

When the farm and ranch work is done, or it's time for locals to party, chislic—deep-fried skewered lamb chunks—are on the plate. Wash that down with a draft beer that's mellowed red with a slug of tomato juice, available at most bars. Chislic is an iconic dish in South Dakota.

PASTIES

What's for lunch when you're thousands of feet below the surface of the Black Hills, mining for gold? Answer: a hearty pasty (pahs-tee) from King's Bakery in Lead. Although underground mining stopped decades ago, descendants of the King family still make them—steak and potato, and a breakfast version with ham, egg, cheese, and potato. These meat pies, lunchbox favorites made from Cornish mining district recipes, are available at convenience stores and some coffee shops throughout the Hills.

SWEET TREATS

Sample delicious pastries and rolls at Jerry's Cakes & Donuts in Rapid City and indulge in all manner of chocolate treats at top shops like the Chubby Chipmunk in Deadwood and Rushmore Candy Co., on South Highway 16 between Rapid City and Keystone.

What to Buy in the Black Hills

TERMESPHERES
Unique among the many fine art offerings found in Black Hills galleries are spherical and polyhedron paintings by Dick Termes of Spearfish. Several of his larger works—several feet in diameter—are on display outdoors or inside large public buildings.

STURGIS JERKY
Sturgis jerky is thinly sliced beef from West River ranches spiced and dried to perfection. The recipe was refined in the mid-1960s by suggestions from Sturgis students who would stop by the family shop on their way home from school. It's got just the right amount of kick.

CRAFT BEER
If you like the beer from any of a dozen craft breweries, six-packs or "growlers," 32- or 64-ounce glass or aluminum vessels that function as a mini-kegs, are available from Crow Peak in Spearfish and Sturgis Brewing (six-packs are also available in stores).

BLACK HILLS GOLD
Black Hills–gold jewelry, with its distinctive grape-leaf patterns and tricolor design schemes, has been a high-end souvenir staple since the gold rush era. Increasingly, artisans include other precious metals and gemstones to create designs reflecting the region's cultural and agricultural symbols.

BIKER T-SHIRTS
In case you miss the Sturgis Motorcycle Rally, you can't miss biker T-shirts, leather garments of any design imaginable plus other souvenirs that reflect the live-free, open-road ethos of bikers. The color pallet favors black; however, a full spectrum of hues is available. Shops in downtown Sturgis have the best choice, naturally, but rest easy knowing that Rally swag priced for any pocketbook is available throughout the Black Hills. Discounts start as the Rally ends and continue through the fall.

ROCKS AND MINERALS
Nature left the Black Hills layered with some of the most diverse and collectible mineral specimens in the nation. Rock shops in Keystone, Hill City, and Custer have the best selections. Small fossils are part of the offerings in many stores. To learn the geology of the Hills in detail, check the books in the gift shops of the Journey Museum and S.D. School of Mines Museum, both in Rapid City.

Cowboy gear

ANTIQUES AND AUCTIONS

There's a busy antiques store and auction scene for furniture, collectibles, coins, guns, and artwork—even the pots and pans from family collections going back generations. At least a dozen stores selling antiques can be found in all major Black Hills cities, along with roadside shops, especially on Highway 385 between Hill City and Custer, and Highway 40 in Keystone.

COWBOY GEAR

There are shops throughout the Black Hills that sell hats, boots, belts, and jeans at many price points. For best choices, authentic goods, and savvy customer service about Western wear, including horse tack and rodeo gear, visit locally owned stores in Belle Fourche, Deadwood, Whitewood, and Rapid City. For serious buyers, know that a high-end hat or pair of boots can last a lifetime.

PIECE OF CRAZY HORSE

Sculptor Korczak Ziolkowski's memorial to legendary Lakota leader Crazy Horse was started in 1948 and was designed to be the world's largest work of art. So far, only the warrior's head has been carved, with his extended arm and hand beginning to emerge as skilled sculptors vow to complete Ziolkowski's vision—one day. For a donation of your choosing, visitors can take home a chunk of granite that's been blasted away from the mountain. Find the size that will fit in your luggage from a big pile inside the original visitor center.

NATIVE AMERICAN CRAFTS

Native American crafts are widely available, especially painting, sculpture, beadwork, and assemblages that combine things found in nature. For good variety, quality, and price try Prairie Edge in Rapid City.

Outdoor Activities in the Black Hills

DAY TRIP TO DEVILS TOWER

The Black Hills do not end at the South Dakota–Wyoming border. Near Hulett, Wyoming, you'll find the stunning Devils Tower National Monument rock formation. It's more than 100 miles—one way—from Rapid City, so plan for a full day.

MICKELSON AND CENTENNIAL TRAILS

Each trail is more than 100 miles long. The Mickelson starts in Deadwood and ends in Edgemont (there's a user fee to hike this trail). The more challenging Centennial Trail starts atop Bear Butte and ends in Wind Cave National Park.

VISIT THE TOWN SQUARES

Rapid City, Sturgis, Deadwood, and Spearfish all have new town squares that provide free, year-round outdoor entertainment, including ice-skating in Rapid City and Deadwood. Look for music, food, craft vendors, movies, and other family-friendly events.

CLIMB A NEEDLE

The Needles in Custer State Park offer rock-climbing challenges for all skill levels. Outfitters in Hill City, Spearfish, and Rapid City can fix you up with lessons, gear, and suggestions for other prime climbing locations, near Mount Rushmore National Memorial, in Spearfish Canyon and, of course, Devils Tower in Wyoming.

GOLFING

There are more than a dozen courses in the Black Hills. High elevation and rolling terrain provide plenty of challenges for all skill levels. Among the area's top courses are the Southern Hills Golf Course in Hot Springs, and the Elkhorn Ridge Golf Club near Spearfish.

KAYAKING

From Silver City, coast into Jenny Gulch, which is full of beaver dams, herons, bald eagles, and osprey. Paddle through tall grass into hidden ponds. Bismarck Lake is another serene spot, as is Canyon Lake. Outfitters have rentals and season-smart suggestions.

HORSEBACK RIDING

From the dude ranch experience to a couple of hours in the saddle, there are outfitters that can meet your needs. Custer State Park and elsewhere in the central Black Hills, as well as the Badlands, are popular riding spots.

Winter sports

FIND INSPIRATION AT POET'S TABLE

There's a secluded spot for poets—with a great view—in Custer State Park. Leave your vehicle at the Little Devils Tower trailhead that's east of Sylvan Lake. It's a bit of a scramble, but hike from there and find the green table and chairs and sit and reflect.

WINTER SPORTS

Head to the Northern Hills for downhill and cross-country skiing. The snowmobile season runs in conjunction; you'll find rentals in Lead, Deadwood, and Spearfish. There is ice fishing on the lakes and nearby prairie reservoirs—and even fly-fishing on Rapid and Spearfish creeks.

HANSON-LARSEN MEMORIAL PARK

Convenience, variety, and challenge are highlights of this 300-acre park that looms high over the creek in Rapid City. Enjoy 20 miles of marked trails for hiking and mountain biking, including many family-friendly ones. The city's paved, creek-side walk-run bike path is adjacent.

History You Can See

Whether from the era before written history, through the gold rush and until the present time, dedicated Black Hills residents and other scholars have worked diligently to record and display the region's history. There are museums in every community, along with sculpture and other displays that tell distinct stories. Don't be shy about asking locals for their versions.

MINING

Rumors of gold in the Black Hills were circulating before the Civil War. Experts traveling with the 1874 Custer Expedition verified the hunches. Two years later, a rip-roarin' gold rush was on and the action focused on Deadwood and Lead. Leap ahead more than a century to when casino-style gambling in Deadwood was legalized in 1989; the town boomed again. Officials fenced off a portion of revenues to support sustained infrastructure improvements and historic preservation. Today, carefully restored 19th- and early-20th-century structures form the backdrop for skilled re-enactors who bring the stories of Wild Bill Hickok, Calamity Jane, Poker Alice, and others to Main Street. In nearby Lead, hardrock miners stopped blasting in 2001 at 8,000 feet below the surface. Scientists eventually took over and today operate a sophisticated lab at the 4,800-foot level. Among other experiments, they are researching dark matter. Stop first at the Sanford Lab Homestake Visitor Center on Main Street, then tour the nearby Black Hills Mining Museum; finally, visit the Homestake Opera House to see and hear how miners and their families appreciated the arts.

CITY OF PRESIDENTS

On 44 street corners in downtown Rapid City you can see, touch, and photograph life-size bronze statues of our nation's presidents. Use your phone or obtain a pocket map from merchants to identify them all. Kids' favorite is William Howard Taft on 8th and Main; they like to mimic his "First Pitch" pose and rub the baseball for luck. City officials and the local arts community are committed to the creation of additional sculptures at the conclusion of each new president's final term.

CUSTER STATE PARK HIDEAWAYS

Take a break from seeing the popular places in Custer State Park and check out the Badger Hole, the interpreted cabin home of Badger Clark, South Dakota's first poet laureate and author of "The Cowboy's Prayer," among other works (it's a short drive off Highway 16A or you can walk in southeast from the Badger Clark Trail around Legion Lake). It's a quiet, out-of-the-way place where you can lose yourself in the verse of the early- to mid-20th-century West and see how this bachelor lived his last 30 years. Just off Highway 87 in the park is the Mount Coolidge Fire Tower. You drive up a short, gravel road to reach this stone lookout that's still in service, providing a multistate view of the hills and countryside. Another less-traveled spot is the 1881 Courthouse Museum in downtown Custer. Sharp staff members interpret the rich history of the community and area—gold, timber, cattle ranching, and plenty of local character stories. The Pioneer Museum is another artifact- and story-filled town museum located in Hot Springs, 32 miles south of Custer on Highway 385.

MORE THAN DUSTY RELICS

The Black Hills are home to several professionally staffed museums that offer year-around programs for adults and children. The Journey Museum and Learning Center in Rapid City is one of the largest, with collections covering geology, Native Americans, early pioneers, and significant events in local and regional history. A 200-seat auditorium is available for speakers and musical performance. Three long-established museums in Deadwood recently joined forces to tell the colorful story of the town's mining, commercial, and social history. Newest of the features is an upstairs and forthright tour of the brothel district. In Hot Springs, visitors who are interested in paleontology should visit The Mammoth Site for a hands-on experience of learning and digging or see rare discoveries at the Black Hills Institute in Hill City. Elsewhere throughout the Hills there are museums devoted to railroading, geology, motorcycles, cars, ranch life, pioneers, Native Americans, and galleries for fine arts.

MILITARY INFLUENCE

Lt. Col. George A. Custer—later of Little Bighorn infamy—led the first expedition of troops into the Black Hills during an 1874 trek to validate the potential for mining and other resources. The 7th Cavalry contingent consisted of 1,200 soldiers plus several civilians. Once the inevitable gold rush started, the Army created a permanent installation near freight wagon trails just south of Bear Butte Mountain. The camp town of Sturgis followed soon thereafter. Today "Old" Fort Meade is a Veterans Administration hospital and regional Army National Guard leadership academy. There's a museum in the regimental headquarters building that tells the Army's story through the end of World War II. The Air Force has been part of the region since the early World War II creation of a B-17 training base northeast of Rapid City. Ellsworth Air Force Base now is home to the 28th Bomb Wing and its B-1 Lancers and will soon be home to the new B-21 Raider bomber. The South Dakota Air and Space Museum is just outside the main gate. Dozens of aircraft and missiles are on display along with three hangars full of indoor exhibits.

MOUNT ROOSEVELT FRIENDSHIP TOWER

The stone tower was built in 1919 by legendary Deadwood sheriff Seth Bullock to memorialize his close friend Theodore Roosevelt. The location, originally called Sheep Mountain, offers a vista of the Black Hills so admired by both men. It's a moderately strenuous mile-long round-trip trek from the Mount Roosevelt trailhead, located about one mile north of Deadwood on Highway 85 at the turnoff for The Lodge at Deadwood. Bear to the right on Forest Road 133 at the turnoff, then proceed another two miles to the Mount Roosevelt Picnic Area. The tower was placed on the National Record of Historic Places in 2005 and underwent structural stabilization in 2010.

What to Watch and Read

GREAT WHITE FATHERS

Among the several books that have been written about the carving of Mount Rushmore and its sculptor Gutzon Borglum, John Taliaferro's work is the most recent and unflinching examination of the entire project. The chapters faithfully reveal details of Borglum's complex life and answer many "why" and "how'd they do it?" questions. The creation of Mount Rushmore involved everything from politics to money to dynamite. No small amounts of ego and ambition are part of the story, too.

GOLD IN THE BLACK HILLS

Black Hills native and history professor Watson Parker came to know the region through a lifetime of research and exploration. Dr. Parker first tells the story of how gold was discovered. Next he highlights tales of the early prospectors and miners, and finally he explains the 125-year run of the Homestake Mine, for decades the largest and deepest (they stopped at 8,000 feet) underground gold mine in the western hemisphere. Today, portions of the mine serve as a world-class physics laboratory.

RATTLESNAKE UNDER HIS HAT

Really? Sam Hurst answers with this biography of Earl Brockelsby, an eccentric and tireless promoter of tourism in the Black Hills. The story traces Brockelsby from his ranch beginnings—where venomous rattlers were a regular occurrence—to the creation of the world-famous Reptile Gardens. In between there are chapters about Army service in World War II, an innate willingness to take risks plus the parallel accounting of how the tourist service industry grew to match the attraction of nearby Mount Rushmore.

THE JOURNEY OF CRAZY HORSE: A LAKOTA HISTORY

Uniquely sourced from oral history transcripts and equally well told, college professor Joseph M. Marshall's story of Crazy Horse provides readers with compelling insight into the full life of one of the Lakota people's most celebrated and determined leaders.

GOING OVER EAST, REFLECTIONS ON A WOMAN RANCHER

Whether Black Hills visitors arrive by air or vehicle, you travel over vast stretches of cattle country. Award-winning author Linda Hasselstrom weaves the story of her affection for the parcel of inherited prairie where she grew up. Her narration takes readers from pasture to pasture as she explains the challenges, rewards, and heartbreak of being a modern-day rancher.

MOON OF POPPING TREES

Ranch-raised author Rex Alan Smith earned lasting acclaim for his recounting of the 1890 Wounded Knee Massacre. Smith's chapters build to the coldest time of the year, the Moon of Popping Trees, when bark would burst, and tragedy befalls Spotted Elk and his band of Miniconjou and Hunkpapa Lakota.

DEADWOOD AND DEADWOOD: THE MOVIE

The 36-episode HBO series Deadwood and a movie sequel made more than a decade later portray a gritty, history-based depiction of life in the Black Hills mining boomtown. Action starts in the roaring year of 1876 and then shows how the gold-fevered new arrivals make their way in the emerging economy of mining and growth of the town. The movie of the same name sets the action a decade later in the growing town's history.

NOMADLAND

A contemporary movie with significant scenes shot in the South Dakota Badlands and nearby famous Wall Drug is Chloe Zhao's *Nomadland*. This modern Western drama, starring Oscar-winning Frances McDormand as Fern, tells the haunting story of people who live their lives as laboring nomads. The sweeping landscape of the Badlands and the famed tourist attraction create visual reinforcement for the status of McDormand and other characters.

DANCES WITH WOLVES

Shot in western South Dakota ranch country and the Black Hills, this drama starring Kevin Costner earned seven Oscars for its compelling portrayal of Native Americans and Civil War–era Army life on the frontier.

NATIONAL TREASURE: BOOK OF SECRETS 2

Fact and fiction are woven into this story that spans from the assassination of President Lincoln to the present. Scenes shot in the Black Hills and atop Mount Rushmore conclude the film as characters search for a lost city of gold beneath the iconic carving. When you visit you'll learn about the real tunnel behind the faces, carved at Gutzon Borglum's direction as a storage place for the nation's founding documents.

NORTH BY NORTHWEST

North by Northwest is Alfred Hitchcock's classic thriller with Mount Rushmore as the visually captivating backdrop for the closing scenes. Look for the boy's blooper in the visitor center dining room scene. He's one of many local residents cast as extras; the lad knows in advance that something loud is about to happen.

PREHISTORIC ROAD TRIP

Emily Graslie, the Chicago Field Museum's energetic chief curiosity correspondent and Black Hills native, wrote and narrates all three episodes of this PBS special. Shot in South Dakota and surrounding states, the series explores the geology and paleontology of the region.

EXPLORING WITH CUSTER: THE 1874 BLACK HILLS EXPEDITION

Writer-historian Ernest Grafe and photographer Paul Horsted have spent more than two decades researching the 1874 Black Hills Expedition by Gen. George Armstrong Custer and the 7th Cavalry. Grafe and Horsted combine diaries, personal accounts and newspaper articles of the day with the already well-documented reports of the two-month long expedition, which led to the discovery of gold in the Black Hills.

WAR PONY

Filmed on the Pine Ridge Reservation in South Dakota and written by Bill Reddy and Franklin Sioux Bob, who grew up there, *War Pony* is the intertwined tale of two Lakota boys and their struggle to come of age in a troubled world. The indie film, co-directed by Riley Keough and Gina Gammell, received the Camera d'Or Award (Best First Feature Film) at the 2022 Cannes Film Festival.

The Black Hills of South Dakota with Kids

In addition to experiencing all the natural beauty of hiking, lake swimming, fishing, and trail riding (horses or motorized), many attractions continue to add kid-focused features such as alpine slides, zip lines, and climbing walls. It can be chilly after sundown, especially in campgrounds and places like Custer, Hill City, or Deadwood, so bring something warm for the kids when attending the Mount Rushmore lighting ceremony and other events.

FOR LITTLE KIDS

Take the family to Rapid City's Storybook Island. This free park was founded in 1959 and has grown into a multi-acre playground full of bigger-than-life storybook exhibits. There are modest fees for some of the extras like a ride on the train. Check the schedule; children's theater can be part of the experience.

DINOSAURS AND MORE

Who wants to sit on a *Triceratops* or hug the leg of a *Brontosaurus*? On top of a mountain ridge in the center of Rapid City, the free Dinosaur Park has been entertaining young and old since the mid-1930s. There are seven concrete sculptures of dinosaurs, maintained by the city. A $3.5 million upgrade will provide much easier access to the park when complete in mid-2024. The view is well worth the climb, providing a vista of the entire city and its forested countryside to the west, and eastward for more than 100 miles across the prairie. The tourist-friendly City Trolley makes stops at the visitor center.

GAME FISH AND PARKS OUTDOOR CAMPUS–WEST

In Rapid City, the South Dakota Department of Game, Fish and Parks operates its free Outdoor Campus–West. There's a pond full of fish, amphibians, and waterfowl. The paths lead to hiking trails and outdoor exhibits. Inside, the big building is a nature classroom with touchable exhibits of mounted wildlife, an aquarium full of game fish, and a carpeted room where little kids can burn off energy. Wildlife experts are on duty to answer questions. With some advance planning and connections via the website, you can sign up for classes. The emphasis is on enjoying the outdoors and the ethics of safe and responsible hunting and fishing.

PANNING FOR GOLD AND FOSSIL HUNTING

Visitors can share some of the gold rush experience at several attractions that will teach you how to look for "color" in the bottom of your pan. Many also have rock and mineral samples for sale. The best spots are in Keystone and Deadwood. Looking for fossils? Along with displays and museums in Badlands National Park, Rapid City, and Hill City, one of the best places to learn about fossil hunting is The Mammoth Site in Hot Springs.

GO UNDERGROUND

There are five family-friendly places where everyone can cool off and experience wonders beneath the earth's surface. The biggest are in the Southern Hills: Jewel Cave National Monument west of Custer and Wind Cave National Park near Hot Springs. Fees are charged for tours. Check before booking a tour at Wind Cave, with an ongoing repair and upgrade of its elevator system. Privately operated show caves include Rushmore Cave east of Keystone, a facility that includes a theme park and campground. Black Hills Caverns is a short distance from Rapid City, and Wonderland Cave is reached on highways from either Nemo or the Vanocker Canyon Road. The private caves all charge fees.

Chapter 2

TRAVEL SMART

Updated by
Jim Holland

★ **CAPITAL:**
Pierre

♔ **POPULATION:**
910,000; the combined, approximate population of the Black Hills region is 190,000.

💬 **LANGUAGE:**
English

$ **CURRENCY:**
U.S. Dollar

☎ **AREA CODE:**
605

⚠ **EMERGENCIES:**
911

🚗 **DRIVING:**
On the right

⚡ **ELECTRICITY:**
120–220 v/60 cycles; plugs have two or three rectangular prongs

🕓 **TIME:**
Mountain Time Zone, two hours behind New York

🌐 **WEB RESOURCES:**
www.travelsouthdakota.com, www.blackhillsbadlands.com, www.visitrapidcity.com

✈ **AIRPORT:**
Rapid City Regional Airport (RAP)

SOUTH DAKOTA

Spearfish
Sturgis
Deadwood
Rapid City *Mount Rushmore Nat'l Memorial*
◆ PIERRE
Badlands National Park
Wind Cave Nat'l. Park
Jewel Cave Nat'l. Mon.

Know Before You Go

The Black Hills's many sights and its natural beauty attract visitors from all over the country and beyond. Getting to know more about this beautiful and historically rich region of South Dakota before you visit can enrich your stay. These tips will help you get the most out of your experience.

STAYING HEALTHY

Even with the pandemic behind us, ever-changing COVID-19 variants still warrant diligence for visitors, who are encouraged to stay current with vaccines, and monitor symptoms before and after travel. Common-sense CDC guidelines for hand washing, social distancing and personal mask use still apply. Other precautions, drinking plenty of water to stay hydrated and applying sunblock when outdoors, are also appropriate.

WEATHER

Summer (June through mid-September) typically provides consistent days of sunshine and hot daytime temperatures with comfortable nights. Afternoon thunder- and hailstorms are common in the Black Hills throughout the spring and summer. Be mindful that, statistically, the area around Rapid City has some of the most unpredictable weather in the United States, especially through winter and spring.

Government forecasters are frequently challenged when analyzing the region's weather in order to make reliable forecasts. Pay attention to local forecasts and dress accordingly. Local conditions can change quickly, any time of the year. Spearfish still holds the world record for the fastest recorded temperature change: from -4°F to 45°F in two minutes, January 22, 1943. Dial 511 or 866/697–3511 for road conditions.

SPEED LIMITS

You can drive 80 mph on long stretches of interstate highway across South Dakota, but note that speed limits are reduced for several miles through the Rapid City metro area and other communities. During the August Motorcycle Rally, the limit on I–90 is 65 mph from Ellsworth Air Force Base all the way to the Wyoming state line.

VAST DISTANCES

Be conservative when making travel-time calculations between Black Hills communities and various attractions. The area rarely endures metropolitan-scale traffic jams, but curvy highways, heavy tourist traffic, a slow-moving logging truck, or a herd of buffalo on a Custer State Park road can turn what you think should be a short ride into something much longer. Give yourself plenty of time to travel between destinations. Enjoy the scenery and ask locals for alternative routes if you encounter road construction or some other unexpected delay.

VISITING PINE RIDGE RESERVATION

The Pine Ridge Reservation Visitor Center is west of the community of Kyle and serves as an educational starting point for appreciating the vast, 2.2 million-acre landscape that is home for Oglala Lakota Tribe members. Kyle is 90 miles east-southeast of Rapid City. You also can travel south of the Badlands National Park to reach Kyle and other historic places.

RALLY AWARENESS

After more than 80 years of growth, the August Motorcycle Rally in Sturgis has become—throttle open—the region's largest attraction. By many calculations, the 400,000-plus who attend each year make the Rally one of the biggest attractions in the nation.

It's loud, busy, exciting, and fun, especially if you like motorcycles or simply want to sample biker life for a few days. But it might not be for everyone. Nightly, big-name entertainment acts have become part of the festivities, especially at the major campgrounds around Sturgis and nearby Deadwood. Expect to pay more for just about everything during the Rally, a price bump that extends across many communities in the region. Law enforcement officials from multiple jurisdictions are very visible in their campaign to keep everyone safe.

GOLD PANNING/ROCK COLLECTING

There's still gold in the hills, including big-money commercial mining around Lead. Amateur prospectors, some of them very skilled and with sophisticated equipment, profitably work their legal claims on public and private land. Check with officials at Forest Service offices for recommendations about places where it is legal to prospect on your own. You can't just grab a shovel and head for the nearest stream. Claim jumping remains a serious crime. Fossils? Along with displays and museums in the Badlands National Park, Rapid City, and Hill City, one of the best places to learn about—and experience—fossil hunting is The Mammoth Site in Hot Springs.

OFF-ROADING

Off-road or all-terrain vehicles are popular throughout the Black Hills. Rentals are available in most communities. Know the regulations that govern travel on public highways and designated trails. Careless off-roading, especially in wet weather, contributes to erosion and can result in fines from state or federal authorities. Because private land is so intermingled with state and federal public property, obtain a Forest Service map of the Black Hills and be confident of your navigation skills. The power and speed of these vehicles can turn you into a trespasser before you know it.

TRAVELING WITH PETS

Pets are not allowed at Mount Rushmore, although pets on short leashes are permitted in exercise areas that are part of the parking garages. Service dogs, as defined by the Americans with Disabilities Act requirements, are permitted to accompany visitors with disabilities. Although incidents of pet or human interaction are rare, be advised there are mountain lions throughout the Black Hills.

RECHARGE YOUR RIDE

Battery electric vehicles, or EVs, are becoming more common on the roads. EV owners can rest assured they'll be able to find charging stations, especially along major highways and the interstates. Stations can be found at convenience stores, restaurants, motels, auto repair shops, and dealerships. Most larger towns in the Black Hills offer multiple stations. Check ⊕ chargehub.com to find specific locations to boost your battery.

BEWARE OF BUFFALO AND OTHER WILD CRITTERS

Well-publicized human-bison encounters—usually ending badly for the humans involved—should be more than enough warning to give these unpredictable and powerful wild animals a wide berth. Officials recommend keeping at least 100 yards between you and the animals, especially in the spring and early summer when calves may be present. Visitors should also be aware of the aforementioned mountain lions, although encounters with these magnificent big cats are rare. Brown and black bears have also been known to make an appearance but are not thought to reside in the hills in any great numbers. Finally, know that poisonous prairie rattlesnakes reside in both the Black Hills and on the South Dakota plains.

Getting Here and Around

Air

Five major carriers provide daily, non-stop commercial service to the Rapid City Regional Airport from major hub airports: Allegiant Air (Las Vegas and Phoenix), American Airlines (Chicago, Dallas, and Charlotte), Delta (Minneapolis, Salt Lake, and Atlanta), United (Chicago, Denver, and Houston) and Sun Country Air (Minneapolis). Some carrier operations and routes to some cities are seasonal. Check airline schedules for precise flight information.

AIRPORT

The Rapid City Regional Airport is the only airport in the area with commercial service. The airport is located approximately 10 miles east of city center on Highway 44. Five airlines fly daily to major hub cities. General aviation is served by WestJet Air Center at the Rapid City Regional Airport. There are municipal airports and landing strips adjacent to the larger Black Hills communities, most affiliated with fixed-base operators providing fuel, maintenance, and other services.

AIRPORT TRANSFERS

Need a ride to or from the airport? Two curbside taxi companies will get you where you need to be. Additional transfer services are available from five major franchise hotel locations in Rapid City as well as two hotels in Deadwood. Ride-sharing services, Lyft, Uber, and Wridz are also available.

Bicycle

Off-road mountain biking is king in the Black Hills, with hundreds of miles of A-grade trails offering that adrenaline-rush ride surrounded by breath-taking scenery from trailhead to finish. Check ⊕ alltrails.com to find the ride matching your ability. And paved-road cyclists, you aren't left behind. The most popular road tours will take riders through the Badlands one hour east of Rapid City, the Wildlife Loop Road in Custer State Park, and Spearfish Canyon Scenic Byway in the northern Black Hills. Bike rentals and tours are available throughout the area.

Bus

Jefferson Lines provides commercial bus service east–west along I–90 and is the regional service provider for Greyhound Lines. There is no commercial bus on north–south routes. The bus transportation hub is the Milo Barber Transportation Center in downtown Rapid City. Jefferson Lines also makes a routine stop in downtown Spearfish (50 miles northwest along I–90) and in Wall (50 miles east).

Car

Unless you arrive in the Black Hills via an escorted package tour or connect with any of several local tour companies, a car is essential. Interstate 90 crosses all of South Dakota from west to east, connecting the Northern Hills towns of Spearfish, Sturgis, and Deadwood (which lies about 14 miles off the interstate) with Rapid City. From Rapid City the interstate runs due east, passing Wall and Badlands National Park on its way to Sioux Falls, or west across the Wyoming border.

Regional highways of importance include U.S. 385, which connects the interior of the Black Hills from south to north, and U.S. 16, which winds south of Rapid City toward the Mount Rushmore and Crazy

Horse memorials. Highway 44 is an alternate route between the Black Hills and the Badlands. On the eastern slope of the Black Hills, Highway 79 leads south, eventually connecting with Denver. Within the Black Hills, seven highway tunnels have limited clearance; they are marked on state maps and in the state's tourism booklet.

Snowplow operators work hard to keep the roads clear in winter, but you may have trouble getting around immediately after a major snowstorm. Unlike the Rockies, where even higher elevations make some major roads impassable in winter, the only Black Hills roads that close permanently in the snowy months are some unimproved Forest Service roads.

Contact the South Dakota State Highway Patrol by dialing ☎ 511 for information on road conditions anytime of the year. If you are experiencing an emergency, dial ☎ 911. The Highway Patrol has the authority to close roads during stormy conditions. Do not drive around barriers and strike out on your own.

CAR RENTALS

Rapid City Regional Airport is the best place to find car rentals. Make rental reservations early; Rapid City is visited by many tourist and business travelers. Rental agencies are often fully booked during the summer season.

GASOLINE

Gasoline and diesel fuel are readily available at service stations throughout the Black Hills. Expect to pay somewhat higher prices for fuel purchased outside of the Rapid City metro area. Charging points for electric vehicles slowly are becoming more prevalent, especially at major lodging establishments.

ROAD CONDITIONS

It can be windy in South Dakota and surrounding states, especially on the prairie, in all seasons. Prevailing winds come from the northwest, so that often means crosswinds if you are traveling in either direction along I-90. Pay attention to local forecasts for high-wind warnings, especially if you are operating a high-profile vehicle such as an RV or towing a trailer.

ROADSIDE EMERGENCIES

If you are experiencing an emergency or are involved in an accident, call 911. For road conditions (example: snow, ice, flooding, and construction zones), call ☎ 511 or ☎ 866/697–3511.

Ride-Sharing

Ride-sharing services, Uber, Lyft, and Wridz, can be booked through their respective apps and are available at airports in the state's three largest metro areas, Sioux Falls, Rapid City, and Aberdeen. Check with each service to find out how far their drivers may take riders into more remote areas.

Taxis

Local taxis and airport shuttle services are readily available by phone or online booking, with more than a half-dozen companies in Rapid City. Some offer Black Hills tour options as well. Most towns in the Hills are also served by city taxi and shuttle services.

Essentials

🍴 Dining

Like neighboring Wyoming, restaurants in the Black Hills are not known for culinary diversity, and no matter where you go in this part of the world, beef is king. Nevertheless, thanks to a growing population and increasing numbers of visitors, the area is beginning to see more dining options. Rapid City and Spearfish have an abundance of national chain restaurants, and all communities have local eateries that specialize in contemporary and traditional American cooking. Look for locally sourced dishes, too. There are many dining options in Deadwood, most of them affiliated with casinos. Fare is typical American bar food, some of it upscale. A few casinos offer all-you-can-eat buffets. Chain fast-food restaurants are sparse in Deadwood, Lead, Hill City, and Custer. However, local establishments make it easy to find typical burger-and-fries meals. Don't be afraid to try wild game dishes, including buffalo (bison), pheasant, and elk, plus Native American–themed offerings.

DISCOUNTS AND DEALS

If you eat early or late in the evening you may be able to take advantage of deals not offered at peak hours. For breakfast and lunch specials, ask the waitstaff for details. Similarly, ask for details about discounts that may be available for active-duty military and veterans, plus senior citizens. If you've found a coupon in a tourist brochure or elsewhere, ensure it will be honored by the restaurant when you place your order, not after you have been served and finished the meal.

PAYING

Most restaurants take credit cards, but a few do not. It's worth asking and learning the location of the nearest ATM. Servers appreciate 20% tips at restaurants that provide table service; some add an automatic gratuity for groups of six or more. Tip jars are common at local establishments where counter service is provided.

RESERVATIONS AND DRESS

Some high-end restaurants accept reservations or offer call-ahead seating. During the peak summer season or in communities that are hosting a popular event like the Buffalo Roundup in Custer, expect lengthy wait times. Generally speaking, dress is casual at all restaurants. Summertime temperatures can cool into the 50s in the Hills, so you'll be more comfortable dining outside or waiting for a table if you bring a sweater or light jacket. Fair or not, the way you dress can influence how you're treated—and where you're seated—in the nicer establishments. If you have doubts about what to wear, call the restaurant and ask.

MEALS AND MEALTIMES

During the summer and early fall seasons, evening meal service is generally available until 9 pm. Local eateries and big-name chain restaurants can keep later hours. Fast-food establishments in Rapid City, Sturgis, and Spearfish often keep their drive-through windows open around the clock. The major exception for late-night dining is Deadwood, where a few restaurants never close. Breakfast starts as early as 6 am in most Black Hills communities.

SMOKING

Smoking is banned in all restaurants and bars.

⇨ *Restaurant reviews have been shortened. For full information, see Fodors.com. Restaurant prices are the average cost of a main course at dinner, or if dinner is not served, at lunch.*

What It Costs

$	$$	$$$	$$$$
AT DINNER			
under $13	$13–$23	$24–$35	over $35

⊕ Health and Safety

DON'T BE BUGGED

Mosquitoes can be a bothersome summertime pest in the Black Hills. Their bites aren't just itchy and uncomfortable, they can spread potentially serious diseases, such as West Nile Virus. Their peak active hours are early morning and just after dusk. Wear long clothing and apply repellent to help protect yourself from insects, which also includes deer ticks. Avoid hiking in tall grasses, which can harbor ticks, especially in the cool-season spring and early summer.

PERSONAL SAFETY

South Dakota is known for a relatively low crime rate, but that doesn't mean common sense personal precautions should be ignored. Hide valuable items and lock your lodging and vehicle doors wherever you might be. City street and remote trail alike are generally safe, but again, let common sense prevail. Travel in groups and stick to well-lighted public spaces after dark.

📶 Internet

Wi-Fi is available at most lodging establishments and campgrounds. Cell phone service is reliable in all communities and along major highways. Reliable cell phone service is not available across the entirety of the Black Hills. Lack of cell towers and the terrain can limit service in various areas, especially if you are far away from communities or major highways. During the Motorcycle Rally, many telephone companies set up temporary towers in the Sturgis area to better meet increased demand for cell service.

Lodging

New chain hotels with modern amenities are plentiful in the Black Hills, but when booking accommodations consider a stay at one of the area's historic properties. From grand brick downtown hotels to intimate Queen Anne homes converted to bed-and-breakfasts, historic lodgings are easy to locate. Many have been carefully restored to their late-19th-century grandeur, down to antique Victorian furnishings and authentic Western art. Other distinctive lodging choices include the region's mountain lodges and forest retreats. Usually built along creeks or near major trails, these isolated accommodations often attract outdoor enthusiasts. There's glamping in a few spots near Rapid City. Try HipCamp to locate small, unique cabins, or camping establishments.

FACILITIES

You can assume that all rooms have private baths, phones, TVs, and air-conditioning, unless otherwise indicated. Breakfast is noted when it is included in the rate. There are a few hotels with pools. Some are indoors, an acknowledgement of cooler evening temperatures and a winter that can arrive early and stay late.

PRICES

There is a noticeable increase in lodging costs during the high season, with an added bump at many locations during events such as the Sturgis Motorcycle Rally, Custer State Park Buffalo Roundup, and Kool Deadwood Nites. Remember to

Essentials

ask about additional costs for state and local taxes and resort fees charged by some establishments.

RESERVATIONS

Black Hills Central Reservations, also known as CenRes (☎ 866/601–5103), offers vacation packages and handles reservations for air travel, car rental, hotels, campgrounds, lodges, ranches, and B&Bs in the Black Hills.

⇨ *Hotel reviews have been shortened. For full information, see Fodors.com. Hotel prices are the lowest cost of a standard double room in high season.*

What It Costs			
$	$$	$$$	$$$$
FOR TWO PEOPLE			
under $150	$150–$200	$201–$250	over $250

Packing

Pack rain gear for spring, summer, and fall travel. Include jackets or windbreakers and gloves for chilly days and nights (even in summer). Winter travelers should prepare for temperatures that can slip below zero, especially at night. Periods of deep winter cold can last for several consecutive days.

$ Taxes

The general sales tax rate for goods and services across South Dakota is 4.2%. Many jurisdictions add local taxes, bringing the standard rate to 6.2%. Rapid City, Deadwood, and other communities have lodging taxes that boost the rate for a room to 8.5% plus $2 Business Improvement District fees. Hotels also can add their own "resort fees" to your bill. When you make a reservation, ask for the total amount you will be paying to avoid surprises at check-out time.

Tipping

⇨ *See our handy tipping guide for the Black Hills on the opposite page.*

🗓 When to Go

Low Season: The winter months from mid-November through April. Parks remain open, but know that many commercial attractions and services shut down for the winter or operate with reduced hours. Downhill and cross-country skiing, snowmobiling, ice fishing, and hunting are popular activities for locals and visitors.

Shoulder Season: Mid-September through early November. Weather is generally more settled and moderate. Tree leaves change color, providing picturesque driving through places like Spearfish Canyon and Vanocker Canyon. Springtime (late April and May) is a secondary shoulder season, especially for visits to the Badlands National Park when wildflowers are blooming.

High Season: Memorial Day through mid-September. Expect rates throughout the Black Hills to be noticeably higher during the Sturgis Motorcycle Rally (mid-August). You can also expect much higher traffic on many Black Hills highways during the Rally. Town by town, rates for lodging will reflect the high demand during major rodeos, festivals, and the increasingly popular Custer State Park Buffalo Roundup in late September.

Tipping Guides for the Black Hills

Bartender	$1–$5 per round of drinks, depending on the number of drinks
Bellhop	$1–$5 per bag, depending on the level of the hotel
Coat Check	$1–$2 per coat
Hotel Concierge	$5 or more, depending on the service
Hotel Doorstaff	$1–$5 for help with bags or hailing a cab
Hotel Maid	$2–$5 a day (in cash, preferably daily since cleaning staff may be different each day you stay)
Hotel Room Service Waiter	$1–$2 per delivery, even if a service charge has been added
Porter at Airport	$1 per bag
Restroom Attendants	$1 or small change
Skycap at Airport	$1–$3 per bag checked
Spa Personnel	15%–20% of the cost of your service
Taxi Driver	15%–20%
Tour Guide	10%–15% of the cost of the tour, per person
Valet Parking Attendant	$2–$5, each time your car is brought to you
Waiter	15%–20%, with 20% being the norm at high-end restaurants; nothing additional if a service charge is added to the bill

WEATHER

Expect the daytime thermometer to range between 80°F and 100°F in summer. In the Hills, summer and early fall nights can cool into the 40s. Afternoon thunderstorms, often with hail, are not uncommon in the spring and early summer. Most visitors come in the warmer months, June to September, which is an optimal time for outdoor activities. The prairies of the Dakotas have earned a reputation for enduring attention-getting winter weather. However, the Black Hills region enjoys a Banana Belt nickname for often having milder winter weather. Inversions can raise winter temperatures in places like Deadwood and Lead comfortably higher than the lower-elevation communities and surrounding prairie. Snow can fall in the upper elevations every month of the year, and temperatures in January occasionally register above 60°F. However, anomalies like these rarely last more than a day or two. Know that winter temperatures can plunge below 0°F and the average annual snowfall exceeds 150 inches in the higher northern Black Hills.

◉ Visitor Information

Information to enhance your stay in the Black Hills abounds. Welcome Centers, offering brochures and knowledgeably seasonal guides, are located close to Interstate 90 both on the eastern outskirts of Rapid City (westbound) and just inside the South Dakota–Wyoming border (eastbound) near Spearfish. Visitor Centers are also easily found in national and state parks as well as in local community chamber of commerce storefronts. Black Hills and Badlands Tourism Association office in Rapid City, and Black Hills Vacations in Deadwood can assist online and in-person. And don't hesitate to ask a local resident for advice on anything from travel shortcuts to off-the-beaten-track eateries and attractions.

Great Itineraries

The national parks of southwestern South Dakota—along with the state park and two national memorials nearby—deliver a surprising variety of sights: the swaying grasses and abundant wildlife of one of the country's few remaining intact prairies, the complex labyrinth of passages and unique geologic formations in one of the world's longest caves, and some of the richest fossil beds on Earth.

Day 1: Wind Cave National Park

48 miles or a one-hour drive from Rapid City Regional Airport.

Arrive in the morning to pick up your rental car at the airport and make the drive to **Wind Cave National Park,** with more than 33,000 acres of wildlife habitat above ground (home to bison, elk, pronghorn, and coyotes) and one of the world's longest caves below. Take an afternoon cave tour and a short drive through the park. Spend the night in Hot Springs, about 7 miles from the park's southern boundary.

Day 2: Custer State Park

20 miles or a 40-minute drive from Hot Springs.

Spend today at **Custer State Park,** which is adjacent to Wind Cave. The 71,000-acre park has exceptional drives, lots of wildlife (including a herd of 1,300 bison), and fingerlike granite spires rising from the forest floor (they're the reason this is called the Needles region of South Dakota). While you're in the park, be sure to visit Limber Pine Natural Area, a National Natural Landmark containing spectacular ridges of granite. If you have time, check out the Cathedral Spires trail,

3 miles round-trip. Overnight in one of five mountain lodges at the Custer State Park Resort.

Day 3: Jewel Cave National Monument and Crazy Horse Memorial

About 16 miles from Custer State Park to Jewel Cave; 19 miles from Jewel Cave to Crazy Horse Memorial.

Today, venture down U.S. 16 to **Jewel Cave National Monument,** 13 miles west of the town of Custer, an underground wilderness where you can see beautiful nailhead and dogtooth spar crystals lining its more than 195 miles of passageways.

After visiting Jewel Cave, head back to Custer and take U.S. 16/385 to **Crazy Horse Memorial** (about 5 miles north of Custer), home to a colossal mountain carving of the legendary Lakota leader and the Indian Museum of North America. Afterward, head 10 miles north to the former gold- and tin-mining town of Hill City, where you'll spend the night.

Day 4: Mount Rushmore National Memorial

12 miles or about a 30-minute drive from Hill City.

This morning, travel to **Mount Rushmore National Memorial,** where you can view the huge carved renderings of Presidents Washington, Jefferson, Theodore Roosevelt, and Lincoln. Afterward, head northwest for 23 miles back to Rapid City, the eastern gateway to the Black Hills. Spend the night here.

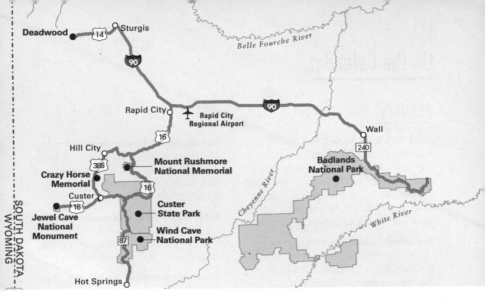

Day 5: Badlands National Park

75 miles or a 1-hour, 15-minute drive from Rapid City to the northeast entrance of Badlands.

Begin your day early and drive east (via Interstate 90) to **Badlands National Park**, a 244,000-acre geologic wonderland. The Badlands Highway Loop Road (Highway 240) wiggles through the moonlike landscape of the park's north unit for 32 miles. Stop in at the Ben Reifel Visitor Center, at the far eastern edge of the park, to pick up a trail map and head out on a hike. The Notch Trail, 1½ miles round-trip, offers spectacular views of the White River Valley, but is definitely not for anyone with a fear of heights. The Cliff Shelf trail, ½-mile round-trip, is a more mellow option that showcases rock formations and juniper forest as well as occasional wildlife sightings.

After you leave the park, head back to Rapid City to spend the night—or if you have the wherewithal, enjoy the nightlife in Deadwood (less than an hour's drive from Rapid City). This bustling Old West town (and former hangout of Wild Bill Hickok and Calamity Jane) brims with saloons, steak houses, and casinos.

Day 6: Deadwood

Less than one hour west of Rapid City. 14 miles from I–90 Exit 30 on SD 14A, or 10 miles from Exit 17 on SD 85. Both scenic drives.

Even after a vibrant night in Deadwood, there is still plenty to see and do during the day. Those hankering for history may visit the **Adams House** and **Adams Museum**, the **Days of '76 Museum** and **The Brothel** (an acknowledgement of the town's bawdy past—prostitution was legal as late as 1980). Also try your luck again at the downtown casinos and dine in popular steak houses.

With the day winding down, it's back to Rapid City, with Rapid City Regional Airport another 20 minutes southeast of town.

On the Calendar

January

Black Hills Stock Show & Rodeo. One of the nation's biggest livestock shows and sales. Most events are conducted indoors, including the rodeo performances. The Rapid City show starts in late January and continues into early February each year. ⊕ *blackhillsstockshow.com*

Deadwood Snocross Showdown. Professional snowmobile racing in the rodeo grounds arena. ⊕ *www.deadwood.com/event/pro-snocross-races*

February

Nemo 500 Outhouse Races. Fun, outdoor winter fundraiser in the tiny town of Nemo, northwest of Rapid City on Route 234. ⊕ *www.nemo500.com*

March

Mountain West Whiskey Festival. Industry experts and connoisseurs gather in Rapid City for whiskey tasting, upscale catering, and live music. ⊕ *mountainwestwhiskeyfestival.com*

April

Black Hills Film Festival. See films shot and produced in the Black Hills. The festival headquarters are in Rapid City. ⊕ *www.blackhillsfilmfestival.org*

May

Sound of Silence Tesla Rally. The only event of its kind nationally invites owners of the innovative battery electric vehicles to tour the Black Hills. ⊕ *www.custersd.com*

June

West Boulevard Summer Festival. Artists and artisans gather in Rapid City's historic neighborhood park for this early-summer favorite event. ⊕ *www.westblvdrc.com/festival*

Annual Crazy Horse Volksmarch. During the first weekend in June, visitors can hike up to the outstretched arm of the carving. ⊕ *crazyhorsememorial.org*

Black Hills Bluegrass Festival. Two days of American bluegrass and acoustic music. Also, workshops, jams, craft vendors, and kids activities. ⊕ *facebook.com/blackhillsbluegrassfestival*

July

Black Hills Roundup. Held for more than a century, the rodeo in Belle Fourche takes place over the long Fourth of July weekend. ⊕ *www.blackhillsroundup.com*

Gold Discovery Days. Custer celebrates the discoveries made by the earliest prospectors. ⊕ *www.custersd.com/Gold-Discovery-Days*

Western Dakota Gem and Mineral Show. Rockhounds and gem and mineral fans gather to buy, sell, trade and display their collections. ⊕ *www.wdgms.org*

Days of '76 Rodeo. The best of Professional Rodeo Cowboys Association gather for one of the PRCA's marquee events of the summer at the storied Deadwood Rodeo Grounds. Daily downtown parades are a can't-miss as well. ⊕ *www.daysof76.com*

August

Sturgis Motorcycle Rally. Expect some 400,000 motorcycle enthusiasts spread out over two weeks for socializing, music, and racing. ⊕ *www.sturgismotorcyclerally.com*

Central States Fair and Rodeo. This is the region's largest late-summer fair and features exhibits, entertainment, racing, and rodeo. ⊕ *www.centralstatesfair.com*

Kool Deadwood Nites. Classic cars, oldies music, a parade, and auction are part of this event. ⊕ *www.deadwood.com/event/kool-deadwood-nites*

September

Black Hills Photo Shootout. Professional and amateur photographers gather in a different community each year for a long weekend of all things camera related. ⊕ *www.facebook.com/blackhillsohotoshootout*

Buffalo Round-Up and Arts Festival. Custer State Park staff and volunteers saddle up to move its herd of 1,300 buffalo; artists and artisans set up nearby. ⊕ *gfp.sd.gov/buffalo-roundup*

Sturgis MusicFest. Two solid days of live music by local and regional artists at numerous venues around town, with multiple genres represented. ⊕ *officialsturgisevents.com*

October

Black Hills Pow Wow. Premier American Indian cultural festivities featuring dancing, artists, speakers, and other events for all ages. ⊕ *www.blackhillspowwow.com*

November

Buffalo Auction. After the September roundup, Custer State Park auctions the excess of its herd in the sales ring and online. ⊕ *gfp.sd.gov/buffalo-auction*

December

Lakota Nation Invitational. This basketball tournament is comprised of 32 high schools from South Dakota and the Upper Midwest, which will fill Rapid City's Summit Arena at The Monument for four days of Lakota culture as well as sports. ⊕ *www.lakotanationinvitational.com*

Trees and Trains Exhibit. The South Dakota State Railroad Museum in Hill City is filled with locally decorated trees, adding a festive holiday atmosphere to the large collection of railroad memorabilia. Book a one-hour, round trip vintage rail tour on the 1880 Train's Holiday Express, right next door to the Museum. ⊕ *1880train.com*

Contacts

Air

AIRLINES Allegiant Airlines. ✉ *4550 Terminal Rd., Rapid City* ☎ *702/505–8888* ⊕ *www.allegiantair. com.* **American Airlines.** ✉ *4550 Terminal Rd., Rapid City* ☎ *800/433–7300* ⊕ *www.aa.com.* **Delta Air.** ✉ *4550 Terminal Rd., Rapid City* ☎ *800/221–1212* ⊕ *www.delta.com.* **United Airlines.** ✉ *4550 Terminal Rd., Rapid City* ☎ *800/241–6522* ⊕ *www. ual.com.* **Sun Country Airlines.** ✉ *4550 Terminal Rd.* ☎ *651/905–2737* ⊕ *www. suncountry.com.*

AIRPORT Rapid City Regional Airport (RAP). ✉ *4550 Terminal Rd., Rapid City* ☎ *605/394–4195* ⊕ *www.rapairport.org.*

Bus

CONTACTS Dakota Tours. ✉ *Rapid City* ☎ *605/342–4461.* **Greyhound Lines.** ✉ *333 Sixth St., Rapid City* ☎ *800/231–2222* ⊕ *www. greyhound.com.* **Jefferson Lines.** ✉ *333 Sixth St., Rapid City* ☎ *858/800–8898* ⊕ *www.jefferson-lines.com.*

Car

HIGHWAY CONDITIONS South Dakota Highway Patrol. ✉ *Rapid City* ☎ *605/394–2286* ⊕ *dps. sd.gov.*

CAR RENTALS Alamo. ✉ *4550 Terminal Rd., Rapid City* ☎ *800/651–1223* ⊕ *www.alamo.com.* **Avis.** ✉ *4550 Terminal Rd., Rapid City* ☎ *800/230–4898* ⊕ *www.avis.com.* **Black Hills Car Rentals.** ✉ *1600 E. Hwy. 44, Rapid City* ☎ *605/342–6696* ⊕ *blackhillscarrental. net.* **Budget.** ✉ *4550 Terminal Rd., Rapid City* ☎ *800/218–7992* ⊕ *www. budget.com.* **Casey's Auto Rental Service.** ✉ *1318 5th St., Rapid City* ☎ *605/343–2277.* **Enterprise.** ✉ *4550 Terminal Rd., Rapid City* ☎ *855/266–9289* ⊕ *www. enterprise.com.* **Hertz.** ✉ *4550 Terminal Rd., Rapid City* ☎ *800/654–3131* ⊕ *www.hertz. com.* **National.** ✉ *4550 Terminal Rd., Rapid City* ☎ *877/222–9058* ⊕ *www. nationalcar.com.*

Lodging

RESERVATIONS Black Hills Central Reservations. ✉ *68 Sherman St., Deadwood* ☎ *866/601–5103* ⊕ *www. blackhillsvacations.com.*

◉ Visitor Information

CONTACTS Black Hills and Badlands Tourism Association. ✉ *1851 Discovery Circle, Rapid City* ☎ *605/355–3700* ⊕ *www. blackhillsbadlands.com.*

Chapter 3

RAPID CITY AND THE CENTRAL BLACK HILLS

Updated by
Jim Holland

👁 Sights	🍴 Restaurants	🛏 Hotels	🛍 Shopping	🍸 Nightlife
★★★★★	★★★☆☆	★★★☆☆	★★☆☆☆	★★☆☆☆

WELCOME TO RAPID CITY AND THE CENTRAL BLACK HILLS

TOP REASONS TO GO

★ **Monumental appeal:** Mount Rushmore National Memorial and Crazy Horse Memorial are bucket-list mountain carvings that draw millions of visitors per year.

★ **Attractions galore:** From bear encounters to helicopter tours, this region is abundant with adventures for travelers of all types.

★ **Rugged beauty:** Scenic drives and recreational trails abound here. The mountains, streams, lakes, and granite formations that punctuate the pine-clad Black Hills National Forest beckon motorists, hikers, climbers, mountain bikers, horseback riders, anglers, and paddlers.

★ **Urban comforts:** Rapid City is the largest population center in the area, offering extensive lodging, dining, and shopping options on the edge of the Black Hills. For a centrally located home base try Keystone or Hill City.

★ **Culture:** Museums and other attractions illuminate the region's geography, Native American heritage, and gold-rush past.

1 Rapid City. South Dakota's second-largest city is the only large metro area in the Black Hills, featuring the region's biggest selection of hotels, restaurants, and entertainment.

2 Keystone. The main street through this small town near the base of Mount Rushmore is a walkable outdoor mall lined with shops, restaurants, and attractions.

3 Mount Rushmore National Memorial. No visit to the Black Hills is complete without a pilgrimage to the Shrine of Democracy. See the enormous carved faces, then take in the restaurant, shops, and walkway.

4 Hill City. This town's central location makes it an ideal home base or stopover while exploring the Black Hills. It features a walkable main street brimming with eclectic shops and it's also the main depot for the scenic 1880 Train.

5 Crazy Horse Memorial. Between Hill City and Custer, this memorial to renowned Lakota Sioux warrior Crazy Horse offers a chance to view a massive mountain carving in progress.

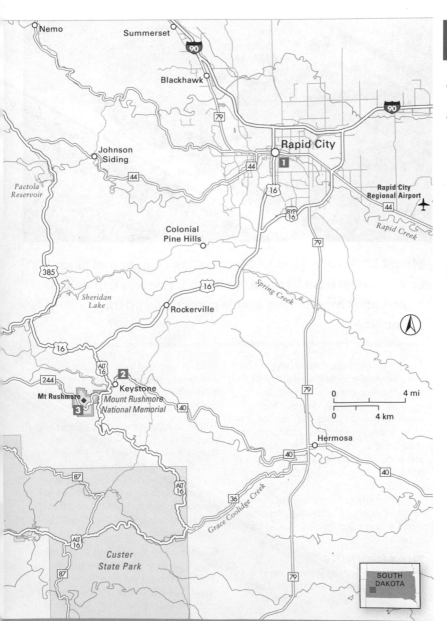

Nemo

Summerset

90

Blackhawk

79

Rapid City

1

Johnson
Siding

Rapid City
Regional Airport

Pactola
Reservoir

44

44

16

BYP
16

Rapid Creek

Colonial
Pine Hills

79

385

16

Spring Creek

Sheridan
Lake

Rockerville

16

ALT
16

2

244

Keystone

Mt Rushmore

3

Mount Rushmore
National Memorial

40

79

0   4 mi
0   4 km

87

ALT
16

Hermosa

40

36

Grace Coolidge Creek

40

ALT
16

Custer
State Park

87

79

SOUTH
DAKOTA

MOUNT RUSHMORE: CARVING A MOUNTAIN

Mount Rushmore National Memorial is a complicated place. It's on land taken from Native Americans. Its carvers dynamited, drilled, and chiseled away a large portion of a pristine mountain.

Two of the men depicted on the mountain were slave owners. Another's presidential legacy had yet to be established when his likeness was added to the sculpture. Yet, as a work of sculpture, the success of Mount Rushmore is undeniable. The colossal and accurate likenesses of Washington, Jefferson, Roosevelt, and Lincoln draw two million visitors annually. Gazing up at the mountain, people experience a range of reactions, including patriotism, wonder, and curiosity at how it all came to be.

THE BEGINNING

The long and arduous task of carving the mountain began with South Dakota historian Doane Robinson's idea in 1923. He wanted to carve sculptures of legendary Western heroes into the Black Hills stone formations known as the Needles.

Robinson invited the noted painter and sculptor Gutzon Borglum for a visit. Borglum was embroiled in difficulties with the Stone Mountain carving of Confederate leaders in Georgia (where he had associations with Ku Klux Klan members). Borglum abandoned that unfinished project and decamped for South Dakota.

Borglum convinced Robinson and other project backers to carve presidential figures into the granite face of a mountain called Rushmore. The prominence had been named previously for Charles E.

Rushmore, a New York mining attorney who had conducted business in the Black Hills. He would have no formal role in the mountain carving, other than providing a donation when asked.

South Dakota's legendary U.S. senator and former governor, Peter Norbeck, joined the fundraising effort with other local leaders. They were eager to establish a Black Hills destination for the burgeoning automobile tourism industry. .

RUSHMORE'S FIRST PRESIDENT: COOLIDGE

Although the project was dedicated in 1925, it languished until 1927 without any actual carving taking place.

Then, President Calvin Coolidge did something unexpected. Needing to placate farmers and ranchers in the middle of the country who were angry about his veto of a farm bill, and also needing a long-term escape from renovations in the White House, Coolidge chose the Black Hills for a summer-long vacation.

Borglum convinced the president to attend a rededication ceremony (it was called a "consecration," to distinguish it from the earlier dedication) at Mount Rushmore. Thus, Coolidge—not Washington, Jefferson, Roosevelt,

or Lincoln—was the first presidential "face" at Mount Rushmore.

On the day of Coolidge's visit, Borglum scaled a long stairway to the top of the mountain, dangled in front of the rock face on a swinglike contraption called a bosun chair, and drilled the first holes into the mountainside. The presidential visit breathed new life into the fundraising effort, and Coolidge later approved the first federal matching funds for the project. .

THE FACES EMERGE

Carving continued with 400 workers for 14 years, through Borglum's death in 1941. His son, Lincoln, declared the memorial finished that year. Original plans to carve full-bodied presidential figures were scrapped in favor of busts that each stand four stories tall. A plan to carve words onto the mountain relating a brief history of America was also scrapped, as was a plan to store archival national documents in a "Hall of Records," bored into the wall of a narrow gulch behind the sculpture. The waste rock and rubble from the blasting and carving was left at the base of the mountain, forming a talus slope that remains today.

Three of the presidential faces on the mountain represent well-known eras in the nation's history: its founding during

the presidency of George Washington, the "father of the country"; its expansion under Thomas Jefferson, who executed the Louisiana Purchase; and its preservation by Abraham Lincoln, who steered the country through the Civil War.

The reasons for including Theodore Roosevelt are less obvious. Borglum said Roosevelt brought unification of America's East and West coasts, and unification of America with the world, thanks to his support of the Panama Canal's construction. Additionally, Borglum and Norbeck were Roosevelt devotees. Roosevelt's death just six years prior to Mount Rushmore's dedication meant there were still many other Roosevelt admirers around from which to seek donations.

A COMPLEX LEGACY

The total cost to carve the memorial was about $1 million, with funding mostly from the federal government. Modern estimates say the memorial contributes about $200 million in annual visitor spending to the Black Hills economy.

Although the memorial is the linchpin of Black Hills tourism, it is not without controversy. The Black Hills are important in the traditional religions of multiple Native American tribes, and some Native Americans consider the mountain carving a desecration of sacred land. Mount Rushmore, the Black Hills, and all of western South Dakota were once part of the Great Sioux Reservation, established by a treaty that the United States broke soon after signing it in 1868.

A Lakota medicine man, Nicolas Black Elk, named the mountain The Six Grandfathers, from his vision of the six directions: north, south, east, west, above, and below.

The National Park Service, which manages Mount Rushmore, attempts to include Native American perspectives with exhibits, speakers, and performances on the memorial grounds.

On the eastern side of the Black Hills, there's a break in a hogback ridge where the cool, clear waters of Rapid Creek emerge onto the plains. In 1876, a group of failed prospectors established a settlement there called Hay Camp. Today, it's known as Rapid City. With more than 77,000 people, it's the largest city for hundreds of miles around on the sparsely populated Northern Great Plains.

That status—along with its proximity to the Black Hills, Badlands, and Ellsworth Air Force Base—has helped Rapid City develop amenities and attractions rivaling larger urban centers.

Entertainment options run the gamut from an intimate community theater to a new, 12,500-seat arena. Live music is common at multiple venues in the rejuvenated downtown district, including a public outdoor square. Native American powwows, art, and exhibitions add vibrancy to the cultural scene. Local museums tell the story of the region's complex, 2-billion-year-old geology; its Native American heritage; the 1870s gold rush; and the 20th-century tourism boom inspired by Mount Rushmore.

In 1972, a devastating Rapid Creek flood in Rapid City killed 238 people, including many who lived along the creek. Remains of six victims were never found. The city emerged with a determination to avoid a repeat disaster. Today, the creek is bounded by an undeveloped greenway and paved recreational path stretching across the entire city, interspersed with parks. On the forested mountain ridges towering above the creek, dirt trails offer a natural escape for hikers and bikers without ever having to leave the city.

Rapid City's role as a gateway to the Black Hills inspired its former nickname, the Gate City. The central Black Hills directly west of the city contain the region's ancient granite heart, where mountain carvers found the perfect settings for the Mount Rushmore and Crazy Horse memorials.

Hill City, Keystone, and other towns and villages high up in the central Black Hills are built on tourism and timber. Man-made attractions line their streets, along with the highways leading to Mount Rushmore. Yet natural beauty is ever-present. The central Black Hills exist within the Mystic District of the Black Hills National Forest, where locals and visitors flock to recreational trails, remote mountain peaks, quiet canyons, spring-fed streams, and placid lakes. Weather is generally cooler in the Black Hills than in Rapid City; it's not uncommon to experience a drop of 10 degrees during a drive into the higher elevations, where summer days are pleasant and bug-free.

As those first settlers of Hay Camp realized back in 1876, and as Native Americans have known since time immemorial, the central Black Hills are a special place imbued with uncommon natural beauty and variety.

Planning

Getting Here and Around

AIR

Although there are several landing strips and municipal airports in the Black Hills, the only airport with commercial service is in Rapid City. Rapid City Regional Airport (RAP), one of the fastest-growing airports in the United States, is 11 miles east of town on Highway 44.

CAR

If you're comfortable doing the driving, your own car or a rental is the best way to see the area. Day trips from Rapid City into the Black Hills are a great way to explore. Several main roads lead west from Rapid City and into the central Black Hills, and then on to the main attractions. The popular routes are Highway 44, toward Pactola Reservoir; Sheridan Lake Road, toward Sheridan Lake and Hill City; and Highway 16, toward Keystone, Mount Rushmore, and Hill City. Highway 385 cuts north and south through the Black Hills and links Hill City with the Crazy Horse Memorial.

This area caters to visitors, so there is ample signage to help you with wayfinding and tempt you with an unplanned stop at a roadside attraction. Highways are steep and curvy in the Black Hills, with lots of scenic distractions and motoring tourists, so it's wise to obey the speed limits and be extra careful. It's also smart to have a printed map. Cell service is generally good, but there are dead spots in the highly varied and mountainous topography. Be sure to check the weather forecast, too, because severe thunderstorms—some carrying hail—can roll in quickly from the surrounding plains. Also be aware that South Dakota ranks fourth in the nation for car-deer collisions. Prime times for deer movement are predawn and at dusk, especially during the fall mating season, called the rut, and in the early spring.

TAXI

Uber and Lyft operate in Rapid City, as do a few taxi services, but few people use them for transport to attractions in the Black Hills. There are many miles between attractions here, so visitors who want to explore the area are better off doing their own driving, or going with a tour operator.

Hotels

An almost overwhelming array of lodging is available in Rapid City, which advertises more than 4,000 rooms for rent, and in the central Black Hills.

Rapid City has budget motels, boutique motels, water-park hotels, all the major chain hotels, and grandly historic properties like the Hotel Alex Johnson. If you're looking for predictable amenities and easy highway access, try the franchise hotels close to Interstate 90. For a hotel with more character and walkable proximity to shops and restaurants, look downtown.

If you'd rather stay closer to nature, there are lodges, resorts, cabins, campgrounds, and even luxury canvas tents scattered across the central Black Hills. Additionally, hundreds of homeowners offer rentals through Airbnb and other online services, ranging from single rooms to mountaintop mansions.

Keystone and Hill City have a similar variety of options, but on a lesser scale.

Restaurants

Tourism ranks second behind agriculture on South Dakota's list of largest industries. Much of the restaurant scene throughout the state—and in Rapid City and the central Black Hills—reflects the state's agricultural heritage and its hardworking, no-nonsense farmers and ranchers. In other words, steaks and burgers are the staples of local fare, and it takes a little digging to find other options.

In the central Black Hills, the culinary variety exists mostly in Rapid City, with options including Asian, Mexican, Indian, and Italian cuisine. Because Rapid City, Keystone, and Hill City are so dependent on tourists—some of whom are on vacation from their diets—there are numerous shops selling locally made pizza, chocolates, cookies, and ice cream. Rapid City also has a thriving food-truck scene, and although the area was late to the nation's craft brewery and winery craze, breweries and wineries are now popping up rapidly.

HOTEL AND RESTAURANT PRICES

⇨ *Hotel and restaurant reviews have been shortened. For full information, see Fodors.com. Restaurant prices are the average cost of a main course at dinner, or if dinner is not served, at lunch. Hotel prices are the lowest cost of a standard double room in high season.*

What It Costs			
$	$$	$$$	$$$$
RESTAURANTS			
under $13	$13–$23	$24–$35	over $35
HOTELS			
under $150	$150–$200	$201–$250	over $250

Tours

If you'd rather leave the driving to others, there are tour operators in the Black Hills ready and waiting to chauffeur you around to all the major sites and attractions. You can take a day-long tour of the Black Hills by bus or van; let a driver ferry you between wineries and breweries; take a hike or ride a bicycle on the Mickelson Trail, with shuttle service to and from the trailheads; or even see the Black Hills by helicopter. In the Black Hills, the tour operators are many and varied, which means there's a tour to match almost any traveler's tastes.

ADVENTURE

Black Hills Adventure Tours

ADVENTURE TOURS | A local guide takes guests on guided hikes, kayaking excursions, and sightseeing tours throughout the Black Hills and Badlands. All tours include pickup and drop off at Rapid City—area hotels, plus bottled water, snacks, and any gear or equipment needed for the excursion. ✉ *550 Berry Blvd., Rapid City* ☎ *605/209–7817* ⊕ *www.blackhillsadventuretours.com* 🎫 *From $325.*

BUS AND VAN TOURS

Black Hills Open-Top-Tours

DRIVING TOURS | Focusing on public and private Jeep tours, this company offers tours to Black Hills area attractions such as Mount Rushmore and Crazy Horse Memorial. One of the most unique excursions is a six-hour Bison Safari Tour through all of Custer State Park with an alpine lake picnic lunch. The Bison Safari and other public tours are family friendly. Reservations required. ✉ *635 Creek Dr., Rapid City* ☎ *605/644–6736* ⊕ *blackhillsopentoptours.com* 🎫 *From $259.*

Black Hills Tour Company

BUS TOURS | This locally owned business offers Black Hills and Badlands tours, bicycle tours, and winery/brewery tours for small groups in unique vehicles ranging from a vintage, Volkswagen stretch limousine to a sleek Mercedes van. The young, energetic owners of the business focus on fun, adventurous tours filled with authentic flavor. Tour destinations range from the typical to the novel, with a Badlands Sunset Tour in the latter category. ⊠ *3434 W. Main St., Rapid City* ☎ *605/389–2092, 605/515–3237* ⊕ *www.blackhillstourcompany.com* ✉ *From $325.*

Fort Hays and Mount Rushmore Tours

BUS TOURS | This nine-hour bus tour amid the Black Hills begins at Fort Hays on the *Dances with Wolves* film set and visits Mount Rushmore, Custer State Park, and the Crazy Horse Memorial. Guests are responsible for their own lunches at the State Game Lodge; a pre-trip breakfast and a post-trip cowboy dinner show are add-on options. Other tour options are available. ⊠ *2255 Fort Hayes Dr., Rapid City* ☎ *605/343–3113* ⊕ *www.mountrushmoretours.com* ✉ *$125.*

MULTIDAY HORSEBACK TOURS
Gunsel Horse Adventures

HORSEBACK RIDING | Specializing in extended, backcountry pack-trips into Custer State Park and other parts of the Black Hills, this company offers adventure-seeking riders a chance to dive deep into nature, camp out under the stars, and experience cowboy cooking, campfire songs, and Western poetry. A special package brings riders in close proximity to the Buffalo Roundup each September in Custer State Park. Just be warned: multiday horseback tours can be physically taxing and are not for the faint of heart. ⊠ *Box 1575, Rapid City* ☎ *605/343–7608* ⊕ *www.gunselhorseadventures.com* ✉ *From $350.*

Visitor Information

Staff offer trip planning, maps, brochures, travel guides, and sales of recreational-vehicle permits in the Black Hills Visitor Information Center, which also houses a gift shop and interpretive exhibits about the Black Hills and Badlands.

CONTACTS Black Hills Visitor Information Center. ⊠ *1851 Discovery Circle, Rapid City* ☎ *605/355–3700 information center, 888/945–7676 booking information* ⊕ *www.blackhillsbadlands.com.*

Rapid City

23 miles northeast of Mount Rushmore, 43 miles northeast of Wind Cave National Park, 42 miles southeast of Deadwood, 62 miles west of Badlands National Park.

The central Black Hills, one of the most developed and best-traveled parts of the region, is anchored by Rapid City. The largest population center in a multistate area, it's the cultural, educational, medical, and economic hub of a vast region. Most of the numerous shops, hotels, and restaurants in the city cater specifically to tourists, including a steady flow of international visitors. Locals refer to western South Dakota as "West River," meaning "west of the Missouri." Cowboy boots are common here, and business leaders often travel by pickup truck or four-wheel-drive vehicle. At the same time, the city supports a convention center and a modern, acoustically advanced performance hall.

GETTING HERE AND AROUND

With its location on Interstate 90 at the eastern edge of the Black Hills, Rapid City is the main gateway to the region's many natural and man-made attractions. It's also one of the only major population centers around, being 347 miles west of Sioux Falls, 300 miles southwest of Bismarck, 318 miles southeast of Billings, and 387 miles northeast of Denver.

TOURS
City View Trolley

BUS TOURS | Walking is the best way to see Rapid City's downtown, but taking the City View Trolley is the easiest way

At Bear Country U.S.A., a drive-through wildlife park, you'll not only be able to see black bears but also elk, sheep, and red foxes.

to see other attractions in the city. The narrated tour includes stops at points of interest and historical sites. The tour begins and ends downtown at the Milo Barber Transportation Center (though you can board it at any of the stops) and includes the Dahl Arts Center, Journey Museum, Storybook Island, and Dinosaur Park. Tours run Thursday through Monday, from late May through September. ⊠ *333 Sixth St., Rapid City* ☎ *605/718–8484* ⊕ *www.visitrapidcity.com* ✉ *$15.*

VISITOR INFORMATION
Visit Rapid City is a one-stop source for visitors seeking maps, brochures and guidance on where to go and what to do in Rapid City, as well as the Black Hills.

CONTACTS Visit Rapid City. ⊠ *512 Main St., Rapid City* ☎ *605/718–8484* ⊕ *www.visitrapidcity.com.*

Sights

Bear Country U.S.A.
OTHER ATTRACTION | FAMILY | Encounter black bear, elk, sheep, and wolves at this drive-through wildlife park just outside Rapid City, which has been entertaining guests for more than 40 years. There's also a walk-through wildlife center with red foxes, porcupines, badgers, bobcats, and lynx. The Babyland area features bear cubs and young otters. ⊠ *13820 S. U.S. 16, Rapid City* ☎ *605/343–2290* ⊕ *www.bearcountryusa.com* ✉ *$20* ⊗ *Closed late Nov.–late Apr.*

Black Hills Caverns
CAVE | FAMILY | Amethysts, logomites, calcite crystals, and other specimens fill this 60-million-year-old, privately owned cave, formed slowly by water trickling through limestone rock and first documented by gold seekers in 1882. Half-hour and hour-long walking tours, as well as gemstone and fossil mining, are available. Tours depart approximately every 20 minutes. ⊠ *2600 Cavern Rd., Rapid City*

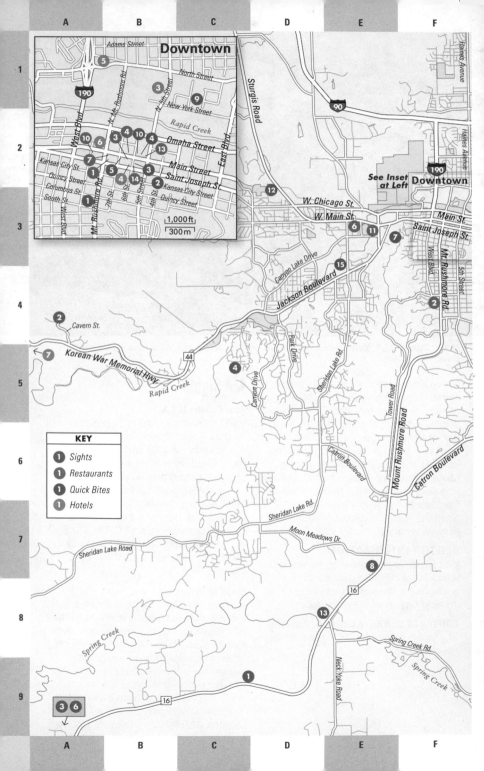

Downtown

KEY
- **1** Sights
- **1** Restaurants
- **1** Quick Bites
- **1** Hotels

Adams Street

North Street

New York Street

Rapid Creek

West Blvd

Kansas City St.

Quincy Street

Columbus St.

South St.

Omaha Street

Main Street

Saint Joseph St

Kansas City Street

Quincy Street

Mt. Rushmore Rd.

4th Street

East Blvd

7th St.

6th St.

5th St.

4th St.

1,000 ft
300 m

Sturgis Road

See Inset at Left

Downtown

W. Chicago St.

W. Main St.

Main St.

Saint Joseph St.

West Blvd

Mt. Rushmore Rd.

5th Street

Canyon Lake Drive

Jackson Boulevard

Korean War Memorial Hwy.

Cavern St.

Rapid Creek

Canyon Drive

Park Drive

Sheridan Lake Rd

Tower Road

Mount Rushmore Road

Catron Boulevard

Catron Boulevard

Sheridan Lake Rd.

Sheridan Lake Road

Moon Meadows Dr.

Spring Creek

Neck Yoke Road

Spring Creek Rd.

Spring Creek

Haines Avenue

Haines Avenue

Rapid City

Sights ▼

1 Bear Country U.S.A. **C9**
2 Black Hills Caverns **A4**
3 Black Hills National Forest **A9**
4 Chapel in the Hills **C5**
5 City of Presidents **B2**
6 Cosmos Mystery Area **A9**
7 Dinosaur Park **E3**
8 Ft. Hays Dances with Wolves Movie Set **E7**
9 The Journey Museum and Learning Center **C1**
10 Main Street Square **B2**
11 Museum of Geology **G3**
12 Outdoor Campus – West **D2**
13 Reptile Gardens **D8**
14 South Dakota Air and Space Museum **I2**
15 Storybook Island **E3**

Restaurants ▼

1 Bokujo Ramen **A2**
2 Colonial House Restaurant and Bar **F4**
3 Delmonico Grill **B2**
4 Firehouse Brewing Company **B2**
5 Fuji Steakhouse & Sushi Bar **H2**
6 Golden Phoenix **E3**
7 Kathmandu Bistro **B2**
8 Millstone Family Restaurant **G2**
9 Minervas **G2**
10 Murphy's Pub and Grill **A2**
11 The Park **E3**
12 Pauly's Pizzeria & Sub Co **H4**
13 Que Pasa Cantina **B2**
14 Tally's Silver Spoon **B2**

Quick Bites ▼

1 Black Hills Bagels **A3**
2 Harriet & Oak **B2**
3 Mary's Mountain Cookies **B2**
4 Silver Lining Creamery **B2**

Hotels ▼

1 Cambria Hotel Rapid City **I2**
2 Comfort Suites Conference Center Rapid City **I2**
3 Holiday Inn Rapid City–Downtown Convention Center **B1**
4 Hotel Alex Johnson **B2**
5 Howard Johnson by Wyndham Rapid City **A1**
6 The Rushmore Hotel **A2**
7 Summer Creek Inn **A5**

⊹ *About 5 miles west of Rapid City on Hwy. 44 to Cavern Rd.* ☎ *605/343–0542, 800/837–9358* ⊕ *blackhillscaverns.com* 🎫 *From $16* ⊙ *Closed weekdays. Closed Nov.–mid-May.*

Black Hills National Forest

FOREST | Hundreds of miles of hiking, mountain biking, ATVing, snowmobiling, and horseback-riding trails crisscross this million-acre forest. The boundaries encompass most of the Black Hills, but there are many "inholdings"—pockets and parcels of privately owned land, most of which are old mining claims that predate the national forest designation. For advice on how to best explore the forest, as well as trail maps, motorized-trail permits, books, and forest-themed gifts, stop in at the Mystic Ranger District Office, which houses the U.S. Forest Service employees who manage the central portion of the Black Hills National Forest. There are also district offices in Custer, Spearfish, and even Sundance, Wyoming, if you venture across the border on a day trip. There's an additional center open seasonally at the Pactola Reservoir. ⊠ *8221 Mt. Rushmore Rd., Rapid City* ☎ *605/343–1567* ⊕ *www.fs.usda.gov/ blackhills* 🎫 *Free.*

★ Chapel in the Hills

RELIGIOUS BUILDING | Hidden away in a residential neighborhood lies this most unexpected gem—an exact replica of the centuries-old Borgund Stavkirke in Norway. Rapid City's version, a high, angular, wooden structure, was built in 1969 as a place for the area's numerous Norwegian Lutherans to worship. If you're looking for a bit of calm, are a fan of unique architecture, love finding unexpected places, or want to take in a service, you won't be sorry. There's a prayer walk around the property, a museum, and a charming Nordic- and religious-themed gift shop. ⊠ *3788 Chapel La., Rapid City* ☎ *605/342–8281* ⊕ *www.chapel-in-the-hills.org* ⊙ *Closed Oct.–May.*

City of Presidents

PUBLIC ART | Started in 2000 to honor "the legacy of the American presidency," a visit to this series of life-size bronze statues ties in nicely with a visit to Mount Rushmore. Located throughout downtown Rapid City, the statues of the country's past presidents can be found on the downtown street corners. Each privately funded sculpture has a creative nod to each president: JFK is with his son, Ronald Reagan has a cowboy hat, and Gerald Ford is with his dog. Some statues may have been moved or placed in storage because of ongoing construction downtown. Check out the website for information about each statue and an interactive map of each statue's location; or, check with Visit Rapid City offices. ⊠ *512 Main St., Rapid City* ☎ *605/718– 8484* ⊕ *visitrapidcity.com.*

Cosmos Mystery Area

OTHER ATTRACTION | **FAMILY** | See water that appears to flow uphill, and try to keep your balance while walking up a wall at this illusion-filled, family-friendly attraction located about 15 miles southwest of Rapid City. This is a busy place that fills up fast with families and kids during the summer, so prospective visitors are encouraged to buy advance tickets on the website. ⊠ *24040 Cosmos Rd., Rapid City* ☎ *605/343–9802* ⊕ *www. cosmosmysteryarea.com* 🎫 *From $14* ⊙ *Closed part of Oct. and Nov.–Apr.*

Dinosaur Park

OTHER ATTRACTION | Seven life-size statues of dinosaurs built by a 1930s government works program stand atop a high ridge overlooking all of Rapid City. The views also extend to the plains in the east and the Black Hills in the west, including a view of South Dakota's highest point, Black Elk Peak. The trip up to the park on Skyline Drive is a scenic one, and the park includes a seasonal visitor center with restrooms and a gift shop. Scheduled construction to add easier walkway access to the statues should

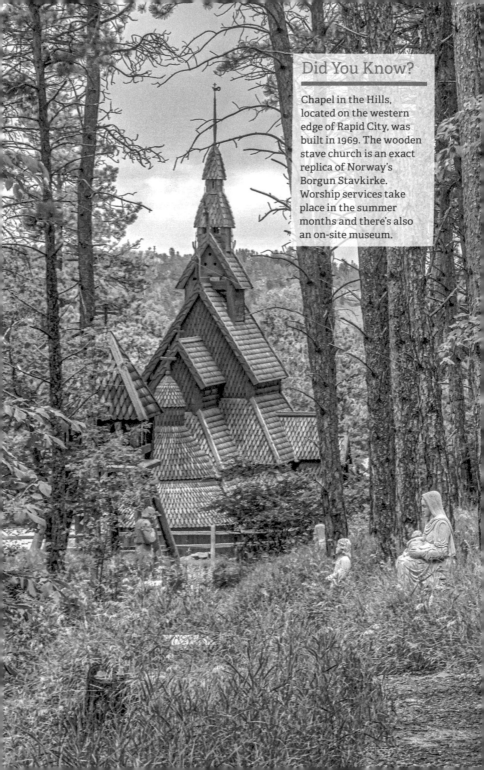

Reptile Gardens has the world's largest private reptile collection, including these hungry crocodiles.

be complete by mid-2024. ✉ *940 Skyline Dr., Rapid City* ☎ *605/343–8687* ⊕ *www.rcgov.org* ⊙ *Visitor center/gift shop closed Oct.–Apr.*

Ft. Hays *Dances with Wolves* Movie Set

FILM/TV STUDIO | Starting with movie sets from the epic *Dances with Wolves,* this attraction is evolving into the South Dakota Film Museum, chronicling some 50 films produced in the state since 1914. See props, posters, and historical photos. A seasonal chuckwagon dinner show is also held here, and a Buffalo Hunt coaster ride soars above the surrounding scenery. ✉ *2255 Fort Hayes Dr., Rapid City* ☎ *605/343–3113* ⊕ *www.mountrushmoretours.com* ✉ *Free; chuckwagon dinner and show, from $44; coaster ride, from $11* ⊙ *Dinner and show closed mid-Oct.–mid-May.*

The Journey Museum and Learning Center

HISTORY MUSEUM | The interactive exhibits at this museum explore the history of the Black Hills from the age of the dinosaurs to the days of the pioneers. Its five permanent collections cover Native

American and pioneer history, geology, paleontology, and archaeology. Special programming and exhibitions occur throughout the year. ✉ *222 New York St., Rapid City* ☎ *605/394–6923* ⊕ *www.journeymuseum.org* ✉ *$14* ⊙ *Closed Mon. in summer, Mon.–Wed. Oct.– Apr.*

Main Street Square

PLAZA/SQUARE | This attractive, outdoor plaza in downtown Rapid City is a focal point for a wide array of special events throughout the year, including movies under the stars, food festivals, musical performances, and, in the winter, ice skating and fire pits. In the summer, the square features interactive fountains, gardens, and a large oval lawn. Giant, sculpted stone slabs called Passage of Wind and Water surround the site, and there are shops and restaurants all around. ✉ *512 Main St., Rapid City* ☎ *605/716–7979* ⊕ *www.mainstreetsquare.org.*

Museum of Geology

SPECIALTY MUSEUM | This museum on the university campus of South Dakota Mines has a fine collection of fossilized bones

Nature in the City

Rapid City is unusually blessed with natural beauty inside its city limits, all of it freely accessible to visitors. Public parks and recreational opportunities abound along the cool, clear waters of Rapid Creek and atop the line of high, forested ridges that run through the city.

Springs, aquifers, and precipitation high up in the mountains feed Rapid Creek, which flows down through Rapid City on its way out to the plains. On the western side of the city, an impoundment forms Canyon Lake, a scenic area with an expansive park, a walking path, and lots of places to fish. Kayakers and canoers also love this small lake, and a lodge on the shore offers paddleboat rentals.

Farther east along the creek, the parks continue. There's Jackson Park, with its disc golf course; Sioux Park, with an herb and flower garden, and a long stretch of tall trees where locals love to hang hammocks; Founders Park, where the city's founders camped under the shelter of limestone rock formations in 1876; and Memorial Park, where the creek is diverted into a small pond next to the city's arena complex, The Monument. The paved Leonard Swanson Memorial Parkway lines the entire length of the creek, connecting all the parks for walkers, joggers, and bicyclists.

At Founders Park, the creek cuts through a line of hogback ridges. To the north of the creek is "M Hill," named for the big white "M" placed atop it by students from the local university, South Dakota School of Mines. Numerous hiking and mountain biking trails wind up and around the hill in Chuck Lien Family Park and Hanson-Larsen Memorial Park.

To the south of the creek is Dinosaur Hill (so named for the dinosaur sculptures in Dinosaur Park), also known as Cowboy Hill. Skyline Drive takes motorists up this hill on a scenic climb several hundred feet above the city. On the way up, keep an eye out for a petrified-looking tree trunk marking the spot of Hangman's Hill, where three horse thieves were hanged in the 1870s. Farther up Skyline Drive, stops include the Skyline Wilderness Area, which contains more hiking and mountain biking trails, and several designated lookout areas to stop and enjoy the views.

From atop M Hill or Skyline Drive, all of Rapid City is visible below, as are the vast plains to the east and the Black Hills to the west. The high point visible to the far west is Black Elk Peak, South Dakota's tallest mountain, which stands 7,242 feet above sea level.

from giant dinosaurs. It also contains extensive collections of agates, fossilized cycads, rocks, gems, and minerals. Younger travelers love the hands-on Kids' Zone exhibits. Shop for a sparkly treasure in the gift shop. ⊠ O'Harra Building, 501 E. St. Joseph St., Rapid City ⊹ From St. Joseph St., turn onto University Loop and right on Technology Ct. Park on

East side of building. ☎ 605/394–2467 ⊕ www.sdsmt.edu ✉ $5 (suggested) ⊗ Closed Sun., seasonal hours after Labor Day.

Outdoor Campus – West

NATURE PRESERVE | A project of the South Dakota Department of Game, Fish, and Parks, this attractive education center opened in 2011. It couples a hands-on museum featuring native habitats—including a freshwater aquarium—with a 32-acre outdoor campus offering outdoor activity classes and equipment rentals year-round. There are 1½ miles of hiking trails on the property. ⊠ *4130 Adventure Trail, Rapid City* ☎ *605/394–2310* ⊕ *gfp. sd.gov/toc-west* ⊘ *Closed Sun.*

★ Reptile Gardens
OTHER ATTRACTION | FAMILY | In a valley just outside Rapid City is western South Dakota's answer to a zoo. In addition to the world's largest private reptile collection, it also has giant tortoises, prairie dogs, and a bald eagle, as well as animal presentations and shows. You can also see more than 50,000 orchids, tulips, and banana trees on the grounds and in the giant Sky Dome. ⊠ *8955 S. U.S. 16, Rapid City* ☎ *605/342–5873, 800/335–0275* ⊕ *www.reptilegardens.com* ⌷ *$24* ⊘ *Closed Dec.–Feb.*

★ South Dakota Air and Space Museum
SPECIALTY MUSEUM | You won't find many free museums with as much to take in as this one. See General Dwight D. Eisenhower's B-25 bomber, a B-1 Bomber, and more than 30 planes, helicopters, and missiles on the outdoor grounds. Inside, there are interactive exhibits, including one about the experimental, stratospheric balloon launches from the Black Hills during the 1930s. During the summer, tours of Ellsworth Air Force Base and a preserved Minuteman missile silo are available for a nominal fee. ⊠ *Ellsworth Air Force Base, 2890 Davis Dr., Bldg. #5208, Box Elder* ☎ *605/385–5189* ⊕ *www.nps.gov/places/sdaasm.htm* ⌷ *Free.*

Storybook Island
CITY PARK | FAMILY | On the west side of Rapid City is Storybook Island, a park on the banks of Rapid Creek that lets children romp through scenes from fairy tales and nursery rhymes. A children's theater troupe, sponsored by the Black Hills Community Theater, performs regular shows on a modest outdoor stage here and hosts workshops and acting programs. Open during the summer and for a Christmas Night of Lights display during the holiday season. ⊠ *1301 Sheridan Lake Rd., Rapid City* ☎ *605/342–6357* ⊕ *storybookisland.org* ⌷ *Free, with nominal fees for carousel and other rides* ⊘ *Closed Labor Day–Memorial Day.*

Restaurants

★ Bokujo Ramen
$$ | JAPANESE | Food Network TV celebrity chef Justin Warner and his wife Brooke (a Rapid City native) have added an American touch to traditional dishes built around slender Japanese noodles made from wheat flour, egg, salt, and *kansui* (an alkaline substance) mineral water, which gives ramen its distinctive texture, flavor, and color. This intimate Far East–themed bistro is located on a busy street. **Known for:** traditional Japanese dishes with an American touch; popular local lunch stop; selection of beer, wine, and sake. ⑤ *Average main: $15* ⊠ *518 Mt. Rushmore Rd., Rapid City* ⊕ *bokujo-ramen.com.*

Colonial House Restaurant and Bar
$$ | AMERICAN | For a good, simple, hearty, and affordable meal, this locally owned restaurant is a popular place among Rapid Citians for breakfast, lunch, and dinner. It's conveniently located on the street that eventually leads out of town toward Mount Rushmore. **Known for:** house-made caramel rolls; generous portions; down-home and friendly atmosphere. ⑤ *Average main: $20* ⊠ *2315 Mt. Rushmore Rd., Rapid City* ☎ *605/342–4640* ⊕ *www.colonialhousernb.com.*

★ Delmonico Grill
$$$$ | STEAK HOUSE | Known as perhaps the best restaurant in Rapid City (in competition with establishments including its sister restaurant, Tally's Silver Spoon), Delmonico is the place to go for delicious steak. Upon entering this downtown steak house, you'll see it's a cut above

Check out more than 30 vintage military aircraft at the South Dakota Air and Space Museum just outside the main gate of Ellsworth Air Force Base.

many other local restaurants. **Known for:** high-end, delectable desserts, including crème brûlée; attentive service; the Delmonico, a massive bone-in rib eye for two. ⑤ *Average main: $40* ✉ *609 Main St., Rapid City* ☎ *605/791–1664* ⊕ *www. delmonicogrill.com* ☽ *No lunch.*

Firehouse Brewing Company

$$ | **AMERICAN** | Brass fixtures and fire-fighting equipment ornament the state's first brewpub, located in the city's original 1915 firehouse. The house-brewed beers are the highlight here, and the menu includes such hearty pub dishes as pastas, salads, gumbo, and buffalo burgers. **Known for:** fun, boisterous atmosphere; large outdoor seating area; live music. ⑤ *Average main: $16* ✉ *610 Main St., Rapid City* ☎ *605/348–1915* ⊕ *www. firehousebrewing.com.*

Fuji Steakhouse & Sushi Bar

$$ | **JAPANESE** | Watch your food cooked on the hibachi or take a seat away from the action and order from the menu, which includes sushi, rolls, soups, and

other traditional Japanese selections. This restaurant is located just off Interstate 90 near lots of other restaurants and shopping. **Known for:** fun atmosphere around the hibachi; one of the few full-service Japanese restaurants in town; quick and affordable lunch specials. ⑤ *Average main: $20* ✉ *1731 Eglin St., Rapid City* ☎ *605/721–8886* ⊕ *www.fujisteakhouse-sd.com.*

Golden Phoenix

$ | **CHINESE** | Great food, low prices, and relaxed, friendly, and quick service make this one of Rapid City's most popular Chinese restaurants. The friendly chef-owner seasons traditional dishes from all over China with spices from his native Taiwan. **Known for:** efficient service; loved by locals; wallet-friendly prices. ⑤ *Average main: $12* ✉ *2421 W. Main St., Rapid City* ☎ *605/348–4195* ⊕ *goldenphoenixrc.com.*

Kathmandu Bistro

$$ | **NEPALESE** | Nepalese, Indian, and Tibetan food are on the menu at this small downtown eatery, which is

a favorite lunch spot for locals. The exposed-brick wall and other decor is unassuming, and the focus is on the food. **Known for:** daily lunch buffet; laid-back atmosphere; fast service. ⑤ *Average main: $16* ✉ *727 Main St., Rapid City* ☎ *605/343–5070* ⊕ *www.kathmandubistro.com.*

Millstone Family Restaurant

$ | AMERICAN | Depending on your early-morning energy level, walk or drive to the Millstone for a satisfying country breakfast before starting your day. Breakfast is so beloved here that it's served all day and includes an extensive array of omelets, waffles, pancakes, and more, but the skillets menu is most worth your attention. **Known for:** soup and salad bar; friendly waitstaff; local favorite. ⑤ *Average main: $12* ✉ *1520 N. Lacrosse St., Rapid City* ☎ *605/348–9022* ⊕ *www.bhmillstone.com.*

Minervas

$$$ | ECLECTIC | Minervas is a regional chain of elegant restaurants that began in South Dakota, where multiple locations are known and loved by local diners for high-quality food and service. Minervas focuses on Midwest steaks, fresh-made pizza and pasta, signature salads, and house-made desserts. **Known for:** elegant atmosphere; outstanding reputation; high-end quality and service. ⑤ *Average main: $24* ✉ *2111 N. LaCrosse St., Rapid City* ☎ *605/394–9505* ⊕ *www.minervasrestaurants.com.*

Murphy's Pub and Grill

$$ | AMERICAN | Chow down on local ingredients that produce hearty regional favorites like buffalo meat loaf, while relaxing in a laid-back, pub atmosphere. Feel free to pair a couple pints with your meal—you can walk back to your hotel if you're staying downtown. **Known for:** great appetizers; outdoor seating area; many beers on tap. ⑤ *Average main: $15* ✉ *510 Ninth St., Rapid City* ☎ *605/791–2244* ⊕ *www.murphyspubandgrill.com.*

The Park

$$ | AMERICAN | Westside Rapid Citians can call this lavish Las Vegas–style dining and entertainment complex their own and visitors can also relax and revel in the 32,000 square-foot centerpiece of the newly renovated Baken Park Shopping Center. The Park features breakfast, lunch, dinner, and dessert quick-bite options as well as a Sunday brunch buffet. **Known for:** steaks, burgers and pasta; craft beer and hand-crafted cocktails; lavish desserts. ⑤ *Average main: $20* ✉ *707 Mountain View Rd., Rapid City* ☎ *605/791–1702* ⊕ *www.thepark707.com.*

Pauly's Pizzeria & Sub Co.

$ | PIZZA | Go here for some of the best pizza in Rapid City, plus other choices including salads, gyros, subs, and a nice selection of craft beer. The many televisions playing sports in this eastern Rapid City establishment make it a cross between a pizzeria and sports bar, but it retains a family atmosphere appreciated by locals. **Known for:** handmade pizzas; self-serve craft beer wall; meaty, hearty deli subs. ⑤ *Average main: $11* ✉ *1624 E. St. Patrick St., Rapid City* ☎ *605/348–7827* ⊕ *www.paulys.com* ⊙ *Closed Sun.*

Que Pasa Cantina

$$ | MEXICAN | Every day is a fiesta at Rapid City's most popular and spacious Mexican restaurant, with its upbeat servers and its focus on gathering people together around food and drink. The Fifth and Main location makes this one of the most visible businesses in the city and puts guests within walking distance of everything in the downtown area, including Main Street Square. **Known for:** outdoor patio and rooftop dining; city's best selection of tequila; happy-hour margaritas. ⑤ *Average main: $16* ✉ *502 Main St., Rapid City* ☎ *605/716–9800* ⊕ *www.quepasarc.com.*

After a day of touring, stop into the Firehouse Brewing Company, located in a 1915 firehouse, for a craft beer and a bite to eat.

★ Tally's Silver Spoon

$$ | ECLECTIC | Ask locals where they like to eat, and many will mention Tally's because of the chef-driven menu, the high-quality food, and the "fine diner" atmosphere (where "cherry pie and foie gras co-exist"). This small, downtown, corner building fills up fast, so consider making reservations. **Known for:** hearty breakfasts served until 2 pm daily; homemade pies; popular local breakfast and lunch stop. ⑤ *Average main: $20* ⊠ *530 Sixth St., Rapid City* ☎ *605/342–7621* ⊕ *www.tallyssilverspoon.com.*

☕ Coffee and Quick Bites

Black Hills Bagels

$ | AMERICAN | Start your day early at this local favorite breakfast spot, where the bagels range from cinnamon raisin to white chocolate chip and can be enhanced with an array of toppings on the build-your-own sandwich menu (or just choose from the five signature sandwiches if endless options aren't your thing). If you're heading off to explore the Badlands or Mount Rushmore, take your breakfast sandwich to go, and consider grabbing something extra for the long morning ahead. **Known for:** more than 20 bagel varieties; fast options for lunch in addition to breakfast; serves Dark Canyon coffee. ⑤ *Average main: $9* ⊠ *913 Mt. Rushmore Rd., Rapid City* ☎ *605/399–1277* ⊕ *www.blackhillsbagels.com.*

★ Harriet & Oak

$ | AMERICAN | For a delicious cup of coffee or a quick sandwich and chips for lunch, this chic coffee shop and café is a great choice in downtown Rapid City. There's bar-stool seating at windows looking out on Main Street, and quiet nooks in a loft overlooking the main dining area. **Known for:** 1960s Volkswagen van inside the restaurant; signature coffee, espresso, cappuccino, and more; distinctive, stylish interior. ⑤ *Average main: $10* ⊠ *329 Main St., Rapid City* ☎ *605/791–0396* ⊕ *www.harrietandoak. com.*

Mary's Mountain Cookies

$ | **BAKERY** | Indulge yourself with a flavor-packed treat at this small downtown shop, where the quarter-pound cookies are baked fresh on-site. The Hotel Alex Johnson, several restaurants, and the historic Elks Theatre are all close by, making this a convenient and tasty stopover. **Known for:** giant cookies; friendly, hometown atmosphere; unique and seasonal flavors. $ *Average main: $5* ✉ *526 Sixth St., Rapid City* ☎ *605/791–0463* ⊕ *marysmountaincookies.com.*

Silver Lining Creamery

$ | **AMERICAN** | Few visitors to Main Street Square can resist the temptation of this shop, where local workers make small batches of ice cream daily. Order at a window overlooking the square and enjoy your treat outdoors, or take advantage of the small seating area inside. **Known for:** changing flavors daily; next to outdoor seating, fountains, and stage at Main Street Square; windows to watch the production process. $ *Average main: $5* ✉ *512 Main St., Rapid City* ☎ *605/791–1141* ⊕ *www.silverliningcreamery.com.*

Hotels

Cambria Hotel Rapid City

$$ | **HOTEL** | Rates are only a little higher here than a typical brand-name hotel, but the accommodations are noticeably more upscale, with sizable suites, a pool area with a large hot tub, and a stylish restaurant-bar featuring craft beers. **Pros:** nice lounge-bar-restaurant for unwinding after a day of sightseeing; ample parking; easy to find and easy access from interstate. **Cons:** on the edge of the city, miles from downtown; not a walkable area; in a developing section of town prone to construction. $ *Rooms from: $165* ✉ *3333 Outfitters Rd., Rapid City* ☎ *605/341–0101* ⊕ *www.choicehotels.com* ⇆ *111 suites* ❯❮ *No Meals.*

Comfort Suites Conference Center Rapid City

$$ | **HOTEL** | This hotel receives high marks across the board for cleanliness, service, and value, and it's also conveniently located at Interstate 90's junction with the highway bypass that goes around Rapid City toward Mount Rushmore. **Pros:** easy access from the interstate; a restaurant, Dakotah Steakhouse, is across the parking lot; close to lots of shopping and dining options. **Cons:** very busy, high-traffic area; one of the least walkable parts of the city; a standard chain hotel without much character. $ *Rooms from: $169* ✉ *1333 N. Elk Vale Rd., Rapid City* ☎ *605/791–2345* ⊕ *www.choicehotels.com* ⇆ *92 suites* ❯❮ *Free Breakfast.*

Holiday Inn Rapid City–Downtown Convention Center

$ | **HOTEL** | This eight-story hotel has a central lobby with an atrium, glass elevators, and a 60-foot waterfall; rooms are spacious and contemporary, done in soothing neutral tones with small colorful touches. **Pros:** the only hotel that's directly next door to the civic center; good food in restaurant; nice bartenders in lounge. **Cons:** sterile feel; fairly long walk to other restaurants; limited parking when the civic center is busy. $ *Rooms from: $149* ✉ *505 N. 5th St., Rapid City* ☎ *605/348–4000, 888/465–4329* ⊕ *www.rushmoreplaza.com* ⇆ *205 rooms* ❯❮ *No Meals.*

★ Hotel Alex Johnson

$$$ | **HOTEL** | Built in 1927 at the same time carving was getting underway at Mount Rushmore, this 11-story hotel stands as a testament to the ambition of its namesake railroad executive, who insisted on elaborate decorative tributes to Native Americans and the Black Hills; historic elegance oozes from every part of this grand old hotel, which is the anchor of downtown Rapid City. **Pros:** updated rooms in a historic

setting; next to Main Street Square and numerous shops and restaurants; Starbucks on the property. **Cons:** smaller rooms, as expected for a hotel built in the 1920s; given its location in the heart of downtown, parking can be challenging; includes a street-level bar that gets rowdy. ⑤ *Rooms from: $210* ✉ *523 Sixth St., Rapid City* ☎ *605/342–1210* ⊕ *www. alexjohnson.com* ⌁ *143 rooms* ❙❍❙ *No Meals.*

Howard Johnson by Wyndham Rapid City

$$ | **HOTEL** | This reasonably priced hotel has clean, brightly decorated rooms and a quiet location tucked into the edge of a residential area, yet it's near an expressway, the city's arena, and the downtown core. **Pros:** predictable quality from a chain hotel; great location for anyone attending events at the arena; just off the short I–190 freeway, with easy access to both downtown. **Cons:** not within walking distance of restaurants or shopping; may fill up with louder guests when there's a concert at the arena; on-site dining is limited to a basic continental breakfast. ⑤ *Rooms from: $150* ✉ *950 North St., Rapid City* ☎ *605/646–0734* ⊕ *www. hojorapidcity.com* ⌁ *98 rooms* ❙❍❙ *Free Breakfast.*

The Rushmore Hotel

$$$ | **HOTEL** | This locally owned hotel has all the amenities you'd expect from a top-notch national chain, including modern and stylish rooms with locally themed decor, a lounge (frequently featuring live music), and two on-site restaurants. **Pros:** close to downtown shops and restaurants; locally owned; uniquely designed rooms. **Cons:** nearby railroad tracks with infrequent but noisy trains; located at one of downtown's busiest intersections; lounge with music can be boisterous. ⑤ *Rooms from: $200* ✉ *445 Mt. Rushmore Rd., Rapid City* ☎ *605/348–8300* ⊕ *therushmorehotel.com* ⌁ *177 rooms* ❙❍❙ *No Meals.*

Summer Creek Inn

$$$ | **B&B/INN** | Escape into nature at this secluded, exceedingly well-reviewed spot with luxuriously decorated rooms and manicured grounds, surrounded by the Black Hills National Forest. **Pros:** away from crowds; in the mountains and forest; fireplaces, private hot tubs, and other extravagances. **Cons:** expensive, especially if staying multiple nights; 15-minute drive to nearest city; deposit of 50% required with reservation. ⑤ *Rooms from: $250* ✉ *23204 Summer Creek Dr., Rapid City* ☎ *605/574–4408* ⊕ *www.summercreekinn.com* ⌁ *10 suites* ❙❍❙ *No Meals.*

Nightlife

Dakota Point Brewing

BREWPUBS | English, Scottish, Irish, and American ales are brewed here, and relaxed conversation is fostered either indoors or, during summer evenings, on a large outdoor patio. No food service at the pub, but food trucks often set up in the parking lot. ✉ *405 Canal St., Rapid City* ☎ *605/791–2739* ⊕ *www.dakota-pointbrewing.com.*

Firehouse Wine Cellars

WINE BAR | Located next door to the Firehouse Brewing Company pub and restaurant, this winery in a busy but relaxed setting offers wine tasting and sales of bottled wine and wine-related merchandise. ✉ *620 Main St., Rapid City* ☎ *605/716–9463* ⊕ *www.firehousewinecellars.com.*

Hay Camp Brewing Co.

BREWPUBS | At this downtown, corner brewpub bearing Rapid City's original moniker (Hay Camp), local brewers craft small-batch ales and customers enjoy an unusually spacious interior decorated with rough-hewn timber. Food trucks often park nearby. ✉ *601 Kansas City St., Rapid City* ☎ *605/718–1167* ⊕ *www. haycampbrewing.com.*

Exclusive Hangouts

Two of the best places to get a relaxed drink in downtown Rapid City are never seen by most visitors, but they're worth a little extra effort to get in the door.

One is the Vertex Sky Bar, perched atop the roof of the historic, 11-story Hotel Alex Johnson. The hotel was built in 1927, and the glamorous decor and feel of the Vertex are evocative of the Prohibition era. Patrons can sit inside and enjoy the view through tall panes of glass, or settle around the fireplaces on the outdoor, rooftop patio.

But don't expect to just stroll in, because the Vertex is open only to guests of the hotel and locals who've purchased a membership. If you're neither of those, you can gain access with a dinner reservation and a $25 cover charge. It's worth the price if you have the time on a nice evening, because there's no other place like it in the Black Hills.

The other little-known downtown Rapid City hideaway is even more evocative of the Prohibition era, and purposely so. That's the Blind Lion Speakeasy, in the basement below Murphy's Pub & Grill.

The Blind Lion transports patrons back to the speakeasy era with its "secret" location, period decor, bartenders who dress and act the part, and Prohibition-era cocktails. Even getting in the door is a "secretive" Prohibition-style task. Prospective guests have to text ☎ 605/939–0095 for reservations, and you'll get a reply with a code to gain entry. Don't be intimidated, because the extra steps are intended as a fun part of the experience rather than roadblocks.

The Blind Lion often hosts live music and has a menu of food available from Murphy's, making it a great place to hide away and unwind.

★ **Independent Ale House**
BREWPUBS | Choose from 50 rotating beer taps and a smaller wine list at this trendy downtown nightspot featuring exposed-brick decor, where you can also eat a tasty, handcrafted pizza. The place fills up fast, so it's best to go in the late afternoon if you want a place to sit and a quieter atmosphere. There's window seating, plus booths, bar stools, and even couches and comfy chairs in the basement. ⊠ *625 St. Joseph St., Rapid City* ☎ *605/718–9492* ⊕ *www.independentalehouse.com*.

Wobbly Bobby
PUB | Drop in for cordial revelry at an Old English pub, named for those early English police officers, nicknamed "Peelers" or "Bobbies," who would excessively imbibe while on duty. The Wobbly Bobby greets customers with traditional rich darkwood decor and checkerboard table ambience. Even the main entrance, in a brick-paved, period-lighted alley behind The Shops at Main Street Square, evokes the atmosphere of a quiet neighborhood pub. Inside, a full selection of craft beers and wines and an impressive array of whiskeys awaits. The pub grub menu highlights Irish nachos and classic fish-'n-chips, or you can order from the Mexican cantina next door. ⊠ *510 Main St., Rapid City* ☎ *605/721–7468* ⊕ *www.wobblybobbypub.com*.

🎭 Performing Arts

PERFORMANCE VENUES

Dahl Arts Center

PERFORMANCE VENUES | At the Dahl Arts Center across from the downtown Rapid City Public Library, exhibits by local artists rotate regularly, and there is a permanent piece: a 180-foot oil-on-canvas panoramic mural depicting United States economic history from the colonization by the Europeans to the 1970s. A small performance space features emerging artists, and a gift shop sells the work of local artisans. ⊠ 713 7th St., Rapid City ☎ 605/394–4101 ⊕ www.thedahl.org.

The Monument Fine Arts Theater

THEATER | This 1,690-seat theater is the local venue for touring Broadway shows, big-name comedians, and the Vucurevich Speaker Series, which has attracted prominent names such as the violinist Itzhak Perlman and Apple co-founder Steve Wozniak. The theater is part of the sprawling Monument complex, which also includes an ice arena for a minor-league hockey team, a convention center, and two arenas, The Summit Arena and Barnett Fieldhouse. ⊠ 444 Mt. Rushmore Rd., Rapid City ☎ 605/394–4115 ⊕ www.themonument.live/plan-your-visit/venue-information/fine-arts-theatre.

Performing Arts Center of Rapid City

CONCERTS | Black Hills Community Theater and the Black Hills Symphony Orchestra are both based in this historic, renovated school building that includes an 830-seat main theater and a 175-seat studio theater, where performances are scheduled throughout the year. The facility stands on the site of the demolished former high school that President Calvin Coolidge used as his office during his 1927 vacation in the Black Hills. ⊠ 601 Columbus St., Rapid City ☎ 605/394–6191, 605/394–1786 box office ⊕ performingartsrc.org.

🛍 Shopping

Dakota Drum Company

ART GALLERY | Lakota artist Sonja Holy Eagle, who grew up on the Cheyenne River and Pine Ridge reservations in South Dakota, has been selling handmade drums, buffalo rawhide paintings, and ledger art for more than two decades in this downtown store filled with her traditional work. ⊠ 603 Main St., Rapid City ☎ 605/348–2421 ⊕ www.dakotadrum.com.

The Market

FOOD | The local owners of this grocery store provide a full selection of healthy, organic, locally sourced products, including produce, grass-fed beef, and South Dakota-made cheeses. Travelers can also find natural bath and body items here. ⊠ 333 Omaha St., Rapid City ☎ 605/341–9099 ⊕ themarketsd.com.

Pawnseum, Presidential Pawn, and The Clock Shop

ANTIQUES & COLLECTIBLES | Forget your preconceived notions about pawn shops before stepping into this three-in-one store, where the Pawnseum was born of a desire to display (and sell) one-of-a-kind items such as a Michael Jackson glove, JFK photos, and a piece of a 1960s space capsule. There's a little bit of everything on the walls and in the display cases of this family-owned, downtown facility. ⊠ 629 St. Joseph St., Rapid City ☎ 605/342–7296 ⊕ www.presidentialpawnshop.com.

★ Prairie Edge Trading Company and Galleries

ART GALLERY | One of the world's top collections of Plains Native American artwork and crafts makes Prairie Edge Trading Company and Galleries seem more like a museum than a store. The collection ranges from books to stunning artwork representing the Lakota, Crow, Cheyenne, Shoshone, Arapaho, and Assiniboine tribes of the Great Plains. You won't find a place like Prairie Edge anywhere else in the Black Hills or, for that matter, hundreds of miles around. But you don't have to go out of your way to find it, since it's in the heart of downtown Rapid City next to Main Street Square. ⊠ *606 Main St., Rapid City* ☎ *800/541–2388* ⊕ *prairieedge.com.*

Rushmore Candy Co.

CANDY | FAMILY | At 13,000 square-feet, this roadside candy shop lays claim as the largest in South Dakota and offers dozens of flavors of current and nostalgic candy brands to satiate any sweet tooth. Made in-house is about anything imaginable slathered in chocolate, from strawberries to pickles and bacon. Anyone spotting the colonial brick architecture will be interested to know the structure, (now minus the cupola), was built as a replica of Philadelphia's Independence Hall for a past attraction. A sister store, Candyland, is located at Three Forks near Hill City. ⊠ *9815 S. Hwy. 16, Rapid City* ☎ *605/342–1489* ⊕ *rushmorecandycompany.com.*

Scheels

SPORTING GOODS | Just off Interstate 90, the enormous Scheels store carries a wide selection of all-weather hiking gear, footwear, and clothes, as well as binoculars suitable for bird-watchers and all manner of other outdoor recreational gear. This is a perfect place to stock up for all of your Black Hills adventures. ⊠ *1225 Eglin St., Rapid City* ☎ *605/342–9033* ⊕ *www.scheels.com.*

 Activities

CAMPING

Hart Ranch Camping Resort Club. This massive yet secluded site about 15 minutes from Rapid City is more like a camping city than a campground. There's a pool, hot tubs, tennis courts, a hiking trail, a restaurant, and other amenities too numerous to mention, and it's all next door to Hart Ranch Golf Course. The campground focuses on members,

but rentals are available to nonmembers. ⊠ *23756 Arena Dr.* ☎ *800/605–4278, 605/399–2582* ⤳ *459 RV/camper sites, 73 cabins, 24 tent sites.*

HTR Black Hills. This conveniently located campground is just outside Rapid City next to the Bear Country U.S.A. attraction on the way to Mount Rushmore. Tall pine trees shade 35 acres that include an outdoor stage and amphitheater, a heated pool and hot tub (open Memorial Day to Labor Day, weather permitting) and activity areas including mini golf and horseshoes. ⊠ *13752 S. U.S. 16* ☎ *605/342–5368* ⤳ *90 RV/camper sites, 24 cabins and guesthouses, 11 tent sites.*

Lake Park Campground and Cottages. Camp without roughing it at this well-shaded area alongside Canyon Lake on the edge of Rapid City, only 4 miles from downtown. The campground offers bicycle rentals to enjoy the 8-mile paved path along Rapid Creek, and a neighboring resort offers paddleboat rentals on the lake. ⊠ *2850 Chapel La.* ☎ *605/341–5320* ⤳ *30 lodges and cottages, 29 RV/camper sites, 7 tent sites.*

FISHING

The Black Hills are filled with tiny mountain creeks, especially on the wetter western and northern slopes, that are ideal for fly-fishing. Rapid Creek, which flows down from the central Black Hills into Pactola Reservoir and finally into Rapid City, is a favorite fishing venue for the city's anglers, both because of its regularly stocked population of trout and for its easy accessibility.

Dakota Angler and Outfitter

FISHING | If you want to try fly-fishing in Rapid Creek or any of the other streams in the Black Hills, stop into this popular shop run by a local fisherman for gear, advice, the latest local fishing reports, or to book a guided fishing trip. ⊠ *1010 Jackson Blvd., Rapid City* ☎ *605/341–2450* ⊕ *www.flyfishsd.com.*

The Rooster

FISHING | The Rooster is a well-established go-to tackle and bait shop for all of your angling needs. You'll find a wide selection of rods, reels, lures, and electronics catering to small stream, river, and lake fishing and live bait from earthworms to minnows. The shop is run by fishermen for fishermen, meaning there are good sources of advice on what's biting and where. ⊠ *1441 W. Main St., Rapid City* ☎ *605/342–3867* ⊕ *www.facebook.com/ roosterlivebait.*

HIKING AND BIKING

Rapid City is unusually rich in free outdoor recreational opportunities inside the city limits, thanks to a paved path along Rapid Creek that stretches the entire width of the city, and a series of interconnected dirt trails atop the forested hogback ridges that run through town.

Chuck Lien Family Park and Hanson-Larsen Memorial Park

HIKING & WALKING | These two "parks" are actually a broad area of hiking and mountain-biking trails covering a high ridge within Rapid City known as M Hill (for the giant "M" placed there by university students from South Dakota Mines). The trails range from easy to strenuous. ⊠ *1510 W. Omaha St., Rapid City* ⊹ *Start at Founders Park along Omaha Street, where there's a map of the trails* ☎ *605/394–4175* ⊕ *www.rcgov.org.*

Leonard Swanson Memorial Pathway

BIKING | This paved path stretches 8 miles across Rapid City, alongside the clear waters of Rapid Creek in a greenway corridor built after a catastrophic 1972 flash flood, and named for the then-city public works director who relentlessly pushed to keep the greenway free of redevelopment after the flood. The mostly flat trail winds through several parks and skirts the downtown area. Walkers, joggers, and cyclists share this popular path, which is at its most scenic in the western part of the city. ⊠ *Entry points include Canyon Lake Park, Sioux Park, Founders Park, and Memorial Park, Rapid City* ☎ *605/394–4175* ⊕ *www.rcgov.org.*

Skyline Drive Wilderness Area

HIKING & WALKING | Drivers love scenic, high-altitude Skyline Drive and its views of Rapid City and the Black Hills, and hikers and mountain bikers love Skyline Drive Wilderness Area, which is a system of forested trails beginning from the various overlooks along the drive. ⊠ *2215 Skyline Dr., Rapid City* ⊹ *Take Quincy Street west from downtown to Skyline Dr.; look for trailheads including Dinosaur Park and Stonewall Overlook* ☎ *605/394– 4175* ⊕ *www.rcgov.org.*

Keystone

21 miles southwest of Rapid City, 3 miles northeast of Mount Rushmore.

Founded in the 1880s by prospectors searching the central Black Hills for gold deposits, this small town wedged into the mountains along Battle Creek now serves the millions of visitors who pass through each year on their way to Mount Rushmore, 3 miles away. The touristy town has some 700 hotel rooms—more than twice the number of permanent residents. Its mall-like main thoroughfare includes dozens of gift shops, restaurants, and attractions that range from wax museums and miniature-golf courses to alpine slides and helicopter rides.

◉ Sights

Big Thunder Gold Mine

MINE | **FAMILY** | Don a hard hat and take a guided tour through an underground gold mine, get some free gold ore samples, explore the mining museum, and do a little gold panning yourself at this authentic-looking facility built into a hillside along Battle Creek. ⊠ *604 Blair St., Keystone* ☎ *605/666–4847* ⊕ *www.bigthundermine.com* ⌑ *Tours from $11; gold panning from $51* ☉ *Closed Nov.–Mar.*

Did You Know?

One of the most stunning drives through the Black Hills is along the 70-mile Peter Norbeck National Scenic Byway, a masterpiece of artistic engineering known for its hairpin turns and numerous tunnels blasted through granite mountains.

Keystone Historical Museum
HISTORY MUSEUM | The main road through Keystone has been transformed into a modern tourist extravaganza, but a bit of the old mining town remains at the Keystone Historical Museum, located in a beautiful 1900 Victorian schoolhouse. Here you can learn about the town's colorful mining history and its connection to the carving of Mount Rushmore, and get directions for a walking tour of the remaining "old town." ✉ *410 Third St., Keystone* ☎ *605/666–4494* ⊕ *www.keystonehistory.com* ⊘ *Closed Oct.–Apr.*

★ Peter Norbeck National Scenic Byway
SCENIC DRIVE | Although there are faster ways to get from Mount Rushmore to the southern Black Hills, this scenic drive in the Black Hills is a more stunning route. Take U.S. 16A south into Custer State Park, where bison, bighorn sheep, elk, antelope, and burros roam. Then drive north on Highway 87 through the Needles, towering granite spires that rise above the forest. Highway 87 finally brings you to U.S. 16/U.S. 385, where you head south to the Crazy Horse Memorial. Because the scenic byway is a challenging drive (with one-lane tunnels and switchbacks) and because you'll likely want to stop a few times to admire the scenery, plan on spending two to three hours on this route. Stretches of U.S. 16A and Highway 87 may close in winter. ✉ *U.S. 16A and Hwy. 87, Keystone* ☎ *605/255–4515* ⊕ *www.fhwa.dot.gov/byways.*

Rush Mountain Adventure Park
CAVE | **FAMILY** | Stalagmites, stalactites, flowstone, ribbons, columns, helictites, and the "Big Room" are all part of the worthwhile tour into this privately owned cave. In 1876, miners found the opening to the cave while digging a flume into the mountainside to carry water to the gold mines below. The cave was opened to the public in 1927, just before the carving of Mount Rushmore began. The attraction also features the Soaring Eagle Zipride, Rushmore Mountain Coaster, Wingwalker Challenge Course, and other theme-park-style activities. ✉ *13622 Hwy. 40, Keystone* ☎ *605/255–4384* ⊕ *www.rushmtn.com* ☞ *From $11* ⊘ *Closed Nov.–Feb.*

Sprockets Fun Foundry
AMUSEMENT PARK/CARNIVAL | **FAMILY** | A family entertainment center with loads of fun for adults as well as children, including a virtual reality platform that brings heat, moving air and movement under your feet to the gaming experience, an arcade with more than 50 games and "duckpin" bowling, a miniature version of traditional bowling. Adults may also find amusement in the second floor Taproom and Treats, with local craft beer and wines, pizza, and ice-cream treats, including beer floats. All in an industrial-chic themed building evoking Keystone's mining heritage. ✉ *221 Swanzey St., Keystone* ☎ *605/666–4242* ⊕ *www.sprockets.fun* ☞ *Fun card (arcade credit) packages start at $10* ⊘ *Closed Mon.– Wed. during winter.*

🍴 Restaurants

Cruizzers
$$ | **PIZZA** | Tasty and hearty made-to-order pizzas, calzones, subs, and pasta make this pizzeria overlooking Keystone's boardwalk a favorite stop for visitors who are hungry from a day of exploring Mount Rushmore and other attractions. There are plenty of menu choices. **Known for:** focus on service; indoor and outdoor balcony seating; pizza that's filling with generous toppings. ⑤ *Average main: $18* ✉ *110B Winter St., Keystone* ☎ *605/666– 4313* ⊕ *www.facebook.com/cruizzers* ⊘ *Closed Oct.–Apr.*

Powder House Restaurant
$$$ | **STEAK HOUSE** | This rustic steak house at the Powder House Lodge is made for quiet mountain evenings with its indoor,

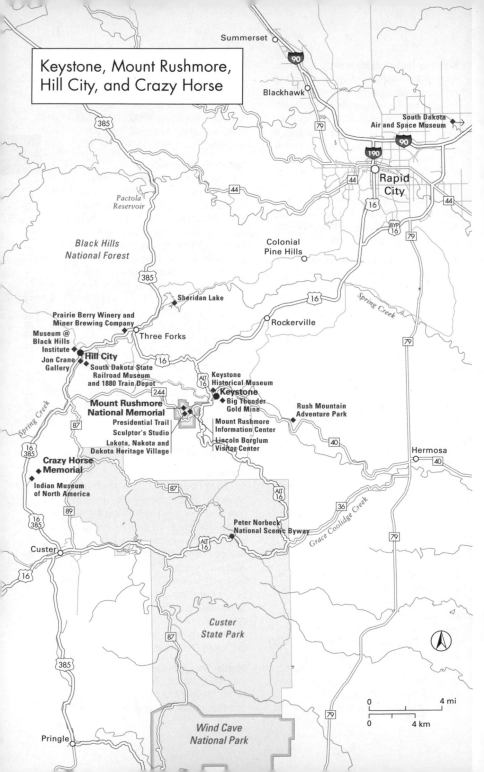

log-cabin-style dining area and expansive, covered, outdoor patio. The menu focuses on quality meats (but with vegetarian options) and relaxing drinks. **Known for:** prime rib, buffalo, wild game; forested, mountainside setting; full bar with wide selection of wine, beer, and spirits. $ *Average main: $25* ⊠ *24125 Hwy. 16A, Keystone* ☎ *800/321–0692* ⊕ *www. powderhouselodge.com* ☉ *Closed Labor Day–Memorial Day.*

☕ Coffee and Quick Bites

Grapes & Grinds
$ | **CAFÉ** | Start your day with some caffeine, get a late-morning pick-me-up, or grab a glass of wine and tasty treat at this quick-stop coffee shop and wine bar along the main road through Keystone, which features indoor seating and an outdoor patio. **Known for:** life-size chessboard and pieces on the outdoor patio; gelato in a variety of flavors; coffee from local roaster Dark Canyon. $ *Average main: $5* ⊠ *609 Hwy. 16A, Keystone* ☎ *605/666–5142* ⊕ *www.grapesgrinds. com* ☉ *Closed Oct.–mid-May.*

Turtle Town
$ | **AMERICAN** | Treat yourself to a delectable dessert item from this tiny shop and enjoy it on one of the nearby boardwalk benches next to the 1880 Train depot. **Known for:** hand-scooped ice cream; specialty chocolates; shakes and malts. $ *Average main: $5* ⊠ *117 Winter St., Keystone* ☎ *605/666–4675* ⊕ *turtletown. com.*

🛏 Hotels

Battle Creek Lodge and Vacation Rentals
$ | **B&B/INN** | This small, simple, well-kept lodge with beautiful outdoor deck and patio areas is tucked up against a forested mountainside just off the main road through Keystone, which makes it a bit quieter in the evenings. **Pros:** away from the busiest part of Keystone;

numerous outdoor seating areas; outdoor gas fire pit. **Cons:** still some road noise, especially during peak season traffic; tight, limited parking in front of the lodge; a helicopter-tour helipad is just up over the hill, making daytime noise. $ *Rooms from: $139* ⊠ *404 Reed St., Keystone* ☎ *605/666–4800, 800/670–7914* ⊕ *battlecreeklodge.us* ⇌ *9 rooms, 9 cabins* ⊘ *No Meals.*

K Bar S Lodge
$$ | **HOTEL** | This contemporary lodge on 45 pine-clad acres feels as if it's been here for a century. **Pros:** excellent staff; exceptional food; amid a wildlife preserve. **Cons:** quite a walk to dining options; pricey rates for the nicer rooms; often full. $ *Rooms from: $150* ⊠ *434 Old Hill City Rd., Keystone* ☎ *605/666–4545* ⊕ *www.kbarslodge.com* ☉ *Closed Nov.–Mar.* ⇌ *96 rooms* ⊘ *Free Breakfast.*

Roosevelt Inn
$$ | **B&B/INN** | This late-Victorian-style inn has some surprisingly updated and modern-looking rooms behind its historic-looking facade, and extra amenities (including a guest laundry) that set it apart. **Pros:** one of the few architecturally interesting hotels in the Black Hills; unique room choices, including some with lofts; one of the closest hotels to Mount Rushmore. **Cons:** like everywhere in tiny, busy Keystone, parking can be difficult; reservations must be guaranteed by a first night's deposit; more expensive than many other Black Hills hotels. $ *Rooms from: $170* ⊠ *206 Old Cemetery Rd., Keystone* ☎ *605/666–4599* ⊕ *www.rooseveltinnkeystone.com* ⇌ *40 rooms* ⊘ *Free Breakfast.*

Under Canvas Mount Rushmore
$$$$ | **RESORT** | Go "glamping" in these luxury tents, which have the amenities of a top hotel and the natural trappings of a campground in a secluded, mountainous, forested setting with views of Mount Rushmore—the tents have

For a true glamping experience, sleep under the stars in a swanky tent at Under Canvas Mount Rushmore.

nearly everything you'd expect from a hotel room, including some with private bathrooms and flushing toilets, while the more expensive tents come with extra space and additional extras like stargazer windows. **Pros:** 4 miles from Mount Rushmore yet very secluded; extras including woodstoves, decks, sitting chairs, fire pit, and adventure concierge; king-size bed in many tents. **Cons:** not a great place to be when extreme weather strikes; rates are high even for the lower-end tents with shared bathrooms; nights can get chilly at this elevation, making the woodstoves necessary. ⑤ *Rooms from: $369* ⊠ *24342 Presidio Ranch Rd., Keystone* ☎ *605/789–5194* ⊕ *www.undercanvas.com* ⊙ *Closed Oct.–Apr.* ⇌ *74 luxury tents* ⊙*❙ No Meals.*

🏃 Activities

There are several ways to add fun and adventure to your Keystone and Mount Rushmore experience, including by train and air.

Black Hills Helicopters

FLIGHTSEEING | See Mount Rushmore, Crazy Horse, and the rugged and rocky majesty of the central Black Hills from the air with this helicopter tour service, run by a local pilot with more than 3,500 hours of flying time. ⊠ *24035 Hwy. 16A, Keystone* ☎ *605/255–4354* ⊕ *www.blackhillshelicopters.com* ⊠ *From $59.99.*

1880 Train, Keystone Depot

TRAIN TOURS | Go back in time and take a leisurely, two-hour, scenic, narrated ride on an old-fashioned passenger train between Hill City and Keystone, getting on and off at either location. The route cuts through the Black Hills, offering rare views of the mountains, forest, and wildlife. ⊠ *103 Winter St., Keystone* ☎ *605/574–2222* ⊕ *www.1880train.com* ⊠ *$39.*

GeoFunTrek Tours

GUIDED TOURS | **FAMILY** | Personalized tours of Black Hills including Mount Rushmore, Crazy Horse, Custer State Park as well as the Badlands are the bread-and-butter for

Keystone's Outdoor, Walkable Mall

Highway 16A connecting Rapid City to Mount Rushmore goes through Keystone, and the people of this small mountain town have made the most of their captive audience just a few miles below the mountain carving.

Along the roughly 1-mile stretch of the highway that serves as Keystone's main street, a bustling and walkable outdoor mall of shops and attractions has sprung up. A long portion of one side of the street is a covered, raised boardwalk. If you're planning to spend a day at Mount Rushmore, you could easily spend another day just strolling, shopping, eating, and adventuring in downtown Keystone.

As you walk from one end of town to the other, you'll encounter opportunities to hop on the 1880 Train; grab an ice-cream cone, taffy, or other sweet treat; have a drink in a saloon; shop for jewelry, T-shirts, Native American art, and souvenirs; dine in local restaurants; play outdoor chess; view chainsaw wood carvings; ride a chairlift; view wax figures of every president; play mini golf; and have old-time Western photos taken.

this family-operated (husband, wife, and adult son) guided tour company based in Keystone. Tours are entirely customizable for families and small groups in vehicles ranging from a small four-wheel-drive SUV to a nine-passenger van. Also available are specialized tours of paleontological sites, gold mines and ghost towns. ⊠ *24430 Nellie La., Keystone* ☎ *605/430–1531* ⊕ *www.geofuntrek.com* ✉ *From $700/day, 2 guests.*

Rushmore Tramway Adventures

ZIP LINING | Fun awaits at this outdoor adventure park with a scenic, all-ages chairlift featuring views of Mount Rushmore. There's also an aerial obstacle course suspended in the trees, an alpine slide, zip line, bungee tower, and tubing hill, all within the town of Keystone. ⊠ *203 Cemetery Rd., Keystone* ☎ *605/666–4478* ⊕ *rushmoretramwayadventures.com* ✉ *From $15* ☺ *Closed Oct.–May.*

Mount Rushmore National Memorial

3 miles southwest of Keystone, 23 miles southwest of Rapid City.

One of the nation's most iconic attractions, with giant likenesses of Washington, Jefferson, Lincoln, and Theodore Roosevelt, this mountain carving lies less than 30 miles southwest of Rapid City. An excellent interpretive center, self-guided audio tours, a trail network, and a Youth Exploration Center make a visit even more memorable. You can also learn about the creation of the monument in the refurbished Sculptor's Studio. The popular Avenue of Flags runs from the entrance of the memorial to the museum and amphitheater at the base of the mountain; this avenue has the flag of each state, commonwealth, district, and territory—arranged alphabetically—of the United States. The site is illuminated at night year-round; in warmer months, a patriotic lighting ceremony is held nightly.

Did You Know?

Sculptor Korczak Ziolkowski's memorial to legendary Lakota leader Crazy Horse was started in 1948 and was designed to be the world's largest work of art. So far, only the warrior's head has been carved, but skilled sculptors vow to complete Ziolkowski's vision—one day.

GETTING HERE AND AROUND

Most visitors arrive from Rapid City, taking Highway 16 and then 16A to Keystone, and then Highway 244 to Mount Rushmore. With its southeasterly exposure, Mount Rushmore is best viewed in the morning light. Early risers also get to have breakfast with the presidents while encountering fewer people than the crowds that flock to the memorial later in the day, as well as to the night lighting ceremony, the busiest interpretive program in the National Park system.

VISITOR INFORMATION

Lincoln Borglum Visitor Center

OTHER ATTRACTION | This giant, granite-and-glass structure underneath the viewing platform shows a repeating introductory film at regular intervals and features fascinating exhibits about the carving of the mountain. It's named for sculptor Gutzon Borglum's son, who was instrumental in the carving project. ⊠ *Mount Rushmore National Memorial, 13000 Hwy. 244, Mount Rushmore* ☎ *605/574–2523* ⊕ *www.nps.gov/moru.*

Mount Rushmore Information Center

OTHER ATTRACTION | Between the park entrance and the Avenue of Flags, the Mount Rushmore Information Center has a small exhibit of photographs detailing the carving of the presidents' faces. The information desk is staffed by rangers who can answer questions about the area. Here you can rent an audio device for a self-guided tour, and a nearly identical building across from the information center houses restrooms and vending machines. ⊠ *Mount Rushmore National Memorial, 13000 Hwy. 244, Mount Rushmore* ☎ *605/574–2523* ⊕ *www.nps. gov/moru.*

RANGER PROGRAMS

There are many ranger programs offered at Mount Rushmore. Some of them include Sculptor's Studio Talk where you learn about the drills, dynamite, and other tools and techniques that carvers used to create the mountain sculpture, and

hear stories about the men who risked their lives to carry out sculptor Gutzon Borglum's vision. These brief talks are repeated throughout the day.

There is an evening program that takes place nightly from late May through September, where you can join a park ranger in the outdoor amphitheater for a talk about the presidents and watch a short film, "Freedom: America's Lasting Legacy," leading up to the nightly lighting ceremony. Ranger programs schedules are posted at the Mount Rushmore Information Center and Lincoln Borglum Visitor Center, where you can also find other information about visiting the site.

 Sights

Lakota, Nakota, and Dakota Heritage Village

TOWN | Along the first section of the Presidential Trail, this gathering area focuses on the culture of the region's indigenous tribes. In summer, rangers and Native American representatives give talks that highlight local Native American traditions. ⊠ *Mount Rushmore National Memorial, 13000 Hwy. 244, Mount Rushmore* ☎ *605/574–2523* ⊕ *www.nps.gov/moru.*

★ Mount Rushmore National Memorial

HISTORIC SIGHT | Abraham Lincoln was tall in real life—6 feet, 4 inches, though add a few more for his hat. But at one of the nation's most iconic sights, Honest Abe, along with presidents George Washington, Thomas Jefferson, and Theodore Roosevelt, towers over the Black Hills in a 60-foot-high likeness. The four images look especially spectacular at night, when they're always illuminated.

Follow the Presidential Trail through the forest to gain excellent views of the colossal sculpture, or stroll the Avenue of Flags for a different perspective. Also on-site are an impressive museum, an indoor theater where an introductory film is shown, an outdoor amphitheater for live performances, an award-winning audio tour, and concession facilities.

The nightly ranger program and special memorial lighting ceremony (June through mid-September) is reportedly the most popular interpretive program in all of the National Park Service system. Be sure to see the Avenue of Flags, running from the entrance of the memorial to the museum and amphitheater at the base of the mountain. This avenue has the flag of each state, commonwealth, district, and territory—arranged alphabetically—of the United States. At the Youth Exploration Area, along the Presidential Trail beneath the towering visage of George Washington, rangers present interactive programs for youngsters. ⊠ *13000 Hwy. 244, Mount Rushmore* ☎ *605/574–2523* ⊕ *www.nps.gov/moru* ⊠ *Free; parking from $10 per vehicle.*

Presidential Trail

TRAIL | This easy hike along a boardwalk and down some stairs leads to the very base of the mountain. Although the trail is thickly forested, you'll have more than ample opportunity to look straight up the noses of the four giant heads. The trail is open year-round, so long as snow and/or ice don't present a safety hazard. ⊠ *Mount Rushmore National Memorial, 13000 Hwy. 244, Mount Rushmore* ☎ *605/574–2523* ⊕ *www.nps.gov/moru.*

Sculptor's Studio

OTHER ATTRACTION | Built in 1939 as Gutzon Borglum's on-site workshop, this studio displays tools used by the mountain carvers, a model of the memorial, and a model depicting the unfinished Hall of Records. ⊠ *Mount Rushmore National Memorial, 13000 Hwy. 244, Mount Rushmore* ☎ *605/574–2523* ⊕ *www.nps.gov/moru.*

🍴 Restaurants

Carvers' Café

$ | AMERICAN | The only restaurant at Mount Rushmore National Memorial, operated by concessionaire Xanterra, affords commanding views of the memorial and the surrounding ponderosa pine forest. It serves good food at reasonable prices. **Known for:** terrific park views; fantastic ice cream; sustainably sourced ingredients. ⑤ *Average main: $10* ⊠ *Mount Rushmore National Memorial, 13000 Hwy. 244, Mount Rushmore* ☎ *605/574–2515* ⊕ *www.mtrushmorenationalmemorial.com.*

🛍 Shopping

Mount Rushmore Bookstores

BOOKS | The Mount Rushmore Bookstores, operated by the Mount Rushmore Society, carry a selection of books, CDs, and videos on the memorial, its history, and the entire Black Hills region. There are also some titles on geology and Native American history. Products are available in the Information Center, Lincoln Borglum Visitor Center, and Sculptor's Studio. ⊠ *Mount Rushmore National Memorial, 13000 Hwy. 244, Mount Rushmore* ☎ *605/341–8883* ⊕ *mountrushmoresociety.com.*

Mount Rushmore Gift Shop

SOUVENIRS | The Mount Rushmore Gift Shop sells souvenirs ranging from shot glasses and magnets to T-shirts and baseball caps. You can also buy Black Hills Gold jewelry and Native American art. ⊠ *Mount Rushmore National Memorial, 13000 Hwy. 244, Mount Rushmore* ☎ *605/574–2515* ⊕ *www.mtrushmorenationalmemorial.com.*

Hill City

12 miles northwest of Mount Rushmore, 27 miles southwest of Rapid City.

This small mountain town has reinvented itself several times over. Born as a gold-mining camp during the rush of 1876, it was all but abandoned when the search for gold moved to the northern Black Hills. A tin-mining boom briefly rejuvenated Hill City after that, and

All aboard! A beloved experience is a ride aboard the old-fashioned 1880 Train that goes back and forth between Keystone and Hill City.

logging has long been a mainstay of the local economy. Today, the town caters largely to visitors with a thriving local winery scene, access to the popular Mickelson Trail, a depot for the 1880 Train, and other attractions and businesses frequented by tourists.

Sights

Jon Crane Gallery

ART GALLERY | Nationally known water-color artist Jon Crane's paintings of nostalgic rural scenes and realistic Black Hills landscapes are displayed and sold here, along with the work of other local artists, sculptors, potters, and craftspeople. Custom framing is also available. ⊠ *256 Main St., Hill City* ☎ *605/574–4440* ⊕ *joncranegallery.net.*

Museum @ Black Hills Institute

SPECIALTY MUSEUM | The plains of western South Dakota are one of the world's prime fossil areas, and the local geologists and fossil hunters at the Black Hills Institute of Geological Research display some of their top finds here. That includes a 65% complete T. rex skeleton nicknamed "Stan" that was unearthed in the northwestern corner of the state. Numerous other fossils, minerals, meteorites, and other treasures can also be seen in this downtown Hill City facility. ⊠ *117 Main St., Hill City* ☎ *605/574–3919* ⊕ *www.bhigr.com* ✉ *$7.50* ⊙ *Closed Sun.*

★ Prairie Berry Winery and Miner Brewing Company

WINERY | Prairie Berry is South Dakota's premier winery and an attraction unto itself. The company has built up a sophisticated and spacious campus in Hill City where visitors can taste and buy wines (in addition to beer at the affiliated Miner Brewing Company). You can also have a meal and enjoy a view of South Dakota's highest mountain, Black Elk Peak, from the outdoor patio. Many of the wines include native South Dakota ingredients, such as the popular Red Ass Rhubarb, while the Anna Pesä–branded wines offer more sophisticated flavors. ✉ *23837 U.S. 385, Hill City* ☎ *877/226–9453* ⊕ *prairieberry.com.*

Sheridan Lake

BODY OF WATER | Just 7 miles from Hill City, this picturesque, 375-acre lake surrounded by mountains in the Black Hills National Forest is ringed by a campground, two beaches, picnic areas, fishing piers, and hiking trails. ✉ *U.S. 385, Hill City* ✛ *7 miles northeast of Hill City* ☎ *605/673–9200* ⊕ *www.fs.usda.gov.*

South Dakota State Railroad Museum and 1880 Train Depot

HISTORY MUSEUM | American expansion into Dakota Territory occurred not as much by covered wagons as by the extension of railroads, and by the arrangement of towns around depots. Here, visitors can learn that story and also buy a ticket for a leisurely, narrated sightseeing ride on the old-fashioned 1880 Train from Hill City to Keystone and back. ✉ *222 Railroad Ave., Hill City* ☎ *605/574–9000* ⊕ *www.1880train.com/railroad-museum.html* ⌲ *$8.*

 ## Restaurants

★ Alpine Inn

$$ | **STEAK HOUSE** | With its pastoral paintings, lacy tablecloths, and beer steins, the rustic Alpine Inn brings a version of old-world charm to the Old West. The lunchtime menu changes daily but always has selections of healthful sandwiches and salads—and no fried food; the dinner menu has just two dishes: filet mignon, which is one of the best steaks around, and a vegetarian pasta primavera option. **Known for:** family-friendly; local atmosphere; really good beef. ⑤ *Average main: $15* ✉ *133 Main St., Hill City* ☎ *605/574–2749* ⊕ *www.alpineinnhillcity.com* ▭ *No credit cards* ◔ *Closed Sun.*

Pizzeria Mangiamo

$$ | **ITALIAN** | Step inside the door and the tantalizing aroma leaves no doubt of Pizzeria Mangiamo's Italian point of view. The owner and chef is New York–trained in authentic Italian pizza and pasta dishes, while also offering American-style favorite pizza and calzones, all served on hand-tossed dough crusts. **Known for:** wood-fired Italian and American pizza; pasta and salads; local craft beer and wine selection. ⑤ *Average main: $18* ✉ *158 Museum St., Hill City* ☎ *605/574–2564* ⊕ *pizzeriamangiamo.com.*

 ## Hotels

Holiday Inn Express and Suites Hill City

$$ | **HOTEL** | Predictable quality, amenities, and pricing are the hallmarks of this clean and modern hotel, which could serve as a solid and affordable home-base option for exploring the Black Hills. **Pros:** very clean; centrally located within the Black Hills; ample parking. **Cons:** standard chain hotel lacking in character; located next to the railroad tracks used by the 1880 Train; doesn't take advantage of beautiful surroundings. ⑤ *Rooms from: $199* ✉ *12444 Old Hill City Rd., Hill City* ☎ *605/574–4040* ⊕ *www.ihg.com* ⤳ *60 rooms* ❢◯❢ *Free Breakfast.*

Mountain View Lodge and Cabins

$$ | **HOTEL** | There is a lot of added value for a reasonable price here, both in the simple but well-kept lodge and in the associated cabins, all located on a forested hillside just outside of Hill City. **Pros:** cabins offer seclusion with convenience near Hill City; price is low when considering the extras; close access to 1880 Train, Mickelson Trail, and Sheridan Lake. **Cons:** the lodge fronts a busy highway; some lodge rooms are on the small side; easy to get confused and rent a lodge room instead of a cabin. ⑤ *Rooms from: $175* ✉ *12654 S. Hwy. 16, Hill City* ☎ *800/789–7411* ⊕ *www.mountainviewlodge.net* ◔ *Closed Nov.–Mar.* ⤳ *13 rooms, 5 cabins* ❢◯❢ *Free Breakfast.*

The orientation center at Crazy Horse Memorial is a mini-museum that tells the story of how this massive still-in-progress monument came to be.

Activities

CAMPING

Mount Rushmore KOA at Palmer Gulch Resort. This huge, commercial KOA campground on Route 244 west of Mount Rushmore offers shuttles to the mountain, bus tours, horse rides, and car rentals. There are also large furnished cabins and primitive camping cabins, as well as a lodge shadowed by the massive granite ramparts of Black Elk Peak. With its pools, waterslide, outdoor activities, on-site rodeos, and kids' programs, this is a great place for families, and parents will appreciate the three hot tubs. A shuttle takes you to Mount Rushmore and Crazy Horse for a nominal charge. ⊠ *12620 Hwy. 244* ☎ *605/574–2525* 🛏 *500 sites including RV, tent, and cabins.*

HIKING AND BIKING

Burlington Northern Hill City Trailhead, Mickelson Trail

BIKING | Next to Hill City's Tracy Park is one of the most centrally located

and easily accessible trailheads for the 109-mile Mickelson Trail, a crushed-rock bicycle path made from a former rail line that stretches south-to-north through the Black Hills with many scenic bridges and rock tunnels. Because it was a former rail line, the grade is never too steep, making the Mickelson Trail a favorite among bicyclists of varying abilities. There's a self-pay station where you'll need cash for the $4 daily trail fee or $15 annual pass. Don't have a bike? Rent one from a local service near the trail. ⊠ *Tracy Park, 512 S. Newtown Ave., Hill City* ☎ *605/584–3896* ⊕ *gfp.sd.gov.*

Rabbit Bicycle

BIKING | If you didn't bring your bicycle along to the Black Hills but still want to ride the Mickelson Trail, you can rent one from this business that is conveniently located near the trail in Hill City. Hybrid, electric, tandem, and youth bikes are available for rent. Shuttle service is also offered if you'd like to get dropped off somewhere along the trail and ride back

Crazy Horse Up Close: The Volksmarch

Twice a year, the Crazy Horse Memorial offers what it describes as the most popular organized hike in the United States, with up to 15,000 people participating annually.

That's the Crazy Horse Volksmarch, when memorial officials open a trail that goes way up onto the arm of Crazy Horse, right next to the mountain carving's emerging face. The view of Crazy Horse's giant visage is surreal from that vantage point, and the panorama of the surrounding Black Hills is spectacular.

Because the events are so popular, you'll want to plan ahead if you'd like to participate. Check the memorial website for the dates, which are typically in early June and late September. Pay close attention to the instructions on the website, which explain the time window allowed for starting your hike, and also the discounted memorial admission fee and small hiking fee (which you'll want to bring in cash).

The memorial grounds and parking areas fill up fast during these events, so plan to go early, leave plenty of time, and don't be in a rush. Bring as much water as you think you'll need, and then add more. On the non-shaded parts of the trail, it can get quite hot. The trail is steep in some places, so take your time and pace yourself at your own ability (you'll see a wide range of people on this hike, from children to the elderly).

Your reward at the top, where you'll experience a "summit" like no other, will be worth the effort.

to your starting point. ⊠ *175 Walnut St., Hill City* ☎ *605/574–4302* ⊕ *www.rabbit-bicyclessd.com.*

Samelius Trailhead, Centennial Trail
HIKING & WALKING | This is one of the most conveniently located trailheads along the 111-mile Centennial Trail, a single-track, dirt hiking trail (separate from the crushed-rock Mickelson Trail) that stretches north-to-south through the entirety of the Black Hills. Park in the small parking area along the highway and hike up into the pine-forested mountains as far as you like. If you're feeling ambitious (and have plenty of water), it's about 3 miles and 800 vertical feet up to 5,889-foot Mount Warner, a little-known and quiet peak where there are panoramic views of the Black Hills National Forest. ⊠ *U.S. 16, Hill City* ⊹ *Look for the trailhead sign 6 miles east of Hill City on U.S. 16* ☎ *605/673–9200* ⊕ *www.fs.usda.gov.*

Crazy Horse Memorial

39 miles southwest of Rapid City, 12 miles southwest of Hill City.

Crazy Horse Memorial gives visitors a rare opportunity to see a mountain carving in progress, along with a plethora of educational programs and exhibits on Native Americans.

GETTING HERE AND AROUND
From Rapid City take U.S. 16 to Hill City and then U.S. 385 from Hill City to Crazy Horse.

Sights

★ **Crazy Horse Memorial**
HISTORIC SIGHT | Designed to be the world's largest work of art (the face alone is 87 feet tall), this tribute to the spirit of the North American Native people

depicts Crazy Horse, the legendary Lakota leader who helped defeat General Custer at Little Bighorn. A work in progress, thus far the warrior's head has been carved from the mountain. His extended left arm is emerging from the rock along with the colossal head of his horse. Self-taught sculptor Korczak Ziolkowski started this memorial in 1948. After his death in 1982, his family carried on the project. Near the work site stands an exceptional orientation center, the Indian Museum of North America, and Ziolkowski's home and workshop. ⊠ *12151 Ave. of the Chiefs, Crazy Horse Memorial* ✛ *Hwy. 385, 5 miles north of Custer* ☎ *605/673–4681* ⊕ *crazyhorsememorial.org* ☜ *$15.*

Indian Museum of North America

SPECIALTY MUSEUM | When Korczak Ziolkowski agreed to carve Crazy Horse at the invitation of a Lakota elder, he determined that he wouldn't stop with the mountain. He wanted an educational institution to sit at the base of the mountain, complete with a center showcasing examples of Native American culture and heritage. The construction in 1972 of the Indian Museum of North America, built from wood and from stone blasted from the mountain, was the initial step in that direction. The permanent collection of paintings, clothing, photographs, and artifacts represents many of the continent's tribes. There is also a space for temporary exhibits that often showcase works by modern Native American artists. ⊠ *Crazy Horse Memorial, 12151 Ave. of the Chiefs, Crazy Horse Memorial* ☎ *605/673–4681* ⊕ *crazyhorsememorial. org.*

Restaurants

Laughing Water

$$ | **AMERICAN** | With windows facing the mountain sculpture, this airy pinewood restaurant is noted for its buffalo burgers. There's a soup-and-salad bar, but you'd do well to stick to the Native American offerings and other dishes in the buffet. **Known for:** monumental views; Tatanka (buffalo) stew; Native American tacos. ⑤ *Average main: $18* ⊠ *Crazy Horse Memorial, 12151 Ave. of the Chiefs, Crazy Horse Memorial* ☎ *605/673–4681* ⊕ *crazyhorsememorial.org.*

Shopping

Korczak's Heritage

CRAFTS | With handmade items representing the Lakota, Navajo, Huichol, Acoma, and other tribes, Korczak's Heritage is more than a simple gift shop. In addition to handcrafted items such as jewelry and dream catchers, Korczak's carries sculpture and prints by Native American artists. The store also sells food and clothing, and gift items hewn from stones blasted from the mountain. ⊠ *Crazy Horse Memorial, 12151 Ave. of the Chiefs, Crazy Horse Memorial* ☎ *605/673–4681* ⊕ *crazyhorsememorial. org.*

Chapter 4

THE NORTHERN BLACK HILLS

4

Updated by
Jim Holland

⦿ Sights	🍽 Restaurants	🛏 Hotels	🛍 Shopping	🍸 Nightlife
★★★★☆	★★★☆☆	★★★☆☆	★★☆☆☆	★★★☆☆

WELCOME TO THE NORTHERN BLACK HILLS

TOP REASONS TO GO

★ **Geographic wonders:** From the high limestone cliffs and roaring waterfalls of Spearfish Canyon to the strangely striated rocks of Devils Tower, this is a place to be awed by nature.

★ **Mining marvels:** This region is the epicenter of Black Hills gold mining, where an educational visitor center now stands next to a jaw-dropping, half-mile-wide pit known as the Open Cut.

★ **Gaming:** Wild Bill and Calamity Jane tried their luck here during the 1870s gold rush, and you can try yours in the gambling mecca of Deadwood.

★ **Cowboy central:** The sprawling plains around the Northern Black Hills are prime cattle country. For visitors, that means world-class rodeos and other opportunities for immersion in Western culture.

★ **Year-round fun:** When summer fades, autumn leaves put on a show in Spearfish Canyon. In the winter, the northern slopes of the Black Hills are a regional destination for skiers, snowshoers, and snowmobilers.

1 Deadwood. The modern and historic are blended in this mountain town full of Western lore. Gambling is legal here and casinos are numerous. There are also first-rate museums and historical sites.

2 Lead. The Homestake Gold Mine made the city of Lead world-famous; now, the mine is an underground science lab. The Sanford Lab Homestake Visitor Center illuminates the city's rich past and scientific present.

3 Sturgis. The world knows Sturgis for its annual August motorcycle rally that draws hundreds of thousands of bikers. This small city also provides access to an extensive network of recreational trails.

4 Spearfish. Mountain culture predominates in this scenic city, the second-largest in the Black Hills. Spearfish Canyon and Spearfish Creek attract sightseers, climbers, and anglers.

5 Belle Fourche. This small town is home to cowboys and a museum dedicated to Western history and culture. The pride of the city is its annual summertime professional rodeo.

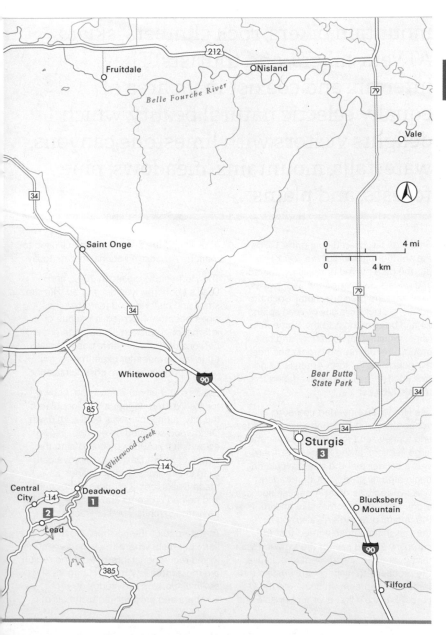

The northern Black Hills is an eclectic brew of miners, Western legends, gamblers, cowboys, motorcycle riders, mountain bikers, rock climbers, skiers, ATVers, hikers, and tourists. They intermix and coexist in an area of equally eclectic natural beauty, which delights visitors with limestone canyons, waterfalls, mountains, meadows, pine forests, and plains.

Gold was discovered during the 1870s in the southern portion of the Black Hills, but the rush moved north as prospectors and miners discovered the best places to extract the precious metal. Soon the northern Black Hills city of Lead sprang up and became host to the Homestake Mine, which sprawled above and below ground, becoming the largest and deepest gold mine in North America. Miners extracted 41 million ounces during the mine's 126-year life.

The Homestake needed timber to support its mind-boggling array of shafts and tunnels, and that meant clear-cutting large sections of the Black Hills. There was a danger that the forest would be decimated by greed, but that tragedy was averted by a great American success story. Leaders at Homestake and in the federal government, alarmed by the vanishing timber, agreed that the company should pay for the timber it was taking, and the government should use the proceeds to manage and sustain the forest. That agreement spawned the U.S. Forest Service's first-ever timber sale and established the system that's still used to manage America's national forests today.

The Homestake closed in 2002, and Lead's economy was decimated. But the small and historic mountain town has since been transformed into a hub of international science. Deep underground portions of the mine have been converted to laboratories for experiments that require protection from cosmic radiation.

Lead's sister city is Deadwood, known for the Western legends who populated the city during its rowdy gold-rush days. Deadwood survived an economic lull of its own in the 1980s by convincing the voters of South Dakota to approve gambling in city limits. Today, casinos have made Deadwood a modern visitor hub and helped preserve and restore much of its historic architectural character.

At the edge of the northern Black Hills lies Spearfish, where the varied economic and recreational interests of the region are most intensely mixed. Loggers and sawmill workers live alongside rock climbers and environmentalists, all of them drawn to the area's bountiful natural resources.

Another city on the edge of the northern Black Hills is Sturgis, where a small gathering of motorcycle racers decades ago has grown into America's best-known annual biker rally. Belle Fourche is a bit farther outside the Black Hills, with a cultural gap to match, owing to its identity as a trade center for cattle ranchers.

And, of course, no description of the northern Black Hills would be complete without an acknowledgement of its most iconic natural wonder: Devils Tower, just over the border in Wyoming. The one-of-a-kind, towering rock formation stands as a representation of all that's unique and alluring about this region.

Planning

Getting Here and Around

AIR
Although there are many private air strips, the closest airport to the northern Black Hills offering scheduled service is Rapid City Regional Airport (RAP).

CAR
The best way to see the northern Black Hills is by car, because of the many miles to cover between towns and attractions. Interstate 90 winds around the mountains and goes through Sturgis and Spearfish, and then on toward Devils Tower. The main roads up into the Black Hills eventually converge on Lead and Deadwood, including Highways 14, 85, and 385.

Hotels

There is a lodging style for everyone in the northern Black Hills. Spearfish and Sturgis have standard hotels to serve as a vacation home base. Deadwood

is chock-full of hotel-casinos for those who like to stay and play, and some of the rooms are priced affordably, on the assumption that guests will gamble their extra money away. Lead is replete with lodges that get skiers close to Terry Peak. And the entire area is populated with campgrounds, cabins, and home rentals, the latter ranging from spare rooms to sprawling mansions.

Restaurants

What the northern Black Hills lack in sheer numbers of restaurants, the region makes up for in quality, especially in Deadwood. A good restaurant is a way for a casino to stand out from its competitors, and that reality has enlivened Deadwood's culinary scene. You'll find a lot of top-quality steaks, seafood, and some international flavor in Deadwood, and decadent desserts. In other northern Black Hills towns, standard local fare like steak and burgers is common. Other than Deadwood, Spearfish is another bright spot, with a wide variety of restaurants infused with local character.

HOTEL AND RESTAURANT PRICES
⇨ *Hotel and restaurant reviews have been shortened. For full information, see Fodors.com. Restaurant prices are the average cost of a main course at dinner, or if dinner is not served, at lunch. Hotel prices are the lowest cost of a standard double room in high season.*

What It Costs			
$	$$	$$$	$$$$
RESTAURANTS			
under $13	$13–$23	$24–$35	over $35
HOTELS			
under $150	$150–$200	$201–$250	over $250

Safety

Like everywhere inside the Black Hills, the mountain highways here are steep, winding, and deserving of caution from visiting drivers. This is especially so in the winter and even the early spring and late fall, when unpredictable winter storms blow in quickly. The northern Black Hills receive more snow than the rest of the area, and roads shadowed by canyons and mountains may get only a brief period of sunlight each day, making them prone to icy conditions.

Deadwood

42 miles northwest of Rapid City via I–90 and U.S. 14A.

Its brick-paved streets plied by old-time trolleys, illuminated by period lighting, and lined with original Victorian architecture, Deadwood today owes much of its historical character to casinos. In 1989 South Dakota voters approved limited-stakes gaming for the town, on the condition that a portion of revenues be devoted to historic preservation. Since then, more than $200 million has been dedicated to restoring and preserving this once infamous gold-mining boomtown, which has earned recognition as a National Historic Landmark. Small gaming halls, good restaurants, and hotels occupy virtually every storefront on Main Street, just as they did back in Deadwood's late-19th-century heyday. You can walk in the footsteps of legendary lawman Wild Bill Hickok, cigar-smoking Poker Alice Tubbs, and the fabled Calamity Jane, who swore she could outdrink, outspit, and outswear any man—and usually did.

Several of the storefronts on Main Street belong to souvenir shops that peddle cheap trinkets to tourists. Some of the more upscale stores carry high-quality Western wear, Black Hills–gold jewelry, and fine art. Ice-cream parlors are never hard to find during summer.

GETTING HERE AND AROUND

Because most of Deadwood was laid out before the advent of automobiles, the city today is entirely walkable. Strung in a roughly straight line along the bottom of a gulch, the main points of interest are difficult to miss. The best strategy is to park in one of the lots on Main or Sherman Streets and begin your pedestrian adventure from there.

The narrow confines of Deadwood Gulch can make parking a problem. Especially during busy weekends, a spot can be hard to find. Be patient, check the city lots (there is a parking ramp off Main Street), and have your money ready for the parking meters that can gulp it as fast as the slot machines.

TOURS

One of the best ways to learn the history of Deadwood and enjoy its historic architecture, all while being entertained with colorful tales of times past, is to book one of the many tours available in the city.

Archaeological Collections of Deadwood: An Ethnic Oasis

SPECIAL-INTEREST TOURS | Take a guided walking tour of Deadwood's historic places, with special emphasis on the city's former Chinatown, and get a behind-the-scenes tour of the world-class archival and archaeological collections at Deadwood City Hall. ⊠ *108 Sherman St., Deadwood* ☎ *800/999–1876* ⊕ *www. deadwood.com* ⌷ *$15.*

Boot Hill Tours

SPECIAL-INTEREST TOURS | Ride a converted, open-air school bus for a one-hour tour of Deadwood and its famed Mount Moriah Cemetery. Local hosts provide narration about past and current gold mining, historic buildings, George Armstrong Custer's military expedition to the

Take a tour of the Adams House, an 1892 Queen Anne–style mansion that was once the home of the Adamses, one of Deadwood's founding families.

Black Hills, Native American resistance to white settlement, Chinese settlement of Deadwood, the killing of Wild Bill Hickok, and more. Tours depart from the Deadwood History and Information Center. ⊠ *3 Siever St., Deadwood* ☎ *605/580–5231* ⊕ *boothilltours.com* ⊠ *$25.*

Lawman's Patrol: Guided Walking Tour

WALKING TOURS | A re-enactor portraying Deadwood's first marshal, Con Stapleton, provides a walking tour lasting up to an hour while explaining the gold rush, Deadwood's infamous brothels and bars, the town's unique architecture, and the destructive history of local floods and fires. ⊠ *Deadwood* ✛ *Tours operate on Main Street; call or book on the website for a meeting place* ☎ *800/344–8826* ⊕ *www.deadwoodalive.com* ⊠ *$25.*

VISITOR INFORMATION

Although the modern Deadwood Welcome Center on the edge of the city is the main place for local visitor information, there's another place

downtown—the Deadwood History & Information Center—to get even more help. The center inhabits a historic former railroad depot and houses interpretive exhibits in addition to informational resources.

On the doorstep of Deadwood's historic downtown district, the spacious Deadwood Welcome Center provides information about local attractions and points of interest. With a large parking lot, public restrooms, and a trolley stop, it's the perfect place to leave your car and launch your exploration of the city. The visitor center also houses the offices of the local Chamber of Commerce.

CONTACTS Deadwood History and Information Center. ⊠ *3 Siever St., Deadwood* ☎ *800/344–8826, 605/578–1876* ⊕ *www.deadwood.com.* **Deadwood History and Information Center.** ⊠ *501 Main St., Deadwood* ☎ *800/344–8826, 605/578–1876* ⊕ *www.deadwood.com.*

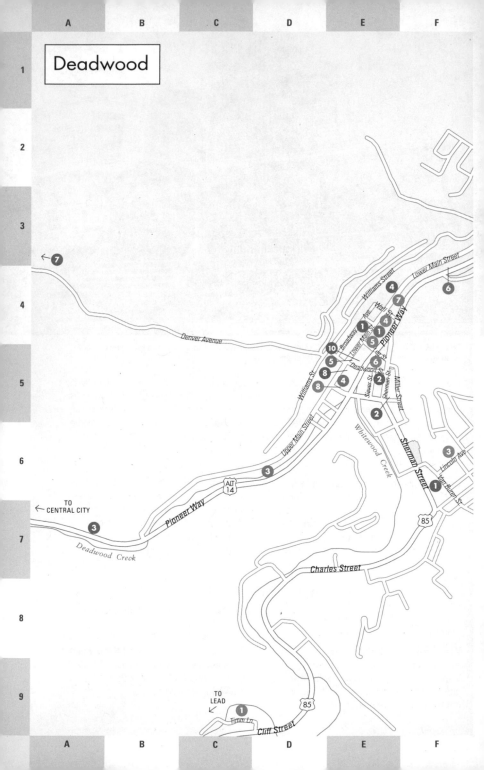

KEY

1 Sights
1 Restaurants
1 Quick Bites
1 Hotels

Sights

★ Adams House

HISTORIC HOME | A tour of the restored Adams House includes an explanation of the tragedies and triumphs of two of the community's founding families (the Franklins and the Adamses) who lived here. The 1892 Queen Anne–style mansion was closed in the mid-1930s and sat empty for more than 50 years, preserving the original furniture and decor that you see today. ⊠ *22 Van Buren St., Deadwood* ☎ *605/578–3724* ⊕ *www.deadwoodhistory.com* ⊡ *$12.*

★ Adams Museum

HISTORY MUSEUM | Between the massive stone-block post office and the old railroad depot, there are three floors of displays at the Adams Museum, including the region's first locomotive, photographs of the town's early days, and an exhibit featuring Potato Creek Johnny's Gold Nugget, the second-largest nugget ever discovered in the Black Hills. The Adams Museum is affiliated with Deadwood History, Inc., which also oversees the Days of '76 Museum, the Historic Adams House, and a cultural center and archives. ⊠ *54 Sherman St., Deadwood* ☎ *605/578–1714* ⊕ *www.deadwoodhistory.com* ⊡ *Free but $5 suggested donation.*

Broken Boot Gold Mine

MINE | You're guaranteed to find gold on a panning experience here. If you take the short, guided, underground mine tour, you'll also get a souvenir stock certificate. Tours begin every 30 minutes from the small surface buildings perched on the hillside. ⊠ *1200 Pioneer Way, Deadwood* ☎ *866/601–5103, 605/578–9997* ⊕ *www.brokenbootgoldmine.com* ⊡ *Tours $8; gold panning $10* ⊙ *Closed early Sept.–late May.*

The Brothel

OTHER ATTRACTION | Brothels operated in Deadwood from the city's founding in 1876 until federal agents raided the last one in 1980 (yes, they lasted that long); today, that history is preserved inside this historic building outfitted to look like the house of ill-repute that it once was. ⊠ *610 Main St., Deadwood* ☎ *605/559–0231* ⊕ *www.deadwoodbrothel.com* ⊡ *$15.*

Days of '76 Museum

HISTORY MUSEUM | Days of '76 Museum began almost by accident as the horse-drawn carriages and stagecoaches used in the namesake annual event's parade became an attraction in their own right. Over the years, cowboy memorabilia, photographs, and historical clothing have been added to the collection. The Days of '76 celebration, commemorating the 1876 gold rush, is held each July with a professional rodeo, parade, and other events. ⊠ *18 76th Dr., Deadwood* ☎ *605/578–1657* ⊕ *daysof76.com* ⊡ *$10.*

Mount Moriah Cemetery

CEMETERY | Mount Moriah Cemetery, on a high spot known as Boot Hill, is the final resting place of Wild Bill Hickok, Calamity Jane, and other notable Deadwood residents. The aging landmark was revitalized by extensive restoration work in 2003, including the addition of a visitor center that houses a leather Bible, a stained-glass window, and pulpit chairs from the town's old Methodist churches. From the top of the cemetery, you'll have the best panoramic view of the town. ⊠ *10 Mount Moriah Dr., Deadwood* ☎ *605/722–0837* ⊕ *www.cityofdeadwood.com* ⊡ *$2.*

Mount Roosevelt Friendship Tower

VIEWPOINT | Legendary Deadwood lawman Seth Bullock spearheaded the erection of this picturesque, mountain-top, stone observation tower in honor of the friendship he forged with Theodore Roosevelt during Roosevelt's ranching era in North Dakota. The drive to the tower from Deadwood is only a few miles, and the hike from the parking area is about a mile on a moderately sloped trail in the Black Hills National Forest. ⊠ *Forest Service Rd. 133, Deadwood*

No trip to Deadwood would be complete without a visit to Mount Moriah Cemetery, the final resting place of Wild Bill Hickok and Calamity Jane.

⚓ From Deadwood, 1½ miles on U.S. 85 north, then west 2 miles on Forest Service Rd. 133 ☎ 605/673–9200 ⊕ www. fs.usda.gov.

Outlaw Square
PLAZA/SQUARE | FAMILY | Concerts, movie nights, historical presentations, and other summertime events occur in this outdoor gathering area with a stage in the downtown area; during the winter, the venue transforms into an outdoor rink for skating and ice bumper cars. ✉ 703 Main St., Deadwood ☎ 605/578–1876 ⊕ www. outlawsquare.com.

Rocksino by Hard Rock Deadwood
CASINO | Rocksino brings something new for a Deadwood casino—entertainment hosted on stage at Outlaw Square, located just across the street. The first acts to celebrate its August, 2023 grand opening included alternative rock's Sublime With Rome and country music's Lady A. Inside the former Hickok's Hotel and Gaming is a spacious casino with 86 new slot machines in a bright, clean

layout designed to feel less crowded. The restaurant at Hickok's Tavern highlights roasted walleye, wings, and pizza, and its full-service bar specializes in hand-crafted cocktails. ✉ 685 Main St., Deadwood ⊕ rocksino.hardrock.com.

Tatanka: Story of the Bison
PUBLIC ART | A heroic-scale bronze sculpture of three Native Americans on horseback driving 14 bison off a cliff is the centerpiece of Tatanka: Story of the Bison, on a ridge above Deadwood. The attraction, owned by Dances with Wolves star Kevin Costner, also includes an interpretive center; Lakota guides explain Plains Indian life circa 1840. ✉ 100 Tatanka Dr., Deadwood ☎ 605/584–5678 ⊕ storyofthebison.com 🎟 $12.

🍽 Restaurants

★ Deadwood Social Club
$$$ | ITALIAN | On the second floor of historic Saloon No. 10, this warm restaurant surrounds you with wood and old-time

Deadwood's Most Famous Residents

Deadwood's gold-rush days during the 1870s were filled with a cast of colorful characters, none more famous—or infamous—than Wild Bill Hickok and Calamity Jane. Today, there's no better place than Deadwood to learn about the two Wild West legends.

Wild Bill Hickok

After gold was discovered near Deadwood in 1876, miners and camp followers swarmed the area. In a region that was still reserved by treaty for the Sioux Native American people, all the newcomers were illegal squatters.

Among them was James Butler "Wild Bill" Hickok—a sometime soldier, scout, cattle rustler, stagecoach driver, showman, actor and sheriff. He fought and spied for the Union during the Civil War and was renowned as a gunman in Kansas.

On August 2, as Hickok sat in a poker game with his back to the door at Nuttal & Mann's Saloon No. 10, a failed gambler named Jack McCall shot Hickok in the back of the head. The dying Hickok supposedly spilled pairs of black aces and eights—now known as "the dead man's hand."

McCall was captured, and a vigilante jury was assembled, but the defendant argued that Hickok had recently killed McCall's brother. To everyone's surprise, the jury acquitted McCall. It was an illegal trial because of its location in a town with no legal right to exist.

McCall was captured again and turned over to Dakota Territory. A Yankton jury found him guilty, and he was hanged. Meanwhile, Hickok's body was laid to rest above Deadwood in Mount Moriah Cemetery. Nearby are the resting places of other legends of Deadwood Gulch, including Calamity Jane.

Calamity Jane

Martha Canary, aka "Calamity Jane," has been the subject of so many stories and legends that it's difficult to distinguish fact from fiction.

Notorious for gun-toting, drinking, cussing, and a preference for wearing men's clothing, she scraped her way through life on the northern Great Plains any way she could. But she was also known for generosity, including her care for the sick during a smallpox outbreak.

She was born in 1852 in Missouri and moved with her family to Montana during that state's 1864 gold rush. Both of her parents died soon after, setting her on a course for a hard-knock life.

Her survival instincts and attraction to excitement eventually brought her into contact with military excursions as a camp follower. It was in that capacity that she encountered and glommed onto Wild Bill's party as it traveled to the Black Hills in 1876. Later in her life, she starred in Buffalo Bills's Wild West Show.

Contrary to popular myths, she apparently had no meaningful relationship with Wild Bill Hickok. But she took every opportunity to profit from such tales told in dime-novel fiction. Today her fame is as strong as ever, aided by the decision of the people of Deadwood to bury her near Hickok in Mount Moriah Cemetery.

On a ridge above Deadwood is large-scale bronze sculpture called Tatanka: Story of the Bison, featuring Native Americans on horseback driving bison off a cliff.

photographs of Deadwood. Light jazz and blues play over the sound system. **Known for:** eclectic Italian menu; great martinis; historic setting. ⑤ *Average main: $26* ✉ *657 Main St., Deadwood* ☎ *605/578–3346* ⊕ *www.saloon10.com.*

FLYT Steakhouse

$$ | **AMERICAN** | **FAMILY** | Hill City's iconic Alpine Inn has brought its culinary prowess to Deadwood, this time with modern American fare in a chic, almost futuristic setting. The menu includes breakfast, lunch and dinner, but if you can't make up your mind on just one selection, you can choose a flight of up to three smaller samples of different dishes for your meal. **Known for:** flights of food and drink; top quality steaks and burgers; intimate, futuristic ambiance. ⑤ *Average main: $18* ✉ *Cadillac Jack's Gaming Resort, 372 Main St., Deadwood* ☎ *605/571–1263* ⊕ *www.cadillacjacksgaming.com/dining/flyt.*

Gold Country Inn Cafe

$ | **AMERICAN** | For a change of pace from Deadwood's upscale dining options, try this affordable, comfort-food café with a small-town, unassuming atmosphere and a menu full of traditional options like eggs, hash browns, chicken-fried steak, burgers, and chicken salad sandwiches. **Known for:** friendly, hard-working waitstaff; raspberry French toast on the breakfast menu; one of the most affordable dining options in Deadwood. ⑤ *Average main: $8* ✉ *801 Main St., Deadwood* ☎ *800/287–1251, 605/578–2393* ⊕ *goldcountrydeadwood.com* ⊗ *No dinner.*

Legends Steakhouse

$$$ | **STEAK HOUSE** | The atmosphere is historic elegance in this intimate, fine-dining establishment where steak, seafood, and dessert are served up with pride and style in the basement of the 1903 Franklin Hotel. With its stone walls, dark wood finishes, and large wine list,

Legends Steakhouse is a great place to step out and spend a little extra on a relaxing evening meal. **Known for:** surprising choices such as elk meat and rack of lamb; thick, juicy steaks, both beef and bison; lobster, salmon, and other unexpected seafood options. $ *Average main: $28* ✉ *709 Main St., Deadwood* ☎ *800/584–7005, 605/578–3670* ⊕ *www. silveradofranklin.com.*

Mavericks Steaks and Cocktails
$$ | **AMERICAN** | Recycled barn wood decorates this casual bar-and-grill establishment in the heart of downtown, where steaks are the star of the menu and big-screen TVs are tuned to ballgames. **Known for:** 30-day aged, certified black Angus beef; slow-roasted baby back ribs; signature specialty drinks. $ *Average main: $18* ✉ *688 Main St., Deadwood* ☎ *605/578–2100* ⊕ *maverickssteak.com.*

Snitches
$$$$ | **CONTEMPORARY** | Upscale, chef-inspired cuisine is on the short menu at this small, art deco–style restaurant with a clean, elegant, 1920s vibe inside the Tin Lizzie Gaming Resort. The restaurant bills itself as a "gastronomic experience" featuring "exotic ingredients" that dress up steak, chicken, and seafood. **Known for:** elaborate presentation; thoughtful extras like grilled baguettes with entrées; three-course dinner with tastings from every part of the menu. $ *Average main: $35* ✉ *555 Main St., Deadwood* ☎ *605/571–2255* ⊕ *www.tinlizzie.com* ⊘ *No lunch.*

Coffee and Quick Bites

Main Street Espresso/Big Dipper Ice Cream
$ | **ICE CREAM** | **FAMILY** | Check out the many flavors of hand-dipped ice cream and a full range of hot and cold drink specials at this warm and inviting eatery on Deadwood's Main Street. The shop features Black Hills Blend coffee and is also the home of a Deadwood icon,

a historic 1902 soda fountain. **Known for:** flavored seasonal hot beverages; hand-dipped ice cream; an antique soda fountain. $ *Average main: $5* ✉ *652 Main St., Deadwood* ☎ *605/717–3354* ⊕ *www. facebook.com/deadwoodespresso.*

Pump House at Mind Blown Studio
$ | **DINER** | This eclectic, locally owned establishment is a combination coffee shop, deli, and glassblowing studio all housed in a retro Texaco station that looks like something straight out of the 1950s, complete with old gas pumps and period signage. **Known for:** locally roasted coffee; opportunities to watch glassblowing in action; one of the few non-casino-affiliated, truly local shops in town. $ *Average main: $5* ✉ *73 Sherman St., Deadwood* ☎ *605/571–1071* ⊕ *mind-blownstudio.godaddysites.com.*

🛏 Hotels

Deadwood Gulch Gaming Resort
$ | **RESORT** | Pine-clad hills, a creek, and a deck from which to view the mountains are at your disposal at this family-style resort about a mile from downtown Deadwood. **Pros:** away from downtown bustle; spacious rooms; attentive staff. **Cons:** more hotel than resort; busy with bus tours; more than a mile's walk from downtown. $ *Rooms from: $99* ✉ *304 Cliff St., Deadwood* ☎ *605/578–1294, 800/695–1876* ⊕ *deadwoodgulchresort. com* 🛏 *87 rooms* ⦿ *No Meals.*

★ DoubleTree by Hilton Deadwood at Cadillac Jack's
$$ | **RESORT** | The recently renovated DoubleTree by Hilton centers this expansive gaming resort, with 107 spacious rooms, each with a microwave, mini-refrigerator and coffeemaker. **Pros:** spacious rooms, stylish decor; fitness center with pool and hot tub; outdoor patio. **Cons:** hotel is above an often noisy casino and sports lounge; more suited to adults than families with children; mid-range

priced rooms book more quickly than the other two hotels in the resort complex. $ *Rooms from: $199* ✉ *360 Main St., Deadwood* ☎ *605/571–1245* ⊕ *www.hilton.com* 🠖 *107 rooms* ❘◎❘ *Free Breakfast.*

1899 Inn

$$$ | B&B/INN | To get away from the casinos and buffets at seemingly every Deadwood hotel, try this historic bed-and-breakfast for a taste of the local authenticity and character that's been scrubbed away from much of the rest of this increasingly corporatized town. **Pros:** located in a quieter part of the city; homemade food; 19th-century character without the intrusion of corporate-gambling culture. **Cons:** comes with some of the quirks common to old buildings; the beauty, privacy, and quiet come with a high price; lacks some of the on-site amenities of other Deadwood hotels. $ *Rooms from: $250* ✉ *21 Lincoln Ave., Deadwood* ☎ *605/920–0626* ⊕ *1899inn. com* 🠖 *7 rooms, 2 cottages* ❘◎❘ *Free Breakfast.*

Historic Bullock Hotel

$$ | HOTEL | A casino occupies the main floor of this meticulously restored hotel, a pink granite structure built by Deadwood's first sheriff in 1895; rooms are furnished in Victorian style with reproductions of the original furniture. **Pros:** central location; historic property; unusual rooms. **Cons:** some rooms are dated; remote parking across a busy highway; a bit of traffic noise. $ *Rooms from: $199* ✉ *633 Main St., Deadwood* ☎ *605/578–1745, 800/336–1876* ⊕ *www. historicbullock.com* 🠖 *28 rooms* ❘◎❘ *No Meals.*

Holiday Inn Express & Suites Deadwood-Gold Dust Casino

$$ | HOTEL | Although the exterior of this four-story hotel in a prime location resembles the brick facades of Deadwood's Main Street, its interior is contemporary, with guest rooms that have Wi-Fi, free high-speed Internet connection, and other modern amenities. **Pros:** in the heart of town; contemporary comforts; reliable brand. **Cons:** street-facing rooms can be loud; no on-site parking; standard chain decor. $ *Rooms from: $150* ✉ *22 Lee St., Deadwood* ☎ *605/578–3330* ⊕ *www.ihg.com* 🠖 *78 rooms* ❘◎❘ *Free Breakfast.*

★ Martin & Mason Hotel

$$$ | HOTEL | The Martin & Mason incorporates all the best aspects of Deadwood: history, in a beautifully restored, 1890s, Victorian, boutique hotel; luxury, in spacious rooms decorated with period-appropriate fabrics and antiques; and a downtown location, within walking distance of dozens of casinos and restaurants. **Pros:** free, dedicated parking for guests; ideal location for anyone wanting to explore on foot; historic charm with modern comfort. **Cons:** pricey, especially if booking the higher-end suites; fills up fast and stays booked; downtown location means the area is always busy. $ *Rooms from: $220* ✉ *33 Deadwood St., Deadwood* ☎ *605/722–3456* ⊕ *www. martinmasonhotel.com* 🠖 *8 rooms* ❘◎❘ *No Meals.*

Mineral Palace Hotel & Casino

$$ | HOTEL | As at the other hotels built in town since gaming was reintroduced in 1989, the architecture of Mineral Palace blends in with the historic buildings of Deadwood while the rooms have modern furnishings, but with floral bedspreads, burgundy carpeting, and hardwood trim that give them a slightly Victorian look. **Pros:** easy to walk everywhere in Deadwood from here; on-site steak house is one of the tastiest in town; liquor store and gift shop on-site. **Cons:** some no-smoking rooms still have a hint of smoke smell; street noise is common in this very walkable area; parking is limited and can be problematic. $ *Rooms from: $180* ✉ *601 Main St., Deadwood* ☎ *800/847–2522* ⊕ *www.mineralpalace. com* 🠖 *69 rooms, 4 suites* ❘◎❘ *No Meals.*

Rochford Ghost Town

The town of Rochford likely would have gone the way of countless Black Hills mining camps which faded into history after the gold played out but it carries on, thanks to the pluck of the citizens who still live there, about 22 miles south of Deadwood (drive south on SD-14A/85 from Deadwood to North Rochford Road, then continue south to Rochford).

In August of 1876, a trio of hunters, M.D. Rochford, Richard B. Hughes, and William Van Fleet, stumbled upon a gold-bearing rock on nearby Montezuma Hill. When word spread, hundreds of prospectors descended and laid claims. Rochford and Hughes formally laid out the town in 1878 with a church, three saloons, six stores, and 100 homes already in place. The following year, hotels, restaurants, blacksmith shops, a butcher shop, theater, drug store, and sawmill served a population of 1,000.

More than a dozen mining operations worked the nearby hills and Rapid Creek but by 1890, gold production had dwindled. Ten years later only about 40 residents remained. Today, about 15 residents maintain the town's frontier legacy. Visitors can enjoy a hamburger and soda at the Moonshine Gulch Saloon, between the Rochford General Store and the self-proclaimed Rochford University, a single-room schoolhouse.

Silverado Franklin Historic Hotel & Gaming Complex

$$ | HOTEL | Opened in 1903, this imposing Victorian-style hotel has welcomed many famous guests, including John Wayne, Teddy Roosevelt, and Babe Ruth; it still has its original banisters, ceilings, and lobby fireplace, thanks to a $6 million main floor restoration, and the guest rooms are a mix of old and new, with reproduction furniture, lace on hardwood tables, and contemporary bedspreads. **Pros:** at the top of Main Street; spacious rooms; historic. **Cons:** guest rooms are tired and lack amenities; service can be patchy; casino-hotel vibe not for everyone. ⑤ *Rooms from: $160* ⊠ *709 Main St., Deadwood* ☎ *605/578–3670, 800/584–7005* ⊕ *www.silveradofranklin. com* 🛏 *68 rooms* ⑩ *No Meals.*

ⓨ Nightlife

There are more than 80 gaming establishments in Deadwood, some of them small and personal and others large and rowdy. They generally serve other functions as well—as restaurants, saloons, and gift shops—and sometimes have only a few blackjack and poker tables and slot machines. Although gambling is pervasive in Deadwood, there are still a few local spots to escape the sound of slots and enjoy a relaxing drink.

BARS

Belle Joli' Winery Tasting Room

WINE BAR | The family-owned Belle Joli' Winery, based in Sturgis, grows and produces its wines in the Black Hills and serves them from a former vintage automotive business tucked into the hillside in downtown Deadwood, with an outdoor patio from which visitors may enjoy its offerings. The main Sparkling House facility is in Sturgis. ⊠ *594 Main St., Deadwood* ☎ *605/571–1006* ⊕ *www. bellejoli.com.*

Buffalo Bodega

LIVE MUSIC | Expect a family crowd in the day and a rowdier bunch at night in this saloon, where most evenings you can listen to live country or rock music. The entertainment moves outdoors

While Deadwood's Saloon #10 isn't the same saloon where Wild Bill Hickok was shot, it does have plenty of Old West artifacts.

in summer, when bands play in the stockade section. The Bodega has a rough past; from the 1890s until 1980, the upper floors were used as a brothel. ⊠ *658 Main St., Deadwood* ☎ *605/578–1162* ⊕ *buffalobodega.com.*

★ Old Style Saloon No. 10
BARS | Although it carries the name of the bar where Wild Bill was shot and also purports to have the chair he was shot in, this Old West saloon-style establishment is not actually on the site where the shooting occurred (that was at 624 Main St.); nevertheless, it's filled with fascinating artifacts making it "the world's only museum with a bar." One of Deadwood's best restaurants, the Deadwood Social Club, is upstairs. ⊠ *657 Main St., Deadwood* ☎ *800/952–9398* ⊕ *www.saloon10.com.*

🎭 Performing Arts

From gunslinging re-enactments on the street to local bands in Outlaw Square and big-name acts at Deadwood Mountain Grand, the performing arts options are plentiful year-round in Deadwood and especially in the summer. Beyond the listings here, some local bars also feature live music.

Deadwood Alive
THEATER | A troupe of local Old West re-enactors gives free performances daily during the summer, including Main Street shootouts and Wild Bill Hickok shooting re-enactments inside Saloon No. 10; additionally, the troupe performs paid shows, such as a re-enactment of the trial of Jack McCall (the man who murdered Will Bill). Check the website for show times and further details. ⊠ *Deadwood* ☎ *800/344–8826* ⊕ *www.deadwoodalive.com* ⊠ *From $10.*

Deadwood Mountain Grand Events Center
CONCERTS | Investors including Kenny Alphin of the country music duo Big & Rich developed a former mining facility into a gaming resort and casino with a cavernous entertainment hall that routinely hosts nationally recognizable

music acts and comedy performers. Past shows have included the likes of Nitty Gritty Dirt Band, Peter Frampton, Larry the Cable Guy, Three Dog Night, Cheech and Chong, Foreigner, and Tanya Tucker. ☒ *1906 Deadwood Mountain Dr., Deadwood* ☏ *605/559–0386* ⊕ *deadwoodmountaingrand.com.*

Shopping

Deadwood's downtown is packed with gift shops hawking trinkets and T-shirts to tourists, but there are some hidden gems offering higher-quality, one-of-a-kind items.

Dakota Sky Stone

JEWELRY & WATCHES | A longtime family-owned business, this store in downtown Deadwood specializes in locally produced turquoise jewelry and also sells Western clothing, decor, and art, including a wide selection of bison paintings and photographs. There's another store in Wall. ☒ *671 Main St., Deadwood* ☏ *605/877–2128* ⊕ *www.dakotaskystone.com.*

★ Jacobs Brewhouse & Grocer

WINE/SPIRITS | Taking inspiration from Napa Valley, this rustic-chic, one-of-a-kind shop in a renovated 1895 building sells craft beers, fine wines, and specialty meats, cheeses, and other food to pair with the drinks. There's also a curated selection of other high-end grocery items, and a bakery and kitchen serving lunch and dinner. If you're a gambling high roller, there's a lavish, three-bedroom penthouse upstairs that rents for $1,000 a night. ☒ *79 Sherman St., Deadwood* ☏ *605/559–1895* ⊕ *jacobsbrewhouse.com.*

Madame Peacock's Beer & Bling

CLOTHING | An oasis of trendy in the heart of downtown Deadwood, Madame Peacock's is a women's boutique featuring fine western wear and accessories, from hats, dresses and tops, to boots, jewelry and bags. In the midst of the clothing and bling is a full-service beer bar, where customers can enjoy a cool mug of suds while they shop. ☒ *638 Main St., Deadwood* ☏ *605/559–1002* ⊕ *madamepeacocks.com.*

Miss Kitty's Mercantile

SPECIALTY STORE | Treat your senses to a line of locally made, handcrafted, buffalo-tallow soaps, beer soap, lotion, and lip balm from the Prairie Soap Company in this downtown shop, which is also filled with other unique Western clothing, jewelry, and gift items. ☒ *649 Main St., Deadwood* ☏ *605/559–0599* ⊕ *www.misskittysmercantile.com.*

Activities

Deadwood makes a good base for a winter sports vacation in the Black Hills, particularly if you like snowmobiling and skiing. The surrounding Northern Hills are especially popular, both for their stunning scenery and heavy snows. The rocky peaks and deep canyons are most dramatic here, and the snowfall is the heaviest. In some years, the area around Deadwood sees as much as 180 inches of the white stuff, although the yearly average hovers around 150 inches. The climate here is more variable than in the Rockies, so snow doesn't blanket the region all winter. Warm spells of 50°F, 60°F, or even 70°F weather often hit the region for a week or so after big snowfalls, quickly melting the fresh powder. Before you make firm plans, be sure to check weather reports.

There's also plenty of adventure to find in the summer. A trailhead for the Mickelson Trail beckons cyclists, while hiking trails abound in the area, and ATV rentals and trails are available to those who prefer thrills of the motorized kind.

★ Mickelson Trail, Deadwood Trailhead

BIKING | Deadwood is the northern terminus of the 109-mile Mickelson Trail, a former railroad line that's now a crushed-rock bicycle path stretching

Deadwood's Main Street is lined with saloons, steak houses, and casinos, recalling the town's late-19th-century gold rush heyday.

all the way through the Black Hills with modest grades, wood bridges, and rock tunnels. Because it was a railroad line, no portion of the trail is very steep, and it attracts cyclists of all abilities. Bring some cash to pay a small daily or yearly access fee at a self-service deposit box. Don't have a bike? The trail is also great for walking and hiking and hosts an annual marathon and half-marathon in early June. ✉ *Deadwood* ✛ *On Sherman St., turn at the trailhead sign near Homestake Adams Research and Cultural Center* ☎ *605/584–3896* ⊕ *gfp.sd.gov.*

Lead

5 miles southwest of Deadwood.

The mile-high city of Lead was the home of the world-famous Homestake Gold Mine; these days, the mine is closed, but parts of it have been reborn as the Sanford Underground Research Facility, which attracts scientists from around the globe. Public and private investments

in the lab are bringing jobs back to the city, and many historic and architecturally significant sites are benefiting from renewed care and attention. Meanwhile, there's still an active, open-pit gold mine, the Wharf Mine, that employs 260 workers just west of the city.

GETTING HERE AND AROUND

There are two ways most visitors reach Lead (which is pronounced "leed," for a mining term referring to an outcrop of gold-bearing ore). One route is via Interstate 90 around the Black Hills to U.S. 14 or 85, both of which lead up into the mountains to Deadwood and on to Lead. The other is up through the heart of the Black Hills on U.S. 385. Both require navigating some steep roads and sharp curves, so visiting motorists should be cautious.

VISITOR INFORMATION

CONTACTS Lead Area Chamber of Commerce. ✉ *160 W. Main St., Lead* ☎ *605/580–7393* ⊕ *www.leadmethere. org.*

Learn about the legendary Homestake gold mine at the Sanford Lab Homestake Visitor Center.

 Sights

Visiting Lead is a bit like traveling back in time. Much of the city is filled with 19th-century housing perched precariously on hills and mountainsides, characteristic of a town that formerly boomed with miners. But today there's a different kind of rush in Lead, and this time it's driven by science, as experiments deep down in the old mine shafts bring new people and new opportunities to the community. Visitors can get a taste of old Lead and new Lead by taking in the town's fascinating sights.

Black Hills Mining Museum

SPECIALTY MUSEUM | The memories, tools, and mementoes of dozens of former gold miners are gathered together in this facility, where visitors can view the collections, watch a video explaining the history of mining in Lead, take an underground gold mine tour, and learn to pan for gold. ⊠ 323 W. Main St., Lead ☎ 605/584–1605 ⊕ blackhillsminingmuseum.com ⛏ From $8 ☉ Closed winter.

Historic Homestake Opera House

PERFORMANCE VENUE | Phoebe Hearst, the widow of mining magnate George Hearst, and her immense wealth were the driving forces behind this ornate architectural jewel that was inspired by the opulence of the Gilded Age. After serving as a cultural center for Lead and the Black Hills for decades, the opera house fell into decline along with the mining industry, and in 1984 the facility was nearly destroyed by fire. Today the citizens of Lead are lovingly restoring the opera house to its original, 1914 glory. Tours are available on weekdays, and the facility hosts concerts and other events. ⊠ 313 W. Main St., Lead ☎ 605/584–2067 ⊕ www.homestakeoperahouse.org ⛏ Tours $10.

★ Sanford Lab Homestake Visitor Center

OTHER ATTRACTION | Perched on the edge of the half-mile-wide, 1,200-feet-deep "Open Cut"—a barren pit left over from the mining era—this ultramodern visitor center uses interpretive exhibits to tell the story of the legendary

Homestake Mine and its recent rebirth as an international hub for underground, scientific research. Here you can hit a golf ball into the Open Cut for a "hole in one," and trolleys depart from the facility for informative tours of the city and its historic districts. ⊠ *160 W. Main St., Lead* ☏ *605/584–3110* ⊕ *www.sanfordlab.org* ☽ *Closed Sun. in winter.*

Terry Peak Lookout Tower

VIEWPOINT | At 7,064 feet above sea level, Terry Peak is the sixth-highest point in the Black Hills. But its stone fire-lookout tower, viewing platform, and panoramic views are easily accessible for anyone willing to take a short drive and a jaunt up several dozen stone stairs. The gravel road that leads close to the summit is typically well maintained but may be impassable in winter. ⊠ *Terry Peak Summit Rd., Lead* ✛ *5 miles south of Lead on U.S. 85, go north on Terry Peak Summit Rd. for 3 miles to the parking area* ⊠ *Free.*

🍴 Restaurants

Dining options have been limited since the late 1990s and early 2000s, when the Homestake Mine closed and Lead's population fell. The city also has a tough time competing with the gambling-powered culinary scene in Deadwood. But as the growing underground science lab in Lead brings in global workers and visitors, dining options are expanding.

The Latchstring Restaurant

$$$ | **AMERICAN** | This restaurant with a simple menu focusing on buffalo meat, beef, fish, soup, and salads is built in a log-cabin style with a stone fireplace and animal mounts on the walls. It's in an unbeatable setting 14 miles from Lead, next to Spearfish Canyon Lodge in Spearfish Canyon. **Known for:** locally caught trout and walleye dishes; buffalo stew; outdoor seating available with beautiful canyon views. ⑤ *Average main:*

$25 ⊠ *10619 Roughlock Falls Rd., Lead* ☏ *605/584–3333* ⊕ *spfcanyon.com.*

Stage Stop Cafe at Cheyenne Crossing

$$ | **AMERICAN** | Located at a crossing that can take you west to Wyoming, north into Spearfish Canyon Scenic Byway, or east to Lead, this country café, rebuilt after a September, 2022 kitchen fire, serves up hearty, home-cooked food without pretension. It's 8 miles southwest of Lead on a site that also includes a small lodge and an extensive gift store. **Known for:** Native American tacos; decadent carrot cake; popular stop for motorists driving Spearfish Canyon. ⑤ *Average main: $16* ⊠ *21415 U.S. 14A, Lead* ☏ *605/584–3510* ⊕ *www.cheyennecrossing.org.*

Stampmill Restaurant & Saloon

$$ | **AMERICAN** | Pub food is served in a relaxed setting in this downtown Lead establishment, located in a lovingly preserved 1897 building with exposed-brick walls, wood floors, high ceilings, and a fireplace. There are two Victorian-style rooms for rent on the upper floors. **Known for:** laid-back vibe; lovely patio seating available; bleu cheese-and-olive burgers and chicken sandwiches. ⑤ *Average main: $15* ⊠ *305 W. Main St., Lead* ☏ *719/250–6555* ⊕ *www.stampmillsd.com* ☽ *Closed winter.*

☕ Coffee and Quick Bites

Lotus Up Espresso & Deli

$ | **CAFÉ** | In a building that looks like a ski lodge, this multilevel coffeehouse has lots of private nooks and comfy chairs to settle in with a hot cup of coffee or tea. It's also in a great location with windows looking out to the Sanford Lab Homestake Visitor Center and the Open Cut. **Known for:** outdoor deck seating available; quick breakfast and lunch items; Italian sodas. ⑤ *Average main: $8* ⊠ *95 E. Main St., Lead* ☏ *605/722–4670* ⊕ *www.lotusuplead.com.*

Hotels

Lead caters to wintertime skiers and snowmobilers and doesn't get as many summertime tourists as Deadwood, which is reflected in the lodging options. You won't find many standard hotels in Lead. You're more likely to end up in a lodge, inn, bed-and-breakfast, or private home rental.

Blackstone Lodge & Suites

$ | HOTEL | Several outdoor hot tubs (open year-round) and a craft beer-and-wine lounge add character to this locally owned hotel that provides the cleanliness, predictability, and value you'd expect from a brand-name property. **Pros:** free shuttle service to Deadwood; minutes away from casinos and ski area; mountain and forest views from outdoor hot tubs. **Cons:** not in a walkable area; alongside noisy highway that connects Deadwood and Lead; have to walk outside for hot tubs. ⓈRooms from: $130 ✉ 395 Glendale Dr., Lead ☎ 605/584–2000 ⊕ www.blackstonelodgehotel.com ➴ 70 rooms ⧾ Free Breakfast.

The Historic Town Hall Inn

$ | B&B/INN | Lodging options don't get much more authentically local than this former city hall building, constructed in 1912 with a stone-column entrance and brick walls—inside, the rooms are a mix of modern and historic with large windows, original wood trim, and decorative wood or brass bed frames. **Pros:** close to Deadwood, but away from the bustle and noise; in a walkable area downtown; drastically reduced bargain rates during the off-season. **Cons:** despite overall historic charm, some rooms are quite plain; very expensive rates during the summer peak season; as an old building, it lacks an elevator. ⓈRooms from: $120 ✉ 215 W. Main St., Lead ☎ 866/258–4872, 605/584–1112 ⊕ townhallinn.com ➴ 12 suites ⧾ Free Breakfast.

★ Spearfish Canyon Lodge

$$ | RESORT | Midway between Spearfish and Lead-Deadwood, this lodge-style hotel commands some of the best views in the Black Hills and rooms are furnished in natural woods, and fabrics are dark maroon and green. **Pros:** wonderful location; adventure rentals on-site (snowmobiles, snowshoes, mountain bikes, ATVs, and more); as pretty as it gets with limestone cliffs that rise nearly 1,000 feet in all directions.. **Cons:** remote location; half-hour drive to restaurants (other than the Latchstring next door); standard rooms. ⓈRooms from: $190 ✉ 10619 Roughlock Falls Rd., Lead ☎ 877/975–6343 ⊕ www.spfcanyon.com ➴ 55 rooms ⧾ No Meals.

Terry Peak Chalets

$$$$ | RESORT | Experience some of the most luxurious lodging in the Black Hills in these large, modern, timber-and-stone chalets along the slopes of Terry Peak that include multiple bedrooms, full kitchens, fireplaces, big-screen TVs, decks, and garages—the chalets are perfect for ski trips, and some include ski-in, ski-out access; in the summertime, the rates drop. **Pros:** on the ski slopes; no expense spared in the construction; privacy in a mountain setting. **Cons:** very expensive; conveniently located in winter, but feels remote in summer; snow conditions are unpredictable when booking in advance. ⓈRooms from: $323 ✉ 21150 Stewart Slope Circle, Lead ☎ 605/728–5942 ⊕ www.facebook.com/terrypeakchalets ➴ 7 chalets ⧾ No Meals.

Ⓨ Nightlife

Dakota Shivers Brewing

BREWPUBS | Enjoy a selection of locally-brewed ales, stouts and IPAs in this friendly, intimate taproom nestled in a vintage wood-frame house with a frontier-style facade. The beer selection changes seasonally. The taproom opens at 2 pm and serves until 8 pm, making it a good place to end your day. ✉ *717 W. Main St., Lead* ☎ *605/580–7403* ⊕ *dakotashiversbrewing.com.*

Lewie's Burgers & Brews

BARS | One of several roadhouse-style establishments in the Lead area, Lewie's is popular among snowmobilers (who can ride a trail right to it) and motorcycle riders joyriding through the Black Hills during the annual Sturgis Motorcycle Rally. The rest of the year, it's a place for anybody to unwind with a burger and a brew. ✉ *711 S. Main St., Lead* ☎ *605/584–1324* ⊕ *www.lewiesburgers. com.*

The Sled Haus

BEER GARDENS | With a style that's a cross between an American roadhouse and a German beer garden, the Sled Haus caters, as the name implies, to snowmobilers looking for hearty pub food (including German-inspired choices such as bratwurst). There's also a large selection of beer and wine. ✉ *209 Glendale Ave., Lead* ☎ *605/639–5322* ⊕ *www.facebook. com/thesledhaus.*

🛍 Shopping

Lynn's Dakotamart

FOOD | If you're looking for a standard, affordable, full-service grocery store with all the essentials in Deadwood or Lead, this is the only one you'll find. It's part of a small chain of family-owned South Dakota stores founded in 1941. ✉ *145 Glendale Dr., Lead* ☎ *605/584–2905* ⊕ *www.lynnsdakotamart.com.*

Miners & Merchants Trading Post

ANTIQUES & COLLECTIBLES | A historic former bank building now houses a store selling locally made crafts, antiques, and other gift items. Vintage furniture, wall decor, novelty coffee mugs, clothing, handmade bags, and candles are among the wares sold here. ✉ *300 W. Main St.,*

Lead ☎ *605/641–2762* ⊕ *www.facebook. com/minersandmerchants.*

Activities

Lead is the winter-sports capital of South Dakota. Terry Peak is the main attraction with its downhill ski runs, but there's also a network of groomed trails nearby for cross-country skiers and snowshoers, and there are miles of snowmobile trails snaking through the area. If you prefer motorized recreation without snow, Lead is also a great place to rent a UTV or ATV and explore Black Hills trails designated for motorized travel.

WINTER SPORTS

There are several popular ski areas near Lead, which is a center for winter sports, including snowmobiling.

Black Hills Motorized Trail System

FOUR-WHEELING | More than 700 miles of trails in the Black Hills are designated for motorized use, and one of the best ways to explore is on a utility-terrain vehicle (UTV) or all-terrain vehicle (ATV). There are several outfitters in the Lead area that rent the machines, provide maps, and sell the necessary permits to access the trails. Maps are also available on the Black Hills National Forest website. ✉ *Lead* ☎ *605/673–9200* ⊕ *www.fs.usda. gov.*

Black Hills Snowmobile Trail System

SNOW SPORTS | The state Department of Game, Fish, and Parks maintains the world-class, 416-mile network of snowmobile trails that ranges all over the high, western plateau of the Black Hills. Lead and Deadwood are the epicenter of the network, where you'll find places to rent snowmobiles and gas them up, and even restaurants and bars situated right along the groomed trails. ✉ *Lead* ⊹ *A map is available from the state Department of Game, Fish, and Parks* ☎ *605/223–7660* ⊕ *gfp.sd.gov/snowmobiling.*

Eagle Cliff Trails

SNOW SPORTS | A local ski club maintains 13 miles of interlocking, groomed trails for cross-country skiing and snowshoeing during the winter in this remote mountain wonderland. During the summer, the trails are open to hikers, horseback riders, and mountain bikers. ⊠ *Hwys. 14 and 85, Lead ✛ 15 miles southwest of Lead via Hwys. 14 and 85* ☎ *605/415–1479* ⊕ *eagleclifftrails.com.*

Mad Mountain Adventures

SNOW SPORTS | Rent a utility terrain vehicle (UTV) or a snowmobile to explore the trails designated for each activity in the Black Hills. ⊠ *11201 U.S. 14A, Lead* ☎ *605/578–1878* ⊕ *www.madmountainadventure.com* ✉ *From $275.*

Terry Peak Ski Area

SNOW SPORTS | Perched on the sides of a 7,064-foot mountain, Terry Peak claims the Black Hills' sixth-highest summit and high-speed quad lifts. The runs are challenging for novice and intermediate skiers and should also keep the experts entertained. From the top, on a clear day, you can see Wyoming, Montana, and North Dakota. Facilities: 30 trails; 450 acres; 1,100-foot vertical drop; 5 lifts. ⊠ *21120 Stewart Slope Rd., Lead ✛ 2 miles south of Lead on U.S. 85* ☎ *605/584–2165* ⊕ *www.terrypeak.com* ✉ *Lift ticket $65.*

Trailshead Lodge

SNOW SPORTS | Near the Wyoming border, this lodge has a small restaurant and bar, cabins, a gas station and garage, and dozens of brand-new snowmobiles for rent by the day. This is a favorite pit stop for snowmobilers exploring the Black Hills' popular 400-mile trail network. ⊠ *22075 U.S. 85 S, Lead ✛ 21 miles southwest of Lead on U.S. 85* ☎ *605/584–3464* ⊕ *www.trailsheadlodge.com* ✉ *From $250/day.*

Sturgis

14 miles east of Deadwood.

When most people hear "Sturgis," they think "motorcycle rally." The 10-day event draws more than 400,000 people every August to this town of only 7,000 residents. But Sturgis is quietly developing an alter ego during the non-Rally summer months as a mecca for nonmotorized travel, with an extensive and growing network of trails branching out from the city. Sturgis is also the closest city to Bear Butte, one of South Dakota's most iconic geologic formations.

GETTING HERE AND AROUND

Sturgis is on Interstate 90, about halfway between Rapid City and Spearfish (roughly 20 miles from both). The town serves as a crossroads: it sits at the edge of the Black Hills, where Highway 14 leads west into the mountains toward Deadwood, and Highway 34 leads east onto the vast plains of western South Dakota.

VISITOR INFORMATION

CONTACTS Sturgis Area Chamber of Commerce & Visitors Bureau. ⊠ *2040 Junction Ave., Sturgis* ☎ *605/347–2556* ⊕ *sturgisareachamber.com.*

 Sights

★ Bear Butte State Park

MOUNTAIN | On the plains outside Sturgis, there's a mountain where it seemingly should not be: Bear Butte rises more than 1,200 feet above its surroundings (and 4,400 feet above sea level). It formed millions of years ago when lava pushed up from underground but never erupted. The Lakota named the resulting laccolith "Mato Paha"—translated as Bear Butte—because from some vantage points, it looks like a bear resting on its side. Today the site is a state park with a challengingly vertical, 1.85-mile trail to

On the plains outside Sturgis lies Bear Butte, a 4,426-foot-high mountain considered sacred to many Native American tribes.

the summit, where the panoramic views are incredible. Visitors are asked to be respectful of the butte as a sacred site in the traditional religions of many Native Americans, and hikers are asked not to photograph or disturb Native American tobacco or cloth prayer-ties adorning tree branches along the trail. ✉ *20250 Hwy. 79, Sturgis ✛ 6 miles northeast of Sturgis on Hwy. 79* ☎ *605/347–5240* ⊕ *gfp. sd.gov* ✇ *$8/vehicle.*

Belle Joli' Winery Sparkling House
WINERY | Tours and tastings are available in this serene setting just outside of Sturgis on the edge of the Black Hills, where *méthode champenoise* (a secondary fermentation in the bottle) sparkling wines crafted next to the family-owned winery's 5-acre vineyard. To enjoy the wines and the scenery to the fullest, take a seat on the expansive outdoor patio. ✉ *3951 Vanocker Canyon Rd., Sturgis ✛ ½ mile south of I-90 Exit 32* ☎ *605/347–9463* ⊕ *www.bellejoli.com.*

Black Hills Petrified Forest
NATURE SIGHT | A 15-minute video and a self-guided nature walk teach you about the geologic evolution of western South Dakota. Allow about an hour for your visit to this forest, which opened to the public in 1929, and is about halfway between Rapid City and Sturgis. ✉ *Elk Creek Resort, 8220 Elk Creek Rd., Piedmont* ☎ *605/787–4884* ⊕ *elkcreekresort.net* ✇ *$12* ⊘ *Closed Nov.–Mar.*

Old Fort Meade Museum
HISTORY MUSEUM | After the Sioux destroyed the 7th Cavalry in 1876 at the Battle of Little Bighorn in present-day Montana, the regiment was reconstituted and stationed at a new frontier outpost on the edge of the Black Hills: Fort Meade. That outpost remains today, functioning primarily as a Veterans Affairs medical center. The campus retains many historic structures, including the former commanding officer's headquarters, which now houses the museum and its

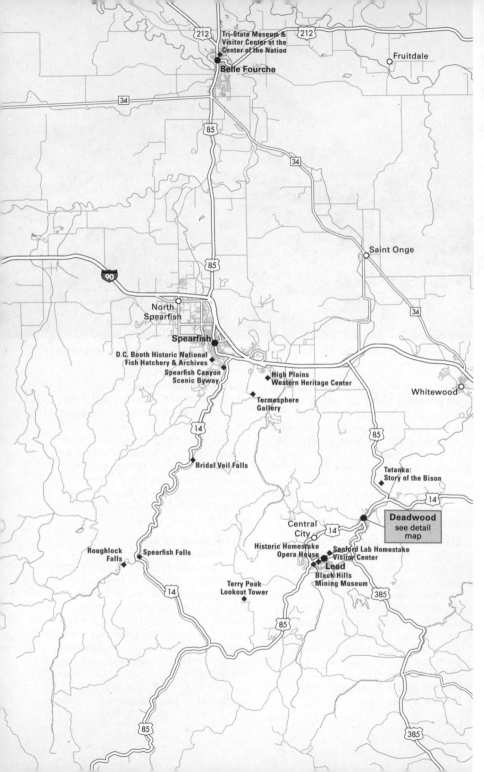

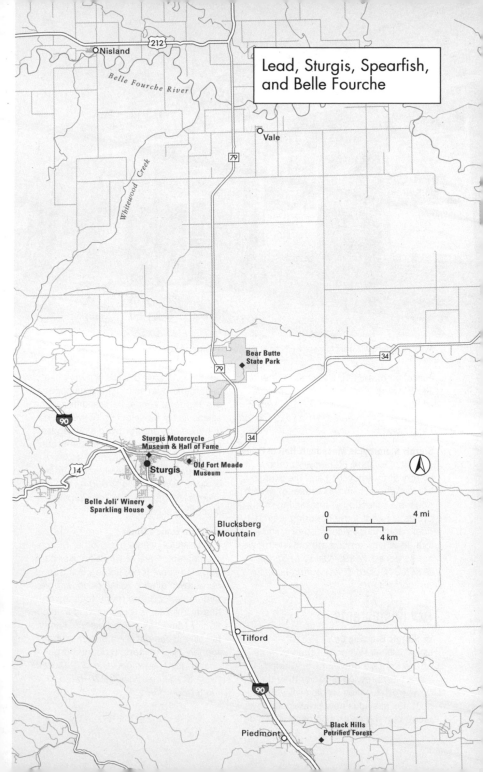

Motorcycle fans will want to make a pitstop at the Sturgis Motorcycle Museum & Hall of Fame.

collection of military artifacts. ✉ *Sheridan St., Bldg. 55, Fort Meade* ✛ *Just east of Sturgis on Hwy. 34* ☎ *605/347–9822* ⊕ *fortmeademuseum.org* ✉ *$5* ⊙ *Closed Oct.–May.*

Sturgis Motorcycle Museum & Hall of Fame
SPECIALTY MUSEUM | Learn about the history of motorcycling and the Sturgis Motorcycle Rally in this museum, which houses a collection of interesting motorcycles, a hall of fame honoring legendary riders and industry contributors, and a lounge where famous motorcycle movies are screened. ✉ *999 Main St., Sturgis* ☎ *605/347–2001* ⊕ *www.sturgismuseum.com* ✉ *$10.*

🍴 Restaurants

★ Sturgis Brewing Co.
$$ | **AMERICAN** | When the then-owners of The Knuckle Brewing Co. needed more beer brewing capacity than their downtown location would allow, they built this spacious new brewery and restaurant on the south side of town. Since opening in 2021, Sturgis Brewing has become known as much for its appetizers, burgers, wings, flatbread pizza, and salads as for its selection of wines and in-house and area-brewed ales, lagers, porters, and IPAs. **Known for:** generous food portions; wide selection of local craft beer and wine; lively atmosphere. ⑤ *Average main: $14* ✉ *600 Anna St., Sturgis* ☎ *605/720–2337* ⊕ *sturgisbrewingcompany.com.*

★ Uncle Louie's Diner
$ | **AMERICAN** | While many other Sturgis "restaurants" are essentially biker bars that also serve food, Louie's is a true hometown diner offering good, simple, affordable food. The menu focuses on hearty breakfasts, burgers, and a selection of Mexican-inspired dishes. **Known for:** all-you-can-eat soup and salad bar; friendly local owners; 6-pound burger challenge. ⑤ *Average main: $10* ✉ *1039 Main St., Sturgis* ☎ *605/720–6475* ⊙ *No dinner Sun.–Tues.*

☕ Coffee and Quick Bites

Emma's Ice Cream Emporium

$ | **AMERICAN** | There is so much more than multiple flavors of ice cream and luscious desserts at this retro downtown shop. Emma's also offers a daily lunch special with sub sandwiches and salads. **Known for:** many flavors of ice cream and desserts; daily lunch specials; beer and wine tap house with live music. $ *Average main: $10* ✉ *1063 Main St., Sturgis* ☎ *605/561–0165* ⊕ *emmasicecream.net.*

🛏 Hotels

Baymont Inn & Suites by Wyndham Sturgis

$ | **HOTEL** | A clean, trusted brand hotel with a friendly, attentive staff, located close but not adjacent to the interstate highway for easy access. **Pros:** restaurant options within easy walking distance; in-house whiskey and seltzer bar; laundry service. **Cons:** no pool or sauna; standard brand rooms; close to rail tracks, noise from occasional passing trains. $ *Rooms from: $125* ✉ *2721 Lazelle St., Sturgis* ☎ *605/206–5400* ⊕ *wyndhamhotels.com* ⤴ *84 rooms* ⦿ *Free Breakfast.*

★ The Hotel Sturgis

$$$ | **HOTEL** | The common areas and rooms in this historic, multistory, 1906 building are thoroughly renovated in the style of chic, downtown loft apartments, with exposed brick walls and sleek metal staircases and railings. **Pros:** in a walkable area downtown; coffee and sandwich shop on-site; some rooms have outdoor balconies. **Cons:** limited off-street parking, especially during the motorcycle rally; boisterous downtown bar scene may mean a noisy stay; some rooms lack windows. $ *Rooms from: $225* ✉ *1144 Main St., Sturgis* ☎ *605/561–0116* ⊕ *thehotelsturgis.com* ⤴ *22 rooms* ⦿ *No Meals.*

Sturgis Lodge & Suites

$ | **HOTEL** | Clean, updated, affordable rooms and common areas make this hotel a top choice for anyone seeking standard accommodations at a good price in Sturgis. **Pros:** heated indoor pool; poolside rooms available; easy access right off I–90. **Cons:** nearby interstate causes some noise problems; not within walking distance of restaurants or shopping; renovated older motel rooms still on the small side. $ *Rooms from: $140* ✉ *2431 Junction Ave., Sturgis* ☎ *605/347–3604* ⊕ *sturgislodgeandsuites.net* ⤴ *55 rooms* ⦿ *Free Breakfast.*

🍸 Nightlife

For a small city, Sturgis has an unusually large number of bars, saloons, and roadhouses. They make much of their income during the 10 days of the annual Motorcycle Rally. During the rest of the year, some remain open, catering to locals and tourists.

The Knuckle Saloon

BARS | Vintage highway signs, old gas pumps, and antique bicycles adorn this large, roadhouse-style saloon where thirsty patrons can have a steak, burger, or other bar food for supper, listen to live music, and play pool. There is also a large selection of area craft beers and wines. ✉ *931 1st St., Sturgis* ☎ *605/347–0106* ⊕ *www.theknuckle.com.*

Loud American Roadhouse

BARS | This large, modern hall is built for the crowds that pack it during the annual Motorcycle Rally, but it remains open throughout the year as a bar and restaurant featuring live music on its stage. The restaurant specializes in steak tips and has other bar staples on its menu, including burgers, wings, and appetizers. ✉ *1305 Main St., Sturgis* ☎ *605/720–1500* ⊕ *loudamericanroadhouse.com.*

🛍 Shopping

The Farm Stand at Bear Butte Gardens

SPECIALTY STORE | A local couple uses this country retail location with a panoramic view of the Black Hills out the front door

The Sturgis Motorcycle Rally

There are certain kinds of tourists who show up every summer in the Black Hills and elicit snickering from locals. They're the tourists who book their trips for early to mid-August, not realizing every road will be blanketed with bikers who fill the air with the unceasing roar of their motorcycles.

Not many people make that mistake, because it's tough to book any lodging in the Black Hills during the annual Sturgis Motorcycle Rally, naively or otherwise. The event brings more than 400,000 people to a region with about half that many residents, and unless you book well in advance, you won't find a place to stay (or, if you do, the rates will be greatly inflated). Nevertheless, there seem to be a few tourists who show up unaware every year.

The rally began humbly in 1938 as a small motorcycle-racing event. It's since exploded into 10 days of adult-themed revelry with lots of booze, bearded bikers, scantily clad biker babes, tattoos, and big-name concerts.

Many bikers stay at massive campgrounds near Sturgis that are open only for the rally. The campgrounds typically include bars and concert venues that draw large nighttime crowds. During the day, bikers stroll around Sturgis and joyride around the Black Hills, creating traffic congestion that otherwise never occurs.

So, if you're a biker, you might love the Rally. If you're not, you might want to avoid western South Dakota during the 10 days beginning with the first Friday each August, and also the few days immediately before and after.

and Bear Butte looming to the north to sell produce, eggs, meat, and other products from their own certified organic farm. They also offer products from other nearby farmers, ranchers, and gardeners, including jams and jellies, local wines, honey, spice mixes, and tea. There's even a large farm cottage and a full commercial kitchen for rent. ✉ 20445 Hwy. 79, Sturgis ✛ 5 miles northeast of Sturgis on Hwy. 79 ☎ 605/490–2919 ⊕ bearbuttegardens.com.

🏃 Activities

If you prefer the nonmotorized version of two-wheeled travel, or if you love the freedom offered by your own two feet, you might be surprised to learn that the city known for motorcycle mania is also one of the best places in South Dakota for nonmotorized adventure. A web of

recreational trails surrounds Sturgis, with numerous trailheads in and around the city.

Centennial Trail

HIKING & WALKING | Created and named for South Dakota's centennial year of 1989, this single-track trail runs for 111 miles through the entirety of the Black Hills. It stretches from the summit of Bear Butte to Wind Cave National Park, and through a stunning array of plains, mountains, forests, and rock outcroppings along the way. There are several access points in the Sturgis area, including trailheads in Bear Butte State Park and the Fort Meade Recreation Area. ✉ Sturgis ☎ 605/223–7660 ⊕ gfp.sd.gov.

Deadman Trail System

HIKING & WALKING | Leading up into the pine-covered mountains on the western edge of Sturgis, these trails feature outstanding views and seclusion just a short distance outside the city. The most convenient trailhead (and a map of the trail system) is near the Belle Joli' Winery Sparkling House. ⊠ *Corner of Vanocker Canyon Rd. and Pineview Dr., Sturgis* ☎ *605/347–3916* ⊕ *www.sturgis-sd.gov.*

7th Cavalry Trails at Fort Meade Recreation Area

HIKING & WALKING | Named for the regiment formerly stationed at Fort Meade, this 30-mile system of interconnected trails for hikers, mountain bikers, and horseback riders sprawls across more than 6,000 acres of mixed grasslands, mountains, and forest under the supervision of the U.S. Bureau of Land Management. Access points include a trailhead at Lions Club Park in Sturgis, the Alkali Creek Trailhead just off I–90 Exit 34, and a trailhead on Cemetery Drive just off Highway 34 east of Sturgis. ⊠ *Sturgis* ⊕ *Access the trailhead at Lion's Club Park off E. Lazelle St.* ☎ *605/892–7000* ⊕ *www. blm.gov/office/south-dakota-field-office.*

Spearfish

15 miles northwest of Deadwood.

As a college town (for Black Hills State University) and a favorite destination of people ranging from rock climbers to retirees, Spearfish has a cultured, laid-back, and slightly bohemian vibe. It also boasts the second-largest population—about 12,000 people—of any city in the Black Hills, making it a regional hub for shopping, dining, lodging, and health care.

GETTING HERE AND AROUND

The convenient location of Spearfish on Interstate 90, along with its abundance of hotels and restaurants, makes it an ideal home base for exploring the northern Black Hills. The Spearfish Canyon Scenic Byway begins from the city, and Spearfish also serves as a central point for anyone interested in visiting Deadwood, Lead, and Devils Tower.

TOURS

Eagle Aviation

FLIGHTSEEING | There's a small airport at Clyde Ice Field just outside of Spearfish, where fixed-base operator Eagle Aviation offers scenic airplane tours ranging from 30 minutes to two hours. Available sites include Spearfish Canyon, gold mines, Crazy Horse, Mount Rushmore, Devils Tower, and more. ⊠ *300 Aviation Pl., Spearfish* ☎ *800/843–8010, 605/642–4112* ⊕ *www.eagleaviationinc.com* ▢ *From $129.*

VISITOR INFORMATION

The U.S. Forest Service employees who manage the northern portion of the Black Hills National Forest work in this Spearfish office, where there's a lobby for visitors to find trail maps, permits for motorized trails, advice, and answers to their questions about exploring the national forest.

CONTACTS Northern Hills Ranger District Office, Black Hills National Forest. ⊠ *2014 N. Main St., Spearfish* ☎ *605/642–4622* ⊕ *www.fs.usda.gov.* **Spearfish Visitor Information Center.** ⊠ *603 Main St., Spearfish* ☎ *800/344–6181, 605/717–9294* ⊕ *visitspearfish.com.*

Sights

Bridal Veil Falls

WATERFALL | Looking like a piece of flowing fabric, Bridal Veil Falls makes a delicate descent some 60 feet over the side of Spearfish Canyon. Among several waterfalls inside the canyon (which can all easily be viewed in a day), it's the most conveniently located, immediately alongside Spearfish Canyon Scenic Byway. Be careful while driving through: It's a popular stop for tourists, who aren't always looking as they cross the road carrying their camera-phones and gawking at the falls. Also be on the lookout for resident mountain goats grazing along the roadway, which will draw plenty of attention from camera-wielding tourists.

Did You Know?

Spearfish Canyon Scenic Byway is chock-full of spectacular vistas but the highlights of the route are its many waterfalls, including Bridal Veil Falls. Other waterfalls not to miss include Roughlock and Spearfish.

✉ *Spearfish ✛ 6 miles south of Spearfish on Spearfish Canyon Scenic Byway*
☎ *605/717–9294* ⊕ *visitspearfish.com.*

D.C. Booth Historic National Fish Hatchery & Archives

OTHER ATTRACTION | A picturesque, serene
stroll around the manicured grounds of a
still-active and historically preserved 1896
fish hatchery awaits visitors here. View
fish in the ponds and through a giant
underwater window, take in the historic
architecture of the numerous buildings
on-site, climb onto a historic railcar,
and feed the ducks that freely roam
the grounds. ✉ *423 Hatchery Circle,
Spearfish* ☎ *605/642–7730* ⊕ *dcbooth-
fishhatchery.org.*

High Plains Western Heritage Center

OTHER ATTRACTION | Focusing on a region
now covered by five states—the Dakotas,
Wyoming, Montana, and Nebraska—this
center features artifacts such as a Dead-
wood-Spearfish stagecoach. Outdoor
exhibits include a log cabin, a one-room
schoolhouse, and, in summer, an entire
farm set up with antique equipment.
Often on the calendar are cowboy poetry,
a cowboy supper and show, live music,
and historical talks. ✉ *825 Heritage Dr.,
Spearfish* ☎ *605/642–9378* ⊕ *www.west-
ernheritagecenter.com* ⊒ *$12.*

★ Roughlock Falls

WATERFALL | Little Spearfish Creek tum-
bles down a series of waterfalls both
powerful and tame at Savoy in Spearfish
Canyon. Visitors can park at the head
of the falls and walk a mile-long path
alongside them to enjoy not only the
cascading water, but also the surrounding limestone canyon walls and the
mixed forest of pine, aspen, and birch.
✉ *Spearfish ✛ 1 mile west from Spearfish Canyon Scenic Byway on Roughlock
Falls Rd.* ☎ *605/584–3896* ⊕ *gfp.sd.gov*
☉ *Roughlock Falls Rd. closed Dec.–Mar.*

Spearfish Canyon Scenic Byway

SCENIC DRIVE | This 20-mile scenic route
runs along Spearfish Creek, below

1,000-foot limestone cliffs and some of
the most breathtaking scenery in the
region. Cascading waterfalls quench the
thirst of quaking aspen, gnarled oaks,
sweet-smelling spruce, and the ubiqui-
tous ponderosa pine. The canyon is home
to deer, mountain goats, porcupines, and
mountain lions. Near its middle is the
old sawmill town of Savoy, a jumping-off
point for scenic hikes to Spearfish Falls
and Roughlock Falls. In fall, changing
leaves rival any found in New England.
✉ *Spearfish ✛ Turn onto Spearfish
Canyon Hwy. from East Colorado Blvd. in
Spearfish* ⊕ *visitspearfish.com.*

★ Spearfish Falls

WATERFALL | By far the most powerful of
the three waterfalls in Spearfish Canyon,
Spearfish Falls makes a sudden, 50-foot
drop to the very bottom of the canyon
floor. Visitors can hike a short trail of
about a mile from the Latchstring Inn at
Savoy down to the bottom of the falls,
close enough to hear the roar of the
water and feel bursts of wind and mist.
✉ *Spearfish ✛ Park at Latchstring Inn
along Spearfish Canyon Scenic Byway*
☎ *605/584–3896* ⊕ *gfp.sd.gov.*

Termesphere Gallery

ART GALLERY | Spearfish native and
internationally known artist Dick Termes
creates his magical, mind-bending paintings on spherical canvases and hangs
them from the ceiling on slowly rotating
motors. The result, as Termes describes
it, is an "inside-out view of the physical
world"—"a revolving three-dimensional
space/time exploration of an entirely
closed universe." He calls the creations
Termespheres. Many are on display and
some are for sale in the Termesphere
Gallery, located inside a geodesic dome
structure. Book a visit by phone or on the
website. ✉ *1920 Christensen Dr., Spearfish ✛ 1.7 miles south on Christensen
Dr. from Colorado Blvd.* ☎ *605/642–4805*
⊕ *termespheres.com.*

Towering limestone formations are a common sight along the 19-mile Spearfish Canyon Scenic Byway.

🍽 Restaurants

Antunez

$$$ | SPANISH | Going for the feel of a Spanish or South American café, this small restaurant is one of the few in the Black Hills attempting to elevate Hispanic food into high cuisine. Although the elaborate dinner entrees are quite expensive, the menu also includes more affordable, all-day choices such as enchiladas, quesadillas, and tacos. **Known for:** succulent meat dishes including buffalo rib eye and Wagyu steak; international wine selection; Spanish and Latin background music. ⑤ *Average main: $32* ⊠ *117 E. Illinois St., Spearfish* ☎ *605/722–8226* ⊕ *antunezcuisine.com* ⊗ *Closed Sun. and Mon.*

★ Dough Trader Pizza

$$ | PIZZA | Whether sitting by the fireplace in the small, indoor seating area or by the fire pit on the outdoor patio, you'll get some of the best pizza in the Black Hills at this beloved cash-only Spearfish eatery, located in a remodeled former Tastee Freeze. The gourmet pizza is cooked in a stone oven and served with fresh toppings generously applied. **Known for:** crust made from 1880s sourdough starter; fun signature pizza names like "Dances with Goats" and "Dear Lucille"; associated bakery sells sourdough treats. ⑤ *Average main: $22* ⊠ *543 W. Jackson Blvd., Spearfish* ☎ *605/642–2175* ⊕ *www.doughtraderpizza.com* ⊟ *No credit cards* ⊗ *Closed Tues. and Wed.*

★ Steerfish Steak & Smoke

$$$ | STEAK HOUSE | Western chic is the style of this restaurant, where a buffalo head and cowboy art adorn the walls of a historic, 1893 stone building with wood floors. Steaks, smoked meats, and burgers are the focus, but the menu also includes a large salad section. **Known for:** hand-cut certified Angus beef; steaks grilled over hickory wood; large, decadent dessert menu. ⑤ *Average main: $25* ⊠ *701 5th St., Spearfish* ☎ *605/717–2485* ⊕ *www.steerfish.com* ⊗ *Closed Sun.*

☕ Coffee and Quick Bites

The Green Bean Coffeehouse

$ | CAFÉ | Local character and flavor permeate this hip, comfortable coffeehouse inside a spacious former residential home, where the window seating is plentiful and padded chairs are tucked into corners and alcoves. Besides coffee and tea, there are also quick breakfast and lunch items on the menu. **Known for:** cozy setting and atmosphere; tasty paninis and grilled sandwiches; smoothies, iced coffee, and other cold drinks. ⑤ *Average main: $5 ✉ 304 N. Main St., Spearfish* ☎ *605/717–3636 ⊕ www.spearfishgreenbean.com.*

★ Leones' Creamery

$ | AMERICAN | Leones' is the kind of quiet, locally beloved, hole-in-the-wall place you could easily miss but definitely shouldn't—its handcrafted and ever-evolving ice-cream flavors are the best in the Black Hills. The owners pour their passion into creative creations that often incorporate locally produced beers, produce, and other novel ingredients. **Known for:** transforming ingredients (like rhubarb) into amazing ice cream; small outdoor seating area; rotating specialties including popsicles, floats, and ice-cream sandwiches. ⑤ *Average main: $5 ✉ 722½ Main St., Spearfish* ☎ *605/644–6461 ⊕ leonescreamery.com ☾ Closed Tues.*

Ruby's Roost Bakery & Coffee

$ | AMERICAN | Try this family-owned-and-operated bakery, specializing in organic baked goods and coffee, but don't wait too late in the day. Their caramel and cinnamon rolls, scones, muffins, glazed doughnuts, and pastries are served daily but only from 7 am to noon. **Known for:** organic baked goods and coffee; caramel and cinnamon rolls; chocolate and maple-glazed baked doughnuts. ⑤ *Average main: $5 ✉ 741 Main St., Spearfish ⊕ rubysroostbakery. com ☾ Closed Mon.*

🛏 Hotels

Best Western Black Hills Lodge

$ | HOTEL | Modern, decorative, leaf-pattern carpeting and dark-wood room accents elevate this hotel's decor a bit above standard national-chain accommodations, with rates in line with what you'd expect from a recognizable brand-name property. **Pros:** outdoor heated pool; conveniently located near I–90; less than a 10-minute walk from downtown. **Cons:** noise is possible from the interstate; pool is outdoors and unusable during bad weather; two floors but no elevator. ⑤ *Rooms from: $149 ✉ 540 E. Jackson Blvd., Spearfish* ☎ *800/780–7234, 605/642–7795 ⊕ www.bestwestern.com ⬗ 50 rooms ❙⊙❙ Free Breakfast.*

Rim Rock Lodge

$$ | HOTEL | With cabins dating to the 1930s that the owners describe as "historic on the outside, new on the inside," this secluded spot offers the rare opportunity to stay inside Spearfish Canyon—accommodations are rustic in style but with modern amenities including queen beds, bathrooms, and kitchens. **Pros:** close access to everything in Spearfish Canyon; next to Spearfish Creek; only 5 miles from Spearfish. **Cons:** rates significantly higher during and around Sturgis Motorcycle Rally; books up fast and far in advance; early and late summer nights can be cold in the canyon. ⑤ *Rooms from: $195 ✉ 10900 Rimrock Pl., Spearfish* ☎ *605/642–3192 ⊕ rimrocklodge.com ⬗ 4 cabins, 3 suites ❙⊙❙ No Meals.*

Secret Garden Bed & Breakfast

$$ | B&B/INN | Located in a quiet, residential neighborhood just a stone's throw from Spearfish Creek, this 1892 Queen Anne–style home on the National Register of Historic Places has rooms that are luxuriously outfitted to match the historic character of the house—en suite baths and extra amenities including bathrobes and wine glasses make this a great

Spearfish's Craft Beer Pioneer

South Dakota's beer scene endured a bit of a dry spell until Jeff Drumm came along.

There were some brewpubs in the state, but they mostly served beer on-site, with some growlers to go. Until Drumm founded Crow Peak Brewing Company in Spearfish in 2007, no South Dakota beer maker had distributed beer commercially since 1942.

Drumm moved from the West Coast to Spearfish after completing a craft-brewing program and apprenticeship. He proved to be the spark that South Dakota's craft beer scene needed. Crow Peak's canned beers can now be purchased in states throughout the Northern Great Plains, and many other brewers in the Black Hills and throughout South Dakota have followed his lead.

Besides Crow Peak and its signature ale, porter, and IPA offerings, the Spearfish craft beer scene includes Spearfish Brewing Company, where the lagers, bocks, ales, and other beers have won multiple national awards; and Sawyer Brewing Company, where cans of IPA, ales, and stouts are emblazoned with a four-ax logo representing four generations of the owner's family who've worked as sawyers (people who saw timber) in the local logging industry.

Elsewhere in the Black Hills, the ever-growing list of craft brewers includes Hay Camp, Cohort Craft, Woodland Republic, Last Mile, Lost Cabin, Dakota Point, Zymurcracy, and the Firehouse in Rapid City; Miner and Sick-N-Twisted in Hill City; Sturgis Brewing in Sturgis, Dakota Shivers in Lead; and Mount Rushmore Brewing in Custer. Besides visiting the breweries, beer lovers can find bottles and cans of many locally made beers in the area's grocery and liquor stores, and on tap in some restaurants.

place for couples. **Pros:** outdoor hot tub; 10-minute walk to downtown; garden area with seating. **Cons:** air-conditioning supplied by window units; some surrounding properties not well maintained; limited privacy sharing a house with other guests. $ Rooms from: $160 ⊠ 938 N. Ames St., Spearfish ☎ 605/642–4859 ⊕ www.secretgardenbandbspa.com �j4 rooms ⊙| Free Breakfast.

ⓨ Nightlife

Killian's Food & Drink
BARS | The fun-loving, adventurous, outdoorsy side of Spearfish shines through at Killian's, where the wood on the walls is imbued with character, bicycles are used as decoration, and the carefully curated 17-tap beer and wine lists are ever evolving. A local chef sources local and exotic ingredients to create creative dishes, including some vegetarian options, which add surprising sophistication to the pub-like atmosphere. ⊠ 539 W. Jackson Blvd., Spearfish ☎ 605/717–1255 ⊕ www.killiansfoodanddrink.com.

★ Sawyer Brewing Company
BREWPUBS | Few if any nightspots in the Black Hills can beat the atmosphere at Sawyer Brewing Company, with its modern, sawmill-inspired building and massive outdoor patio, which opens onto a greenway and walking path alongside Spearfish Creek. Besides the craft beer brewed on-site, there's also pizza made in a brick oven. This is one of the newest areas of the city, where great care has been shown to incorporate the natural

surroundings. ✉ *2537 Yukon Pl., Spearfish* ☎ *605/569–2676* ⊕ *www.sawyerbrewingco.com.*

Spearfish Creek Wine Bar

WINE BAR | Although not actually alongside the creek as its name implies, this quiet spot has a wood privacy fence surrounding the outdoor seating area, and vines growing around the entrance. It's a great place to enjoy a relaxing glass of wine on a warm summer evening. There's also a small indoor seating area, and often live, acoustic music from local and regional performers. ✉ *127 W. Grant St., Spearfish* ☎ *605/722–7027* ⊕ *www.facebook.com/spearfishcreekwinebar.*

 Performing Arts

Matthews Opera House & Arts Center

THEATER | Residents of Spearfish have lovingly restored this ornate, 1906 theater, which has architectural and design flourishes including a ceiling dome, a mural-painted arch over the stage, and chandeliers in the lobby. The box offices sells tickets for concerts, locally produced plays, magicians, and film screenings, and there's an attached fine-arts gallery showcasing the work of local and regional artists. ✉ *612 Main St., Spearfish* ☎ *605/642–7973* ⊕ *www.matthewsopera.com.*

Shopping

The Art Nest Gallery

ART GALLERY | Locals banded together to create this space in a former city hall building where 40 local and regional artists display and sell their work. There's also a selection of gifts and souvenirs, and when you're done browsing and shopping, homemade ice cream awaits at Leones' Creamery next door. ✉ *722 N. Main St., Suite 1, Spearfish* ☎ *605/631–0673* ⊕ *www.theartnestgallery.com.*

Good Earth Natural Foods

SPECIALTY STORE | Since the 1970s, local owners have been running this downtown shop stocked with healthy, organic, fair-trade, sustainable groceries and personal-care items. There's also an organic café serving breakfast and lunch, and a loft selling eco-friendly apparel. ✉ *638 Main St., Spearfish* ☎ *605/642–7639* ⊕ *www.goodearthnaturalfood.com.*

Activities

The Spearfish area is a recreational paradise, with a dizzying array of opportunities for outdoor adventure. Name an outdoor pursuit, and it's probable that you can do it here, thanks to the incredible bounty that nature affords.

Some of the most popular summer pastimes revolve around the area's many trails, where hikers have miles to explore and mountain bikers come from around the country to compete in top-level races. Separate trails designated for motorized travel lure ATVers, and the rocks of Spearfish Canyon are a magnet for climbers. Fly-fishers and paddlers love the streams that flow down from the mountains, and there are also plenty of camping opportunities, ranging from primitive tent sites in the forest to large camping resorts.

The winter brings cold weather and snow to the northern Black Hills—the snow piles up higher here than elsewhere in the region—but it doesn't slow down the fun. The focus shifts to winter sports, including snowmobiling, cross-country skiing, snowshoeing, and fat-tire bicycling on trails designated for each activity, and even ice climbing on the trickling water that freezes into ice flows on the walls of Spearfish Canyon.

OUTFITTERS

Two Wheeler Dealer Cycle and Fitness

BIKING | Family-owned and-operated Two Wheeler Dealer Cycle and Fitness, based in Spearfish, stocks bicycles for sale and rent. The store is also a great place to pick up advice on where and how to explore the area's trails by bike. ✉ *305 Main St., Spearfish* ☎ *605/642–7545* ⊕ *www.twowheelerdealer.com.*

SUMMER ACTIVITIES
Elkhorn Ridge Resort

CAMPING | This sprawling resort east of Spearfish has 185 RV sites and 36 cabins, plus tent sites and house rentals with a pub, golf course, outdoor swimming pool, sport courts, and a 4.5-mile recreational trail system. The resort is on a flat plain along Miller Creek, with views of the surrounding Black Hills. ✉ *20189 U.S. 85, Spearfish* ☎ *605/722–1800* ⊕ *elkhornridgeresort.com.*

Iron Creek Trail

HIKING & WALKING | This conveniently located trail begins from a small parking area alongside Spearfish Canyon Scenic Byway and follows an easy to moderate route into a side canyon formed by Iron Creek. The trail is about 3 miles total out and back; along the way, keep an eye out for an abandoned mining tunnel and a picturesque rock formation high atop the canyon (which you're more likely to see on the way back) called the Iron Creek Arch. ✉ *Spearfish Canyon Scenic Byway, Spearfish* ✛ *5½ miles south of Bridal Veil Falls on Spearfish Canyon Scenic Byway* ☎ *605/717–9294* ⊕ *visitspearfish.com.*

Lookout Mountain Park and Trail

HIKING & WALKING | This city "park" consists of more than 700 acres of protected mountain and forest terrain with several miles of trails, including routes to the top of 4,452-foot Lookout Mountain. From the summit, there are spectacular views of Spearfish, the Black Hills, and the surrounding plains. The trail is popular with hikers and mountain bikers, and there's a map at the trailhead. ✉ *Spearfish* ✛ *Just east of the 10th and Nevada St. intersection* ☎ *605/717–1189* ⊕ *www. cityofspearfish.com.*

WINTER SPORTS
Big Hill Trail System

SNOW SPORTS | The Big Hill Complex in the Black Hills National Forest is open for hikers and mountain bikers in the summer, but its real purpose is to serve as the epicenter of winter sports in the Spearfish area, with access to both a snowmobile trail and a 13.6-mile network of groomed trails for cross-country skiers and snowshoers. The trails, which allow users to disappear into a winter wonderland of snow, mountain views, and pine trees, are maintained by a club of local winter-sports enthusiasts in partnership with the Forest Service. ✉ *Spearfish* ✛ *South from Spearfish on Forest Service Rd. 134 about 8 miles to the trailhead* ☎ *605/642–4622* ⊕ *www. fs.usda.gov.*

Belle Fourche

12 miles north of Spearfish.

This city of about 6,000 residents bears a French name for the "beautiful fork" where several local waterways meet, but today the phrase is pronounced by locals as "Bell Foosh," and the local culture is all-American. If you're interested in authentic, Western, cowboy culture, Belle Fourche is the place to sample it. The city lies just outside the Black Hills amid the vast cattle ranges of the Great Plains, and the annual summertime professional rodeo here is one of the biggest and best in South Dakota. The area has also produced a crop of homegrown rodeo stars including Marvin Garrett, who competed in bareback riding and earned a place in the national Pro Rodeo Hall of Fame.

GETTING HERE AND AROUND

Most visitors drive to Belle Fourche by taking Interstate 90 to Spearfish, and then heading north for 12 miles on Highway 85.

Sights

Aladdin General Store

HISTORIC SIGHT | Located 17 miles west of Belle Fourche on SD-34/WY-24, a scenic backroad route to Devils Tower, is a historical gem, the Aladdin General Store (and very much worth a detour). The Victorian-style mercantile, dating back to 1896 and showing its age with creaky wooden floors, stocks groceries, snacks, beverages, souvenirs, outdoor goods, and antiques. There is even a small bar and a functioning post office serving tiny Aladdin, population 15. Also visible nearby is another designated historic site, the Aladdin Mine coal tipple, a wooden structure used to load mined coal into railroad cars. ⊠ *3983 WY-24, Aladdin* ✛ *16 miles west of Belle Fourche on SD-34/WY-24* ☎ *307/896–2226* ⊕ *www.facebook.com/aladdingeneralstore.*

Tri-State Museum & Visitor Center at the Center of the Nation

VISITOR CENTER | Artifacts of regional ranchers and pioneer families are showcased in this museum's interpretive exhibits. You can see historical photos and items from the everyday life of 19th-century homesteaders, such as saddles, branding equipment, dolls, clothing, and dinnerware. The museum occupies a spacious building near the bank of the Belle Fourche River. The grounds include a relocated gold-rush cabin and a monument celebrating the Belle Fourche area's distinction as the geographic center of the United States (when Hawaii is included). ⊠ *415 5th Ave., Belle Fourche* ☎ *605/723–1200* ⊕ *www.thetristatemuseum.com* ⧉ *Free.*

Restaurants

Branding Iron Steakhouse & Saloon

$$$ | STEAK HOUSE | Much of the Belle Fourche–area economy is built on cattle, and when local ranchers and other residents want a good steak, they go to the Branding Iron. This is a no-nonsense, saloon-style facility with wood paneling on the walls, a bar, pool tables, lots of seating, and big food portions. **Known for:** steak tips; slow-roasted prime rib; boisterous local atmosphere. ⑤ *Average main: $25* ⊠ *19079 S. U.S. 85, Belle Fourche* ☎ *605/892–2503* ⊕ *www.facebook.com/brandingironsteakhouse* ⊗ *Closed Sun.*

Rancho Los Agaves Mexican Restaurant

$$ | MEXICAN | FAMILY | Extensive menu of authentic Mexican favorites, from burritos and fajitas to quesadillas and seafood, served dine-in or take-out in a welcoming, warm south-of-the-border atmosphere with a cordial staff. The menu includes lunch specials priced less than $10, desserts, a kids' menu and vegetarian options. **Known for:** authentic Mexican dishes; budget-friendly lunch; friendly waitstaff. ⑤ *Average main: $16* ⊠ *1807 5th Ave., Belle Fourche* ☎ *605/723–1623* ⊕ *www.facebook.com/losagavesmexican.*

Hotels

★ AmericInn by Wyndham Belle Fourche

$ | HOTEL | Timber pillars support the awning and a buffalo head hangs over the stone fireplace in the lobby of this lodge-style hotel, which offers standard hotel furnishings and gets good reviews for service, cleanliness, and price. **Pros:** good option if hotels in the Black Hills are booked; indoor pool; good place to stay for guests with pet allergies. **Cons:** away from Black Hills attractions; nearby dining options are few; no pets allowed. ⑤ *Rooms from: $130* ⊠ *2312 Dakota Ave., Belle Fourche* ☎ *605/892–0900* ⊕ *www.wyndhamhotels.com* ⇌ *61 rooms* ⦿ *Free Breakfast.*

Activities

Black Hills Roundup

HORSE SHOW | FAMILY | If you want to see a rodeo in South Dakota, consider circling the five days ending on July Fourth and attending the Black Hills Roundup, one of the biggest, best, and most historic rodeos on the Great Plains. There are multiple rodeo performances at the city's outdoor rodeo grounds, where professional cowboys and cowgirls come from all over the country to compete in front of a covered grandstand. There's also a slate of other events, including a cattle drive, fireworks, concerts, a parade, and a carnival. ⊠ *301 Roundup St., Belle Fourche* ☎ *605/723–2010* ⊕ *www.blackhillsroundup.com.*

Rocky Point Recreation Area

WATER SPORTS | In 1911, when the federal government finished constructing an impoundment on Owl Creek called Orman Dam, it was the largest earthen dam in the world; today, the dam has lost that distinction, but it still provides irrigation for nearby farms and doubles as a recreational destination. The Belle Fourche Reservoir is an oasis on the semiarid plains, covering 8,000 acres with 58 miles of shoreline and reaching a depth of 25 feet. The state-run Rocky Point Recreation Area is a place to camp, fish, swim on the beach, and launch boats. ⊠ *18513 Fisherman's Rd., Belle Fourche* ✛ *9 miles east of Belle Fourche via U.S. 212 and Fisherman's Rd.* ☎ *605/641–0023* ⊕ *gfp.sd.gov* ◰ *$8 per vehicle.*

Chapter 5

THE SOUTHERN BLACK HILLS

Updated by
Tanya Manus

⊙ Sights	🍴 Restaurants	🛏 Hotels	🛍 Shopping	🍸 Nightlife
★★★★★	★★★☆☆	★★★☆☆	★★☆☆☆	★★☆☆☆

WELCOME TO
THE SOUTHERN BLACK HILLS

TOP REASONS TO GO

★ **Powerhouse park:** With a size and scenery rivaling national parks, Custer State Park is packed with wildlife, hiking trails, lakes, lodges, campgrounds, and fun.

★ **National mammal:** No state has more bison, also known as buffalo, than South Dakota. Viewing opportunities abound in Custer State Park and Wind Cave National Park.

★ **Prehistoric wonder:** About 26,000 years ago, more than 60 mammoths met their demise in a muddy pit in what is now the city of Hot Springs. Watch the excavation in progress at The Mammoth Site.

★ **Rails-to-trails:** Bicyclists of all abilities can hop on the beginning of the Mickelson Trail, a 109-mile former railroad line that stretches south-to-north through the Black Hills.

★ **Underground worlds:** Two of the world's 10 longest caves are in the southern Black Hills. The combined length of the explored passageways in Jewel Cave and Wind Cave is more than 375 miles.

1 **Custer.** This small town hosts some of the best restaurants in the Black Hills. The city also boasts a trailhead for the popular Mickelson Trail, along with the headquarters of the Black Hills National Forest and the 1881 Courthouse Museum.

2 **Custer State Park.** Plan several days or a week if you want to fully explore this 110-square-mile gem. There's something for everyone here: driving the Wildlife Loop, hiking to the state's highest peak, paddling a placid lake, or even taking climbing lessons.

3 **Hot Springs.** Warm mineral springs drew Civil War veterans here in the 1890s. Those springs still feed a public swim center and a spa. Hot Springs also hosts a public archeological dig known as The Mammoth Site. Just down the road is Angostura Reservoir, a popular lake lined with miles of sandy beaches.

4 **Edgemont.** This tiny town at the edge of the Black Hills is short on amenities, but it boasts one of the region's most important trailheads: the southern terminus of the Mickelson Trail. There's also a rare covered bridge here and a much-loved local museum.

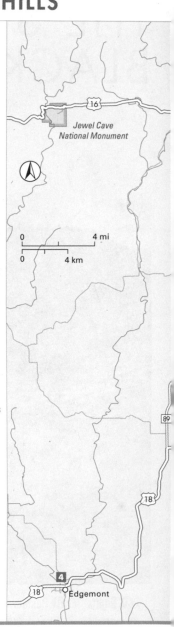

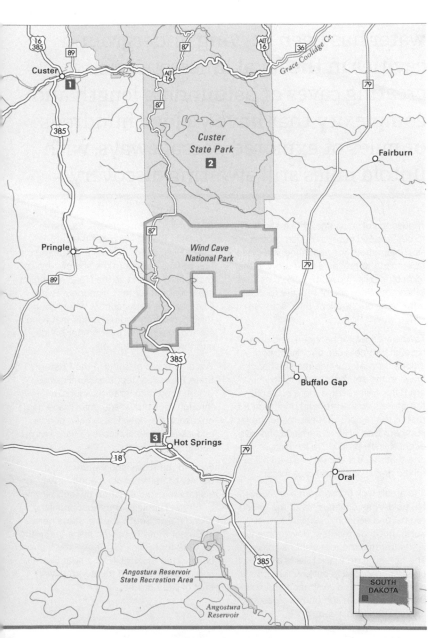

The southern Black Hills is a region shaped by the inexorable forces of nature. For eons, the flow and trickle of water has been carving underground cavities in the local limestone rock, creating caves of astounding length and complexity that have yielded hundreds of miles of explored passageways, with untold miles still awaiting discovery.

Thousands of years ago, those same forces trapped dozens of mammoths in a sinkhole, where they perished in a place tailor-made to preserve their story in the form of fossils. Today, it's known as The Mammoth Site, one of the few tourist attractions on the Black Hills' southern fringe.

Towns are few, far between, and small here, in part because of climatic conditions. In winter, when the sun hangs lower in the southern sky, the southern Black Hills receive more sun and therefore stay warmer and drier than the rest of the region. That has made the far southern Black Hills a semiarid and less economically productive landscape, yet one that's also a starkly beautiful place of mixed grass, sage, and pine forests.

The area's lack of moisture—or recoverable gold—has driven most of the people, towns, and economic activity farther north, but that dearth of development is the intrepid modern visitor's gain. The far southern Black Hills is a place of underappreciated beauty, where it's still possible to escape civilization and pause in silent awe as bison graze across an undisturbed landscape.

But it's not all emptiness. Where the southern Black Hills meet the central Black Hills, the granite core of the region has been eroded into the sharply vertical rock pillars known as the Needles (which are a magnet for rock climbers). This is Custer State Park country, where tourists throng carefully laid-out roads that wind around mountains, over timber bridges, and through rock tunnels.

Water is more plentiful in the Custer State Park area, too. In several places where mountain streams squeeze through rock crevasses, man-made dams hold back the flow. These calm ponds and lakes are ideal places to fish, swim, paddle, and reflect.

Beyond the roads and waterways, a bounty of trails provides another way for visitors to explore nature by foot, bicycle, or off-road vehicle. The most popular hiking trail in South Dakota starts here, in Custer State Park, and leads to the top of 7,242-foot Black Elk Peak—the highest point in the Black Hills, in South Dakota, and in the portion of the country lying east of the Rockies.

It's exactly that kind of opportunity for adventure and sightseeing that leads many people to base their Black Hills vacation in Custer State Park, and also causes many to confine their trip mostly within the park's boundaries, save for an excursion to Mount Rushmore. For those willing to explore a bit farther afield, the unspoiled beauty of the broader southern Black Hills awaits as a bonus.

Planning

Getting Here and Around

AIR
Although there are several landing strips and municipal airports in the Black Hills, the only airport with commercial service is in Rapid City, the fastest growing metro area in the Midwest. Rapid City Regional Airport is 11 miles east of town on Highway 44.

CAR
Traveling the southern Black Hills by car begins with determining where to make an entrance into the mountains. There are several places to do that. A popular route, Highway 16, leads from Rapid City up into the Keystone and Hill City areas; then, from Hill City, Highway 385 goes south through the mountains to the city of Custer. From Custer, Highway 16A leads into Custer State Park.

In Custer State Park, motorists can enjoy the famously scenic Needles Highway and Iron Mountain Road. All of the aforementioned roads are scenic, winding, mountainous routes through forested areas—in other words, they're places to drive carefully, enjoy the scenery, and forget about being in a rush.

Alternatively, Highway 79 is a freeway that skirts the mountains along the eastern edge of the Black Hills. From this highway, motorists can turn west and head up into the mountains on Highway 36 toward Custer State Park. Or, they can head farther south on the freeway and take Highway 18 west to Hot Springs. From Hot Springs, Highway 385 leads to Wind Cave National Park.

Hotels

For many people, staying in the southern Black Hills means renting a room or cabin at one of the lodges in Custer State Park, or renting one of the park's many campsites. For those who'd rather stay outside the park—or if the park is booked up, which is frequently the case—there are good, standard hotel options in the city of Custer and, to a lesser extent, in Hot Springs. The region is also dotted with public and private campgrounds, bed-and-breakfast establishments, and rental cabins.

Restaurants

The city of Custer may be small, but it packs a culinary punch with two restaurants—Black Hills Burger & Bun and Skogen Kitchen—that locals consistently rank as two of the best places to eat in all of the Black Hills. Elsewhere in Custer, and in Hot Springs, there are a number of restaurants that cater to tourists, focusing mainly on burgers, steaks, pizza, and other standard fare intended for broad appeal. Custer State Park has its own restaurants attached to its lodges. Overall, there are fewer places to eat in the southern Black Hills than in the central and northern Black Hills, and there's also less variety in the cuisine.

HOTEL AND RESTAURANT PRICES

⇨ *Hotel and restaurant reviews have been shortened. For full information, see Fodors.com. Restaurant prices are the average cost of a main course at dinner, or if dinner is not served, at lunch. Hotel prices are the lowest cost of a standard double room in high season.*

What It Costs			
$	**$$**	**$$$**	**$$$$**
RESTAURANTS			
under $13	$13–$23	$24–$35	over $35
HOTELS			
under $150	$150– $200	$201– $250	over $250

Tours

Dave's World Tours

DRIVING TOURS | Focusing on the southern Black Hills, this company offers private, personalized full- and half-day van tours with stops including major attractions such as Mount Rushmore, Crazy Horse, and Custer State Park, plus alternatives including winery and brewery tours. They provide shuttle service for bicycling and hiking with drop-offs and pick-ups along the Mickelson Trail, and at Rapid City Regional Airport. Advance reservations required. ⊠ *Custer* ☎ *605/673–1130* ⊕ *davesworldtours.com.*

Custer

41 miles southwest of Rapid City via U.S. 16 and U.S. 385.

Custer is the oldest town in the Black Hills. It dates to 1875, when prospectors illegally staked claims in the area while all of the Black Hills and present-day western South Dakota were still promised to the Sioux by treaty. The prospectors had been excited in 1874 when George

Armstrong Custer's military expedition discovered gold in the area (just two years later, Custer would perish in present-day Montana at the Battle of the Little Bighorn). The gold rush ultimately moved north to more lucrative deposits in the northern Black Hills, leaving the beauty of the Custer area largely unspoiled. Today, the roughly 2,000 residents of Custer mine mostly for tourists' money.

GETTING HERE AND AROUND

Many visitors to Custer get there from nearby Custer State Park, where they're likely to be staying. Highway 16A runs between the park and the city. Otherwise, people making day trips typically arrive from Rapid City via Highway 16 to Hill City, and then Highway 385 the rest of the way to Custer.

VISITOR INFORMATION

Many people assume the Black Hills National Forest is headquartered in the largest city in the region, Rapid City, where there is a Forest Service district office; however, the forest is actually headquartered in a modest complex on the edge of Custer. The lobby of that complex is a place to pick up trail maps, motorized-trail permits, forest-themed books and gifts, and advice on exploring the national forest.

CONTACTS Black Hills National Forest Headquarters. ⊠ *1019 N. Fifth St., Custer* ☎ *605/673–9350* ⊕ *www.fs.usda.gov.* **Custer Chamber of Commerce.** ⊠ *615 Washington St., Custer* ☎ *800/992–9818, 605/673–2244* ⊕ *www.custersd.com.*

 Sights

1881 Courthouse Museum

HISTORY MUSEUM | Looking every bit as historical as its name implies, this Italianate-style structure is built from bricks made in a local kiln. The courthouse was the center of government and justice in Custer for nearly 100 years, until 1973, when it was the site of a notorious

This subterranean passageway in Jewel Cave National Monument showcases the cave's rare crystalline formations.

melee between local law enforcement and the American Indian Movement in the weeks prior to AIM's occupation of Wounded Knee. Today, the building is a museum that houses exhibits on Native Americans, the Custer expedition, mining, and more. ⊠ *411 Mt. Rushmore Rd., Custer* ☏ *605/673–2443* ✉ *$8* ⊘ *Closed Sun.*

Jewel Cave National Monument

CAVE | Jewel Cave's more than 215 miles of surveyed passages made it the third-longest cave in the world as of 2023, while exploration continued. But for tourists who aren't cavers, it's the rare crystalline formations that abound in the cave's passages—not the cave's size—that are the main draw. Take one of the paid, year-round, ranger-led tours, and you'll be rewarded with the sight of tiny crystal Christmas trees, hydromagnesite balloons, and delicate calcite deposits dubbed "cave popcorn." Plan to arrive early in the morning, because summertime tours fill up fast and start at prescheduled intervals. While you wait, scenic surface trails and exhibits in the visitor center can be explored for free. ⊠ *11149 U.S. 16, Custer* ⊹ *15 miles west of Custer* ☏ *605/673–8300* ⊕ *www.nps.gov/jeca* ✉ *Free, tours from $16* ⌘ *Advance reservations strongly recommended.*

🍴 Restaurants

★ Black Hills Burger & Bun

$ | BURGER | The focus on simple, fresh, and delicious food at affordable prices has made this very small establishment into a phenomenon with one of the best reputations of any restaurant in the Black Hills. It's located in a renovated, downtown building with exposed brick walls and stained-glass accents. **Known for:** delicious, juicy burgers made from fresh-ground meat; black-bean vegetarian burger options; rotating selection of mouth-watering desserts. ⑤ *Average main: $10* ⊠ *441 Mt. Rushmore Rd., Custer* ☏ *605/673–3411* ⊕ *www.blackhillsburgerandbun.com* ⊘ *Closed Sun.*

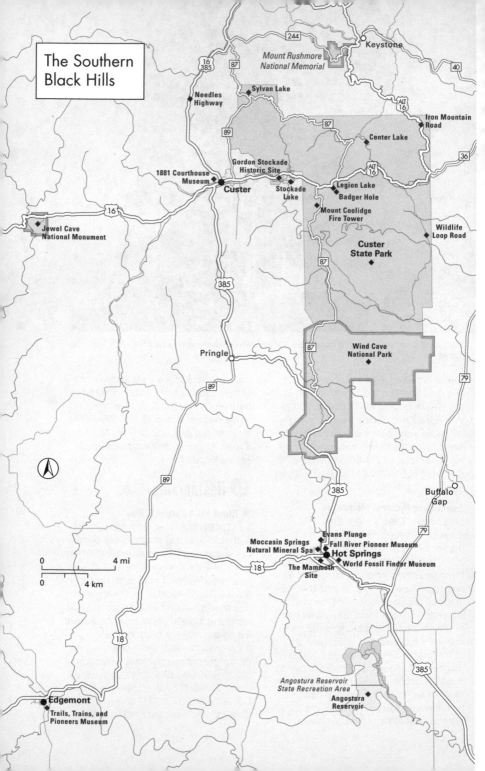

The Southern Black Hills

Keystone

Mount Rushmore National Memorial

Sylvan Lake

Needles Highway

Iron Mountain Road

Center Lake

1881 Courthouse Museum

Gordon Stockade Historic Site

Custer

Stockade Lake

Legion Lake

Badger Hole

Mount Coolidge Fire Tower

Jewel Cave National Monument

Wildlife Loop Road

Custer State Park

Pringle

Wind Cave National Park

Buffalo Gap

Evans Plunge

Moccasin Springs Natural Mineral Spa

Fall River Pioneer Museum

Hot Springs

World Fossil Finder Museum

The Mammoth Site

Angostura Reservoir State Recreation Area

Angostura Reservoir

0 4 mi

0 4 km

Edgemont

Trails, Trains, and Pioneers Museum

The Custer Wolf

$$ | AMERICAN | This bar and grill is in a renovated brick building with wood floors and a long, wooden bar, where the food is elevated a bit beyond standard pub fare. The menu changes seasonally; gluten-free and vegetarian options are available. **Known for:** renovated, dog-friendly outdoor seating area; surprising menu choices for a bar and grill, like the falafel burger and Walleye Chermoula; selection of local and regional craft beers. $ Average main: $18 ☒ 506 Mt. Rushmore Rd., Custer ☎ 605/673–9653 ⊕ www.custerwolf.com ⊗ Closed Sun. and Thurs.

★ Hjem A.M.

$$ | MODERN AMERICAN | "Hjem" means home in Danish—a nod to the restaurant owners' heritage—and the cozy eatery is designed to be a place that feels like home in the morning. They specialize in breakfast fare, and their imaginative menu incorporates a gamut of flavors, including lingonberries, miso butter, and Marcona almonds. **Known for:** inventive spin on breakfast favorites; eggs Benedict, rice pudding, pancakes; friendly service. $ Average main: $20 ☒ 308 Mt. Rushmore Rd., Custer ☎ 605/981–9047 ⊕ www.hjemam.com ⊗ Closed Mon. and Tues. No dinner.

★ Skogen Kitchen

$$$$ | CONTEMPORARY | The small town of Custer is one of the last places a visitor might expect to find gourmet cuisine, but it's available at Skogen Kitchen, where a chef with national experience has settled into a small, modest-looking establishment and built a widespread following. Skogen Kitchen was a 2023 semi-finalist for the James Beard Foundation awards. **Known for:** a quality of heightened cuisine found nowhere else in the Black Hills; inventive menu; carefully curated wine and beer lists. $ Average main: $40 ☒ 29 N. Fifth St., Custer ☎ 605/673–2241 ⊕ www.skogenkitchen.com ⊗ Closed Sun. and Mon.

☕ Coffee and Quick Bites

Calamity Jane's Coffee Shop & Grill

$ | DINER | The wagon wheel and skull, wood walls, and framed facts about South Dakota history immediately create a western vibe to match this coffee shop's name. Calamity Jane's serves the finest coffee and espresso from locally roasted beans, along with smoothies, kombucha, and Italian sodas, and breakfast, lunch, and dinner. **Known for:** coffee, espresso, smoothies; burgers, sandwiches; seasonal selections of local wines. $ Average main: $10 ☒ 512 Mt. Rushmore Rd., Custer ☎ 605/673–2269 ⊕ calamityjanecoffeeshop.com.

Horatio's Homemade Ice Cream

$ | CAFÉ | One of the most interesting examples of early architecture in the city, the 1881 First National Bank building, hosts this old-fashioned ice-cream parlor where local owners make small batches of ice cream and customers enjoy it outside on warm summer days. Inspiration for the name comes from Horatio Nelson Ross, who discovered gold in Custer in 1874. **Known for:** waffle cones; homemade ice-cream sandwiches; daily specials and variety of flavors. $ Average main: $5 ☒ 548 Mt. Rushmore Rd., Custer ☎ 605/673–4009 ⊗ Closed Tues. and Wed.

Miner's Cup

$ | CAFÉ | Stop into this little drive-through joint for a coffee or smoothie to go, or sit down and enjoy it at one of the picnic tables on the lawn. There's also a surprisingly good selection of fresh-made breakfast and lunch sandwiches, wraps, salads, and pastries. **Known for:** signature drinks; fast service; creative breakfast food combos. $ Average main: $5 ☒ 1021 Mt. Rushmore Rd., Custer ☎ 605/673–3882 ⊕ minerscup.com.

Pizza Mill

$ | PIZZA | The handmade doughs, creative toppings and homey atmosphere of this family-run eatery are its recipe for success. Along with signature pizzas such as the Towering Timber supreme pizza, the Healthy Logger vegetarian option and many more, Pizza Mill serves sandwiches, appetizers and salads. **Known for:** specialty sandwiches; take-and-bake pizzas; unique pizza toppings. $ Average main: $14 ⊠ 904 Mt. Rushmore Rd., Custer ☎ 605/673–2020 ⊕ www.pizzamillcuster. com ⊘ Closed Sun. and Mon.

Hotels

Bavarian Inn

$$$ | HOTEL | Living up to its name, this alpine-style inn has flowers hanging over the front balcony and is on a forested lot high above Custer—it offers standard hotel rooms with a bevy of extras, including a café, beautifully landscaped grounds, indoor and outdoor pools, a tennis court, a fitness trail, and guest laundry facilities. **Pros:** hotel accommodations with the extras of an inn; in a quiet spot just outside the main part of the city; complimentary cookie happy hour each afternoon. **Cons:** not within close walking distance to downtown Custer; more expensive than nearby standard hotel options; guests complain of poor soundproofing in some rooms. $ Rooms from: $230 ⊠ 855 N. Fifth St., Custer ☎ 605/961–0203 ⊕ www.bavarianinnsd. com ↙ 64 rooms ⲻ No Meals.

Holiday Inn Express & Suites Custer

$$ | HOTEL | This is one of the newer hotels in Custer, offering the quality expected of a major national chain with some locally inspired extras, a water feature where guests can gaze up at the rocky, forested hillside directly behind the facility. **Pros:** some rooms with private balconies; indoor pool; large parking lot. **Cons:** not as low-priced as you'd expect from a chain hotel; breakfast is typical mass-produced

fare; what you gain in predictability, you sacrifice in local character. $ Rooms from: $175 ⊠ 433 W. Mt. Rushmore Rd., Custer ☎ 605/673–2500 ⊕ www.ihg.com ↙ 91 rooms ⲻ Free Breakfast.

Rock Crest Lodge & Cabins

$$ | HOTEL | With a main lodge set back from the road and private cabins tucked up into a shady hillside, this facility offers the feel of a wooded retreat with the convenience of being a 10-minute walk from downtown shops and restaurants. **Pros:** outdoor pool and playground; unusual amount of privacy for a lodge within city limits; beautiful natural surroundings bordering the national forest. **Cons:** bad weather closes the outdoor pool and hot tub; traffic noise from its location near busy street; cost of first and last night's stay required as a deposit at booking. $ Rooms from: $184 ⊠ 15 W. Mt. Rushmore Rd., Custer ☎ 877/412–2246, 605/673–4323 ⊕ rockcrestlodge.com ⊘ Closed mid-Oct.–May 1 ↙ 14 rooms, 20 cabins, 2 off-site group rentals ⲻ Free Breakfast.

Nightlife

Buglin' Bull Restaurant & Sports Bar

BARS | Featuring a craft beer brewed exclusively for them by the Mount Rushmore Brewing Company, the owners of the Buglin' Bull (named for the sound made by a male elk) also offer a wide selection of other beers, spirits, cocktails, margaritas, martinis, wine, and bourbon. It's all served up in a bustling atmosphere at a renovated downtown building with a bar, tin ceiling, exposed brick walls, and a large outdoor deck on an upper floor. ⊠ 511 Mt. Rushmore Rd., Custer ☎ 605/673–4477 ⊕ www.buglinbull.com.

Mount Rushmore Brewing Company

BREWPUBS | Using malt from North Dakota and hops from the Midwest and Pacific Northwest, this brewery creates a flagship line of four beers with names inspired by the four presidents on Mount Rushmore: American Fabius, a blond ale; Long Tom, an American IPA; Trust Buster, a Scottish export; and Rail Splitter, a London-style porter. All the beers can be enjoyed on-site in the taproom. The expansive facility also include a restaurant and event space. ⊠ *140 Mt. Rushmore Rd., Custer* ☎ *605/673–4200* ⊕ *mtrushmorebrewingcompany.com.*

🎭 Performing Arts

The Custer Beacon

MUSIC | Some of the best musicians in the Black Hills perform at The Custer Beacon, which has become known as the place to eat, sip, gather, and groove. There's a bar, a restaurant that serves hearty lunch, dinner, and late-night appetizers, sandwiches, and salads, and an outdoor seating area, making the Beacon a lively community gathering place. ⊠ *351 Washington St., Custer* ☎ *605/673–3800* ⊕ *custerbeacon.com.*

👜 Shopping

Art Expressions Gallery & Gifts

ART GALLERY | A local cooperative of artists and artisans displays and sells paintings, jewelry, furniture, pottery, glass, quilts, photography, wood, metal, mixed media, and more. The work on display ranges from simplistic to sublime, with art and photography subjects including local wildlife, landscapes, and Native American themes. ⊠ *17 N. Fifth St., Custer* ☎ *605/673–3467* ⊕ *www.artexpressions-gallerycuster.com.*

Good Karma Jewelry

JEWELRY & WATCHES | The name does not encompass the breadth of items sold in this fashionable downtown Custer shop. There's jewelry—much of it turquoise and Western-themed. There's also home decor, a Boho Chic clothing section for women and men, and a rock shop selling gems, fossils, and crystals. While you're

shopping, grab a hot or cold drink and a Black Hills Bagel at Dino Brew Coffee Bar inside the store. ⊠ *507 Mt. Rushmore Rd., Custer* ☎ *605/673–3047* ⊕ *www. goodkarmacusterstore.com.*

🏃 Activities

Adventure Rentals

FOUR-WHEELING | Rent a utility-terrain vehicle (UTV) to explore the more than 700 miles of trails designated for motorized travel in the Black Hills National Forest, or rent a three-wheeled Slingshot roadster to cruise the region's paved roads in style. ⊠ *444 U.S. 16, Custer* ☎ *866/445–5386* ⊕ *adventurerentalssd.com* 💰 *From $200.*

Black Hills Balloons

BALLOONING | Black Hills Balloons has more than 35 years of experience providing bird's-eye views of some of the Black Hills' most picturesque locations. Tours meet up at the Black Hills Balloons Hangar in Custer. Because the balloons can only fly in appropriate weather, reservations are essential, and you'll need to meet up before sunrise. Given the incredible things you'll see, it'll be worth it. Flights last approximately one to two hours. Reservations required. ⊠ *Black Hills Balloons Hangar, 747 Mt. Rushmore Rd., Custer* ☎ *605/673–2520* ⊕ *www. blackhillsballoons.com* 💰 *$375.*

Harbach Trailhead, Mickelson Trail

BIKING | Use this trailhead for access to the Mickelson Trail, a 109-mile, crushed-rock path stretching all the way through the Black Hills from south to north. Because the trail was formerly a rail bed, the grade is never too steep, and bicyclers of all abilities enjoy riding it. Bring some cash to pay a small daily or annual fee at a self-service kiosk. Don't have a bike? Rent one from a local outfitter, or set out on foot. Besides the natural scenery, the Mickelson Trail also features railroad bridges and rock tunnels. ⊠ *On*

Washington St. between Sixth and Seventh Sts., Custer ☎ *605/584–3896* ⊕ *gfp.sd.gov.*

Rockin' R Trail Rides

HORSEBACK RIDING | A local couple and a staff of friendly guides offer trail rides ranging from one to three hours, which are good lengths for anyone not accustomed to the surprising physical demands of horseback riding. The rides begin from the Heritage Village Campground just a mile south of Crazy Horse Memorial, and the routes are on scenic Black Hills National Forest land under the terms of a permit with the U.S. Forest Service. ⊠ *24853 Village Ave., Custer* ☎ *605/673–2999* ⊕ *rockingrtrailrides.com* 🎫 *From $70* ☉ *Closed Oct. 1–Memorial Day weekend.*

Rocky Knolls Golf Course

GOLF | Spectacular views of the Black Hills' rocky vistas, and a wooded landscape of Ponderosa pines along the fairways await golfers on this nine-hole course designed for precision play. After a few rounds of golf, relax over lunch or dinner at Rocky Knolls' on-site bar and grill. ⊠ *12181 W. US-16, Custer* ☎ *605/673–4481* ⊕ *www.rockyknollsgolfcourse.com* 🎫 *From $27* ☉ *Closed Oct. 15–Apr. 15.*

Sylvan Rocks Climbing School & Guide Service

ROCK CLIMBING | This business has been a fixture among the rocks of Sylvan Lake and the Needles in Custer State Park since 1989. It's operated by experienced, local climbing guides who espouse the belief that anyone, from young to old, can experience whatever level of climbing they're ready for. Guided trips include all the necessary training and gear, and they range from several hours of basic instruction to multiday outings. ⊠ *757 Mt. Rushmore Rd., Custer* ☎ *605/484–7585* ⊕ *sylvanrocks.com* 🎫 *From $90.*

Custer State Park

4 miles east of Custer via U.S. 16A

This 71,000-acre park is the crown jewel of South Dakota's state park system. Elk, pronghorns, mountain goats, bighorn sheep, mountain lions, wild turkey, prairie dogs, and the second-largest (behind Yellowstone National Park) publicly owned herd of bison in the world roam this pristine landscape. Scenic drives roll past fingerlike granite spires and panoramic views (try the Needles Highway). Take the 18-mile Wildlife Loop Road to see prairies teeming with animals and some of the beautiful backdrops for several Western films. Accommodations here are outstanding, too, with numerous campgrounds and a resort network that includes five amenities-filled lodges and well-appointed vacation cabins. TravelAwaits named Custer State Park one of the top five best state parks in the U.S. The park is open year-round; some amenities are closed during winter.

GETTING HERE AND AROUND

There are numerous routes into the park, and the one you'll choose may depend on which part of the park you're staying in, or which part you want to see first. One of the most popular routes is to head south from Rapid City along the eastern flank of the Black Hills on Highway 79, and then take Highway 36 west to reach the Custer State Park Visitor Center, Wildlife Loop Road, or State Game Lodge. Another option is Highway 16 to Hill City, and then Highways 385 and 87 to Sylvan Lake. Or, if you've got the time, just grab a map and take any route you please—with beautiful scenery everywhere and lots of signs pointing the way, there's no bad way into the park.

VISITOR INFORMATION

The Custer State Park Visitor Center is a large, modern visitor center, constructed in 2016, houses staff members ready to answer questions, interpretive exhibits, maps, and a 100-seat theater that plays a 20-minute introductory film about the park. The Peter Norbeck Outdoor Education Center is a historic stone structure that formerly served as the park's visitor center and now hosts exhibits, activities, and educational programs geared toward families and children. The building's namesake, Peter Norbeck, was a legendary South Dakota politician who was instrumental in the formation of the park. The Wildlife Station Visitor Center, located in a picturesque former buffalo herdsman's house with a stone foundation and timber frame, has been renovated into a mini-visitor center for motorists who want a break while driving the Wildlife Loop Road.

CONTACTS Custer State Park. ⊠ *13329 U.S. 16A, Custer* ✛ *4 miles east of Custer* ☎ *605/255–4515* ⊕ *gfp.sd.gov/ parks/detail/custer-state-park.* **Custer State Park Visitor Center.** ⊠ *Custer State Park, Custer* ✛ *Junction of U.S. 16A and Wildlife Loop Rd.* ☎ *605/255–4515* ⊕ *www.custerstatepark.com.* **Peter Norbeck Outdoor Education Center.** ⊠ *Custer State Park, Custer* ✛ *1 mile west of the visitor center* ☎ *605/255–4515* ⊕ *www. custerstatepark.com.* **Wildlife Station Visitor Center.** ⊠ *Wildlife Loop Rd., Custer* ✛ *8 miles south of U.S. 16A on the Wildlife Loop Rd.* ☎ *605/255–4515* ⊕ *www. custerstatepark.com.*

◉ Sights

Every inch of Custer State Park is a sight unto itself, but if you need a destination for your wanderings, there are lots of places to target for a visit.

Badger Hole
HISTORIC HOME | Cowboy poet Charles Badger Clark was the first poet laureate of South Dakota and spent 30 years of his life in a rustic cabin within Custer State Park. He died in 1957, but his cabin is preserved and open to visitors. Badger Clark Historic Trail, a 1-mile hiking trail behind the cabin, is still lined with some of Clark's stonework. ⊠ *Custer State Park, Custer* ✛ *From U.S. 16A, about 1 mile south on Badger Clark Rd.* ☎ *605/255–4515* ⊕ *www.custerstatepark.com.*

Center Lake
BODY OF WATER | As one of the lesser-known and more out-of-the-way lakes in Custer State Park, Center Lake is worth a visit for anyone hoping for a respite from the crowds. The lake has a no-wake designation, which means motorized boats have to take it slow, while swimmers and paddlers rule the water. There's a nice beach and a 71-site campground at the lake, too, all surrounded by hills, rock formations, and the pine forest in the north-central part of the park. ⊠ *Custer State Park, Custer* ✛ *From Needles Hwy., about a mile on Playhouse Rd. to Center Lake Rd.* ☎ *605/255–4515* ⊕ *www.custerstatepark.com* ⌂ *Same-day reservations.*

Gordon Stockade Historic Site
HISTORIC SIGHT | After the discovery of gold in 1874, prospectors rushed into the Black Hills. They were all there illegally, because the area still belonged to the Sioux Native Americans as part of a treaty. Knowing that, a group of prospectors called the Gordon Party built a log fortress as protection against attacks. Within several months, the Army removed the party from the Black Hills; today, a replica of the log fortress stands on the site. ⊠ *Custer State Park, Custer* ✛ *3 miles east of Custer on U.S. 16A, just inside the park's western boundary* ☎ *605/255– 4515* ⊕ *www.custerstatepark.com.*

★ Iron Mountain Road
SCENIC DRIVE | Legendary former governor and U.S. senator Peter Norbeck personally oversaw the layout of this road, which was designed during the 1930s to complement the park's scenic

One of the most idyllic spots in Custer State Park is Sylvan Lake—especially when viewed from a rented kayak or canoe.

beauty. The 17-mile route winds around several wooden, pigtail bridges and passes through three rock tunnels that frame Mount Rushmore. Plan an hour or more on this road, because the going is intentionally slow, and you'll want to stop for pictures. The road forms part of the longer Peter Norbeck Scenic Byway. ⊠ *Custer State Park, Custer* ✛ *Enter from Hwy. 36 near the park's eastern boundary or from U.S. 16A near Mount Rushmore* ☎ *605/255–4515* ⊕ *www. custerstatepark.com* ⊘ *Periodic winter-weather closures.*

Legion Lake
BODY OF WATER | Giant rock formations frame this small lake, which has a swimming beach and is popular with paddlers. Canoe and kayak rentals are available at the back of the Dockside Grill restaurant on the lakeshore. There's a small campground and a cluster of rental cabins just up the hill. ⊠ *Custer State Park, Custer* ✛ *7 miles east of Custer on U.S. 16A* ☎ *605/255–4515* ⊕ *www. custerstatepark.com.*

Mount Coolidge Fire Tower
MOUNTAIN | The 6,023-foot summit known as Sheep Mountain was renamed Mount Coolidge in 1927 when President Calvin Coolidge vacationed in Custer State Park. During the 1930s, the Civilian Conservation Corps built a stone fire-lookout tower atop the mountain, and that tower is still in use today. Visitors willing to brave a steep, narrow, curvy, 1.2-mile gravel road can drive to the summit to see the tower and take in the panoramic views. ⊠ *Custer State Park, Custer* ✛ *3 miles south of U.S. 16A on Hwy. 87 to Mt. Coolidge Lookout Rd.* ☎ *605/255–4515* ⊕ *www.custerstatepark.com* ⊘ *Closed late Sept.–Memorial Day.*

★ Needles Highway
SCENIC DRIVE | Like Iron Mountain Road, the construction of Needles Highway was overseen by the late South Dakota politician Peter Norbeck, who took great care to complement the area's natural beauty. The winding, 14-mile road has numerous scenic overlooks, passes through two rock tunnels, and

showcases the giant, fingerlike granite formations known as the Needles. The most popular stop on the route is the Needle's Eye, where one of the massive Needles formations sports a hole worn away by erosion. Because the Needle's Eye area is often packed with people and vehicles in tight quarters, use extra caution when passing through or stopping for a look. ✉ *Custer State Park, Custer* ⊹ *Enter from Sylvan Lake or from U.S. 16A near Legion Lake* ☎ *605/255–4515* ⊕ *www.custerstatepark.com* ⊙ *Closed winter.*

Stockade Lake
BODY OF WATER | Covering 130 acres, and 45 feet at its deepest point, Stockade Lake is the largest lake in the park and is especially popular for fishing. The lake has a boat ramp and numerous shore-fishing areas, as well as two campgrounds and cabins. ✉ *Custer State Park, Custer* ⊹ *3 miles east of Custer on U.S. 16A* ☎ *605/255–4515* ⊕ *www.custerstatepark.com.*

★ Sylvan Lake
BODY OF WATER | People love to scramble around on the big rock formations that line this small, placid, picturesque mountain lake, which is high up in one of the most scenic parts of the park. The lake is very popular among paddlers, and there are kayak, canoe, and SUP rentals available. Swimmers love the beach, and the campground is always full. A walking path along the shore is great for a relaxing stroll, while several other trails begin near the lake—including the most popular route to Black Elk Peak, the state's highest point. Snacks, drinks, apparel, and other items are available in the general store. All of these things make Sylvan Lake extremely popular, so you might consider getting up early to find parking and beat the crowds. ✉ *Custer State Park, Custer* ⊹ *10 miles south of Hill City via Hwys. 385 and 87* ☎ *605/255–4515* ⊕ *www.custerstatepark.com.*

Wildlife Loop Road
SCENIC DRIVE | Plan a couple of hours to make this 18-mile drive through some of the park's best meadows, where wildlife come to graze. You're likely to see some of the park's 1,400 bison, and you might have to stop for a while as they amble across the road (bison are dangerous, so keep a safe distance). You'll also see prairie dogs and burros (which are small, feral donkeys), and you might spot deer, pronghorns, elk, bighorn sheep, coyotes, and birds of prey. ✉ *Custer State Park, Custer* ⊹ *Enter from U.S. 16A near the visitor center or from Hwy. 87 near the Blue Bell area* ☎ *605/255–4515* ⊕ *www.custerstatepark.com.*

🍴 Restaurants

There are very few dining options in the park to serve thousands of visitors every day, so if you'd like to get a meal inside the park boundaries, it's best to plan ahead and call for reservations.

Blue Bell Lodge Dining Room and Lounge
$$ | AMERICAN | Feast on fresh walleye or buffalo—which you can have as brisket, meatloaf, or stew—in this rustic log-cabin structure with a stone fireplace. There's also a good selection of salads as well as kid-friendly burgers, sandwiches, and wraps. **Known for:** park setting; outdoor patio overlooking French Creek; family-friendly. ⑤ *Average main: $20* ✉ *Custer State Park, 25453 S.D. 87, Custer* ☎ *605/255–4531* ⊕ *custerresorts.com* ⊙ *Closed mid-Oct.–May 1.*

State Game Lodge Restaurant
$$ | AMERICAN | Located in the historic Game Lodge where President Calvin Coolidge and First Lady Grace Coolidge lived for nearly three months on a 1927 vacation, the Game Lodge restaurant has the biggest dining capacity of any restaurant in the park. There are multiple seating areas ranging from basic to elegant to outdoors (be sure to inquire about the options). **Known for:** historic character; gift

store attached to restaurant; interpretive exhibits about the building and famous guests. ⑤ *Average main: $20* ✉ *Custer State Park, U.S. 16A, Custer* ✛ *½ mile west of Custer State Park Visitor Center* ☎ *605/255–4541* ⊕ *custerresorts.com* ⊗ *Closed mid-Oct.–May 1.*

Sylvan Lake Lodge Restaurant

$$ | **AMERICAN** | There's no better setting for dining in Custer State Park than the Sylvan Lake Lodge, which is perched on a hillside above beautiful Sylvan Lake. The dining area has vaulted ceilings, hardwood floors, large windows, and a stone veranda. **Known for:** beautiful outdoor patio; bison steak; great location near Sylvan Lake and Needles Highway. ⑤ *Average main: $20* ✉ *Custer State Park, 24572 S.D. 87, Custer* ☎ *605/574–2561* ⊕ *custerresorts.com* ⊗ *Closed mid-Oct.–May 1.*

☕ Coffee and Quick Bites

Dockside Grill at Legion Lake Lodge

$$ | **AMERICAN** | The restaurant at Legion Lake Lodge is an affordable, faster-food option. You can sit down by the floor-to-ceiling windows inside and enjoy an appetizer, salad, sandwich, burger, or dessert and drinks, or you can order from the picnic menu and take your food to go. **Known for:** simple menu; great views of the lake; fried-pickle appetizer. ⑤ *Average main: $14* ✉ *Custer State Park, 12967 U.S. 16A, Custer* ☎ *605/255–4521* ⊕ *custerresorts.com* ⊗ *Closed late Sept.–May.*

🛏 Hotels

South Dakota's Department of Game, Fish & Parks operates Custer State Park and all of its campgrounds, but a concessionaire operates the lodges, hotels, and nicer cabins. Collectively, the concessionaire-operated facilities are known as the Custer State Park Resort. The resort options range from small, rustic cabins to modern, well-appointed houses that are big enough to accommodate groups.

Blue Bell Lodge

$$$ | **RESORT** | For an Old West-theme lodging experience, pick this complex in the park's more remote western section, where the activities include trail riding, hayrides, and chuckwagon cookouts—the accommodations are log cabins ranging from four-person options to a giant group cabin. **Pros:** less-developed portion of the park; dude-ranch atmosphere; privacy in individual cabins. **Cons:** away from the park's main attractions; lots of horses and horse smells; confusing variety of cabin options. ⑤ *Rooms from: $225* ✉ *Custer State Park, 25453 S.D. 87, Custer* ☎ *888/875–0001* ⊕ *custerresorts.com* ⮑ *29 cabins* ⦿ *No Meals.*

Creekside Lodge

$$$ | **HOTEL** | This facility is not actually a "lodge" in the style of the park's other historic or cabin-style amenities, but rather is a hotel built in 2008 on the grounds of the State Game Lodge complex; rooms are large (described as junior suites) and decorated in earth tones to match the natural surroundings. **Pros:** comforts of a modern hotel in a park setting; ample parking; tucked back from the highway along Grace Coolidge Creek. **Cons:** bland hotel atmosphere; just as expensive as other park options; lacks privacy compared to individual cabins. ⑤ *Rooms from: $230* ✉ *Custer State Park, 13389 U.S. 16A, Custer* ✛ *Next to the State Game Lodge, just west of the visitor center* ☎ *888/875–0001* ⊕ *custerresorts.com* ⮑ *30 rooms* ⦿ *No Meals.*

★ Legion Lake Lodge

$$$$ | **RESORT** | A group of log-style, modernized cabins is perched on a forested hillside, well away from the highway and above Legion Lake, with walking access down to the water; all cabins are at least family sized with kitchens or kitchenettes, private bathrooms, and climate controls, and the options range from basic to luxurious. **Pros:** high degree of privacy; walking distance to trails, lake, and restaurant on lakeshore; even

with added benefits, rates are in line with park's other cabins. **Cons:** activities limited to lake and trails; lots of differing cabin options, can be confusing; books up fast. $ *Rooms from: $283* ✉ *Custer State Park, 12967 U.S. 16A, Custer* ☎ *888/875–0001* ⊕ *custerresorts.com* ⚲ *26 cabins* ⦿ *No Meals.*

State Game Lodge
$$$ | RESORT | Once the "Summer White House" for President Calvin Coolidge, this classic stone-and-wood lodge is the largest of Custer State Park's hotels; cabins, many of them on the banks of a creek, range from simple and spartan to deluxe; hotel rooms are awash in earth tones and natural woods; and historical lodge rooms are stately with elegant hardwood furniture and massive stone fireplaces. **Pros:** historic character; has the regal feel of some of America's great Western lodges; easy-access location near the visitor center. **Cons:** often booked up; small lobby can get busy; must drive to other restaurants. $ *Rooms from: $220* ✉ *Custer State Park, 13389 U.S. 16A, Custer* ✛ *14 miles east of Custer on U.S. 16A* ☎ *888/875–0001* ⊕ *custerresorts.com* ⚲ *47 rooms, 33 cabins* ⦿ *No Meals.*

Sylvan Lake Lodge
$$$ | RESORT | The complex next to beautiful Sylvan Lake consists of a lodge-style hotel built in 1937 and expanded in 1991, with standard-looking rooms, plus a large group of cabins nestled in the woods. **Pros:** smaller lodge rooms have some of the lowest rates in the park; unbeatable scenery; near the lake, beach, restaurant, general store, and trails. **Cons:** some cabins are quite a distance from the lake; an extremely busy and crowded area of the park; weak to nonexistent Wi-Fi. $ *Rooms from: $246* ✉ *Custer State Park, 24572 S.D. 87, Custer* ☎ *888/875– 0001* ⊕ *custerresorts.com* ⚲ *35 rooms, 31 cabins* ⦿ *No Meals.*

◉ Performing Arts

★ Black Hills Playhouse
THEATER | The summertime shows at this nonprofit theater in the woods have been a beloved Black Hills tradition since 1946. The paid cast members and crew, recruited from around the country, stay in on-site dormitories while they stage plays Tuesday through Sunday throughout the summer. The indoor venue is a rustic and wheelchair-accessible, walker and scooter-accessible theater, and the well-landscaped grounds also feature a popular concessions building. Patrons love to come early and relax with a snack or drink on the grounds before showtime. ✉ *Custer State Park, 24834 S. Playhouse Rd., Custer* ✛ *About ½ mile north of Needles Hwy., near Center Lake* ☎ *605/255–4141* ⊕ *www.blackhillsplayhouse.com* ⊗ *Closed mid-Aug.–mid-May.*

◉ Shopping

Coolidge General Store
GENERAL STORE | All of the lodges in Custer State Park have small stores, but the park's main retail outlet is the larger Coolidge General Store. Named for President Calvin Coolidge because it was built in 1927 ahead of his vacation in the park, this structure is packed with a wide selection of locally themed apparel and books, plus personal-care products, basic groceries, beverages, quick food items, and supplies for camping and fishing. ✉ *Custer State Park, 805 U.S. 16A, Custer* ✛ *About ½ mile west of the State Game Lodge* ☎ *605/255–4541* ⊕ *custerresorts.com* ⊗ *Closed mid-Oct.–May 1.*

◉ Activities

Custer State Park not only has numerous hiking and biking trails, it also offers horseback riding, hayrides for the kids, and numerous campgrounds.

Did You Know?

Along the famous Needles Highway, one of the Black Hills' most famous scenic drives, you'll need total concentration to tackle the extremely narrow Needles Eye Tunnel— make sure your car's side mirrors are folded in!

CAMPING

Custer State Park has hundreds of camp-sites and camping cabins spread across nine campgrounds, all managed by the state Department of Game, Fish & Parks (as opposed to the concessionaire that manages the park's lodges, hotels, and fancier cabins). The campground cabins are one-room, log-style structures with a double bed, bunk bed, table, and benches on the inside, plus a wood porch, fire grate, and picnic table on the outside. Several of the best options for camping in the park are listed here.

Blue Bell Campground. This large camp-ground is tucked into the forest near the park's horse stables, making it a good campground for anyone who wants to try horseback riding during their stay in the park. ⊠ *Adjacent to Blue Bell Lodge* ☎ *605/255–4515* ⇆ *31 campsites, 23 camping cabins.*

Game Lodge Campground. If you'd like to camp closer to the park's developed areas, this large campground is near the visitor center and State Game Lodge, along the banks of Grace Coolidge Creek. ⊠ *Near the junction of U.S. 16A and Wildlife Loop Rd.* ☎ *605/255–4515* ⇆ *59 campsites, 11 camping cabins.*

Legion Lake Campground. This single-lane campground stretches back into the forest. The campsites are fairly close together, but because its layout stretches away from the road, and because it's close to Legion Lake and Dockside Grill, it's a good place to park an RV. ⊠ *On U.S. 16A across from Legion Lake* ☎ *605/225–4515* ⇆ *26 campsites.*

Stockade North and South Campground. These campsites are nestled in the forest in the quieter Stockade Lake area of the park, making either the North or South campground a great place to get away from the park's crowds. ⊠ *Just inside the park's western boundary, 4 miles east of Custer* ☎ *605/255–4515* ⇆ *65 campsites, 13 camping cabins.*

TOURS AND TRAIL RIDES
Buffalo Safari Jeep Tour

GUIDED TOURS | One of the best ways to safely see the park's herd of 1,400 bison is from a passenger seat in an open-air jeep. A guide drives the jeep into off-road areas for close-up viewing of not only bison but also pronghorns, elk, and other wildlife. Daily tours during the summer depart from the State Game Lodge and last about two to three hours. ⊠ *Custer State Park, 13389 U.S. 16A, Custer* ☎ *605/255–4541* ⊕ *custerresorts.com* ⌫ *From $58.*

Hayride & Chuck Wagon Cookout

GUIDED TOURS | This tour from Blue Bell Lodge in the western part of the park is conveyed by an open-air hay wagon. The 45-minute ride goes over a back road in a wildlife-rich area to a mountain meadow and canyon, where the tour climaxes with a chuckwagon supper consisting of beans, cornbread, coffee, and other traditional cowboy fare. ⊠ *Custer State Park, 25453 S.D. 87, Custer* ☎ *605/255–4531* ⊕ *custerresorts.com* ⌫ *From $55.*

Trail Rides

GUIDED TOURS | To slow down and enjoy the more serene and remote parts of the park, join one of the trail rides that begin from Blue Bell Lodge. Horseback riding can be physically challenging; fortunately, these tours account for that with rides ranging from one hour to a full day. Be sure to wear long pants and closed-toe shoes, and arrive plenty early to fill out paperwork and get matched to a horse. Call for prices. ⊠ *Custer State Park, 25453 S.D. 87, Custer* ☎ *605/255–4531* ⊕ *custerresorts.com.*

TRAILS

There are more hiking and mountain-biking trails in and around the park than there is time to explore them all. Check the website or stop at the visitor center for more information and trail maps; meanwhile, here are a few of the more popular, scenic, and easily accessible choices.

Black Elk Peak Trail 9

HIKING & WALKING | Standing 7,242 feet above sea level, Black Elk Peak (formerly called Harney Peak), is not only higher than any other point in the Black Hills but is also said to have the highest elevation between the Rocky Mountains and the Pyrenees Mountains in France and Spain. You don't have to be a mountaineer to reach the summit; in fact, thousands of people hike to the stone lookout tower atop the granite peak every year, making this one of the most popular trails in South Dakota. Just be warned that although anyone who's reasonably fit can do this hike, it's 7 miles round-trip and takes about four hours—you'll want to start early in the morning and bring plenty of snacks and lots of water. The trail crosses from Custer State Park into the Black Elk Wilderness within the Black Hills National Forest, and the reward at the top is the best view in the Black Hills. ⊠ *Custer State Park, Custer* ✛ *Trailhead is near the northeast corner of Sylvan Lake, by the swim beach* ☎ *605/255–4515* ⊕ *www.custerstatepark.com.*

Centennial Trail

HIKING & WALKING | This 124-mile hiking trail stretches from north-to-south through the entire Black Hills, with a 22-mile segment inside Custer State Park. There are three trailheads in the park, where you can get on the trail and explore as much or as little as you like: Iron Creek Trailhead, on Camp Remington Road just north of Needles Highway; Badger Hole Trailhead, on Badger Clark Road just south of U.S. 16A; and French Creek Trailhead, on North Lame Johnny Road, 3 miles from Blue Bell Lodge. ⊠ *Custer State Park, Centennial Trail, Custer* ☎ *605/255–4515* ⊕ *www.custerstatepark.com.*

Creekside Trail

HIKING & WALKING | If walking is more your speed than hiking, try this 2-mile (one way) paved path that parallels Grace Coolidge Creek and passes the State Game Lodge, Peter Norbeck Outdoor Education Center, and Coolidge General Store. You'll see lots of natural beauty along the creek, with mountains and pine trees all around, without ever having to venture away from the developed areas of the park. The trail is also bike- and roller-blade-friendly. ⊠ *Custer State Park, Custer* ✛ *Access at various points along U.S. 16A from the visitor center to the Coolidge General Store* ☎ *605/255–4515* ⊕ *www.custerstatepark.com.*

Hot Springs

32 miles south of Custer, 7 miles south of Wind Cave National Park.

Noted for its striking sandstone structures, the small and historic community of Hot Springs (population approximately 3,400) is the gateway to Wind Cave National Park. It is also the entry point to scores of other natural and historical sites, including Evans Plunge, a naturally heated indoor-outdoor pool; The Mammoth Site, where more than 60 mammoths have been unearthed; and one of the state's premier golf courses.

GETTING HERE AND AROUND

The easiest and fastest way to reach Hot Springs from Rapid City is to skirt the Black Hills on Highway 79 and then take a short stretch of Highway 18. If you're already up in the mountains, scenic Highway 385 goes south from Custer through Wind Cave National Park and on to Hot Springs.

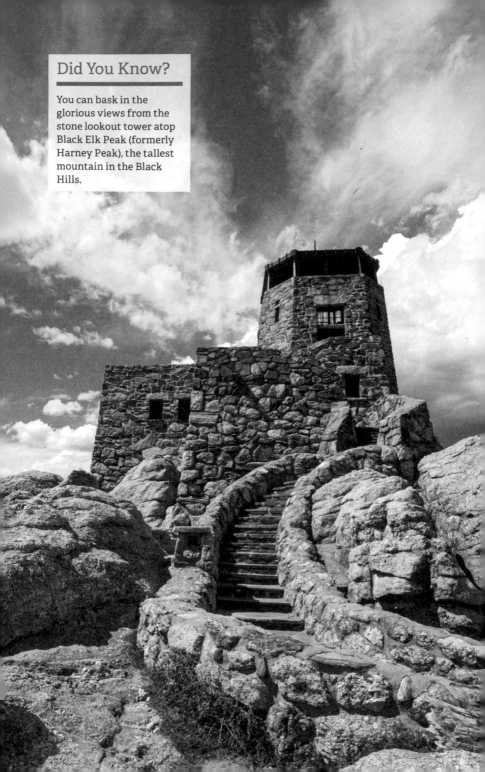

Did You Know?

You can bask in the glorious views from the stone lookout tower atop Black Elk Peak (formerly Harney Peak), the tallest mountain in the Black Hills.

All About the Buffalo

The 1,400-animal-strong Custer State Park bison herd got its start in 1914 when two legendary South Dakotans got together. Peter Norbeck, the governor and later U.S. senator who was instrumental in the park's creation, obtained 36 bison (commonly known as "buffalo") from Scotty Philip, who safeguarded some of the last remaining bison on the Great Plains after they were nearly hunted into extinction by the U.S. government in the 1800s.

By 1965, the park's bison herd numbered in the thousands, and it was overwhelming the park's ability to support it. Thus, the park held its first-ever roundup and auction, to cull the herd back to a manageable size.

The roundups have continued annually ever since and have grown into a visitor spectacle. Thousands of people come to the park in late September every year, where they arrive early in the morning to a roped-off viewing area on a hillside and wait for the herd to come thundering by, pushed along by wranglers on horseback. There's an art festival, held outdoors near the State Game Lodge, in conjunction with the roundup. See the park website (⊕ www.custerstatepark.com) for the festival dates and more information.

But you don't have to attend the roundup to see the bison. They roam freely across much of the park and are especially visible along the Wildlife Loop Road.

There are signs all over the park warning visitors to keep a safe distance when they encounter bison, and those warnings can't be stressed enough. Bison typically couldn't care less about you, as evidenced by their propensity to stand on or amble across roads, causing traffic jams in the park. But if you approach them and make them feel threatened, you'll quickly find out how dangerous they are. They have sharp horns and powerful necks, and they can run up to 35 mph. Seemingly every summer, a few tourists ignore the warnings and do incredibly ill-advised things, like attempting to pet a bison. The consequence of such behavior is often serious injury and, sometimes, death.

That doesn't mean you can't enjoy viewing these wild, majestic beasts. Just give them the respect and the wide berth they deserve.

VISITOR INFORMATION

Summertime visitors are welcome to stop by this historic former railroad depot, built in 1891 from the locally quarried sandstone that makes so many Hot Springs buildings architecturally significant. Maps and advice are dispensed here by friendly locals.

CONTACT Hot Springs Chamber Seasonal Visitor Center. ⊠ 630 N. River St., Hot Springs ☎ 605/745–6974 ⊕ www.visithotspringssd.com.

Sights

Angostura Reservoir

BODY OF WATER | Thirty-six miles of shoreline, much of it consisting of sandy beaches, surround this man-made lake fringed by forested hills near Hot Springs. Here you can stay in an RV, camping cabin, or tent campsite in one of several large campgrounds operated by the state Department of Game, Fish & Parks. The campgrounds offer kayak rentals, and

The remains of partially excavated mammoths, which got trapped in a sinkhole here 26,000 years ago, are on display at The Mammoth Site in Hot Springs.

you can inquire about motorized boat and pontoon rentals with the concessionaire at the marina. If you like fishing, that's also popular here, and if you get hungry, there's a restaurant near the marina. ⊠ *13157 N. Angostura Rd., Hot Springs* ✛ *Go 3 miles south of Hot Springs on U.S. 18 and follow the signs* ☎ *605/745–6996* ⊕ *gfp.sd.gov.*

Evans Plunge

HOT SPRING | FAMILY | Hot Springs grew up around the warm, mineral springs that inspired its name. Around the turn of the 20th century, visitors came from around the country, hoping mineral baths would cure whatever ailed them. Today, you can still soak in the 87°F waters at Evans Plunge, a large, indoor-outdoor aquatic complex built over the top of the springs that feed it. Relax with a warm dip in the pool, or have fun on the waterslides and rope swings. ⊠ *1145 N. River St., Hot Springs* ☎ *605/745–5165* ⊕ *www. evansplunge.com* ⊠ *$14.*

Fall River Pioneer Museum

HISTORY MUSEUM | The sight of this imposing, Romanesque, sandstone structure built in 1893 is reason enough to visit. Inside, the exhibits are mostly relics of the pioneers who settled the area in the late 1800s and early 1900s, including a re-created pioneer school room and doctor's office, and a collection of antiques. The museum also exhibits paintings, sculptures, and other work by local artists. ⊠ *300 N. Chicago St., Hot Springs* ☎ *605/745–5147* ⊕ *fallriverpioneermuse-um.wordpress.com* ⊠ *$6* ⊘ *Closed Sun., Oct.–May 14.*

★ The Mammoth Site

RUINS | While building a housing development in the 1970s, workers uncovered this sinkhole where giant mammoths came to drink, got trapped, and died about 26,000 years ago. The site has been protected with a high, domelike structure so archaeologists can dig up and study the bones. To date, the remains of 60-plus mammoths have been discovered, and most have been left in place, partially excavated, for visitors to see. You can watch the excavation in progress, take guided tours, and learn all about mammoths and archaeology. ⊠ *1800 U.S. 18 Bypass, Hot Springs* ☎ *605/745–6017* ⊕ *mammothsite.org* ⊠ *$14.*

★ Moccasin Springs Natural Mineral Spa

HOT SPRING | The warm, mineral springs that give this city its name are no longer believed to cure a range of ills, but they are definitely good for your soul, especially in a setting as unique and luxurious as this. An entrepreneur built this business atop the stone ruins of the 1890 Minnekahta Bathhouse, incorporating the remains of that long-ago retreat into a chic new spa. You can drop in for a soak, get a massage, or pamper yourself with a variety of spa treatments, salt therapy, and skin care. This is big-city luxury in a beautiful, quiet, small-town atmosphere. ⊠ *1829 Minnekahta Ave., Hot Springs* ☎ *605/745–7625* ⊕ *www.moccasinsprings.com* ⊠ *From $27* ☉ *Closed Mon. and Tues.*

★ Wind Cave National Park

NATIONAL PARK | With more than 160 miles of explored passageways (and counting), Wind Cave ranks as one of the longest caves in the world. Most cave tours at Wind Cave range from one to two hours and are first-come, first-served, so it's advisable to arrive early in the morning. If you miss the tour or want something to do afterward or while you wait, don't miss the opportunity to explore the park's surface area, which is one of the most underappreciated yet ruggedly beautiful parts of the Black Hills. You'll likely see some of the park's bison, prairie dogs, and other wildlife, and there are scenic drives and numerous hiking trails through prairie and forested land.

⇨ *Please see the Wind Cave National Park chapter for more detailed information.* ⊠ *26611 U.S. 385, Hot Springs* ⊕ *For the visitor center, go about 10 miles north of Hot Springs on U.S. 385*

and follow the signs ☎ *605/745–4600* ⊕ *www.nps.gov/wica* ⊠ *Free, cave tours from $14.*

World Fossil Finder Museum

SCIENCE MUSEUM | Debby Sue, the 45-foot-long *Tylosaurus* that museum owner Frank Garcia named after his wife, is one of many treasures housed at the World Fossil Finder Museum. Debby Sue was unearthed in 2018 near Edgemont, SD. She is part of a collection that includes fossils from every continent, and artifacts such as a life-sized *T.rex* head, an Ice Age cave bear skeleton, a Badlands diorama and much more. Collections are rotated every year so there's continually something different to explore. ⊠ *719 Jensen Hwy., Hot Springs* ☎ *605/745–5007* ⊕ *worldfossilfindermuseum.com* ⊠ *$10* ☉ *Closed weekends, May–Sept.; Sun.–Wed. Oct.–Apr.*

🍴 Restaurants

Buffalo Dreamer

$$$ | AMERICAN | Co-located with Moccasin Springs Natural Mineral Spa, this restaurant is run by a local chef who trained in New York and is now attempting to bring high cuisine to the High Plains. The evolving menu promises joyful food prepared with "love and deep intention," including dishes incorporating salmon, grass-fed beef, lamb and locally grown farm vegetables. **Known for:** organic and seasonal ingredients; sophisticated food presentation; elaborate desserts. ⑤ *Average main: $35* ⊠ *1829 Minnekahta Ave., Hot Springs* ☎ *605/745–6100* ⊕ *www.buffalodreamer.com* ☉ *Closed Mon. and Tues.*

The 1891 Steakhouse and Bistro

$$$ | STEAK HOUSE | In a shared location with the Red Rock River Resort, this steak house in a historic building sources produce from local farmers' markets and locally raised beef, buffalo, and pork. The spacious dining room has wood floors and high ceilings with intimate, cloth-covered table settings. **Known for:** filet mignon and rib eye; signature Red Rock River Mud Pie dessert; American food with a French influence. ⑤ *Average main: $25* ⊠ *603 N. River St., Hot Springs* ☎ *605/745–4400* ⊕ *redrockriverresort.com* ☽ *Closed Mon. and Tues. Memorial Day–Labor Day; closed Sun.– Thurs. in off-season.*

☕ Coffee and Quick Bites

Mornin' Sunshine Coffee House

$ | **AMERICAN** | Coffee, tea, smoothies, and quick choices for breakfast, lunch, and dinner are served in a small, historical, and architecturally interesting structure with exposed-stone interior walls. This friendly, locally owned establishment is a great place to stop on your way through Hot Springs, before or after your adventures in the area. **Known for:** wide selection of coffee; hearty breakfast selections; friendly staff, popular with locals. ⑤ *Average main: $10* ⊠ *509 N. River St., Hot Springs* ☎ *605/745–5550* ⊕ *www.morninsunshinecoffee.com.*

Two Cows Creamery & Bistro

$ | **AMERICAN** | Sample some of the best ice cream in the Black Hills at Two Cows Creamery, which hand-crafts ice cream, sorbet, and gelato on-site at its historic downtown Hot Springs location. This casual, unfussy diner focuses on qualify food made with dairy from a family farm, locally sourced meats and locally grown fruits and vegetables. **Known for:** yak chili; burgers, ice cream; laid-back atmosphere; proximity to Hot Springs Riverwalk. ⑤ *Average main: $10* ⊠ *237 N. River St., Hot Springs* ☎ *605/745–3838* ⊕ *www.twocowscreamery.com.*

🛏 Hotels

★ Flatiron Historic Sandstone Inn

$ | **B&B/INN** | This is a hidden gem in the Black Hills, with richly decorated, apartment-style rooms in a historic, sandstone building accompanied by a courtyard and gazebo; rooms range from small studios with shared baths to large suites with bathrooms, full kitchens, fireplaces, and dining tables. **Pros:** unexpected luxury in a small lodging market; small-town setting; historic charm with modern comfort. **Cons:** right below the busy Hot Springs VA Medical Center; some rooms have a shared bathroom; no overall booking website; rooms booked individually on Airbnb. ⑤ *Rooms from: $125* ⊠ *745 N. River St., Hot Springs* ☎ *605/890–0641* ⊕ *www.flatiron.us* ⇨ *9 rooms* ⑪ *No Meals.*

Hills Inn

$ | **HOTEL** | There's nothing grand about this motel, and that's kind of the point: it specializes in clean, simple, affordable rooms with good service, and it consistently does well on all those fronts. **Pros:** some of the lowest rates in the Black Hills; local owners take great pride in the property; extras include an outdoor pool, mini golf, and a walking path along a river. **Cons:** no luxury here—just the basics; limited privacy with all outdoor-entrance rooms; spartan furnishings. ⑤ *Rooms from: $110* ⊠ *640 S. 6th St., Hot Springs* ☎ *605/745–3130* ⊕ *www.hotspringshillsinn.com* ⇨ *35 rooms* ⑪ *Free Breakfast.*

The Historic Burdette House

$$ | **HOUSE** | This eye-popping, three-story, 1891 Victorian home is a prime example of the hidden gems that can be found in the less-visited southern Black Hills— guests stay in the second-floor apartment, with two bedrooms, a bathroom, and a full kitchen and also have access to the redwood dry sauna, landscaped yard, nature pond, fire pit, and barbecue/smoker. **Pros:** one of the most grandly historic homes in the Black Hills; great views and setting; comfortable outdoor seating areas. **Cons:** owners occupy the third floor; only available through Airbnb; like a classic bed-and-breakfast, but without

the breakfast. $ Rooms from: $184 ⊠ 1729 Minnekahta Ave., Hot Springs ☎ 605/440–3512 ⊕ www.airbnb.com ⟿ 1 apartment ❖ No Meals.

River Falls Lodging
$$ | B&B/INN | Three lovely little lodging options—a suite, a studio apartment, and a cozy cabin—are located on three hillside acres on the outskirts of Hot Springs, with a river running through the property. **Pros:** comfortable, homelike accommodations; out of the city, but only a few minutes' drive away; beautiful surroundings. **Cons:** have to drive into town for restaurants and shopping; some noise from the highway; can be tough to book with only three choices. $ Rooms from: $150 ⊠ 13223 Fall River Rd., Hot Springs ☎ 530/368–7429, 303/883–6537 ⊕ riverfallslodging.com ⟿ 3 suites ❖ No Meals.

🛍 Shopping

Art-House
ART GALLERY | Discover unexpected and contemporary artwork by local and regional artists, and pieces by international artists. It's all beautifully displayed and sold in one of the grandest structures in Hot Springs, the 1911 Morris Grand Theater, built by a Russian-Jewish immigrant jeweler. The art includes paintings, pottery, and sculpture showcased in galleries on two levels in this historic venue. ⊠ 405 N. River St., Hot Springs ☎ 605/348–7761 ⊕ www.arthouseblackhills.com.

Earth Goods Natural Foods
SPECIALTY STORE | A local staple since 1996, this store sells a wide variety of natural foods, vitamins, supplements, herbs, spices, gluten-free foods, organic produce, local grass-fed meats, and personal-care products. Honey, from local producers and around the globe, is a specialty. ⊠ 738 Jennings Ave., Hot Springs ☎ 605/745–7715 ⊕ www.facebook.com/earthgoodsnaturalfoods.

🏃 Activities

In addition to campsites and activities along the Mickelson Trail, Hot Springs has one of the best golf courses in the state of South Dakota.

CAMPING

There are hundreds of campsites in the Hot Springs area, in public and private campgrounds. Here are a few of the most popular choices.

Angostura Recreation Area. This sprawling, state-operated complex includes several campgrounds along the eastern shoreline of Angostura Reservoir, which is one of the most popular beach hangouts in the Black Hills. ⊠ 13157 N. Angostura Rd. ☎ 605/745–6996 ⟿ 4 campgrounds, 169 campsites, 12 camping cabins.

Hidden Lake Campground and Resort. For a quieter camping experience, try this privately owned campground on the shores of a small lake at the edge of Hot Springs. Guests here love to spend lazy days paddling rented canoes and kayaks and fishing from the shore. The resort offers cabins that range from small camping huts to full-size homes, while most of the campsites are made for campers and RVs. ⊠ 27291 Evans St. ☎ 605/745–4042 ⟿ 23 campsites, 10 cabins.

Hot Springs KOA. This large, well-shaded campground just off Highway 79 about 5 miles from Hot Springs offers all the typical amenities of a KOA site—pool, lots of campsites, cabins ranging from basic to deluxe, a guest laundry facility, and more. ⊠ 27585 S.D. Hwy. 79 ☎ 800/562–0803 ⟿ 60 campsites, 13 cabins.

GOLF
Southern Hills Golf Course
GOLF | Few Black Hills golf courses incorporate their natural surroundings as well

Did You Know?

Immerse yourself in spectacular Black Hills scenery during a hike or bike ride along the Mickelson Trail. The 109-mile trail, on a former Gold Rush rail line, was named for the late South Dakota governor George S. Mickelson.

The Mickelson Trail Trek

If you're an avid bicycler, one of the best ways to bicycle the Mickelson Trail while seeing loads of Black Hills scenery and making connections with other bicycling enthusiasts is to plan ahead and book a spot in the Mickelson Trail Trek.

The annual, three-day June and September events (see for dates and registration details) starts in Edgemont and covers much of the 109-mile Mickelson Trail. With the aid of shuttles, participants spend the day riding, ending up each evening in a city where they've booked lodging.

Registration includes an annual trail pass, shuttle service, snacks, and several meals.

If you're interested, be sure to plan ahead. Registration opens months in advance, and the spots fill up fast.

The Mickelson Trail, named for the late South Dakota governor George S. Mickelson, is a crushed-rock path built on a former rail line stretching all the way through the Black Hills, from south to north. Grades are generally slight, and the trail includes numerous railroad bridges and rock tunnels.

as this gem, which many golfers consider the top public course in the state. The 18 holes are surrounded by mountains, pine trees, natural grasses, and red-rock canyon walls, all spread out under the big, blue South Dakota sky. Golfers sometimes see wildlife here, including deer, turkeys, and rabbits. ⊠ *1130 Clubhouse Dr., Hot Springs* ☎ *605/745–6400* ⊕ *www.hotspringssdgolf.com* ⊠ *From $37.*

TRAILS AND OUTDOOR ADVENTURING

Minnekahta Trailhead, Mickelson Trail

BIKING | Near Hot Springs is the second-most southern trailhead on the Mickelson Trail. This crushed-rock path stretches 109 miles from the southern to the northern end of the Black Hills, on a former railbed where grades are never too steep. The trail offers close-up views of some of the best scenery in the Black Hills, and there are numerous railroad bridges and rock tunnels. ⊠ *U.S. 18, Hot Springs* ⊕ *About 11 miles west of Hot Springs on U.S. 18* ☎ *605/584–3896* ⊕ *gfp.sd.gov.*

Edgemont

25 miles southwest of Hot Springs, 34 miles southwest of Wind Cave National Park.

Edgemont is a small town of about 700 residents on the southern edge of the Black Hills. These days, it's mostly supported by ranchers from the surrounding plains, but from the 1950s through the '70s, it was the site of a uranium-mining boom. Numerous mines sprung up throughout the countryside, and there was a mill that processed the material in Edgemont, all in service to the Cold War (uranium is the main ingredient in nuclear warheads). That brief boom of prosperity has long since vanished, and Edgemont's population today is less than half of what it was in 1960.

GETTING HERE AND AROUND

One of the main reasons visitors travel to Edgemont is because it hosts the southernmost trailhead for the 109-mile Mickelson Trail; if that's your reason for visiting, your most likely route to

Edgemont goes down the eastern flank of the Black Hills on Highway 79 and then through the southern portion of the Black Hills on Highway 18.

Sights

Trails, Trains, and Pioneers Museum

SPECIALTY MUSEUM | If you like going a little off the beaten path, and if you dig quirky, small-town museums, consider checking out this facility, operated by local volunteers and showcasing finds "from the Stone Age to the Atomic Age." Those items include fossils, Native American artifacts, pioneer tools, and relics from Edgemont's uranium-mining boom of the 1950s through the 1970s. If you're lucky, you might encounter a talkative local volunteer who lived through some of the history that's on display. ⊠ *603 2nd Ave., Edgemont* ✛ *Next to the Edgemont Trailhead of the Mickelson Trail* ☎ *605/662–5858* ⊕ *www.edgemontmuseum.com* ☒ *Free* ☾ *Closed Mon. and Labor Day–Memorial Day.*

 Restaurants

The New Hat Creek Grill

$$ | AMERICAN | For a convenient place to eat while you're checking out the local museum or the Mickelson Trail in Edgemont, try the Hat Creek Grill, which is right next door to both. This is a bar and grill, serving a basic selection of pub-style food for dinner at affordable prices. **Known for:** laid-back atmosphere; friendly local service; burgers, steak, brick-fired pizza. ⑤ *Average main: $20* ⊠ *521 2nd Ave., Edgemont* ☎ *605/662–5888* ⊕ *www.facebook.com/hatcreekgrill* ☾ *Closed Sun.–Wed.*

Activities

Edgemont Trailhead, Mickelson Trail

BIKING | If you want to bicycle the entire, 109-mile Mickelson Trail from south to north, or if you just want to see its southern end, this is the place to start. The trailhead is in Edgemont City Park, next to a pond spanned by a 120-foot-long wooden covered bridge. The Mickelson Trail is a crushed-rock path built on a former railbed, with gradual grades and lots of railroad bridges and tunnels. The Edgemont Trailhead, at about 3,500 feet above sea level, is the lowest point of the trail. To gain access to the trail, bring some cash to pay a nominal daily or annual fee at a self-service dropbox. ⊠ *1948 2nd Ave., Edgemont* ☎ *605/584–3896* ⊕ *gfp.sd.gov.*

Chapter 6

THE BADLANDS

Updated by
Jim Holland

👁 Sights	🍴 Restaurants	🛏 Hotels	🛍 Shopping	🍸 Nightlife
★★★★☆	★★☆☆☆	★★☆☆☆	★★☆☆☆	★☆☆☆☆

WELCOME TO THE BADLANDS

TOP REASONS TO GO

★ **Scenic grandeur:**
With its sweeping vistas, pointed spires, vast grasslands, and stark desolation, there is nothing quite like the visual feast of the Badlands region of South Dakota.

★ **Native America:**
Encounter the Lakota Sioux people and their culture and traditions on the Pine Ridge Reservation, home of the Oglala Sioux Tribe.

★ **Americana:** Any Great American Road Trip includes roadside attractions. The pinnacle of that tradition is Wall Drug, a free attraction next to the Badlands.

★ **Cold War history:**
Underground nuclear missile silos once dotted western South Dakota, but only one remains. Go underground to see the preserved launch-control facility at the Minuteman Missile National Historic Site.

★ **Wildlife:** Wide-open spaces in the Badlands provide a window into the natural world. Sightings of bison, antelope, prairie dogs, and birds of prey are common.

1 Wall. Wall is home to Wall Drug, a small-town pharmacy turned tourist mall that defies easy description. Shops hawk everything from boots to books. The restaurant offers homemade doughnuts, buffalo burgers, and yes, 5-cent coffee. The "Backyard" features a time-honored South Dakota tradition: the chance to take your picture on a jackalope.

2 Interior. Isolation makes the Badlands beautiful. It also means there aren't many places to find services. One of the few is Interior, a tiny town just outside the national park. Here you'll find gas for your car, a shop selling Native American artwork, and a KOA campground.

3 Pine Ridge. The vast and remote Pine Ridge Reservation includes the little-visited South Unit of Badlands National Park and its Lakota-themed White River Visitor Center. The Heritage Center at Maȟpíya Lúta | Red Cloud in Pine Ridge houses a collection of Native American art and culture.

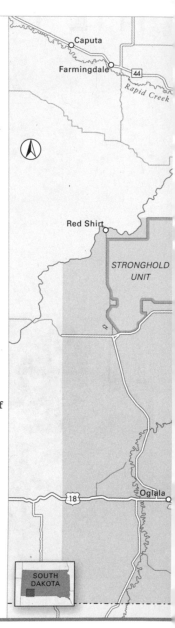

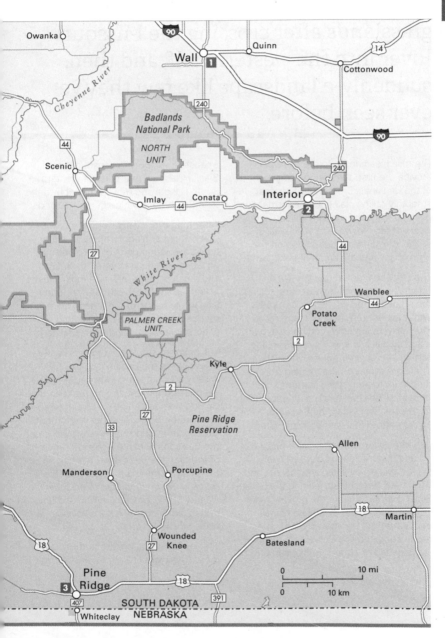

Driving across South Dakota on Interstate 90, travelers see tidy farms in the state's eastern half, sprawling grasslands after crossing the Missouri River into the western half, and then, suddenly, a landscape like few they've ever seen before.

The miles leading up to the city of Wall provide the first, tantalizing glimpses of the Badlands. From the otherwise smoothly rolling plains, these formations poke up jaggedly in clearly discernible layers of tan, brown, and yellow, all of which look different depending on the time of day and the angle of sunlight.

The Badlands formations are like an open-air natural history museum, telling the stories of the past 75 million years with their layered mud, dirt, and rock. Those layers are now eroding away with every rainfall and windstorm, revealing further secrets in the form of fossils. There are remains here ranging from dinosaurs to prehistoric mammals and fantastical sea creatures, dating to a time from eons past when the Badlands were at the bottom of a vast body of water.

As long as human beings have been around, natural resources have been scarce in the Badlands, and the sun and wind have been harsh, leading the Lakota Sioux people to name the region "mako sica"—"bad lands." It was no coincidence that the U.S. government, after finally subduing the Oglala Lakota following decades of armed conflict and broken treaties, took away the resource-rich Black Hills and other parts of western South Dakota and moved the tribe to the Pine Ridge Reservation in the Badlands.

After the Lakota were confined to the reservation, settlers temporarily clambered over other parts of the Badlands, engaging in a quixotic attempt to farm and ranch in these infertile lands. Most failed, leaving much of the abandoned land in the hands of the federal government, ultimately to become parts of national grasslands and a national park.

The onset of automobile tourism brought a new era to the Badlands in the 1920s, when part of the area was declared a national monument around the time that carving was beginning on Mount Rushmore in the Black Hills. The monument later became Badlands National Park, and the Badlands became a place for millions of tourists to stop or drive through on their way to the Black Hills. ⇨ *For more detailed information about Badlands National Park, including hiking and driving routes and maps, see our Badlands National Park chapter.*

That remains the region's primary identity today. There are still some ranchers in the Badlands, but making a living in this sparsely vegetated region requires huge tracts of land, so the ranches are few and far between.

Thus, the Badlands remain basically the same lonely, quiet, and beautiful place they've been for millennia, and likely will be for millennia to come.

Planning

Getting Here and Around

AIR
Although there are many private air strips in South Dakota, the closest airport to the Badlands offering scheduled service is Rapid City Regional Airport (RAP).

CAR
You'll need a car to explore the Badlands. If you didn't arrive by car, then you'll need to rent one, so reserve as far in advance as possible. The easiest and most popular route to the Badlands is Interstate 90, from which travelers can exit onto a loop road that dips down into the Badlands and returns to the interstate.

Hotels

Quality hotel options in the Badlands region are found mostly in the small town of Wall, where one end of the Badlands Loop Road connects with Interstate 90, or in Badlands National Park.

Restaurants

Dining options are extremely few and far between in the Badlands and, like hotel options, are located mostly in the small town of Wall or in the national park.

HOTEL AND RESTAURANT PRICES
⇨ *Hotel and restaurant reviews have been shortened. For full information, see Fodors.com. Restaurant prices are the average cost of a main course at dinner, or if dinner is not served, at lunch. Hotel prices are the lowest cost of a standard double room in high season.*

What It Costs			
$	$$	$$$	$$$$
RESTAURANTS			
under $13	$13–$23	$24–$35	over $35
HOTELS			
under $150	$150–$200	$201–$250	over $250

Safety

The Badlands are a mostly treeless and undeveloped place, leaving them exposed to extremes of sun, wind, and weather. Summertime temperatures often climb above 100°F, and there are dozens of miles between services. You should bring plenty of water on all of your Badlands adventures and keep an eye on your vehicle's temperature gauge, allowing for time to pull over and let it cool down if necessary. Winter storms can also be brutal, because the wind pushes snow for miles across the plains and piles it up in huge drifts wherever anything stands in the way. In both spring and summer, violent plains thunderstorms can roll up quickly. Watch for wildlife on roadways especially in early morning and after dusk, when visibility is poor. Keep at least 100 yards between you and buffalo (bison) anywhere these magnificent, yet unpredictable animals are encountered. Venomous prairie rattlesnakes are also prevalent on the South Dakota plains.

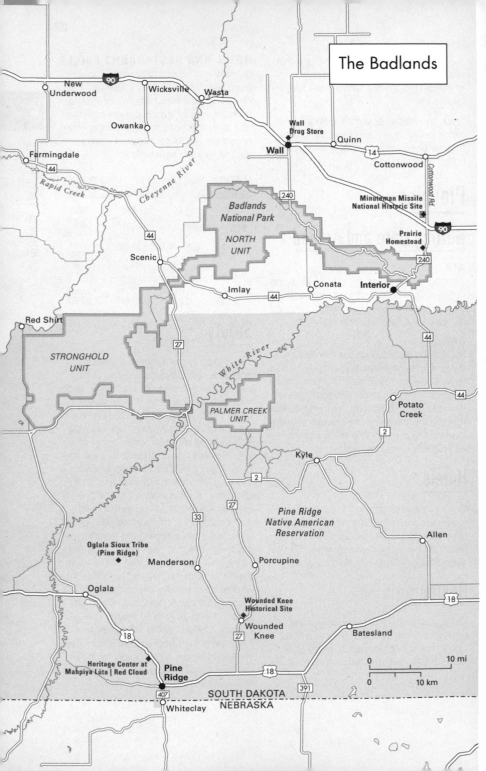

The Badlands

See a deactivated Cold War-era nuclear missile site at the Minuteman Missile National Historic Site.

Wall

55 miles east of Rapid City, 7½ miles north of Badlands National Park.

Built near the edge of a steep "wall" of layered badlands dirt and rock, Wall was founded in 1907 as a railroad station, and is the biggest town with close proximity to Badlands National Park, about 8 miles from the Pinnacles entrance to the North Unit. Wall is home to about 800 residents and the world-famous Wall Drug Store, best known for its fabled jackalopes (a fanciful combination of a jackrabbit and antelope) and free ice water. Wall is also the place most Badlands visitors will stop for a place to eat and gas up their vehicle, and find a hotel room if they're interested in staying near the national park.

GETTING HERE AND AROUND
Finding Wall couldn't be easier, although it requires a long drive no matter where you start from. Wall is on Interstate 90, and it's one of the few towns with a full range of businesses and services located in the vast expanse of plains between the Black Hills and the Missouri River.

VISITOR INFORMATION
Many of the areas immediately surrounding Badlands National Park are part of the Buffalo Gap National Grassland. At the National Grasslands Visitor Center in Wall, operated by the U.S. Forest Service, there are exhibits and a short film about the history and purposes of America's publicly owned national grasslands. The local Chamber of Commerce in Wall publishes a visitor guide and offers advice on exploring the Badlands region.

CONTACTS National Grasslands Visitor Center. ✉ *708 Main St., Wall* ☎ *605/279–2125* ⊕ *www.fs.usda.gov.* **Wall Badlands Area Chamber of Commerce.** ✉ *501 Main St., Wall* ☎ *605/279-2665, 888/852-9255* ⊕ *www.wall-badlands.com.*

The famous Wall Drug Store, which opened its doors in 1931, is a must-stop before or after a visit to nearby Badlands National Park.

◉ Sights

★ Minuteman Missile National Historic Site

HISTORIC SIGHT | Treaties with the Soviet Union caused the removal of the nuclear missiles that formerly stood ready to launch in underground silos across western South Dakota, but one silo and disarmed missile, and its underground launch-control facility, were preserved as part of this historic site. The site consists of three spots along a 15-mile stretch of Interstate 90: a modern visitor center, which is full of exhibits about the Cold War, and the silo and launch-control facility. The visitor center and silo are free and open to the public, but there's a fee and a required reservation for the launch-control tour. ✉ *24545 Cottonwood Rd., Philip* ✛ *The visitor center is 20 miles east of Wall on I–90* ☎ *605/433–5552* ⊕ *www. nps.gov/mimi* 🕓 *Closed 4 pm weekdays, 3 pm on weekends.*

★ Wall Drug Store

STORE/MALL | **FAMILY** | This South Dakota original got its start in 1931 by offering free ice water to road-weary travelers headed for Mount Rushmore. Today, its dining rooms seat 530 visitors at a time. A life-size mechanical Cowboy Orchestra and Chuckwagon Quartet greet you inside, and, in the back, you'll find an animated *T. rex*, a replica of Mount Rushmore, and a panning and mining experience. The attached Western Mall has 14 shops selling all kinds of keepsakes from cowboy hats, boots, and Black Hills gold jewelry to T-shirts, Western-themed books, and fudge. Just don't skip the doughnuts. ✉ *510 Main St., Wall* ☎ *605/279–2175* ⊕ *www.walldrug.com* ✉ *Free.*

Wall Drug's Billboards Explained

You'll notice it as you drive on Interstate 90: Wall Drug's hand-painted, nostalgic-looking billboards are seemingly everywhere.

Wall Drug's original owners, Ted and Dorothy Hustead, put up the first one in 1936 while they were struggling to transform their drug store into a tourist magnet. Dorothy had the idea to put a sign on Route 16—this was decades before the interstate system, or the regulation of billboards—to advertise a string of offerings including free ice water. The sign worked so well that the Husteads put up more ... and more, and more.

Eventually, there were several hundred of the distinctive billboards across South Dakota and beyond, advertising the store and its attractions and telling tourists how many more miles they had to travel to get there. The billboards also seeped into South Dakota's culture, becoming something of an inside joke. To this day, soldiers deployed overseas and other international travelers from South Dakota often display or post comical, makeshift signs bearing messages like "4,000 miles to Wall Drug," with an arrow pointing the way.

🍴 Restaurants

Badlands Saloon and Grille

$$ | **AMERICAN** | Meat and potatoes are the mainstays of the menu at this Western-themed restaurant, which is a modern take on an Old West saloon. The location is across the street from Wall Drug. **Known for:** steaks and burgers; craft beer on tap; big portions. ⑤ *Average main: $20* ✉ *509 Main St., Wall* ☎ *605/279–2210* ⊕ *www.visitbadlandssaloon.com.*

Salty Steer

$$$ | **AMERICAN** | As the name insists, steak is the star at Wall's newest eatery, located just one block from Wall Drug Store. But don't sleep on the other culinary attractions, including burgers, pasta, and seafood, including an instant hit: lobster mac 'n cheese. **Known for:** steaks and burgers; local craft beer selection; "modern rustic" decor. ⑤ *Average main: $27* ✉ *600 Main St., Wall* ☎ *605/279–2700* ⊕ *www.visitsaltysteer.com.*

Western Art Gallery Restaurant

$$ | **AMERICAN** | More than 300 original oil paintings, all with a Western theme, line the dining room of this eatery in the Wall Drug complex. For a tasty meal, try a hot beef sandwich or a buffalo burger. **Known for:** road-trip classic; Western memorabilia; friendly service. ⑤ *Average main: $15* ✉ *510 Main St., Wall* ☎ *605/279–2175* ⊕ *www.walldrug.com.*

☕ Coffee and Quick Bites

Stompin' Grounds Coffeehouse

$ | **AMERICAN** | A full selection of hot or iced drinks are a great way to start your day or keep it going at this modest (on the outside) kiosk near downtown Wall. A full beverage menu includes hot or iced coffees, and specialty teas and lemonades to accompany breakfast and lite-lunch sandwiches and ice cream. **Known for:** hot and cold beverage selection; friendly service; breakfast sandwiches. ⑤ *Average main: $9* ✉ *112 South Blvd., Wall* ☎ *605/279–1055* ⊘ *Closed Feb.–Mar.*

For a glimpse of the hardscrabble life of settlers in the Badlands, visit Prairie Homestead, which includes an original 1909 home and outbuildings.

Hotels

Badlands Frontier Cabins

$$$$ | **MOTEL** | **FAMILY** | Sit back and enjoy a South Dakota sunset from the front porch of a custom log cabin at this recently updated resort. **Pros:** parking close to cabin; kitchenettes available; picnic area with grill, wet sink, and table. **Cons:** close to interstate off-ramp, traffic noise; no free breakfast on-site; cabins close together. ⑤ *Rooms from: $299* ✉ *1101 Glenn St., Wall* ☎ *605/279–2619* 📞 *33 cabins* ⑩ *No Meals.*

Best Western Plains

$$ | **HOTEL** | **FAMILY** | A couple of blocks from downtown Wall and just 8 miles from Badlands National Park, this pleasant motel has both standard hotel rooms as well as two-bedroom family suites that sleep up to six people. **Pros:** continental breakfast; great indoor and outdoor pools; good location for families. **Cons:** chain motel; no restaurant on-site; close enough to the interstate to hear some noise. ⑤ *Rooms from: $185* ✉ *712 Glenn St., Wall* ☎ *605/279–2145, 800/528–1234* ⊕ *bestwestern.com* 📞 *74 rooms, 8 family suites* ⑩ *Free Breakfast.*

Travelodge by Wyndham Wall

$$ | **MOTEL** | **FAMILY** | This longtime Wall motel is being renovated by a new local owner—all 39 extensively remodeled rooms feature new beds and Western-chic decor reflecting the South Dakota plains. **Pros:** newly renovated rooms; seasonal outdoor pool; playground. **Cons:** highway noise from nearby interstate; second floor accessible only by stairs; dated exterior appearance. ⑤ *Rooms from: $199* ✉ *211 10th Ave., Wall* ☎ *605/550–4806* ⊕ *wyndhamhotels. com* 🕙 *Closed Jan.–Mar.* 📞 *39 rooms* ⑩ *No Meals.*

Shopping

Dakota Sky Stone

JEWELRY & WATCHES | A longtime family-owned business, this store in

Wounded Knee Massacre

By 1890, the Indian Wars were ending. The U.S. government violated the 1868 Treaty of Fort Laramie and split the Great Sioux Reservation, which had encompassed all of western South Dakota, into separate, smaller reservations. Dakota Territory joined the union in 1889 as two states, North and South Dakota. Settlers would soon swarm across western South Dakota, starting towns and laying claim to land that Native Americans had fought for decades to keep.

With their lands taken and their wild game diminished, many of the last free bands of Sioux people found themselves in desperate situations as they retreated onto the new reservations. The environment was ripe for a new religious movement that swept parts of Indian Country. It was known as the Ghost Dance, and some practitioners believed it would reverse their fortunes.

The U.S. government, fearing trouble, made a show of force to subdue the holdout bands and push them onto reservations. Into this tense environment came a group of more than 350 Lakota Sioux, who made camp along Wounded Knee Creek as they prepared to meet federal officials at the nearby Pine Ridge Agency.

A force of 490 soldiers kept watch over the encampment. When the soldiers attempted to disarm the camp on December 29, 1890, a skirmish broke out. The soldiers opened fire as chaotic fighting ensued.

Thirty-one soldiers died, but those losses paled in comparison to the estimated 300 Native Americans who lost their lives, including a large number of women and children. Some of the Native American dead remained frozen on the ground for days, until a military burial party dumped them into a mass grave.

That grave is now marked by a weathered obelisk at the Wounded Knee Massacre Site. A collection of short, dirt paths leads up to the hilltop grave from the highway below, where local Sioux people sometimes sell arts and crafts along the roadside.

Those who visit the grave should be quiet and respectful, because its's not only the site of a terrible massacre and mass burial, but it also symbolizes the painful loss of land, culture, and freedom that Native Americans suffered in the face of America's westward expansion. For a more in-depth account of the massacre as well as a comprehensive history of Native Americans in the American West, read Dee Brown's acclaimed book *Bury My Heart at Wounded Knee*.

downtown Wall specializes in locally produced turquoise jewelry and also sells Western clothing, decor, and art, including a wide selection of bison paintings and photographs. There's a sister store in Deadwood. ⊠ *511 Main St., Wall* ☎ *605/390–5500* ⊕ *www.dakotaskystone.com.*

Wall Food Center

FOOD | If you're in or near the Badlands and need to stock up on food or other supplies, this is the place to go. It's a fully stocked, locally owned, small-town grocery store. ⊠ *103 W. South Blvd., Wall* ☎ *605/279–2331.*

Activities

Wheelin' To Wall
BIKING | **FAMILY** | The only recreational cycling event to include Badlands National Park trails is scheduled around National Public Lands Day in September. Two days of rides are designed for all ages and abilities, both on paved and mixed surface (gravel) roads. Proceeds go for improvements to hiking and cycling opportunities in the Wall-Badlands area. ✉ *Wall* ☎ *605/685–3882* ⊕ *wheelintowall. com* 🍽 *$50–$60.*

Interior

32 miles southeast of Wall, 2 miles southeast of Badlands National Park.

Interior, population roughly 50, is what passes for a town in the sparsely populated heart of the Badlands. There's not much here, but there are basic services, including gas for your car and convenience-store food. If you've ventured off the Badlands Loop Road to see more of the area's scenery, Interior is one of the only places you'll find a respite from the road.

GETTING HERE AND AROUND
From the Badlands Loop Road near the Cedar Pass Campground, go a couple of miles south on Highway 377.

 ## Sights

Prairie Homestead
OTHER ATTRACTION | Most of the attempts to homestead in the Badlands were doomed to failure because of the area's extreme climate, infertile soil, and sparse grasses. Settlers suffered an incredibly hardscrabble existence, and today a glimpse into that existence is preserved at the Prairie Homestead. The site includes an original 1909 sod home and outbuildings, with tools and furnishings appropriate to the homestead era. ✉ *21070 S.D. 240* ✛ *3 miles south of I–90 Exit 131 on the Badlands Loop Rd. (Hwy. 240)* ☎ *605/433–5400* ⊕ *www.prairiehomestead.com* 🕙 *Closed Nov.–Apr.*

 ## Hotels

Badlands Inn
$ | **HOTEL** | At this inn with beautiful views of Badlands National Park, you can awaken to a panoramic sunrise over Vampire Peak and the rest of the rugged landscape, 1½ miles from the park's visitor center and just outside the park boundary—this is one of the few lodging options with modern-looking, upgraded rooms in the heart of the Badlands. **Pros:** exceptional views; affordable rates; friendly staff. **Cons:** basic rooms; often fills up by early afternoon; very remote. ⑤ *Rooms from: $140* ✉ *20615 Hwy. 377, Interior* ☎ *877/386–4383* ⊕ *www.badlandsinn. com* 🕙 *Closed mid-Oct.–mid-May* 🛏 *26 rooms* 🍽 *Free Breakfast.*

Circle View Guest Ranch
$$ | **B&B/INN** | **FAMILY** | Located in the heart of the badlands, this B&B on a working cattle ranch has spectacular views; rooms have big beds and en suite baths and kitchens, and there's free Wi-Fi throughout the property. **Pros:** friendly people; beautiful views; great for groups. **Cons:** small and isolated; long drive from any attractions other than Badlands National Park; minimum $40 charge for cancellations. ⑤ *Rooms from: $180* ✉ *20055 Hwy. 44 E, Interior* ☎ *605/433–5582* ⊕ *www.circleviewranch.com* 🛏 *8 rooms, 2 cabins, bunkhouse with 4 rooms* 🍽 *Free Breakfast.*

 ## Shopping

Native West Trading Company
SPECIALTY STORE | The owner, Jennifer Reisser, of Creek and European ancestry, provides a place for artists and artisans from the nearby Pine Ridge Reservation

to sell their work. The store is brimming with authentic, Native-made products, including art, bead and quillwork, moccasins, buffalo robes, jewelry, pottery, and more. ⊠ *251 S.D. 44, Interior* ☎ *605/433–5003* ⊕ *www.nativewest-trading.com.*

Activities

RODEOS
Frontier Days Rodeo
HORSE SHOW | FAMILY | Two days of pro and amateur rodeo action fill the storied Interior Rodeo Grounds in August. The event lays claim as the oldest rodeo in South Dakota and was listed as the second largest rodeo in the world in the 1920s. Organizers added top PRCA athletes from around the world to the event in 2023. Also on the schedule are parades, dances, clowns, and a ranch rodeo. ⊠ *East S.D. 44, Interior* ☎ *605/441–6027* ⊕ *www.muddycreekprorodeo.com* ⊠ *$12.*

CAMPING
Badlands/White River KOA. The owners of this campground have cleverly taken advantage of the White River, which is one of the few places where trees grow in abundance near the Badlands. The campground has a pool, bike rentals, mini golf, laundry rooms, and other amenities, all about 4 miles from the southeast corner of the national park. ⊠ *20720 S.D. Hwy. 44* ☎ *605/433–5337, 800/562–3897* ⊕ *koa.com* ⊋ *77 RV/camper sites, 48 tent sites, 12 cabins, 2 tipis, 1 yurt.*

Pine Ridge

84 miles southwest of Interior, 45 miles south of Badlands National Park.

The village of Pine Ridge, population approximately 3,300, is in the southwest portion of the Pine Ridge Reservation, just a couple of miles from the Nebraska border. The U.S. government forced the Oglala Sioux Tribe onto the reservation in the 1870s and 1880s as the government broke a treaty and split the former Great Sioux Reservation—which originally encompassed all of western South Dakota—into several smaller reservations.

Covering more than 3,000 square miles, the Pine Ridge Reservation is one of the largest Native American reservations in the country. It's also home to some of the worst poverty in America, along with chronically high levels of unemployment, alcoholism, and crime. Because of those and other problems, the tribe has had difficulty developing a thriving visitor industry.

GETTING HERE AND AROUND
For a route to Pine Ridge that includes a couple of other destinations, take Highway 44 from Rapid City or Badlands National Park to the tiny Badlands map dot of Scenic. From there, turn south on Bombing Range Road, which becomes BIA 27 when it crosses onto the reservation. On your long drive south, you'll pass the Lakota-themed White River Visitor Center of Badlands National Park, and the Wounded Knee Massacre Site. When you reach Highway 18, go west about 8 miles to the village of Pine Ridge.

VISITOR INFORMATION
Oglala Sioux Tribe (Pine Ridge)
INDIGENOUS SIGHT | The Pine Ridge Reservation is home to more than 20,000 Oglala Lakota, members of a major Sioux division known as the Western or Teton Sioux, who live in nine tribal districts on 2 million acres of land. They are led by a Tribal Council president who is advised by an executive committee and a tribal council. ⊠ *Pine Ridge* ☎ *605/867–5821* ⊕ *oglalalakotanation.net.*

Sights

Heritage Center at Maȟpíya Lúta| Red Cloud
HISTORY MUSEUM | Construction of a new Heritage Center museum on the grounds of the former Red Cloud school

Did You Know?

The U.S. government forced the Oglala Sioux Tribe onto the Pine Ridge reservation in the 1870s and 1880s as the government broke a treaty and split the former Great Sioux Reservation—which originally encompassed all of western South Dakota—into several smaller reservations.

is expected to be complete in 2025. The current museum, containing changing exhibits highlighting Native American culture and art, including a permanent collection of 10,000 contemporary and historical pieces, remains open in nearby Drexel Hall. In July 2023, Red Cloud Indian School administrators changed the name to Maȟpíya Lúta, Lakota language translation of Red Cloud. ⊠ *100 Mission Dr., Pine Ridge* ☎ *605/867–8257* ⊕ *www. redcloudschool.org/museum* ☒ *Free.*

Wounded Knee Historical Site
INDIGENOUS SIGHT | A stone obelisk marks the mass grave at the site of the 1890 massacre at Wounded Knee, where several hundred Sioux—including many women and children—were killed by U.S. Army soldiers after a skirmish broke out at what had been a peaceful encampment. Only a handful of visitors make pilgrimages to the remote site today, which is simple and largely unchanged from its 1890 appearance. The short dirt road leading up the hill to the site from the highway is sometimes too rutted to drive. If you go, be advised that this is a place of deep solemnity for many people. Visitors should be quiet and respectful. ⊠ *U.S. 18, Pine Ridge* ✛ *15 miles northeast of Pine Ridge via Hwys. 18 and 27* ☒ *Free.*

Chapter 7

BADLANDS NATIONAL PARK

Updated by
Jim Holland

SOUTH
DAKOTA

🏕 Camping	🏨 Hotels	🏃 Activities	👁 Scenery	👥 Crowds
★★★☆☆	★★★☆☆	★★★☆☆	★★★★★	★★★★☆

WELCOME TO BADLANDS NATIONAL PARK

TOP REASONS TO GO

★ **Fossils:** From the mid-1800s, the fossil-rich Badlands area has welcomed paleontologists, research institutions, and fossil hunters who have discovered the fossil remnants of numerous species from ancient days.

★ **A world of wildlife:** Badlands National Park is home to a wide array of wildlife: bison, pronghorn antelope, deer, black-footed ferrets, prairie dogs, rabbits, coyotes, foxes, and badgers.

★ **Missiles:** The Minuteman Missile National Historic Site, north of the entrance to the park, represents the only remaining intact components of a nuclear missile.

★ **Stars aplenty:** The park contains some of the clearest and cleanest air in the country, which makes it perfect for viewing the night sky.

★ **Moonscape:** With hundreds of square miles of ragged ridgelines and sawtooth spires, Badlands National Park touts a landscape that is otherworldly.

The park is divided into three units: the North Unit and the southern Stronghold and Palmer units. The two southern units are within Pine Ridge Indian Reservation and are jointly managed by the National Park Service and the Oglala Sioux Tribe. Much of the southern park is accessible only on foot, horseback, or a high-clearance four-wheel-drive vehicle.

1 North Unit. This is the most accessible unit and includes the Badlands Wilderness Area.

2 Stronghold Unit. This was used as a gunnery range for the United States Air Force and the South Dakota National Guard from 1942 until the late 1960s. Discarded remnants and unexploded ordnance make this area potentially dangerous. Do not handle fragments; report the location to a ranger instead.

3 Palmer Creek Unit. This is the most isolated section of the park—no recognized roads pass through its borders. You must obtain permission from private landowners to pass through their property (contact the White River Visitor Center). Allot one day to hike in and one day to hike out.

Pine Ridge Indian Reservation Boundary

Stronghold Unit

Stronghold Table

SOUTH DAKOTA

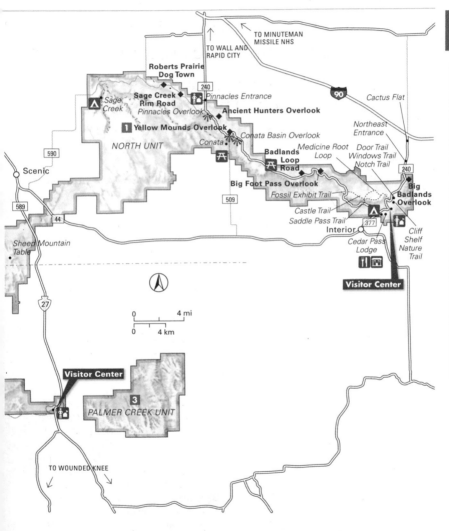

TO MINUTEMAN
MISSILE NHS

TO WALL AND
RAPID CITY

Roberts Prairie
Dog Town

240

Pinnacles Entrance

Cactus Flat

Sage Creek
Rim Road

Sage
Creek

Pinnacles Overlook

Ancient Hunters Overlook

Northeast
Entrance

1 Yellow Mounds Overlook

NORTH UNIT

Conata

Conata Basin Overlook

Door Trail
Windows Trail

590

Medicine Root
Loop

Badlands
Loop
Road

Notch Trail

240

Scenic

Big Foot Pass Overlook

Big
Badlands
Overlook

509

589

Fossil Exhibit Trail

44

Castle Trail

Saddle Pass Trail

377

Sheep Mountain
Table

Interior

Cedar Pass
Lodge

Cliff
Shelf
Nature
Trail

27

Visitor Center

0   4 mi
0   4 km

Visitor Center

3

PALMER CREEK UNIT

TO WOUNDED KNEE

Ravaged over time by wind and rain, the 380 square miles of chiseled spires, ragged ridge lines, and deep ravines of South Dakota's Badlands continue to erode and evolve. Prairie creatures thrive on the untamed territory, and animal fossils abound. The rugged, desolate terrain looks more like moonscape than prairie.

The South Dakota Legislature summarized its value well in a 1909 petition to Congress: "This formation is so unique, picturesque, and valuable for the purpose of study that a portion of it should be retained in its native state." After several tries, the area was ultimately designated a national monument in 1939 and national park in 1978.

Badlands National Park features the largest mixed-grass prairie in the National Park System. It's home to prairie dog towns as well as bison, bighorn sheep, pronghorn, mule deer, coyotes, jackrabbits, the endangered black-footed ferret, and numerous bird species. There's also fossil evidence of prehistoric creatures, including the three-toed horse, camel, saber-toothed cat, and an ancestral rhinoceros.

Despite its vastness, most of the park is relatively accessible. Several shorter trails are wheelchair-friendly, and visitors are allowed to walk through formations made of sand, silt, clay, and mudstone. Though there are only about 20 miles of formal trails, hikers and backpackers are free to explore and camp off the paths

(⇨ *see camping regulations later in the chapter*) because of the park's open-hike policy. The North Unit, one of three that comprise the park, attracts the most visitors. It's home to the park headquarters and offers the easiest access by vehicle over the Badlands Loop Road. Buffalo Gap National Grassland surrounds most of the North Unit. The other two units to the south, Stronghold and Palmer Creek, lie within the Pine Ridge Indian Reservation, and the Oglala Sioux Tribe can limit access, so check the park website for updates.

The area around Badlands National Park is rich in Native American and Cold War history. In the 1890s, Sioux warriors performed the Ghost Dance rituals on what is now the Stronghold Unit. When they refused to end the practice, the U.S. Army was called in. On December 29, 1890, soldiers shot and killed 300 Lakota men, women, and children at nearby Wounded Knee, the last confrontation between Native Americans and the United States Army. If you do venture to the park's southern districts, you can visit the Wounded Knee Massacre Memorial, which marks the mass grave and is

AVERAGE HIGH/LOW TEMPERATURES					
Jan.	Feb.	Mar.	Apr.	May	June
34/11	40/16	48/24	62/33	72/44	82/56
July	Aug.	Sept.	Oct.	Nov.	Dec.
91/60	92/55	81/46	65/34	48/21	39/17

a somber reminder of that part of our nation's history. North of the park, the Minuteman Missile National Historic Site is a decommissioned nuclear missile site with a visitor center. An hour's drive west are Rapid City and the Black Hills, home to Mount Rushmore and the Crazy Horse Memorial.

Planning

When to Go

Most visitors see the park between Memorial Day and Labor Day. The park's vast size and isolation prevent it from ever being too packed—though it is usually crowded the first week of August, when hundreds of thousands of motorcycle enthusiasts flock to the Black Hills for the annual Sturgis Motorcycle Rally (⇨ see Wind Cave chapter for more info). In summer, temperatures typically hover around 90°F—though it can get as hot as 116°F—and sudden mid-afternoon thunderstorms are not unusual. Storms put on a spectacular show of thunder and lightning, but it rarely rains for more than 10 or 15 minutes (the average annual rainfall is 16 inches). Autumn weather is generally sunny and warm. Snow usually appears by late October. Winter temperatures can be as low as −40°F. Early spring is often wet, cold, and unpredictable. By May the weather usually stabilizes, bringing pleasant 70°F days.

FESTIVALS AND EVENTS

Black Hills Stock Show and Rodeo. Watch world-champion wild-horse races, bucking horses, timed sheepdog trials, draft-horse contests, and steer wrestling during this two-week-long professional rodeo at the Rushmore Plaza Civic Center in Rapid City and Central States Fairgrounds (the festival's headquarters). ⊕ www.blackhillsstockshow.com

Central States Fair & Rodeo. Held every August, the fair features a midway with rides and games; concerts and the Range Days Rodeo; craft, art, and culinary exhibits; cattle shows; horse events; and kids' entertainment. ⊕ www.centralstatesfair.com

Red Cloud Indian Art Show. Native American paintings and sculptures by both emerging and professional artists are the focus of this 11-week-long exhibition, beginning on the first Sunday in June, at the Heritage Center at Maȟpíya Lúta | Red Cloud (formerly Red Cloud Indian School) in Pine Ridge. ⊕ www.redcloudart.show

Getting Here and Around

CAR

The North Unit of Badlands National Park is 75 miles east of Rapid City (with a regional airport) and about 140 miles northeast of Wind Cave National Park in western South Dakota. It's accessed via Exit 110 or 131 off I–90, or Route 44 east to Route 377. Few roads, paved or otherwise, pass within the park. Badlands Loop Road (Route 240) is the most traveled and the only one that intersects I–90. It's well maintained and rarely crowded. Parts of Route 44 and Route 27 run at the fringes of the badlands, connecting the visitor centers and Rapid City. Unpaved roads should be traveled

Badlands in One Day

With a packed lunch and plenty of water, arrive at the park via the northeast entrance (off I–90 at Exit 131) and follow Badlands Loop Road (Route/ Highway 240) southwest toward the **Ben Reifel Visitor Center.** You can pick up park maps and information here, and also pay the park entrance fee (if the booth at the entrance is closed).

Next, stop at the **Big Badlands Overlook,** just south of the northeast entrance, to get a good feel for the landscape. As you head toward the visitor center, hike any one of several trails you'll pass, or if you prefer guided walks, arrive at the visitor center in time to look at the exhibits and talk with rangers before heading over to the **Fossil Exhibit Trail.** The badlands are one of the richest fossil fields in the world, and along the trail are wayside exhibits describing creatures that once lived here. After your walk, drive a couple of miles to the **Big Foot Pass Overlook,** up on the right. Picnic tables here let you enjoy a packed lunch amid grassy prairies, with the rocky badland formations all around you.

After lunch, continue driving along Badlands Loop Road, stopping at the various overlooks for views and a hike or two. Near the Conata Picnic Area, you'll find the **Big Pig Dig,** a fossil site that was excavated by paleontologists through the summer of 2008. When you reach the junction with **Sage Creek Rim Road**, turn left and follow it along the northern border of the 100-square-mile **Badlands Wilderness Area**, which is home to hundreds of bison.

Provided the road is dry, take a side trip 5 miles down Sage Creek Rim Road to **Roberts Prairie Dog Town,** inhabited by a huge colony of the chattering critters. Children will love to watch these small rodents, which bark warning calls and dive underground if you get too close to their colony. The animals built burrow networks that once covered the Great Plains, but since European settlers established ranches in the region during the late 19th century, prairie dogs have become a far rarer sight. The park is less developed the farther you travel on Sage Creek Rim Road, allowing you to admire the sheer isolation and untouched beauty of badlands country. Hold out for a glorious sunset over the shadows of the nearby Black Hills, and keep your eyes open for animals stirring about.

with care when wet. Segments of Sheep Mountain Table Road, the only public road into the Stronghold Unit, are impassable when wet, with deep ruts—sometimes only high-clearance vehicles can get through. Off-road driving is prohibited. There's free parking at visitor centers, overlooks, and trailheads.

Inspiration

Badlands National Park, by Jan Cerney and part of the Images of America Series, uses historical photography to help shed light on a ruggedly surreal landscape that has, over the centuries, been traversed by Native Americans, fur traders, cattlemen, homesteaders, and fossil hunters.

Mount Rushmore, Badlands, Wind Cave: Going Underground, by Mike Graf, with illustrations by Marjorie Leggitt, takes kids on national park learning adventures with the Parker family.

Several movies have featured scenes from South Dakota's badlands, including *Nomadland, Dances With Wolves, Starship Troopers, Armageddon, How the West Was Won, Thunderheart,* and *Badlands.*

Park Essentials

ACCESSIBILITY
Cedar Pass Lodge, the visitor centers, and most overlooks are wheelchair accessible. The Fossil Exhibit Trail and the Window Trail have reserved parking and are accessible by ramp, although they are quite steep in places. The Door and Cliff Shelf trails are accessible by boardwalk. Cedar Pass Campground has two fully accessible sites, plus many other sites that are sculpted and easily negotiated by wheelchair users; its office and amphitheater also are accessible. The Bigfoot Picnic Area has reserved parking, ramps, and an accessible pit toilet. Other areas can be difficult or impossible to navigate by those with limited mobility.

PARK FEES AND PERMITS
The entrance fee is $15 per person or $30 per vehicle and is good for seven days. An annual park pass is $55 and an annual pass for all National Parks is $80. No cash is accepted. Only credit/debit cards. A backcountry permit isn't required for hiking or camping in Badlands National Park, but check in at park headquarters before setting out on a backcountry journey. Backpackers may set up camps anywhere except within a half mile of roads or trails, but must be out of sight. Open fires are prohibited.

PARK HOURS
The park is open 24/7 year-round and is in the Mountain time zone. Ranger programs are offered May to September. For offerings and times, check at the Ben Reifel Visitor Center and the Cedar Pass Lodge; a schedule also be posted on the park's Facebook page.

CELL PHONE RECEPTION
Cell phone service has improved measurably over the last decade in western South Dakota, but you may not get a signal in much of the park. The closest pay phone you'll find will likely be in Wall.

FOSSILS, PLANTS, AND WILDLIFE
It's illegal to collect or disturb fossils, plants, or rocks inside the park. Anyone finding fossils should leave them as found and report the find to the visitor center. If possible, record a GPS location and email a photo of the fossil to badlands_fossil_finds@nps.gov/badl. Feeding wildlife is also prohibited.

SUPPLIES
A good place to stock up is Badlands Grocery, 2 miles south of the Ben Reifel Visitor Center in Interior, and limited groceries and supplies can be found at Cedar Pass Lodge (there's also a vending machine there).

Hotels

If you're determined to bed down within park boundaries, you have only one choice: Cedar Pass Lodge. Though rustic, it's comfortable, inexpensive, and has eco-friendly cabins.

The rustic-but-comfy formula is repeated by the area's few motels, hotels, and inns. Most are chain hotels grouped around the interstate. Whether you stay inside or outside the park, you shouldn't have to worry about making reservations very far in advance, except during the first full week of August, when the entire region is inundated with motorcyclists for the annual Sturgis Motorcycle Rally. Rooms for miles around book up more than a year in advance.

Restaurants

Dining on the prairies of South Dakota has always been a casual and family-oriented experience, and in that sense little has changed in the past century. Even the fare, which consists largely of steak and potatoes, has stayed consistent (in fact, in some towns, "vegetarian" can be a dirty word). But for its lack of comparative sophistication, the grub in the restaurants surrounding Badlands National Park is typically very good. You'll probably never have a better steak—beef or buffalo—outside this area. You should also try cuisine influenced by Native American cooking. In the park itself there's only one restaurant. The food is quite good, but don't hesitate to explore other options farther afield.

RESTAURANT AND HOTEL PRICES

⇨ *Hotel and restaurant reviews have been shortened. For full information, see Fodors.com. Restaurant prices are the average cost of a main course at dinner, or if dinner is not served, at lunch. Hotel prices are the lowest cost of a standard double room in high season.*

What It Costs			
$	$$	$$$	$$$$
RESTAURANTS			
under $13	$13–$23	$24–$35	over $35
HOTELS			
under $150	$150–$200	$201–$200	over $250

Tours

Affordable Adventures Badlands and Wall Drug Tour

GUIDED TOURS | Take a seven-hour narrated tour through the park and surrounding badlands, with a stop at the famous Wall Drug Store for lunch (not included in the fee), the Minuteman II Missile Museum, and the Prairie Homestead Sod House Historical Site. Tours can easily be customized and are available year-round; there's hotel pickup in Rapid City. ✉ *5542 Meteor St., Rapid City* ☎ *605/342–7691, 888/888–8249* ⊕ *www.affordableadventuresbh.com.*

Visitor Information

Park maps and brochures on wide-ranging topics including geology, photography, horseback riding, and other activities are free at the visitor centers and from ⊕ *www.nps.gov/badl.*

PARK CONTACT INFORMATION Badlands National Park. ✉ *Badlands National Park* ☎ *605/433–5361* ⊕ *www.nps.gov/badl.*

North Unit

34 miles from Wall (northeast entrance).

The North Unit hosts most of the major attractions and is most accessible from Interstate 90. The Badlands Loop Road has numerous overlooks that offer varying views as well as the park's formal hiking trails. Ben Reifel Visitor Center is a must-stop with museum exhibits, a fossil preparation lab, a film about the park, and bookstore.

While not technically part of the Badlands National Park, Minuteman Missile National Historic Site and Visitor Center is a prominent fixture close to the northeast park entrance road and definitely worth a stop to learn about the area's prominent role in the Cold War.

The two-lane Badlands Loop Road has more than a dozen scenic overlooks that provide amazing views of the spires and ridges that make the Badlands so distinct.

Sights

HISTORIC SITES

Ancient Hunters Overlook

VIEWPOINT | Perched above a dense fossil bed, this overhang, adjacent to the Pinnacles overlook, is where prehistoric bison hunters drove herds of buffalo over the edge. ⊠ *Badlands National Park ✛ 22 miles northwest of the Ben Reifel Visitor Center* ⊕ *www.nps.gov/badl.*

Big Pig Dig

NATURE SIGHT | Until 2008, paleontologists dug for fossils at this site near the Conata Picnic Area. It was named for a large fossil with a pig-like appearance (it turned out to be a small, hornless rhinoceros). Wayside signs and exhibits, including a mural, provide context on the area and its fossils. ⊠ *Badlands National Park ✛ 17 miles northwest of Ben Reifel Visitor Center* ⊕ *www.nps.gov/badl.*

PICNIC AREAS

Bigfoot Pass Overlook

OTHER ATTRACTION | There is only a handful of tables here and no restrooms, but the incredible view makes it a lovely spot to have lunch. ⊠ *Badlands Loop Rd., Badlands National Park ✛ 7 miles northwest of Ben Reifel Visitor Center* ⊕ *www.nps.gov/badl.*

Conata Picnic Area

OTHER ATTRACTION | A half-dozen or so covered picnic tables are scattered over this area, which rests against a badlands wall ½ mile south of Badlands Loop Road. There's no potable water, but there are bathroom facilities and you can enjoy your lunch in peaceful isolation at the threshold of the Badlands Wilderness Area. The Conata Basin area is to the east, and Sage Creek area is to the west. ⊠ *Conata Rd., Badlands National Park ✛ 15 miles northwest of Ben Reifel Visitor Center* ⊕ *www.nps.gov/badl.*

Peter Norbeck's Park

Much of the credit for setting aside South Dakota's badlands as public lands is owed to Peter Norbeck, a powerful politician who was also largely responsible for establishing nearby Custer State Park and obtaining federal funding for Mount Rushmore National Memorial. Convinced that the state's badlands formations were more distinctive than those in other parts of the American West, Norbeck began lobbying for a new national park almost immediately after he was elected a U.S. senator in 1920. Political maneuvering tied up the proposal in Congress for nearly 10 years, and land issues delayed the measure for another decade. Finally, on March 4, 1939, the region was declared Badlands National Monument by President Calvin Coolidge. It was re-designated as a national park in 1978.

SCENIC DRIVES

For the average visitor, a casual drive is the essential means by which to see Badlands National Park. To do the scenery justice, drive slowly, and don't hesitate to get out and explore on foot when the occasion calls for it.

★ Badlands Loop Road

SCENIC DRIVE | The simplest drive is on two-lane Badlands Loop Road (Route/Highway 240). The drive circles from Exit 110 off I-90 through the park and back to the interstate at Exit 131. Start from either end and make your way around to the various overlooks along the way. Pinnacles and Yellow Mounds overlooks are outstanding places to examine the sandy pink- and brown-toned ridges and spires distinctive to the badlands. The landscape flattens out slightly to the north, revealing spectacular views of mixed-grass prairies. The Cedar Pass area of the drive has some of the park's best trails. ⊠ *Badlands Loop Rd., Badlands National Park* ⊕ *www.nps.gov/badl.*

Sage Creek Rim Road

SCENIC DRIVE | This gravel route near the Pinnacles entrance follows the road less traveled and covers rougher terrain than Badlands Loop Road. Sage Creek Rim Road is completely negotiable by most vehicles, but should be avoided during a thunderstorm when the sudden rush of water may cause flooding. It might also close temporarily after snowstorms. A vast mixed-grass prairie covers the rest. Keep an eye out for free-roaming bison. ⊠ *Sage Creek Rim Rd., Badlands National Park* ⊕ *www.nps.gov/badl.*

SCENIC STOPS

★ Badlands Wilderness Area

NATURE SIGHT | Covering about a quarter of the park, this 100-square-mile area is part of the country's largest prairie wilderness. About two-thirds of the Sage Creek region is mixed-grass prairie, making it the ideal grazing grounds for bison, pronghorn, and other native animals. The Hay Butte Overlook (2 miles northwest on Sage Creek Rim Road) and the Badlands Wilderness Overlook (1 mile south of the Pinnacles entrance) are the best places to get an overview of the wilderness area. Feel free to park at an overlook and hike your own route into the untamed, unmarked prairie. ⊠ *Badlands National Park* ⊹ *25 miles northwest of Ben Reifel Visitor Center* ⊕ *www.nps.gov/badl.*

Big Badlands Overlook

VIEWPOINT | From this spot just south of the park's northeast entrance, the vast majority of the park's 1 million annual visitors get their first views of the White River Badlands. ⊠ *Badlands National Park ⊹ 5 miles northeast of the Ben Reifel Visitor Center ⊕ www.nps.gov/badl.*

Big Foot Pass Overlook

VIEWPOINT | See where Sioux Chief Big Foot and his band traveled en route to the battle at Wounded Knee, December 29, 1890. ⊠ *Badlands National Park ⊹ 7 miles northwest of the Ben Reifel Visitor Center ⊕ www.nps.gov/badl.*

Roberts Prairie Dog Town

NATURE SIGHT | **FAMILY** | Once a homestead, the site today contains one of the country's largest (if not the largest) colonies of black-tailed prairie dogs. ⊠ *Sage Creek Rim Rd., Badlands National Park ⊹ 5 miles west of Badlands Loop Rd. ⊕ www.nps.gov/badl.*

Yellow Mounds Overlook

VIEWPOINT | Contrasting sharply with the whites, grays, and browns of the Badlands' pinnacles, the mounds viewed from here greet you with soft yet vivid yellows, reds, and purples. ⊠ *Badlands National Park ⊹ 16 miles northwest of Ben Reifel Visitor Center ⊕ www.nps. gov/badl.*

TRAILS

If you want a challenge, you might consider trekking this 100-square-mile parcel of grassy steppes and rocky canyons east of the highway and south of Sage Creek Rim Road, near the Pinnacles entrance. There are no services here and very few visitors, even in summer. Before venturing out, check in with park staff at one of the visitor centers.

Castle Trail

TRAIL | The park's longest hike runs 5 miles one way between the Fossil Exhibit trailhead on Badlands Loop Road and the parking area for the Door and Windows

Tips for Multiday Trips

Before you begin a multiday visit to the badlands, stock up on enough drinking water and food; both resources are hard to come by in the park. This is especially true in the backcountry, where water is so laden with silt and minerals that it's impossible to purify. Also bring a compass, topographical map, and rain gear.

trails. Although the Castle Trail is fairly level, allow at least four hours to cover the entire 10 miles out and back. If you choose to follow the Medicine Root Loop, which detours off the Castle Trail, you'll add ½ mile to the trek. Experienced hikers will do this one more quickly. *Moderate.* ⊠ *Badlands National Park ⊹ Trailhead: 5 miles north of Ben Reifel Visitor Center, off Hwy. 240 ⊕ www.nps. gov/badl.*

Cliff Shelf Nature Trail

TRAIL | This ½-mile loop winds through a wooded prairie oasis in the middle of dry, rocky ridges and climbs 200 feet to a peak above White River Valley for an incomparable view. Look for chipmunks, squirrels, and red-winged blackbirds and eagles, hawks, and vultures at hilltop. Even casual hikers can complete this trail in far less than an hour, but if you want to observe the true diversity of wildlife present here, stay longer. *Moderate.* ⊠ *Badlands National Park ⊹ Trailhead: 1 mile east of Ben Reifel Visitor Center, off Hwy. 240 ⊕ www.nps.gov/badl.*

Door Trail

TRAIL | The ¾-mile round-trip trail leads through a natural opening, or door, in a badlands rock wall. The eerie sandstone formations and passageways beckon,

Did You Know?

The Badlands' other-worldly scenery has often been likened to a lunar landscape. The unique rock formations, which proved hard to navigate by explorers and trappers, had already been given the name mako sico, or the bad lands, by the Lakota people.

but it's recommended that you stay on the trail. The first 100 yards of the trail are on a boardwalk. Even a patient and observant hiker will take only about 30 minutes. *Easy.* ⊠ *Badlands National Park* ⊹ *Trailhead: 2 miles east of Ben Reifel Visitor Center, off Hwy. 240* ⊕ *www.nps. gov/badl.*

★ Fossil Exhibit Trail

TRAIL | FAMILY | The trail, in place since 1964, has fossil replicas of early mammals displayed at wayside exhibits along its ¼-mile length, which is completely wheelchair accessible. Give yourself at least an hour to fully enjoy this popular hike. *Easy.* ⊠ *Badlands National Park* ⊹ *Trailhead: 5 miles northwest of Ben Reifel Visitor Center, off Hwy. 240* ⊕ *www.nps.gov/badl.*

Notch Trail

TRAIL | One of the park's more interesting hikes, this 1½-mile round-trip trail takes you over moderately difficult terrain and up a ladder. Winds at the notch can be fierce, but it's worth lingering for the view of the White River Valley and the Pine Ridge Indian Reservation. With breaks to enjoy the views, you'll probably spend more than an hour on this hike. *Moderate–Difficult.* ⊠ *Badlands National Park* ⊹ *Trailhead: 2 miles north of Ben Reifel Visitor Center, off Hwy. 240* ⊕ *www.nps.gov/badl.*

Saddle Pass Trail

TRAIL | This route, which connects with Castle Trail and Medicine Root Loop, is a steep, ¼-mile round-trip route up and down the side of "The Wall," an impressive rock formation. Plan on spending about an hour on this climb. *Difficult.* ⊠ *Badlands National Park* ⊹ *Trailhead: 2 miles west of Ben Reifel Visitor Center, off Hwy. 240* ⊕ *www.nps.gov/badl.*

Window Trail

TRAIL | Please note that Door, Notch, and Window Trails are all accessible at the same trailhead. Window Trail is a ¼-mile

round-trip trail ends at a natural hole, or window, in a rock wall. You'll see more of the distinctive badlands pinnacles and spires. *Easy.* ⊠ *Badlands National Park* ⊹ *Trailhead: 2 miles north of Ben Reifel Visitor Center, off Hwy. 240* ⊕ *www.nps. gov/badl.*

VISITOR CENTERS

Ben Reifel Visitor Center

VISITOR CENTER | Open year-round, the park's main information hub has brochures, maps, and information on ranger programs. Check out exhibits on geology and wildlife, and watch paleontologists at work in the Fossil Prep Lab. View the film, *Land of Stone and Light,* in the 95-seat theater, and shop in the Badlands Natural History Association Bookstore. The facility is named for a Sioux activist and the first Lakota to serve in Congress. Born on the nearby Rosebud Indian Reservation, Ben Reifel also served in the Army during World War II. ⊠ *Badlands Loop Rd., Badlands National Park* ⊹ *8 miles from northeast entrance, near Hwy. 377 junction* ☎ *605/433–5361* ⊕ *www.nps.gov/badl.*

Restaurants

Cedar Pass Lodge Restaurant

$$ | AMERICAN | FAMILY | Cool off within dark, knotty-pine walls under an exposed-beam ceiling, and enjoy a hearty meal of steak or tacos and fry bread. **Known for:** locally sourced fish, meat, and produce; fresh fry bread; decent selection of vegetarian and gluten-free dishes. ⑤ *Average main: $15* ⊠ *20681 Hwy. 240, Interior* ☎ *605/433–5460* ⊕ *www.cedar-passlodge.com* ⊙ *Closed Nov.–mid-Apr.*

🛏 Hotels

Cedar Pass Lodge

$$$ | HOTEL | Besides impressive views of the Badlands, these cabins include modern touches like flat-screen TVs and Wi-Fi connections. **Pros:** new cabins; the best stargazing in South Dakota; pine deck chairs to enjoy the scenery. **Cons:** remote location; long drive to other restaurants; pricey. ⑤ *Rooms from: $176* ✉ *20681 Hwy. 240, Interior* ☎ *605/433–5460, 877/386–4383* ⊕ *www.cedarpasslodge. com* ⊘ *Closed Nov.–mid-Apr.* ⊋ *26 cabins* ⦿ *No Meals.*

Shopping

Badlands Natural History Association Bookstore

BOOKS | The Badlands Natural History Association Bookstore sells everything from books on geology and paleontology to postcards and posters. ✉ *Ben Reifel Visitor Center, Badlands Loop Rd., Badlands National Park* ✛ *Near Hwy. 377 junction, 8 miles from northeast entrance* ☎ *605/433–5489* ⊕ *www.badlandsnha. org.*

Cedar Pass Lodge Gift Store

SOUVENIRS | The shop's extensive collection includes locally made bead- and quillwork, Black Hills gold, and silver-and-turquoise jewelry, as well as postcards, pottery, books, and films. Drinks and snacks are available. ✉ *20681 Hwy. 240, Interior* ☎ *605/433–5460* ⊕ *www. cedarpasslodge.com.*

Stronghold Unit

4 miles from Scenic and 34 miles from Ben Reifel Visitor Center in the North Unit.

With few paved roads and no campgrounds, the park's southwest section is difficult to access without a four-wheel-drive vehicle. If you're willing to trek, its isolation provides a rare opportunity to explore the Badlands rock formations and prairies completely undisturbed. From 1942 to 1968, the U.S. Air Force and South Dakota National Guard used much of the area as a gunnery range. Hundreds

of fossils were destroyed by bomber pilots, who frequently targeted the large fossil remains of an elephant-size brontothere (an extinct relative of the rhinoceros). Beware of unexploded bombs, shells, rockets, and other hazardous materials. Steer clear of it and find another route.

Sights

PICNIC AREAS

White River Visitor Center Picnic Tables

OTHER ATTRACTION | Directly behind this visitor center are four covered tables, where you can picnic simply and stay protected from the wind. There are also restroom facilities. ✉ *Rte. 27, Badlands National Park* ✛ *25 miles south of Rte. 44* ⊕ *www.nps.gov/badl.*

SCENIC STOPS

Stronghold Table

HISTORIC SIGHT | Within the Stronghold Unit, the Stronghold Table, a 3-mile-long plateau, is a historic site, sacred to the Lakota and inaccessible. It was here, just before the Massacre at Wounded Knee in 1890, that some 600 Sioux gathered to perform one of the last known Ghost Dances, a ritual in which the Sioux wore white shirts that they believed would protect them from bullets. ✉ *Badlands National Park* ✛ *North and west of White River Visitor Center; entrance off Hwy. 27* ⊕ *www.nps.gov/badl.*

TRAILS

Sheep Mountain Table Road

TRAIL | This 7-mile dirt road in the Stronghold Unit is ideal for mountain biking, but should be attempted only when dry, and riders must stay on the road. The terrain is level for the first 3 miles, then it climbs and levels out again. At the top you can take in great views of the area. ✉ *Badlands National Park* ✛ *About 14 miles north of White River Visitor Center* ⊕ *www.nps.gov/badl.*

The Fossil Exhibit Trail, featuring fossil replicas of early mammals, is one of the park's most family-friendly trails.

VISITOR CENTER

White River Visitor Center

VISITOR CENTER | Open in summer, this small center serves almost exclusively serious hikers and campers venturing into the Stronghold or Palmer unit. If that's you, stop here to view park videos and for maps and details about road and trail conditions. The center is on the Pine Ridge Indian Reservation. While you're here you can see fossils and Native American artifacts, and learn about Lakota culture. ⊠ *Badlands National Park* ⚓ *25 miles south of Hwy. 44 via Hwy. 27* ☎ *605/455–2878* ⊕ *www.nps.gov/badl.*

Palmer Creek Unit

26 miles from Kyle.

This is a very remote part of the park and accessible only with permission to cross private land. Backcountry camping is allowed, but you have to hike in and follow all rules and regulations.

Activities

Pure, unspoiled, empty space is the greatest asset of Badlands National Park, and it can only be experienced at its best if you're on foot. Spring and autumn are the optimal times of the year to do wilderness exploring, because the brutal extremes of summer and winter can—and do—kill. In fact, the two biggest enemies to hikers and bicyclists in the badlands are heat and lightning. Before you venture out, make sure you have at least one gallon of water per person per day, and be prepared to take shelter from freak thunderstorms, which often strike in the late afternoon with little warning.

BIKING

Bicycles are permitted only on designated roads, which may be paved or unpaved. They are prohibited from closed roads, trails, and the backcountry. Flat-resistant tires are recommended.

Plants and Wildlife in Badlands

The park's sharply defined cliffs, canyons, and buttes are near-deserts with little plant growth. Most of the park, however, is made up of mixed-grass prairies, where more than 460 species of hardy grasses and wildflowers flourish in the warmer months. Prairie coneflower, yellow plains prickly pear, pale-green yucca, buffalo grass, and sideoats grama are just a few of the plants on the badlands plateau. Trees and shrubs are rare and usually confined to dry creek beds. The most common trees are Rocky Mountain junipers and plains cottonwoods.

It's common to see pronghorn and mule deer dart across the flat plateaus, bison grazing on the buttes, prairie dogs and sharp-tailed grouse, and, soaring above, golden eagles, turkey vultures, and hawks. Also present are coyotes, rarely-seen swift foxes, jackrabbits, bats, gophers, porcupines, skunks, bobcats, horned lizards, bighorn sheep, and prairie rattlesnakes. The latter are the only venomous snakes in the park—watch for them near rocky outcroppings and in prairie-dog towns. Backcountry hikers might consider heavy boots and long pants reinforced with leather or canvas. Although rarely seen, mountain lions and the endangered black-footed ferret roam the park.

BIRD-WATCHING

Especially around sunset, get set to watch the badlands come to life. More than 215 bird species have been recorded in the area, including herons, pelicans, cormorants, egrets, swans, geese, hawks, golden and bald eagles, falcons, vultures, cranes, doves, and cuckoos. Established roads and trails are the best places from which to watch for nesting species. The Cliff Shelf Nature Trail and the Castle Trail, which both traverse areas with surprisingly thick vegetation, are especially good locations. You may even catch sight of a rare burrowing owl at the Roberts Prairie Dog Town.

CAMPING

Pitching a tent and sleeping under the stars is one of the greatest ways to fully experience the sheer isolation and unadulterated empty spaces of Badlands National Park. You'll find two relatively easy-access campgrounds within park boundaries, but only one has any sort of amenities. The second is little more than a flat patch of ground with some signs. Unless you desperately need a flush toilet to have an enjoyable camping experience, you're just as well off hiking into the wilderness and choosing your own campsite. You can set up camp anywhere that's at least a half mile from a road or trail and is not visible from any road or trail.

Cedar Pass Campground. With tent sites and 20 RV sites as well as coin-operated showers, this is the most developed campground in the park, and it's near Ben Reifel Visitor Center, Cedar Pass Lodge, and a half-dozen hiking trails. Reservations required. ⊠ *Rte. 377, ¼ mile south of Badlands Loop Rd.* ☎ *605/433–5361* ⊕ *www.cedarpasslodge.com.*

Sage Creek Primitive Campground. If you want to get away from it all, this lovely, isolated spot surrounded by nothing but fields and crickets is the right camp for you. Amenities include picnic tables and pit toilets. Sites available first-come, first-served. ⊠ *Sage Creek Rim Rd., 25 miles west of Badlands Loop Rd.* ⊕ *www.nps.gov/thingstodo/campgrounds-badl.htm.*

The Cliff Shelf Nature Trail is one of the park's top birding spots. Keep an eye out for egrets, hawks, cranes, doves, and falcons.

EDUCATIONAL PROGRAMS
Adventure Hikes
HIKING & WALKING | FAMILY | Park staff often lead daily hikes on established trails. Hikes can vary in length from 30 to 45 minutes to as long as 4 hours and are for hikers of all ages and experience levels. Check with the visitor center for specific details. ⊠ *25216 Ben Reifel Rd., Interior* ⊕ *www.nps.gov/badl.*

Evening Program and Night Sky Viewing
STARGAZING | Watch a 30-minute presentation on the wildlife, natural history, paleontology, or another aspect of the Badlands. Shows typically begin around 9 pm. Stick around afterward for the Night Sky Viewing, a stargazing interpretive program complete with telescopes. ⊠ *Cedar Pass Campground amphitheater, 20681 Hwy. 240, Badlands National Park* ⊕ *www.nps.gov/badl* ⊙ *Closed Sept.–May.*

Fossil Talk
HIKING & WALKING | What were the Badlands like many years ago? This 20-minute talk about protected fossil exhibits will inspire and answer all your questions. It's usually held at 10:30 am and 1:30 pm daily at the Fossil Exhibit Trail. ⊠ *Badlands Loop Rd., Badlands National Park* ⊹ *Fossil Exhibit Trail, 5 miles northwest of Ben Reifel Visitor Center* ⊕ *www.nps. gov/badl.*

Geology Walk
HIKING & WALKING | Learn the geologic story of the White River Badlands in a 30-minute walk, generally departing from the Door Trailhead daily at 8:30 am. The terrain can be rough in places, so be sure to wear hiking boots or sneakers. A hat is a good idea, too. ⊠ *Badlands Loop Rd., Badlands National Park* ⊹ *Door and Window trails parking area, 2 miles south of the northeast entrance* ⊕ *www.nps. gov/badl.*

Junior Ranger Program

HIKING & WALKING | FAMILY | Children can join in this 30-minute adventure, typically a short hike, game, or other hands-on activity focused on badlands wildlife, geology, or fossils. Parents are welcome. Check with the visitor center for schedule, as times and dates vary with staff availability. ✉ *Ben Reifel Visitor Center, 25216 Hwy. 240, Badlands National Park* ⊕ *www.nps.gov/badl.*

HIKING

The otherworldliness of the badlands is best appreciated with a walk through them. Take time to examine the dusty rock beneath your feet, and be on the lookout for fossils and animals. Fossil Exhibit Trail and Cliff Shelf Nature Trail are must-dos, but even these popular trails tend to be primitive. You'll find bathrooms at Fossil Exhibit Trail. Both trails feature boardwalks, so you won't be shuffling through dirt and gravel. Door Trail and Window Trail are also short, easy, and easily accessible treks on the east end of the North Unit. Notch Trail is nearby but is more of a strenuous hike that offers an awesome view of the White River Valley. Castle Trail, the park's longest, takes you deep into the badlands. Extend your hike by connecting with Medicine Root Trail or the steep and strenuous Saddle Pass Trail. Thanks to Badlands National Park's open-hike policy, you can also venture off the trails. One area to consider is the Sage Creek Wilderness Area where the park's bison live.

Because the weather here can be so variable, be prepared for anything. Wear sunglasses, a hat, and long pants, and have rain gear available. It's illegal to pick up or remove any park resources, which include everything from rocks and fossils to plants and artifacts. Stay at least 100 yards away from wildlife. Due to the dry climate, open fires are never allowed. Tell friends, relatives, and the park rangers if you're going to embark on a multiday

expedition. Assume that your cell phone, if you've brought one, won't get a signal in the park. But most important of all, be sure to bring your own water. Sources of water in the park are few and far between, and none of them are drinkable. All water in the park is contaminated by minerals and sediment, and park authorities warn that it's untreatable. If you're backpacking into the wilderness, bring at least a gallon of water per person per day. For day hikes, rangers suggest you drink at least a quart per person per hour.

OUTFITTERS

Scheels All Sport

HIKING & WALKING | If you plan on being in Rapid City before your visit to the Badlands National Park, be sure to visit this enormous shop. Scheels carries a wide selection of all-weather hiking gear, footwear, and clothes as well as binoculars suitable for bird-watchers. ✉ *1225 Eglin St., Rapid City* ☎ *605/342–9033* ⊕ *www. scheels.com.*

HORSEBACK RIDING

The park has one of the largest and most beautiful territories in the state in which to ride a horse. Riding is allowed in most of the park except for designated trails, roads, and developed areas. The mixed-grass prairie of the Badlands Wilderness Area is especially popular, though the weather can be unpredictable. Only

Best Bets for Families

- Badlands Loop Tour
- Fossil Exhibit Trail
- Mount Rushmore
- Robert's Prairie Dog Town
- Wall Drug Store

experienced riders or people accompanied by experienced riders should venture far from more developed areas.

There are several restrictions and regulations that you must be aware of if you plan to ride your own horse. Potable water for visitors and animals is a rarity. Riders must bring enough water for themselves and their stock. Only certified weed-free hay is approved in the park. Horses are not allowed to run free within the borders of the park.

ROCK CLIMBING

Rangers forbid rock climbing in the traditional sense. The rocky walls of the Badlands are sand-like and very fragile. Most people who attempt climbing in the park end up in a pile of clumpy dust before they get very high. More problematically, they sometimes take valuable fossil deposits away during their fall, essentially destroying them. For that reason, climbing in the park is prohibited.

What's Nearby

Located off I–90, 50 miles east of the edge of the Black Hills (and **Rapid City,** the largest community on this side of the state), Badlands National Park allows travelers a unique stop in a highly dense area of national parks, monuments, and memorials including Mount Rushmore National Memorial, Wind Cave National Park, Jewel Cave National Monument, Devils Tower National Monument, and Custer State Park. The Black Hills provide a wonderful backdrop for the dry canyon and dusty buttes of the badlands. Park entrances along I–90 are near the towns of **Wall** on the west (home to the famous Wall Drug) and Kadoka on the east, which have lodging, restaurants, gas and auto repair, and other support services.

Chapter 8

WIND CAVE NATIONAL PARK

8

Updated by
Tanya Manus

SOUTH
DAKOTA

⛰ **Camping**
★★★☆☆

🏨 **Hotels**
★★★★★

🏃 **Activities**
★★★★★

👁 **Scenery**
★★★★★

👥 **Crowds**
★★★★☆

WELCOME TO WIND CAVE NATIONAL PARK

TOP REASONS TO GO

★ **Underground exploring:** Wind Cave offers visitors the chance to view amazing formations on guided tours through a long and complex cave.

★ **The call of the wild:** Wind Cave National Park boasts a wide variety of animals: bison, coyote, deer, pronghorns, elk, and prairie dogs.

★ **Education by candlelight:** Wind Cave offers educational programs, including the Candlelight Cave Tour, which allows guests to explore the cave by candlelight.

★ **Historic cave:** On January 9, 1903, President Theodore Roosevelt signed a bill that made Wind Cave the first cave in the United States to be named a national park.

★ **Noteworthy neighbors:** With its proximity to national and state parks, Wind Cave is situated perfectly to explore some of America's greatest national treasures.

Bounded by Black Hills National Forest to the west and wind-swept prairie to the east, 33,851-acre Wind Cave National Park, in southwestern South Dakota, encompasses the transition between two distinct ecosystems: mountain forest and mixed-grass prairie. Underground, a year-round 54°F temperature gives summer visitors a cool oasis—and winter visitors a warm escape.

1 **Wind Cave.** With an explored maze of more than 160 miles of caverns and passageways, Wind Cave is considered one of the world's longest caves. Notably, scientists estimate that only 5% to 10% of the cave has been explored to date. Most of the world's known boxwork formations are found here, which means that visitors are treated to some of the rarest geological features on the planet. The cave lies at the confluence of western mountains and central plains, which blesses the park with a unique landscape. A series of established trails weave in and out of forested hillsides and grassy prairies, providing treks of varying difficulty.

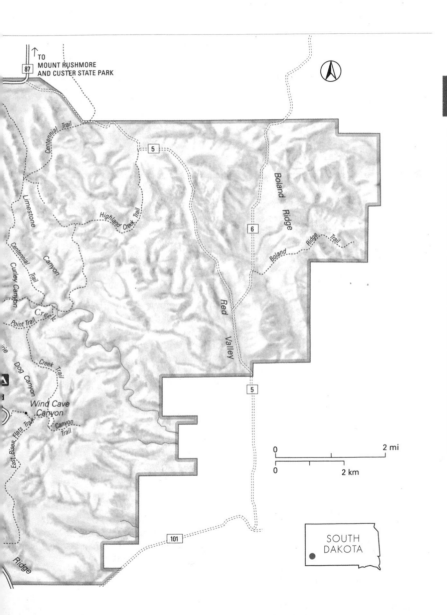

TO
MOUNT RUSHMORE
AND CUSTER STATE PARK
87

Centennial Trail

5

Limestone

Highland Creek Trail

Canyon

Centennial Trail

Curley Canyon

Point Trail

Creek

Creek Trail

Dog Canyon

Wind Cave
Canyon

Canyon
Trail

East Bison Flats Trail

Ridge

101

Boland Ridge

6

Boland Ridge Trail

Red Valley

5

0 ——————— 2 mi
0 ——————— 2 km

SOUTH
DAKOTA

Wind Cave has more than 160 miles of underground passageways. Cave formations include 95% of the world's mineral boxwork, along with cave popcorn and needle-like frostwork. This underground wilderness is part of a giant limestone labyrinth beneath the Black Hills.

Wind Cave ranks as the sixth-longest cave in the world, but experts believe at least 90% of it has yet to be mapped. On the surface, bison, elk and other wildlife roam the rolling hills that demonstrate the biodiversity of grasslands and forest.

One of the country's oldest parks—President Theodore Roosevelt established it in 1903—the National Park Service says it's the world's most complex three-dimensional maze cave with the best boxwork, a rare honeycombed formation of calcite that hangs from the walls and ceilings. Wind Cave's name comes from the air that howls at the natural entrances because of differences in barometric pressure between the cave below and atmosphere above.

Though the cave is the star of the show, make sure you also set aside time to explore the park's more than 50 square miles of surface. The largest known natural opening to the cave is located near the visitor center entrance and is accessible on a self-guided tour. The park has more than 30 miles of hiking trails, open year-round, that offer a close-up view of the forest and rolling prairies as well as bison, elk, pronghorns, and prairie dogs. Bird-watching is popular because the park is home to more than 100 different permanent species, as well as others during spring and fall migration. If you visit in mid-September to early October, you'll see fall colors on display and maybe hear the elk bugling. A 30-mile scenic driving tour is another great way to see the geology of the pristine Black Hills.

The area known as the Black Hills is sacred to Native Americans. Lakota culture believes that humans and bison came from the spirit world in the earth through the natural entrance of the cave, referred to as a "hole that breathes cool air." In 1881, brothers Tom and Jesse Bingham heard the sound of wind coming from one of the holes which, as the story goes, blew Jesse's hat off when he peered inside. Charlie Crary is credited with the first entry into the cave that year. After several legal fights over ownership to the land and cave below, Congress and President Roosevelt created the Wind Cave National Park, making it the world's first cave to be designated as a national park. Tours of the cave had occurred, though, before Wind Cave became a national park.

Planning

When to Go

The biggest crowds come to Wind Cave from June to September, but the park and surrounding Black Hills are large enough to diffuse the masses. Neither the cave nor grounds above are ever uncomfortably packed, although on busy summer days tours sometimes sell out more than an hour ahead of time, so come early in the day and reserve your spot. Park officials contend it's actually less busy during the first full week in August, when the Sturgis Motorcycle Rally brings roughly a half-million bikers to the region, clogging highways for miles around. Most hotels and some campgrounds within a 100-mile radius are booked up to a year in advance.

The colder months are the least crowded, though you can still explore underground, thanks to the cave's constant 54°F temperature. The shoulder seasons are also quieter, though autumn is a perfect time to visit. The days are warm, the nights are cool, and in late September and early October the park's canyons and coulees display incredible colors.

FESTIVALS AND EVENTS

Crazy Horse Volksmarch. This 6.2-mile hike up the mountain where the massive Crazy Horse Memorial is being carved is the largest event of its kind and gives hikers the opportunity to see views of the memorial not otherwise available to the public. It's held the first full weekend in June. Another one-day Volksmarch is held in late September, timed to coincide with the Custer State Park Buffalo Roundup. ⊕ crazyhorsememorial.org

Custer State Park Buffalo Roundup & Arts Festival. The nation's largest buffalo roundup is one of South Dakota's most exciting events. Early on a Friday morning in late September, cowboys, cowgirls,

and rangers saddle up to corral and vaccinate the park's 1,400 head of bison. You'll hear the thunder of thousands of hooves before you even see the bison. Before, during, and after the roundup, a three-day festival showcases works by South Dakota artists and artisans. ⊕ gfp. sd.gov/parks/detail/custer-state-park

Days of '76. This outdoor, award-winning, Professional Rodeo Cowboys Association (PRCA) event is known as one of the best outdoor rodeos in the nation. In addition to the riding, roping, and bull riding, there's two parades with vintage carriages and coaches and Western arts and crafts. This five-day affair is one of the state's most popular, featuring the top cowboys and cowgirls in the sport. ⊕ www.deadwood.com/event/ days-of-76

Deadwood Jam. These free outdoor concerts have filled the streets of Deadwood with live music for more than 30 years. The Black Hills' premier music festival showcases an eclectic collection of country, rock, and blues for two days in mid-September. ⊕ www.deadwood.com/ event/deadwood-jam

Gold Discovery Days. A parade, carnival, car show, biking selfie run, hot air balloon rally, a cornhole tournament and hunting for gold nuggets are all part of the fun at this three-day event in late July in Custer. ⊕ www.custersd.com/ Gold-Discovery-Days

Sturgis Motorcycle Rally. This 10-day event held in early August regularly draws more than 500,000 bikers and non-bikers alike who pack the Black Hills town's streets. It features a variety of music, T-shirt stands, vendors, food and, of course, motorcycles of all varieties. ⊕ www. sturgismotorcyclerally.com

AVERAGE HIGH/LOW TEMPERATURES					
Jan.	Feb.	Mar.	Apr.	May	June
37/11	42/15	50/21	61/32	71/42	81/51
July	Aug.	Sept.	Oct.	Nov.	Dec.
89/57	88/55	78/45	66/34	50/23	40/14

Getting Here and Around

AIR
The nearest commercial airport is in Rapid City.

CAR
Wind Cave is 56 miles from Rapid City, via U.S. 16 and Highway 87, which runs through the park, and 73 miles southwest of Badlands National Park.

U.S. 385 and Highway 87 travel the length of the park on the west side. Additionally, two unpaved roads, NPS Roads 5 and 6, traverse the northeastern part of Wind Cave. NPS Road 5 joins Highway 87 at the park's north border, or take a scenic drive on NPS Road 5 to the park's southern boundary.

Inspiration

Wind Cave National Park is one of the featured destinations in the 2001 IMAX movie *Journey Into Amazing Caves.* Narrated by Liam Neeson, with music by The Moody Blues, the immersive film follows scientists into unique underground worlds.

Wind Cave National Park: The First 100 Years includes more than 200 historic images as well as history and stories about the cave and park.

Wind Cave: The Story Behind the Scenery provides good photos and information about the park; it can be purchased at the visitor center.

Park Essentials

ACCESSIBILITY
The visitor center is entirely wheelchair accessible, but only a few areas of the cave itself are navigable by those with limited mobility. Arrangements can be made in advance for a special ranger-assisted tour for a small fee. The Elk Mountain Campground has two accessible sites.

PARK FEES AND PERMITS
There's no fee to enter the park; standard cave tours cost $14–$16. The requisite backcountry camping and horseback-riding permits are both free from the visitor center. Rates at Elk Mountain Campground are $24 a night per site early spring through late fall (when the water is turned on in the restroom facility); $12 a night per site the rest of the year.

PARK HOURS
The park is open year-round, though visitor center hours and tour schedules vary seasonally. It is in the Mountain time zone.

CELL PHONE RECEPTION
Cell phone reception is hit and miss in the park. You will find a public phone outside the visitor center.

Hotels

Wind Cave has only one campground, and you'll have to look outside park boundaries if you want to bed down in something more substantial than a tent. New chain hotels with modern amenities

Wind Cave in One Day

Pack a picnic lunch, then head to the visitor center to purchase tickets for a morning tour of Wind Cave. Visit the exhibit rooms in the center afterward. Then drive or walk the ¼ mile to the picnic area north of the visitor center. The refreshing air and deep emerald color of the pine woodlands will flavor your meal.

In the afternoon, take a leisurely drive through the parklands south of the visitor center, passing through **Bison Flats** and **Gobbler Pass**, for an archetypal view of the park and to look for wildlife. On the way back north, follow U.S. 385 east toward **Wind Cave Canyon**. If you enjoy bird-watching, park at the turnout and hike the 1.8-mile trail into the canyon, where you can spot swallows and great horned owls in the cliffs and woodpeckers in the trees.

Get back on the highway going north, take a right on Highway 87, and continue ½ mile to the turnout for **Centennial Trail**. Hike the trail about 2 miles to the junction with **Lookout Point Trail**, turn right and return to Highway 87. The whole loop is about 5 miles. As you continue driving north to the top of Rankin Ridge, a pull-out to the right serves as the starting point for 1-mile **Rankin Ridge Trail**. It loops around the ridge, past **Lookout Tower**—the park's highest point—and ends up back at the pull-out. This trail is an excellent opportunity to enjoy the fresh air, open spaces, and diversity of wildlife in the park.

are plentiful in the Black Hills, but when booking accommodations consider a stay at one of the area's historic properties. From grand brick downtown hotels to intimate Queen Anne homes converted to bed-and-breakfasts, historic lodgings are easy to locate. Other distinctive lodging choices include the region's mountain lodges and forest retreats.

It may be difficult to obtain quality accommodations during summer—and downright impossible during the 10-day Sturgis Motorcycle Rally, held in early August every year—so plan ahead and make reservations (three or four months out is a good rule of thumb) if you're going to travel during peak season. To find the best value, choose a hotel far from Interstate 90.

Restaurants

If you're determined to dine in Wind Cave National Park, be sure to pack your own meal, because other than vending machines, the only dining venues inside park boundaries are the two picnic areas, one near the visitor center and the other at Elk Mountain Campground. The towns beyond the park offer additional options. Deadwood claims some of the best-ranked restaurants in South Dakota. Buffalo, pheasant, and elk are relatively common ingredients in the Black Hills. No matter where you go, beef is king.

⇨ *Hotel and restaurant reviews have been shortened. For full information, see Fodors.com. Restaurant prices are the average cost of a main course at dinner, or if dinner is not served, at lunch. Hotel prices are the lowest cost of a standard double room in high season.*

What It Costs

	$	$$	$$$	$$$$
RESTAURANTS				
	under $13	$13–$23	$24–$35	over $35
HOTELS				
	under $150	$150–$200	$201–$250	over $250

Tours

Candlelight Cave Tour
GUIDED TOURS | Available once or twice daily, mid-June through Labor Day, this tour goes into a section of the cave with no paved walks or lighting. Everyone on the tour carries a lantern similar to those used in expeditions in the 1890s. The tour lasts two hours, covers 2/3 mile, and is limited to 10 people, so reservations are essential. Children younger than eight are not admitted. *Moderate. ⊠ 26611 U.S. 385, Wind Cave National Park ✛ Starts at visitor center ⊕ www.nps. gov/wica ☎ $16.*

Fairgrounds Cave Tour
GUIDED TOURS | View examples of nearly every type of calcite formation found in the cave on this 1½-hour, 1/2-mile tour, available at the visitor center from early June through mid-August. There are some 450 steps, leading up and down. *Moderate. ⊠ 26611 U.S. 385, Wind Cave National Park ✛ Off U.S. 385, 3 miles north of the park's southern boundary ⊕ www.nps.gov/wica ☎ $16.*

Garden of Eden Cave Tour
GUIDED TOURS | You don't need to go far to see boxwork, cave popcorn, and flow-stone formations. Just take the relatively easy, one-hour tour, which covers 1/4 mile and 150 stairs. It's available one to four times daily year-round. *Easy. ⊠ 26611 U.S. 385, Wind Cave National Park ✛ 3 miles north of park's southern border ⊕ www.nps.gov/wica ☎ $14.*

Natural Entrance Cave Tour
GUIDED TOURS | This 1¼-hour tour takes you 1/2 mile into the cave, onto more than 300 stairs (most heading down), and out an elevator exit. Along the way are some significant boxwork deposits on the middle level. The tour leaves several times daily except during winter months. *Moderate. ⊠ 26611 U.S. 385, Wind Cave National Park ✛ Off U.S. 385, 3 miles north of park's southern border ⊕ www. nps.gov/wica ☎ $16.*

Visitor Information

PARK CONTACT INFORMATION Wind Cave National Park.
⊠ 26611 U.S. 385, Hot Springs ☎ 605/745–4600 ⊕ www.nps. gov/wica.

Sights

PICNIC AREAS

Elk Mountain Campground Picnic Area
OTHER ATTRACTION | You don't have to be a camper to use this well-developed picnic spot, with more than 70 tables, fire grates (some of them heightened to accommodate people with disabilities), and restrooms. Some of the tables are on the prairie; others sit amid the pines. ⊠ Wind Cave National Park ✛ ½ mile north of visitor center ⊕ www.nps.gov/wica.

Wind Cave Picnic Area
OTHER ATTRACTION | On the edge of a prairie and grove of ponderosa, this is a peaceful, pretty place ¼ mile from the visitor center. Small and simple, it's equipped with 12 tables and a potable-water pump. ⊠ Wind Cave National Park ✛ ¼ mile north of visitor center ⊕ www.nps.gov/wica.

SCENIC DRIVES

Bison Flats Drive (South Entrance)
SCENIC DRIVE | Entering the park from the south on U.S. 385 takes you past Gobbler Ridge and into the hills commonly found in the southern Black Hills region. After a couple of miles, the landscape gently

Did You Know?

Wind Cave, a giant limestone labyrinth beneath the Black Hills, has 160 miles of underground passageways, making it one of the longest caves in the world—but it could be much longer, as experts believe only 5% to 10% of the cave has been mapped. It became a national park in 1903.

Plants and Wildlife in Wind Cave

About three-quarters of the park is grassland. The rest is forested, mostly by the ponderosa pine. Poison ivy is common in wetter, shadier areas, so wear long pants and boots when hiking. The convergence of forest and prairies makes an attractive home for bison, elk, coyotes, pronghorn antelope, prairie dogs, and mule deer. Wild turkey and squirrels are less obvious in this landscape, but commonly seen by observant hikers.

Mountain lions sometimes live in the park; although usually shy, they might attack if surprised or threatened. Make noise while hiking to prevent chance encounters, especially while hiking in low-visibility/forested areas at dawn, dusk or at night. Bison appear docile but can be dangerous. The largest land mammal in North America, they weigh up to a ton and run at speeds in excess of 35 mph.

levels onto the Bison Flats, one of the mixed-grass prairies on which the park prides itself. You might see a herd of grazing bison (the park has between 450 and 550 of them) between here and the visitor center. You can also catch panoramic views of the parklands, surrounding hills, and limestone bluffs. ⊠ *Hwy. 385, Wind Cave National Park* ⊕ *www. nps.gov/wica.*

★ Rankin Ridge Drive (North Entrance)

SCENIC DRIVE | Entering the park across the north border via Highway 87 is perhaps the most beautiful drive into the park. As you leave behind the grasslands and granite spires of Custer State Park and enter Wind Cave, you see the prairie, forest and some of the oldest rock in the Black Hills. The silvery twinkle of mica, quartz, and feldspar crystals dots Rankin Ridge east of Highway 87, and gradually gives way to limestone and sandstone formations. ⊠ *Hwy. 87, Wind Cave National Park* ⊕ *www.nps.gov/wica.*

SCENIC STOPS

Rankin Ridge Lookout Tower

VIEWPOINT | Although some of the best panoramic views of the park and surrounding hills can be seen from this 5,013-foot tower, it's never staffed or open to the public. Still, if you want to stretch your legs on a car ride along

Rankin Ridge Drive, consider following the 1-mile Rankin Ridge loop to the tower and back. ⊠ *Wind Cave National Park* ✛ *6 miles north of the visitor center on Hwy. 87* ⊕ *www.nps.gov/wica.*

★ Wind Cave

CAVE | Known to Native Americans for centuries, Wind Cave was named for the strong air currents that alternately blow in and out of its entrances. The cave's winds are related to the difference in atmospheric pressure between the cave and the surface. When the atmospheric pressure is higher outside than inside, the air blows in, and vice versa. With more than 160 miles of known passageways divided into three different levels, Wind Cave ranks among the longest in the world. It's host to an incredibly diverse collection of geologic formations, including more boxwork than any other known cave, plus a series of underground lakes, though they are located in the deepest parts of the cave not seen on any tours. All tours are led by National Park Service rangers and leave from the visitor center. These tours allow you to see the unusual and beautiful formations with names such as boxwork, cave popcorn, and frostwork. The cave remains a steady 54°F year-round, so wear closed-toe shoes and bring a jacket or sweater.

Above the massive Wind Cave underground network, bison, elk, and other wildlife roam the national park's rolling hills.

Tickets are sold at the visitor center and sometimes sell out more than an hour before each tour during summer, so plan accordingly. Check out the park website for the different tours, times, and pricing. ⊠ *Wind Cave National Park ✛ U.S. 385 to Wind Cave Visitor Center* ⊕ *www.nps. gov/wica.*

TRAILS

Boland Ridge Trail

TRAIL | Get away from the crowds for a half day via this strenuous, 2.6-mile (one way) hike. The panorama from the top is well worth it, especially at night. *Difficult.* ⊠ *Wind Cave National Park ✛ Trailhead: off Park Service Rd. 6, 1 mile north of junction with Park Service Rd. 5* ⊕ *www. nps.gov/wica.*

Centennial Trail

TRAIL | Constructed to celebrate South Dakota's centennial in 1989, this trail bisects the Black Hills, covering about 124 miles from north to south, from Bear Butte State Park through Black Hills National Forest, Black Elk Wilderness, Custer State Park, and into Wind Cave National Park. Designed for bikers, hikers, and horses, the trail is rugged but accommodating (note, however, that bicycling on the trail is not allowed within park boundaries). It will take you at least a half day to cover the 6-mile Wind Cave segment. *Moderate.* ⊠ *Wind Cave National Park ✛ Trailhead: off Hwy. 87, 2 miles north of visitor center* ⊕ *www.nps. gov/wica.*

Cold Brook Canyon Trail

TRAIL | FAMILY | Starting on the west side of U.S. 385, 2 miles south of the visitor center, this 1.4-mile (one way), mildly strenuous hike runs through an active prairie-dog town, the edge of an area burned by a controlled fire in 1986, and through Cold Brook Canyon to the park boundary fence. Experienced hikers can conquer this trail and return to the trailhead in an hour or less, but more leisurely visitors will probably need more time. *Moderate.* ⊠ *Wind Cave National Park ✛ Trailhead: west side of U.S. 385, 2 miles south of visitor center* ⊕ *www.nps. gov/wica.*

Highland Creek Trail

TRAIL | This difficult, roughly 8.6-mile (one way) trail is the longest and most diverse trail within the park, traversing mixed-grass prairies, ponderosa pine forests, and the riparian habitats of Highland Creek, Beaver Creek, and Wind Cave Canyon. Even those in good shape will need a full day to cover this trail round-trip. *Difficult.* ✉ *Wind Cave National Park* ✛ *Southern trailhead stems from Wind Cave Canyon trail 1 mile east of U.S. 385. Northern trailhead on Forest Service Rd. 5.*

Wind Cave Canyon Trail

TRAIL | This easy 1.8-mile (one way) trail follows Wind Cave Canyon to the park boundary fence. The canyon, with its steep limestone walls and dead trees, provides the best opportunity in the park for bird-watching. Be especially vigilant for cliff swallows, great horned owls, and red-headed and Lewis woodpeckers. Deer, least chipmunks, and other small animals also are attracted to the sheltered environment of the canyon. Even though you could probably do a round-trip tour of this trail in less than an hour and a half, be sure to spend more time here to observe the wildlife. *Easy.* ✉ *Wind Cave National Park* ✛ *Trailhead: east side of Hwy. 385, 1 mile north of southern access road to visitor center* ⊕ *www.nps. gov/wica.*

VISITOR CENTERS

Wind Cave Visitor Center

VISITOR CENTER | The park's sole visitor center is the primary place to get park information and embark on cave tours. Located on top of the cave, it has three exhibit rooms, with displays on cave geology and exploration, prairie ecology and management, and Native American culture. The center also hosts ranger programs and has an auditorium that presents the film, *Wind Cave, Two Worlds.* Other than vending machines, there's no coffee or snacks here or elsewhere in the park. ✉ *26611 U.S. 385, Hot*

Hats Off to the Cave

Native Americans knew of Wind Cave long before cowboys Jesse and Tom Bingham stumbled on it when they heard air whistling through the rocky opening. Legend goes that the airflow was so strong that it knocked Tom's hat clean off his head. Jesse came back a few days later to show the trick to some friends, but it didn't happen quite as he'd planned. The wind, now flowing in the opposite direction, stole Jesse's hat and vacuumed it into the murky depths of the cave.

Springs ✛ *Off U.S. 385, 3 miles north of park's southern border* ☎ *605/745–4600* ⊕ *www.nps.gov/wica.*

🛍 Shopping

Wind Cave National Park Store

BOOKS | The only retail establishment on park grounds, this bookstore sells trail maps, guides to the Black Hills, and books on the geology and history of Wind Cave and neighboring Jewel Cave. ✉ *Wind Cave Visitor Center, U.S. 385, Wind Cave National Park* ☎ *605/745–4600* ⊕ *www.nps.gov/wica.*

🏃 Activities

Many visitors come to Wind Cave solely to descend into the park's underground passages. While there are great ranger-led tours for casual visitors—and more daring explorations for experienced cavers—the prairie and forest above the cave shouldn't be neglected.

Common Cave Terms

Sound like a serious spelunker with this cavemen cheat sheet for various *speleothems* (cave formations).

Boxwork: Composed of interconnecting thin blades that were left in relief on cave walls when the bedrock was dissolved away.

Cave balloons: Thin-walled formations resembling partially deflated balloons, usually composed of hydromagnesite.

Flowstone: Consists of thin layers of a mineral deposited on a sloping surface by flowing or seeping water.

Frostwork: Sprays of needles that radiate from a central point that are usually made of aragonite.

Gypsum beard: Composed of bundles of gypsum fibers that resemble a human beard.

Logomites: Consist of popcorn and superficially resemble hollowed-out stalagmites.

Pool Fingers: Deposited underneath water around organic filaments.

Stalactites: Carrot-shape formations formed from dripping water that hang down from a cave ceiling.

Stalagmites: Mineral deposits from dripping water built up on a cave floor.

8

Wind Cave National Park

BIKING

Bikes are prohibited on all of the park's trails and in the backcountry. Cyclists may ride on designated roads, and on the 124-mile Centennial Trail, once it passes the park's northern border.

BIRD-WATCHING
Rankin Ridge

BIRD WATCHING | See large birds of prey here, including turkey vultures, hawks, and golden eagles. ⊠ *Wind Cave National Park ✛ 6 miles north of the visitor center on Hwy. 87* ⊕ *www.nps.gov/wica.*

★ Wind Cave Canyon

BIRD WATCHING | Here's one of the best birding areas in the park. The limestone walls of the canyon are ideal nesting grounds for cliff swallows and great horned owls, while the standing dead trees on the canyon floor attract red-headed and Lewis woodpeckers. As you hike down the trail, the steep-sided canyon widens to a panoramic view east across the prairies. ⊠ *Wind Cave National Park ✛ About ½ mile east of visitor center* ⊕ *www.nps.gov/wica.*

CAMPING

Camping is one of this region's strengths. While there is only one relatively developed campground within the park, there are countless campgrounds in the Black Hills. The public campgrounds in the national forest are accessible by road but otherwise secluded and undeveloped; private campgrounds typically have more amenities, as do some of those in Custer State Park, which has numerous options.

Elk Mountain Campground. If you prefer a relatively developed campsite and some proximity to civilization (the campground is 11 miles north of the town of Hot Springs), Elk Mountain is an excellent choice. Experience the peaceful pine forests and wild creatures of the park without straying too far from the safety of the beaten path. ⊠ *½ mile north of visitor center* ☎ *605/745–4600* ⊕ *www. nps.gov/wica/planyourvisit/campgrounds. htm* ⊊ *62 sites.*

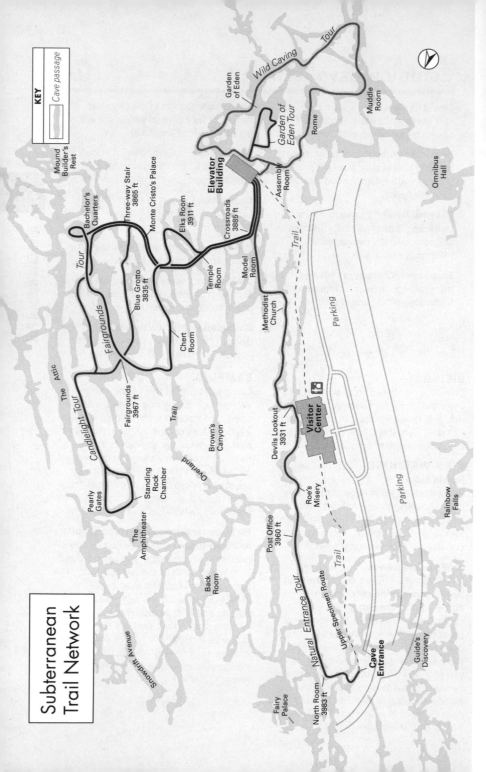

Subterranean Trail Network

KEY

Cave passage

Mound Builder's Rest

Bachelor's Quarters

Three-way Stair 3865 ft

Monte Cristo's Palace

Blue Grotto 3835 ft

Elks Room 3911 ft

Crossroads 3885 ft

Temple Room

Model Room

Chert Room

Fairgrounds 3967 ft

Fairgrounds Tour

The Attic

Candlelight Tour

Brown's Canyon Trail

Overland Trail

Standing Rock Chamber

Pearly Gates

The Amphitheater

Snowdrift Avenue

Back Room

Methodist Church

Elevator Building

Garden of Eden

Garden of Eden Tour

Wild Caving Tour

Assembly Room

Rome

Muddle Room

Omnibus Hall

Trail

Devils Lookout 3931 ft

Visitor Center

Parking

Parking

Roe's Misery

Post Office 3960 ft

Natural Entrance Tour

Upper Specimen Route Trail

Cave Entrance

North Room 3983 ft

Fairy Palace

Guide's Discovery

Rainbow Falls

The lookout tower at Rankin Ridge is a popular place to spot birds of prey, including hawks, turkey vultures, and golden eagles.

EDUCATIONAL OFFERINGS
Adventures in Nature

HIKING & WALKING | Although annual themes and individual program topics vary, nature is always the focus on these seasonally offered adventures held at the visitor center. They're open to children ages 3 to 12, who are divided into groups that participate in age-appropriate activities. ⊠ *26611 Hwy. 385, Wind Cave National Park* ☎ *605/745–4600* ⊕ *www. nps.gov/wica.*

Junior Ranger Program

HIKING & WALKING | **FAMILY** | Visitors of all ages can earn a Junior Ranger badge by completing activities that teach them about the park's ecosystems, the cave, the animals, and protecting the environment. Pick up the Junior Ranger guidebook free of charge at the Wind Cave Visitor Center. ⊠ *26611 Hwy. 385, Wind Cave National Park* ☎ *605/745–4600* ⊕ *www.nps.gov/wica.*

HIKING

There are more than 30 miles of hiking trails within the boundaries of Wind Cave National Park, covering ponderosa forest and mixed-grass prairie. The landscape has changed little over the past century, so a hike through the park is as much a historical snapshot of pioneer life in the 1890s as it is exercise. Be sure to hit the Wind Cave Canyon Trail, where limestone cliffs attract birds like cliff swallows and great horned owls, and the Cold Brook Canyon Trail, a short but fun trip past a prairie-dog town to the park's edge. Besides birds and small animals such as squirrels, you're apt to see deer and pronghorn while hiking, and probably some bison.

Hiking into the wild, untouched backcountry is perfectly safe, provided you have a map (available from the visitor center) and a good sense of direction. Don't expect any amenities, however; bathrooms and a water-bottle filling

Did You Know?

While you can't explore the massive cave system in Wind Cave National Park on your own, you can choose from five ranger-led tours where you'll see all manner of fascinating rock formations—but remember, the cave is 54°F year-round so bring a sweater!

station are available only at the visitor center, and the trails are dirt or gravel. There are no easily accessible sources along the trails, and water from backcountry sources must be treated, so pack your own.

MULTISPORT OUTFITTERS
Granite Sports
HIKING & WALKING | Several miles north of Wind Cave National Park in Hill City, Granite Sports sells a wide range of hiking, climbing, and camping apparel and accessories; they also know the best local guides. This business is not affiliated with Wind Cave National Park. ✉ *201 Main St., Hill City* ☎ *605/574–2121* ⊕ *www.granite-sports.com.*

SPELUNKING
You may not explore the depths of Wind Cave on your own, but you can choose from five ranger-led cave tours, available from June through August; the rest of the year, only one or two tours are available. On each tour you pass incredibly beautiful cave formations, including extremely well-developed boxwork. The least crowded times to visit in summer are mornings and weekends.

The cave is 54°F year-round, so bring a sweater. Note that the uneven passages are often wet and slippery. Rangers discourage those with heart conditions and physical limitations from taking the organized tours. However, with some advance warning (and for a nominal fee) park rangers can arrange private, limited tours for those with physical disabilities. To prevent the spread of white-nose syndrome, a disease that is deadly to bats, don't wear any clothes or shoes or bring any equipment that you might have used to explore other caves (with the exception of the nearby Jewel Cave National Monument).

Curious Crystals

Thin, spidery boxwork and other Wind Cave formations were created when water moved through the cave, dissolving the limestone, then evaporating, leaving behind deposits of crystallized gypsum (calcium sulfate).

Tours depart from the visitor center. A schedule can be found online at ⊕ *www. nps.gov/wica.* To make a reservation, call ☎ *605/745–4600.*

★ Wild Cave Tour
SPELUNKING | For a serious caving experience, sign up for this challenging four-hour tour. After some basic training in spelunking, you crawl and climb through fissures and corridors, most lined with gypsum needles, frostwork, and boxwork. Expect to get dirty. Wear shoes with good traction, long pants, and a long-sleeve shirt. The park provides knee pads, gloves, and hard hats with headlamps. Parents or guardians must sign a consent form for 16- and 17-year-olds. Tours, which are limited to 10 people, are available at 1 pm daily, mid-June through mid-August, and at 1 pm weekends mid-August through Labor Day. Reservations required. *Difficult.* ✉ *26611 U.S. 385, Wind Cave National Park* ✛ *Off U.S. 385, 3 miles north of park's southern boundary* ☎ *605/745–4600* ⊕ *www.nps. gov/wica/planyourvisit/tour-caving.htm* 🎟 *$45.*

Did You Know?

The Black Hills region is known for its spectacular geological formations, as you'll find on the expansive grounds of Wind Cave National Park. The formations often appear to be different colors due to erosion of sedimentary layers. The orange hue seen here is from iron oxide deposits.

What's Nearby

Wind Cave is part of the Black Hills, a diverse region of alpine meadows, ponderosa pine forests, and creek-carved, granite-walled canyons covering 1.2 million acres in western South Dakota and northeastern Wyoming. The Black Hills contrast sharply with the sheer cliffs and dramatic buttes of the Badlands to the north and east, and the wide, windswept plains in most of South Dakota. Though anchored by Rapid City—the largest city for about 350 miles in any direction—the Black Hills' crown jewel is Mount Rushmore National Memorial, visited by more than 2 million people each year. U.S. 385 is the backbone of the Black Hills.

Known as the Mother City of the Black Hills, **Custer** is a great place to stay if you can spend a few days in the southern Black Hills. It's a short drive to world-class attractions like Mount Rushmore, Crazy Horse, Wind Cave National Park, Jewel Cave National Monument, and Custer National Park. With all the lodging, dining and shopping options, you can explore all day and still find time to relax at your hotel or cabin.

Founded in 1877 by prospectors searching for gold deposits, the small town of **Keystone** has an abundance of restaurants, shops, and attractions. To serve the millions of visitors passing through the area, there are more than 900 hotel rooms—that's about three times the town's number of permanent residents.

Chapter 9

CODY, SHERIDAN, AND NORTHERN WYOMING

Updated by
Kelsey Olsen

👁 Sights	🍴 Restaurants	🛏 Hotels	👜 Shopping	🍸 Nightlife
★★★☆☆	★★★☆☆	★★★☆☆	★★☆☆☆	★★☆☆☆

WELCOME TO CODY, SHERIDAN, AND NORTHERN WYOMING

TOP REASONS TO GO

★ **Cody:** Experience Cody's endearing Western style and incomparable museums.

★ **Thermopolis:** Soak in 104°F mineral springs in Wyoming's oldest state park in Thermopolis.

★ **Devils Tower:** Trek around Devils Tower to marvel at one of nature's most impressive monoliths.

★ **State fair:** Watch the rodeo, ride the Ferris wheel, and attend a chuck wagon breakfast at the Wyoming State Fair.

★ **Buffalo:** Check out Buffalo's history museums and the spectacular natural scenery of the surrounding Bighorn Mountains.

1 Thermopolis. The home of popular Hot Springs State Park offers a hint of the hydrothermal features you'll find at Yellowstone National Park, including mineral springs to soak in, without the crowds.

2 Lovell. This otherwise prosaic little town near the Montana border is a base for exploring Bighorn Canyon National Recreation Area.

3 Cody. The eastern gateway to Yellowstone National Park abounds with its own Western charms, including authentic dude ranches, a rollicking nightly rodeo, and exceptional museums.

4 Sheridan. From the largest city in the Powder River Basin, you can learn about the region's complicated Native American and cowboy history at several historic sites.

5 Big Horn. Home to the superb ranching exhibits of the Brinton Museum, this unincorporated hamlet offers easy access to the rugged Bighorn National Forest.

6 Buffalo. Stroll through the engaging historic downtown and museums of this fabled community in the eastern foothills of the scenic Bighorn Mountains.

7 Gillette. Northeastern Wyoming's largest and fastest-growing city and supply center lies at the edge of the Black Hills and is a hub of energy production with several noteworthy attractions.

8 Devils Tower. America's first national monument rises nearly 900 feet above the surrounding countryside

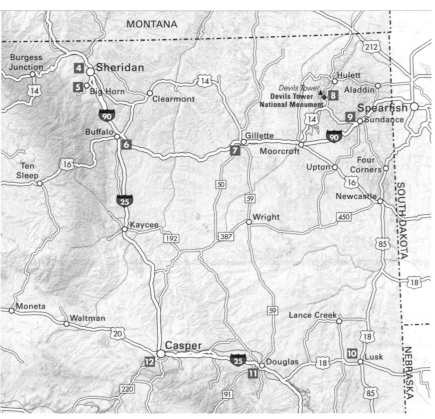

and makes for a fascinating short hike (only 1% of visitors make the technical climb to the top).

9 Sundance. This friendly little Black Hills town with an excellent history museum and a few colorful saloons gave the Sundance Kid his nickname.

10 Lusk. Learn about a key aspect of frontier history at the impressive Stagecoach Museum in this small high-plains town near the Nebraska border.

11 Douglas. Every August, the Wyoming State Fair draws thousands to this bustling railroad town on the North Platte River with some engaging history museums.

12 Casper. The state's second largest city is home to the exceptional National Historic Trails Interpretive Center and Tate Geological Museum and has an eclectic array of shops and restaurants.

Pine-carpeted hillsides and snowy mountain summits give way to windswept prairies and clean-flowing rivers where the Great Plains meet the mighty Rocky Mountains. Northern Wyoming's epic landscape is replete with symbols of the American frontier: the ranch, the rodeo, and the cowboy. Most settlements have no more than a few hundred people; only three—Casper, Gillette, and Sheridan—surpass 15,000 residents.

It may be that no state in the union exalts cowboy life as Wyoming does. The concept of the dude-ranch vacation—where urban folk learn to rope, ride, and rodeo with weathered ranchers and professional cattle drivers—started in northern Wyoming, at the still popular Eatons' Guest Ranch, 18 miles outside Sheridan in the town of Wolf. Numerous other guest ranches are strewn across the grassy plains here, from the dusty prairies east of Cody to the alpine meadows of the Big Horn Mountains. Most Big Horn–area dude ranches run pack trips into these high, rugged peaks, sometimes for days at a time. If you prefer a warm bed to sleeping under the stars, you'll find plenty of distinctive hotels and inns in the region's larger communities, especially Cody, the eastern gateway to Yellowstone National Park.

The outdoors is northern Wyoming's primary draw. Take the time to appreciate the wide-open spaces before you: take a hike, go fishing, ride a bike, or get out into the snow. Much of this territory is just as empty as it was when the first white people arrived here two centuries ago. Even though Europeans settled in Wyoming as early as 1812, the state's population remains the smallest in the nation, at just under 580,000 permanent residents. But many who have dwelt in this place have been history-makers. This part of Wyoming has a rich and storied past that encompasses icons such as gunslingers, gamblers, miners, mule skinners, and warriors. Some of the most famous (and infamous) figures of the Old West passed through here, including Buffalo Bill Cody, Wild Bill Hickok, Calamity Jane, Chief Washakie, Butch Cassidy, and the Sundance Kid, the latter of whom took his name from one of the region's towns.

MAJOR REGIONS

Rich in Native American history, Old West flavor, and natural wonders, the broad **Big Horn Basin** is flanked by the Absaroka and Owl mountains to the west and the Big Horns to the east. The Bighorn River flows north along the eastern edge of the basin and up into Montana. Here, straddling the two states, is Bighorn Canyon National Recreation Area; most of the recreation area lies in Montana, but the southern portion is easily accessible in Wyoming via Highway 37, using the small ranching town of **Lovell** as a base, and has much to offer visitors. **Cody,** with about 10,200 residents, is the largest community between the Big Horn Mountains and Yellowstone National Park, a convenient base with several first-rate attractions that's popular with visitors on their way to the natural treasures farther west. At the southern end of Big Horn Basin, **Thermopolis** is famous for its curative mineral springs, which you can experience in Hot Springs State Park.

The rolling grassland of the **Powder River Basin,** in the northeastern corner of Wyoming, is the ancestral homeland of the Lakota Sioux. On its western edge the Big Horn Mountains are both a popular winter recreational area and a beautiful backdrop for the communities of **Sheridan, Big Horn,** and **Buffalo.** As you drive east the mountains give way to coal mines—particularly around the small city of **Gillette**—oil fields, and family ranches, many of which were established in the 19th century by Basque sheepherders. Now one of the least-populated parts of America, the basin encompasses the vast Thunder Basin National Grasslands. The Black Hills—home to iconic **Devils Tower National Monument** and the small outdoorsy town of **Sundance**—border the Powder River Basin to the east, where a couple of hundred thousand acres of Black Hills National Forest spill out of South Dakota into Wyoming.

Sweeping down from the Colorado Rockies into the very center of Wyoming, the North Platte River was a key waterway for emigrants because its valley was one of the few places where wagons could safely cross the mountains. A deep pioneer legacy survives here, where several trails converged along the Platte and Sweetwater rivers and snaked through South Pass. Some of the travelers put down roots, and the **North Platte River Valley** remains one of Wyoming's important agricultural areas. Much of this area is cattle country, for one simple reason: it's flat, dry, and relatively treeless. The bustling city of **Casper** is the biggest settlement, while to the east lie the high plains ranching and agricultural towns of **Douglas** and **Lusk.** Today a hefty share of central Wyoming's wealth derives from its deposits of oil, uranium, and bentonite.

Planning

Getting Here and Around

AIR

The region has four small airports—Casper–Natrona County International Airport, Gillette's Northwest Wyoming Airport, Sheridan County Airport, and Cody's Yellowstone Regional Airport—with regularly scheduled commercial service to just two cities, although both of them are hubs. Delta Air Lines serves Casper and (in summer only) Cody from Salt Lake City. United Airlines flies from Denver into Casper, Cody, Gillette, and Sheridan.

CONTACTS Casper–Natrona County International Airport. ✉ *8500 Airport Pkwy., Casper* ☎ *307/472–6688* ⊕ *www. iflycasper.com.* **Northeast Wyoming Regional Airport.** ✉ *2000 Airport Rd., Gillette* ☎ *307/686–1042* ⊕ *www.iflygillette. com.* **Sheridan County Airport.** ✉ *908 W. Brundage La., Sheridan* ☎ *307/674–4222*

⊕ *www.sheridancountyairport.com.*
Yellowstone Regional Airport. ⊠ *2101
Roger Sedam Dr., Cody* ☎ *307/587–5096*
⊕ *www.flyyra.com.*

CAR

Many people drive across northern
Wyoming en route to visit the wonders
of Yellowstone National Park, in the
state's northwest corner. Try not to let
the empty spaces between towns and
the wide-open road tempt you to speed
through the region too quickly. Give
yourself enough time to check out the
region's many intriguing attractions, and
to overnight in both the small and larger
towns in the region. If you're headed into
Wyoming from the east along Interstate
90, be sure to stop in Sundance and
make the short detour north to Devils
Tower National Monument. The towns
of Gillette, Buffalo, and Sheridan are
good places to spend the night and have
some excellent museums, too. Take
either U.S. 14 or U.S. 16 through the
mountains and stretch your legs in the
Cloud Peak Wilderness Area, a prime
spot for outdoor recreation, whether it's
a 15-minute hike or a daylong ski trip.
West of the Big Horns, the two highways
meet up near Basin; from here, U.S. 14
is a straight shot to Cody and U.S. 310
is a scenic route through the arid plains
around Lovell.

An alternative route for those interested
in pioneer trails and stagecoach routes is
to head south from Buffalo via Interstate
25 to the eastern Wyoming towns of
Casper, Douglas, and Lusk. They lie in
flatter landscape and—with the exception of Casper—offer less in the way of
visitor services, but this is where you'll
find the National Historic Trails Interpretive Center, Fort Fetterman State Historic
Site, and other notable attractions. From
here, head back north through dramatic
Wind River Canyon on U.S. 20 to Thermopolis, then continue northeast into
the Big Horns on U.S. 16 or northwest

toward Cody and Yellowstone National
Park via Highway 120.

Because the territory in this part of
the world is so sparsely populated, it's
almost impossible to find gas and repair
shops at your convenience. There are
few towns along the major routes here,
even the interstates, so it's prudent to
start out any trip with a full tank of gas
and never to let the tank dip to below
half full. Many small towns lack 24-hour
credit-card gas pumps, and it's uncommon to find a gas station open past the
early evening outside of Gillette, Sheridan, Casper, and Cody. If you're driving
in a particularly remote region, it's wise
to take along extra water. Although the
communities here employ great fleets of
snowplows in the winter, it can sometimes take them time to clear the upper
elevations. Some passes in the Big
Horns close entirely from as early as mid-November to as late as late May. Keep in
mind, too, that locals are used to driving
in a little snow and ice, so plows come
out only if accumulations are substantial.
Plan ahead, and note also that with the
region's current energy-production boom,
it can sometimes be difficult to get
last-minute hotel reservations, especially
in summer.

Hotels

Just as diverse as the area's landscape,
which fades from small Western cities
into vast expanses of open prairie and
forested mountains, are its accommodations. In the population centers along the
interstates, budget and midrange chain
lodgings are the norm, but you'll also
find a smattering of historic stone inns
decorated with buffalo skins and Victorian
furniture. Move beyond these larger
communities, however, and you can
find sprawling guest ranches alongside
cold mountain-fed creeks. In the higher
elevations, look for charming bed-and-
breakfasts on mountain slopes with

broad alpine vistas. And in a few historic towns, Cody in particular, you can find some interesting independent properties, from century-old hotels to inexpensive mom-and-pop motels and roadside cabin compounds. Even most simple budget accommodations offer good Wi-Fi and flat-screen TVs, but you will encounter some remote dude ranches and inns where Wi-Fi is spotty and cell service nonexistent; check in advance if this is important to you.

CAMPING

The opportunities to camp in this region are almost limitless. There are countless campgrounds in the Big Horns, and a few in the prairies below. Most of the public land within the national forests and parks is open for camping, provided that you don't light any fires. Keep in mind when selecting your campsite that the majestic peaks of the Big Horns are home to black bears and mountain lions.

Restaurants

In comparison to more touristy or trendy parts of the Rockies—like Bozeman, Jackson, and even laid-back Laramie—northern Wyoming remains behind the curve when it comes to the kind of dining that most food-driven travelers go out of their way for, the exception being steak houses that dole out impressive cuts of regionally raised beef, elk, bison, and trout, and small-town saloons and taverns where you can find tasty burgers, tacos, fried chicken, and other pub fare along with increasingly good selections of craft beer. In the larger communities along the interstates, chain restaurants dominate the landscape, but you will also find some independent Italian and Mexican restaurants, and a variety of Asian eateries, too. In smaller towns, home-style taverns and diners are the main options, but it's becoming increasingly easier to find a hip brewpub,

coffeehouse, Thai restaurant, or even a bistro with a seasonal menu.

HOTEL AND RESTAURANT PRICES

⇨ *Restaurant and hotel reviews have been shortened. For full information, visit Fodors.com. Restaurant prices are for a main course at dinner, excluding sales tax of 4%–6% (Wyoming only). Hotel prices are for two people in a standard double room in high season, excluding service charges and 4%–11% tax.*

What It Costs			
$	$$	$$$	$$$$
RESTAURANTS			
under $12	$12–$20	$21–$30	over $30
HOTELS			
under $125	$125– $175	$176– $300	over $300

When to Go

People come to experience northern Wyoming in all four seasons—sometimes all in the same week. The weather here is notoriously difficult to predict, as warm Chinook winds can shoot January temperatures into the 70s and freak storms can drop snow in July. On the whole, however, the area enjoys pleasantly warm summers and refreshingly snowy winters. Most travelers visit between June and September, a great time to pursue most outdoor activities. Others come to ski or snowmobile the pristine powder of the Big Horn Mountains in winter.

Temperatures in both seasons can be extreme, however. Thermometers often register a week of triple digits in August in the lower elevations. Snow begins to blanket the mountain slopes in late September and begins to recede only in late May, resulting in the seasonal closure of even some major roads over high-elevation mountain passes—always check conditions and forecasts when traveling in northern Wyoming this time of year. Spring, especially in the mountains, is sometimes nothing more than a week or two of rain and wind between the last winter snowfall and the warm sunshine of summer. Autumn, on the other hand, is full of pleasantly warm days, cooler nights, and vivid foliage. Additionally, the only crowds to fight are small pockets of hunters, anglers, and local leaf peepers.

Thermopolis

132 miles east of Dubois; 85 miles southeast of Cody; 130 miles northwest of Casper.

Native Americans, particularly the Shoshone, considered Thermopolis's hot mineral springs and surrounding land neutral territory. In 1896 they ceded the ground to the U.S. government as a "gift of the waters," stipulating that the springs remain available for the free use of all people. The springs and surrounding countryside were turned into Hot Springs State Park the following year, and you still take the waters gratis at the bathhouse, but a couple of commercially operated pools in the park charge a fee. A 10- to 15-minute walk west of the state park, the community's historic downtown has undergone a bit of a revitalization in recent years and has a handful of inviting eateries and shops. Thermopolis is also a good base for exploring scenic Wind River Canyon to the south and the Bighorn Mountains to the northeast.

GETTING HERE AND AROUND
On U.S. 20 between Shoshoni and Worland, Thermopolis is also the southeastern terminus of Highway 120, which leads northwest to Meeteetse and Cody. You'll need a car to get here, but downtown and the western side of the state park are easily managed on foot.

VISITOR INFORMATION
CONTACTS Thermopolis-Hot Springs Chamber of Commerce. ⊠ *220 Park St., Thermopolis* ☎ *307/864–3192* ⊕ *www. thermopolis.com.*

Sights

★ Hot Springs State Park
HOT SPRING | FAMILY | The land that became Wyoming's first state park in 1897 has always been sacred to Native Americans because of its healing natural hot springs. You can partake of these waters by soaking indoors or outside at the free 104°F mineral pools at the State Bath House, which is a central feature of this impressive 1,104-acre park that's also home to two waterparks (which charge admission fees) with more indoor and outdoor hot mineral pools, waterslides, and other amusements. You can also hike or bike on 6 miles of trails, view the park's sizable bison herd, and traipse across a swinging suspension bridge that traverses the Big Horn River, offering views of the dramatic travertine mineral terraces. ⊠ *220 Park St., Thermopolis* ☎ *307/864–2176* ⊕ *wyoparks.wyo.gov* 🎫 *$12 per vehicle ($7 for Wyoming residents).*

Legend Rock State Petroglyph Site
RUINS | About 30 miles northwest of town, this state park preserves 92 petroglyph panels and more than 300 figures carved into a 1,312-foot-long sheer cliff face anywhere from a few hundred to 10,000 years ago. Interpretative trails lead to and describe the petroglyphs, and there's an informative visitor center and a picnic shelter as well. ⊠ *2861 W. Cottonwood Rd., Thermopolis* ☎ *307/864–2176* ⊕ *wyoparks.wyo.gov* 🎫 *$12 per vehicle ($7 for Wyoming residents).*

Ten Sleep
TOWN | One of the region's quirkiest and most scenic little towns, Ten Sleep lies on the eastern edge of the Bighorn Basin, along scenic U.S. 16 before it

Wyoming's first state park, Hot Springs State Park, preserves the natural mineral pools and travertine terraces along the Big Horn River as well as over 1,000 acres of the surrounding area.

climbs over 9,666-foot Powder Horn Pass en route to Buffalo. It's well worth a stop to stroll through the tiny downtown where you can stop by one of the friendly taverns to grab a bite to eat or drink. A favorite of locals and tourists alike is one of Wyoming's best craft breweries, **Ten Sleep Brewing**, on the west side of town. ⊠ *U.S. 16, Ten Sleep* ✛ *60 miles northeast of Thermopolis, 65 miles southwest of Buffalo* ⊕ *www.townoftensleep.com.*

★ Wyoming Dinosaur Center

RUINS | FAMILY | Among the nearly 60 dinosaur skeletons displayed at this nonprofit museum and research center is the winged "Thermopolis Specimen," the only Archaeopteryx exhibited outside of Europe, and "Stan," one of the most complete *Tyrannosaurus rex* skeletons in the world, measuring 35 feet long and weighing in at nearly 6 tons. Special full-day programs allow kids and adults to try their hand at paleontology by digging in one of the several active dinosaur sites nearby (some 10,000 dinosaur bones have been excavated in the vicinity

since 1993). Tours of the dig site are also offered daily in summer. ⊠ *110 Carter Ranch Rd., Thermopolis* ☎ *307/864–2997* ⊕ *www.wyomingdinosaurcenter.org* ⊠ *From $12.*

★ Wyoming Whiskey

DISTILLERY | The complex small-batch whiskeys produced by this craft distiller have received high marks from top spirits critics around the world. Fans of premium, barrel-age bourbon now flock to tiny Kirby (population 75, 13 miles north of Thermopolis) to sample and buy these smooth sippers and tour the handsome silo-style building in which they're distilled. ⊠ *120 E. Main St., Kirby* ☎ *307/864–2116* ⊕ *www.wyomingwhiskey.com.*

Restaurants

★ Bangkok Thai

$$ | THAI | You could be forgiven for not expecting to find legit Thai food in northern Wyoming, much less in tiny Thermopolis, but this simple downtown eatery

turns out flavorful, authentic curries and stir-fries. Choose from the usual proteins along with duck and lamb—the pineapple curry, pad Thai, and orange chicken are among the specialties. **Known for:** friendly, welcoming service; plenty of vegetarian options; mango sticky rice. $ *Average main: $16* ✉ *512 Broadway St., Thermopolis* ☎ *307/864–3565* ⊕ *bangkok-thai. business.site* ⊗ *Closed Sun. and Mon.*

One Eyed Buffalo Brewing

$$ | **AMERICAN** | As notable for its well-crafted IPA, whiskey stout, and peach blonde ale as for serving reliably good comfort fare, this convivial brew-pub occupies a stately stone building downtown. You could make a meal of a few apps—calamari, potato skins, loaded nachos—or tackle one of the hearty entrées, like the charbroiled garlic lime shrimp skewers or a Cajun-rubbed spicy blackened burger. **Known for:** large, enclosed patio; first-rate craft beer; boneless rib-eye steaks. $ *Average main: $15* ✉ *528 Broadway St., Thermopolis* ☎ *307/864–3555* ⊕ *www.oneeyedbuf-falobrewingwyo.com.*

☕ Coffee and Quick Bites

Audra's Copper Coo

$ | **CAFÉ** | This charming organic coffee shop is tucked away just a short drive from downtown Thermopolis, making it a delightful hidden gem. Housed in a cozy building with a distinctive red door and an inviting outdoor patio, Audra skillfully crafts a diverse selection of specialty organic coffees, teas, and sweet treats. **Known for:** wide assortment of gluten-free treats; freshly made cold brew; exceptionally friendly service. $ *Average main: $6* ✉ *225 Clark St., Thermopolis* ☎ *904/874–2560* ⊕ *www.coppercoo.com* ⊗ *Closed Sun.*

Hotels

★ Best Western Plus Plaza Hotel

$$$ | **HOTEL** | Located in Hot Springs State Park on the banks of the Big Horn River and by far the best hotel in town, this handsomely restored 1918 hotel has spacious rooms with attractive Western log-cabin-style furnishings, and suites have fireplaces. **Pros:** restored historic building; great location inside Hot Springs State Park; seasonal pool and year-round mineral springs hot tub. **Cons:** a 15-minute walk from downtown dining; bare-bones breakfast; no elevator. $ *Rooms from: $220* ✉ *116 E. Park St., Thermopolis* ☎ *307/864–2939* ⊕ *www.bestwestern. com* ⇆ *46 rooms* ⦿ *Free Breakfast.*

Nightlife

★ Ten Sleep Brewing

BREWPUBS | Nestled beneath a red-rock cliff an hour northeast of Thermopolis in the quirky cowboy town of Ten Sleep, this terrific craft brewery makes for a fun side trip or an enjoyable stop while driving through the Cloud Peak Wilderness area. And if you'd rather not drive back after partaking of a local ale, you're welcome to pitch a tent on the property's seasonal campground. ✉ *2549 U.S. 16, Ten Sleep* ☎ *307/366–2074* ⊕ *www. tensleepbrewingco.com.*

Activities

RAFTING

Wind River Canyon Whitewater

WHITE-WATER RAFTING | **FAMILY** | This popular outfitter leads white-water floats—lasting from a couple of hours to a full day with lunch—down the Wind River. Scenic floats and fly-fishing trips are also offered. ✉ *210 Hwy. 20, Thermopolis* ☎ *307/864–9343* ⊕ *www.windrivercan-yon.com* ⊟ *From $79.*

Lovell

49 miles northeast of Cody; 102 miles north of Thermopolis.

This small ranching community makes a convenient, if bare-bones, base for exploring the Bighorn Canyon National Recreation Area, which spans the Wyoming–Montana border. On the Wyoming side, Bighorn Lake is popular with boaters, anglers, and bird-watchers; most of the recreation area's main attractions, including the majority of the Pryor Mountain Wild Horse Range, lie on the Montana side.

GETTING HERE AND AROUND
Lovell lies at the junction of U.S. 14A and Highway 310, about an hour's drive northeast of Cody. Note that U.S. 14A east of town is steep and winding, though beautiful; it's closed due to snow from late November through late May. If you're traveling east toward Sheridan during these months, you'll have to detour south and then east via U.S. 14.

Sights

Bighorn Canyon National Recreation Area
NATIONAL PARK | To learn about this 120,000-acre national park wilderness that was established in 1966 following the creation of Yellowtail Dam, visit the South District's Cal Taggart Visitor Center in Lovell, Wyoming, where you can view geological and historical exhibits on the area, as well as a film about the canyon. Two shorter movies, one on the Pryor Mountain wild horses and the other about Medicine Wheel National Historic Landmark (east of Lovell), are shown on request, and there's a small gift and bookshop. The park's South District is reached by heading north on Highway 37 east of Lovell and encompasses Horseshoe Bend Marina, Devil Canyon Overlook, 12 hiking trails (in both Wyoming and southern Montana), four historic ranches that you can tour on your own, and three campgrounds. The park's North District is 120 miles north, in Fort Smith, Montana. Note that part of the park near Lovell is adjacent to Yellowtail Wildlife Management Area at the southern end of Bighorn Lake. More than 155 species of birds—including white pelicans, pheasants, bald eagles, and great blue herons—inhabit the 19,202-acre refuge, as do numerous other animal species, including red fox, mule deer, and cottontail rabbits. ⊠ *20 U.S. 14A, Lovell* ☎ *307/548–5406* ⊕ *www.nps.gov/bica* ☒ *Free.*

★ **Medicine Wheel/Medicine Mountain National Historic Landmark**
INDIGENOUS SIGHT | A ring of rocks 75 feet in diameter, this ancient site is the best preserved of nearly 150 Native American stone wheels found in Wyoming, South Dakota, Montana, Alberta, and Saskatchewan. Evidence such as the 28 spokes (one for each day of the lunar cycle) leading from the edge of the wheel to a central cairn has persuaded some that the wheel was an ancient spiritual observatory much like England's Stonehenge may have been. To protect the area, access to the wheel is restricted to foot travel; it's a 1½-mile hike on a well-maintained unpaved road to the site from the parking lot (people with disabilities may drive to the site). Up in the Big Horn Mountains, at an elevation of 9,642 feet, the site affords views of the entire Big Horn Basin. Dress warmly, as it's cool up here, even in summer. ⊠ *Forest Rd. 12, off U.S. 14A, Lovell* ✛ *25 miles east of Lovell* ☎ *307/674–2600* ⊕ *www.fs.usda. gov/bighorn* ☒ *Free* ☉ *Road closed mid-Sept.–mid-June.*

Pryor Mountain Wild Mustang Center
WILDLIFE REFUGE | At this interpretive center inside a modern log cabin just up the road from the Bighorn Canyon Visitor Center, photos, printed materials, and helpful volunteers introduce people to the 120 to 140 mustangs that roam over 38,000 acres of range. Although

The best preserved of nearly 150 Native American wheels is at Medicine Wheel/Medicine Mountain National Historic Landmark and may be 10,000 years old.

many of the mustangs will likely be up in the mountains, you're almost sure to see some right from the paved road, Highway 37, which is a short drive east of the center. This could include White Cloud, a stallion featured in two books by Ginger Kathrens. Tours are offered in the summer (May 15 through September). ✉ 1106 Rd. 12, off U.S. 14A, Lovell ☎ 307/548–9453 ⊕ www.pryormustangs. org ✍ Tours from $240 per person ⏱ Closed weekdays Nov.–May.

🍴 Restaurants

Mustang Cafe & Smokehouse

$$ | **AMERICAN** | This homey diner-style grill is a local favorite, where folks come for the kind of down-home cooking that sticks to your ribs: biscuits and gravy, ham-steak eggs Benedict, chicken-fried steaks, and "mustang meatloaf" (dinner only). For lighter meals, consider the several sandwich and salad options. **Known for:** down-home hospitality; steak-and-eggs breakfasts; build-your-own burgers.

$ *Average main: $16* ✉ *483 Shoshone Ave., Lovell* ☎ *307/548–9370* ⊕ *www. mustang-cafe.com.*

Hotels

★ Wyoming High Country Lodge

$$$ | **B&B/INN** | **FAMILY** | Set amid verdant meadows at 9,000 feet elevation in the mountains of Bighorn National Forest, this peaceful compound of attractively outfitted contemporary cabins along with several spacious lodge rooms offers a charming, distinctive alternative to the handful of budget motels in downtown Lovell, about 30 miles away. **Pros:** tranquil location; close to a variety of outdoor activities, from hiking to snowshoeing trails; rates include well-prepared meals. **Cons:** no cell service and spotty Wi-Fi; main road to Lovell is closed in winter; extremely remote setting. $ *Rooms from: $220* ✉ *Forest Rd. 13, Lovell* ☎ *307/529–0914* ⊕ *www.wyhighcountry. com* ⇄ *12 rooms* ⏹ *All-Inclusive.*

⊕ Performing Arts

★ Hyart Theatre

FILM | This striking mid-century modern 975-seat movie palace built in 1950 by film lover Hyrum Bischoff received a full restoration in the early 2000s, thanks to efforts by local volunteers who raised funds to restore the building's spacious lobby, sunken lounge, sloping balcony, and neon painter's palette high above the marquee. Both current and classic films are shown here. ⊠ *251 E. Main St., Lovell* ☎ *307/548–7021* ⊕ *www.hyarttheatre.com.*

Cody

60 miles southeast of Red Lodge, MT; 52 miles east of Yellowstone.

Founded in 1896 and named for Pony Express rider, army scout, Freemason, and entertainer William F. "Buffalo Bill" Cody, Cody lies just east of the Absaroka Range in the high plains of the Bighorn Basin, about a mile above sea level. As the eastern gateway community for Yellowstone National Park, this town of about 10,000 sees a sharp influx of visitors during the summer months when Yellowstone's eastern entrance is open. But at any time of year, this easygoing community with a bustling downtown historic core offers plenty to see and do. Five superb museums under one roof make up the outstanding Buffalo Bill Historical Center, an affiliate of the Smithsonian, and the town exemplifies America's Western style and sensibility with its dude ranches and colorful shops specializing in everything from cowboy hats, landscape paintings, and hand-carved furniture to local beef jerky and outerwear. Part of the fun in Cody is sauntering down Sheridan Avenue, stopping by the Irma Hotel (built in 1902 by Buffalo Bill and named for his daughter) for an ice-cold beer, and attending the summertime nightly rodeo.

GETTING HERE AND AROUND

The North Fork Highway—as the region's span of U.S. 14/16/20 leading west to Yellowstone is known—follows the North Fork of the Shoshone River past barren rock formations strewn with tumbleweeds, then enters lush forests and green meadows as the elevation increases roughly 3,000 feet in 70 miles. Cody is within easy reach of the Shoshone National Forest, the Absaroka Range, the Washakie Wilderness, and the Buffalo Bill Reservoir. Although you can explore downtown, shops, restaurants, and even the Buffalo Bill Historical Center on foot, you need a car to explore the surrounding region.

TOURS

Cody Trolley Tours

BUS TOURS | FAMILY | These hour-long tours on vintage trolley–style buses travel 22 miles and cover Cody's history dating back to the late-19th-century era of Buffalo Bill and Annie Oakley. Tours start at the fabled Irma Hotel, named for Buffalo Bill's daughter, and take in historic sites, scenery, wildlife, and other natural attractions. On summer evenings (except Sunday) at 6, stay to watch the amusing if cheesy 30-minute mock gunfights staged outside the Irma. ⊠ *Irma Hotel, 1192 Sheridan Ave., Cody* ☎ *307/527–7043* ⊕ *www.codytrolleytours.com* ⊠ *From $28.*

★ Red Canyon Wild Mustang Tours

SPECIAL-INTEREST TOURS | From mid-May through mid-October, the well-established outfitter offers morning and early-evening 2½- to 3-hour van excursions out to see the famed wild mustangs who roam freely throughout the McCullough Peaks Herd Management Area, about 20 miles east of Cody. You'll be provided binoculars, and in addition to seeing these stately creatures running and playing in this vast badlands wilderness, you may spy pronghorn, coyotes, prairie dogs, and raptors. Red Canyon's tour menu also includes photography and Yellowstone adventures. ⊠ *Cody*

Part of the Buffalo Bill Center of the West, the Plains Indian Museum focuses on the tribes of the Northern Plains, including the Arapaho, Lakota, Crow, Cheyenne, Blackfeet, and Pawnee.

Wyoming Adventures, 1119 12th St., Cody ☎ *307/587–6988, 800/293–0148* ⊕ *www.codywyomingadventures.com* 🎫 *From $65.*

VISITOR INFORMATION

CONTACTS Cody Country Chamber of Commerce. ✉ *836 Sheridan Ave., Cody* ☎ *307/587–2777* ⊕ *www.codychamber. org.*

 Sights

Bridal Veil Falls Trail

TRAIL | The best hiking in the region tends to be west of Cody and includes this moderately strenuous 4-mile round-trip trek to a dramatic waterfall in Shoshone National Forest, northwest of town. The trail starts out on a wide road that parallels the Clarks Fork of the Yellowstone River before cutting up alongside Falls Creek—the steep final half-mile to the falls will get your blood flowing. ✉ *Cody* ⊹ *Trailhead: end of Hwy. 292, 11 miles west of Hwy. 120.*

★ Buffalo Bill Center of the West

OTHER ATTRACTION | FAMILY | This extraordinary "five-in-one" complex, an affiliate of the Smithsonian Institution, contains the Buffalo Bill Museum, the Whitney Western Art Museum, the Plains Indian Museum, the Cody Firearms Museum, and the Draper Natural History Museum. All are well organized and mount superb exhibitions in their respective subject areas. The flagship Buffalo Bill Museum puts into context the life, era, and activities of its (and its town's) namesake, William F. "Buffalo Bill" Cody (1846–1917), whose numerous careers included guide, scout, showman, and entrepreneur. If you want to understand how the myth of the American West developed, this is the place to come. The other four museums—there's also a research library—are equally absorbing. Plan to spend at least four hours here—and to discover that this isn't enough time to take it all in. Luckily, your admission ticket is good for two days over a seven-day period. ✉ *720 Sheridan Ave., Cody* ☎ *307/587–4771*

⊕ *www.centerofthewest.org* ◪ *$23*
⊙ *Closed Mon.–Wed. in Dec.–Feb.*

Buffalo Bill State Park

STATE/PROVINCIAL PARK | About 6 miles
west of downtown on U.S. 14, you'll pass
through the Shoshone Canyon Tunnel
(the state's largest, at 2.8 miles) and
emerge at the northeast end of Buffalo
Bill Reservoir, which was formed in 1910
by the construction of a 350-foot-tall
dam. The reservoir, which is popular for
boating and fishing, forms the heart of
Buffalo Bill State Park, which also has a
campground and picnic area. Just after
exiting the tunnel, you can also stop by
the visitor center operated by the U.S.
Bureau of Reclamation. Here you can
peer over the immense dam from a
viewing platform and explore exhibits
detailing this impressive feat of engineering and the region's natural and human
history. ⊠ *4192 N. Fork Hwy., Cody*
☏ *307/587–9227* ⊕ *wyoparks.wyo.gov/*
index.php/places-to-go/buffalo-bill ◪ *$12*
per vehicle ($7 for Wyoming residents)
⊙ *Visitor center closed Oct.–Apr.*

★ By Western Hands

SPECIALTY MUSEUM | In a restored down-
town hardware store, this nonprofit juried
artisan guild and museum is devoted
to preserving and showcasing Cody's
profound influence on Western design
as it applies to furniture and decorative
arts. Inside the galleries you can view
pieces by legendary Cody designers like
Edward Bohlin who with his eventual
Hollywood connections become known
as the "saddle maker to the stars," and
furniture craftsman Thomas Molesworth.
Additionally, the showrooms are filled
with ornately crafted works by the guild's
members, who continue to further
Cody's Western design legacy. ⊠ *1007*
12th St., Cody ☏ *307/586–1755* ⊕ *www.*
bywesternhands.org ⊙ *Closed Sun. and*
Mon.

★ Chief Joseph Scenic Byway

SCENIC DRIVE | In 1877, Chief Joseph and
hundreds of the Nez Perce tribe executed

a daring escape from the pursuing United
States Cavalry, who aimed to forcibly
relocate the tribe from their ancestral
lands to a reservation. Fearing capture by
the U.S. Army, Chief Joseph made the
audacious decision to lead his people
on an arduous 1,800-mile journey into
Canada. Their path took them through
what is now Yellowstone National Park,
where the group found themselves
cornered by the U.S. Cavalry. Rather
than surrender, they defied all odds by
descending through a narrow gorge previously considered impassable. Although
the tribe was ultimately apprehended a
mere 40 miles from the Canadian border,
the Chief Joseph Scenic Byway now
stands as a poignant tribute to this heroic
escape. This 46-mile highway winds
through open meadows, pine forests,
and breathtaking vistas, creating an
unforgettable journey through history and
nature. ⊠ *Cody.*

★ Cody Dug Up Gun Museum

HISTORY MUSEUM | The intriguing name of
this museum fully states its unusual mission: to collect and exhibit firearms and
other weapons that have been exhumed
from the earth (or, in the case of an old
musket, entombed inside a tree trunk).
The knowledgeable owner has amassed
some 1,400 items, ranging from rust-
ed-out mid-19th-century revolvers to
rifles used by mobsters in the 1930s.
Every artifact in this fascinating museum
seems to tell a story that might otherwise have been lost to obscurity. ⊠ *1020*
12th St., Cody ☏ *307/587–3344* ⊕ *www.*
codydugupgunmuseum.com ⊙ *Closed*
Oct.–Apr.

★ Heart Mountain Interpretive Center

HISTORIC SIGHT | From 1942 through 1945,
nearly 14,000 Japanese Americans were
relocated to this hastily constructed
incarceration center—one of ten located
throughout the country—at the foot of
Heart Mountain, about 13 miles north
of Cody. Evicted from their West Coast
homes through an executive order issued

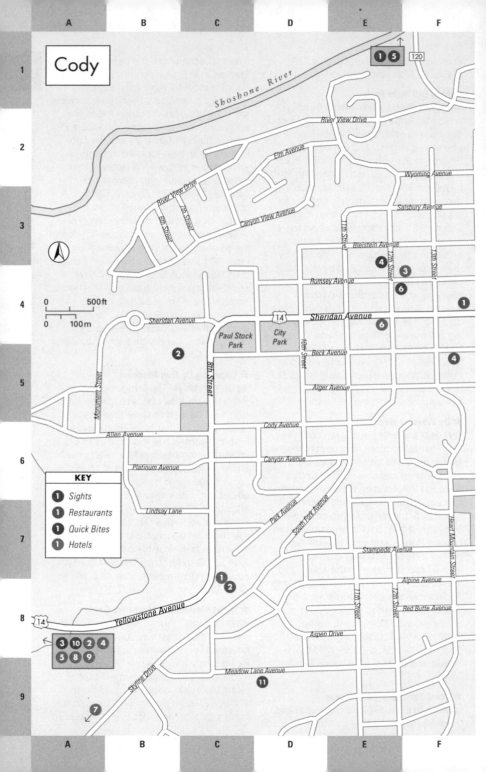

Cody

Shoshone River

River View Drive

Elm Avenue

Wyoming Avenue

River View Drive

Salsbury Avenue

Canyon View Avenue

8th Street

7th Street

11th Street

12th Street

Bleistein Avenue

4 **3**

Rumsey Avenue

6

Sheridan Avenue

6

1

Sheridan Avenue

2

Paul Stock Park

City Park

10th Street

Beck Avenue

4

Alger Avenue

Allen Avenue

Cody Avenue

Canyon Avenue

Platinum Avenue

KEY

1 Sights

1 Restaurants

1 Quick Bites

1 Hotels

Lindsay Lane

Park Avenue

South Fork Avenue

Stampede Avenue

Heart Mountain Street

Alpine Avenue

11th Street

12th Street

Red Butte Avenue

1 **2**

Yellowstone Avenue

3 **10** **2** **4**

5 **8** **9**

Aspen Drive

Skyline Drive

Meadow Lane Avenue

11

7

1 **5** 120

Monument Street

14

500 ft

100 m

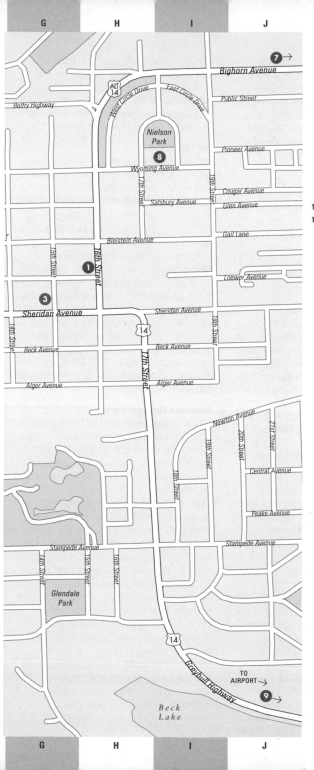

Sights ▼

1 Bridal Veil Falls Trail E1
2 Buffalo Bill Center of the West ... B5
3 Buffalo Bill State Park A8
4 By Western Hands E3
5 Chief Joseph
  Scenic Byway E1
6 Cody Dug Up Gun Museum E4
7 Heart Mountain
  Interpretive Center J1
8 Historic Cody
  Mural & Museum I2
9 Meeteetse Museums J9
10 Old Trail Town A8
11 Shoshone National Forest D9

Restaurants ▼

1 Cody Steak House F4
2 8th Street at the Ivy C8
3 Pat's Brew House G4
4 Trailhead Bar | Grill |
  Wood Fired Pizza F5

Quick Bites ▼

1 The Station by Cody Coffee H4

Hotels ▼

1 Best Western Premier Ivy
  Inn & Suites C7
2 Bill Cody Ranch A8
3 Chamberlin Inn E4
4 Cody Cowboy Village A8
5 The Cody Hotel A8
6 Irma Hotel E4
7 K3 Guest Ranch
  Bed and Breakfast A9
8 Rimrock Dude Ranch A8
9 Yellowstone Valley Inn
  & RV A8

by President Franklin D. Roosevelt shortly after the bombing of Pearl Harbor, the residents lived in small, tightly spaced barracks. In 2011, a museum opened on the long-abandoned site. At the Heart Mountain Interpretive Center, you can learn about this shameful episode of U.S. history by watching an impactful short film and touring both permanent and rotating exhibits that use photographs, letters, news clippings, and other artifacts to bring to life the powerful and inspiring stories of Heart Mountain's inhabitants, who persevered in the face of anti-Asian prejudices and unjust conditions. ⊠ *1539 Rd. 19, Powell* ☎ *307/754–8000* ⊕ *www.heartmountain.org* ✉ *$12* ◷ *Closed Sun.–Wed. in Oct.–mid-May.*

Historic Cody Mural & Museum

PUBLIC ART | The Cody Mural, at the Church of Jesus Christ of Latter-day Saints, presents a larger-than-life artistic interpretation of Mormon settlement in the West. Edward Grigware painted the 36-foot-diameter scene on the domed ceiling in the 1950s. A small museum contains historical artifacts as well as interactive kiosks where visitors can explore their genealogy. ⊠ *1719 Wyoming Ave., Cody* ☎ *307/587–3290* ⊕ *codymural.com.*

Meeteetse Museums

HISTORY MUSEUM | Anchoring the historic downtown of this small community named for the Shoshone term for "meeting place," this collection of three free history museums is well worth a stop on the scenic drive along Highway 120 between Cody and Thermopolis. The most interesting of the group is the Charles Belden Museum of Western Photography, which occupies a 1919 former drugstore and contains photographs, Molesworth furniture, and other items that once belonged to the renowned early-20th-century photographer, whose works are featured prominently in *Life* magazine and *National Geographic.* The Bank Museum and Meeteetse Museum occupy other nearby vintage buildings and present engaging exhibits on the region's human and natural history. ⊠ *1947 State St., Meeteetse* ☎ *307/868–2423* ⊕ *www.meeteetsemuseums.org* ◷ *Closed Sun. and Mon.*

Old Trail Town

MUSEUM VILLAGE | FAMILY | A short drive west of downtown near the Stampede Park rodeo grounds, you can tour this authentic museum that comprises about two dozen historic buildings from Wyoming's frontier days—including a saloon and a blacksmith's shop—many of them housing photos, pioneer, and Native American artifacts. The complex is situated on Cody's original townsite, and there are about 100 horse-drawn vehicles on display and a small original cemetery that serves as a resting place for some of the region's famous mountain men, including Liver Eatin' Johnson. ⊠ *1831 Demaris Dr., Cody* ☎ *307/587–5302* ⊕ *www.oldtrailtown.org* ✉ *$12* ◷ *Closed Oct.–mid-May.*

Shoshone National Forest

FOREST | Established in 1891 as the country's first designated national forest, this 2.4-million-acre tract of alpine woodland, sagebrush flats, and verdant meadows extends west from Cody to Yellowstone National Park (which is roughly the same size). At both the headquarters south of downtown and the Clarks Fork, Greybull, and Wapiti Ranger Districts office on the west side of Cody (⊠ *203A Yellowstone Ave., Cody*), you can pick up maps, buy permits, and obtain advice on the many activities you can pursue in the forest—hiking, camping, fishing, mountain biking, horseback, snowshoeing, snowmobiling, cross-country skiing—and the best places to enjoy them. Some highlights include the well-preserved ghost town of Kirwin, about 65 miles south of Cody, and the Clarks Fork of the Yellowstone, a designated Wild and Scenic River during its 20½-mile course through the forest about 30 miles northwest of Cody.

Old Trail Town preserves some two dozen buildings and about 100 horse-drawn vehicles from the early frontier days on Cody's original townsite.

✉ *Headquarters, 808 Meadow Lane Ave., Cody* ☎ *307/527–6241* ⊕ *www.fs.usda. gov/shoshone* 🎫 *Free* ☉ *Office closed weekends.*

Restaurants

Cody Steak House

\$\$\$ | STEAK HOUSE | This handsome, clubby-feeling restaurant along Cody's main drag is a favorite of carnivores, but there's also a surprising variety of internationally inspired seafood and poultry dishes, including prawns sautéed in a butter, white wine, and garlic sauce. Among the meatier fare, consider the 16-ounce hand-cut buffalo rib-eye or 18-ounce T-bone Angus beef steak. **Known for:** prodigious portions; one of Cody's better wine and beer selections; homemade bread pudding topped with ice cream. ⑤ *Average main: \$25* ✉ *1367 Sheridan Ave., Cody* ☎ *307/586–2550* ⊕ *www.codysteakhouse.com* ☉ *Closed Sun. No lunch.*

8th Street at the Ivy

\$\$\$ | AMERICAN | A short drive west of downtown, this high-ceilinged regional American restaurant with deep booth seats and big windows looking out toward the mountains draws guests but also quite a few locals for breakfast, lunch, and dinner. Regionally sourced meat and seafood are the stars here, including fall-off-the-bone short ribs and flavorful seared ahi tuna. **Known for:** well-curated wine list; creative entrée-size salads; locally sourced, hand-cut steaks. ⑤ *Average main: \$21* ✉ *1800 8th St., Cody* ☎ *307/578–8444* ⊕ *www.8thstreetattheivy.com.*

Pat's Brew House

\$\$ | AMERICAN | Stainless steel brewing vats are the centerpiece of the bar and dining area of this friendly downtown Cody brewpub that also has a large dining patio. The kitchen turns out tasty gastropub fare, from chicken lollipops brined in house beer to amber beer-battered fish and chips, and the ales on tap include both house brews and plenty of visiting craft beers from around the country. **Known for:** Irish-influenced classics like shepherd's pie; hefty cheeseburgers; seasonal brews. $ *Average main: $16* ✉ *1019 15th St., Cody* ☎ *307/586–5410* ⊕ *www.patsbrewhousewy.com* ⊗ *Closed Mon. and Tues.*

★ **Trailhead Bar | Grill | Wood Fired Pizza**
$$$ | **MODERN AMERICAN** | This hip neighborhood bistro a block off Cody's main drag serves some of the most creative fare in town—consider the starter of fried brussels sprouts with a kicky bourbon honey molasses gastrique, followed by grilled elk medallion served on a bed of black truffle and parmesan risotto. There's also a full bar serving first-rate craft cocktails, like the mezcal and basil margarita. **Known for:** live music some evenings; wood-fired pizzas and grills; weekend brunches with a Bloody Mary bar. $ *Average main: $21* ✉ *1326 Beck Ave., Cody* ☎ *307/578–8510* ⊕ *www.trailheadcody.com* ⊗ *Closed Mon.*

 Coffee and Quick Bites

★ **The Station by Cody Coffee**
$ | **CAFÉ** | The downtown branch of this excellent small-batch coffee roaster with a flagship café by the airport occupies a colorfully restored and decorated former gas station with a landscaped patio. In addition to well-crafted espresso drinks, both locations of Cody Coffee offer an extensive menu of sweet and savory crepes and triple-decker sandwiches. **Known for:** egg-ham-cheddar breakfast crepes; banana–bacon–peanut butter dessert crepes; mocha lattes. $ *Average main: $10* ✉ *919 16th St., Cody* ☎ *307/578–6661* ⊕ *www.codycoffee.com* ⊗ *No dinner.*

Hotels

Best Western Premier Ivy Inn & Suites
$$$$ | **HOTEL** | This newer and more upscale member of the ubiquitous Best Western brand offers among the most spacious and attractive rooms in town, in a handsome stone-and-timber building on the west side of town, making it convenient for making the 50-mile drive to Yellowstone's East Entrance. **Pros:** spacious and stylish rooms; good gym and indoor heated pool; full-service restaurant and bar. **Cons:** no pets; not within walking distance of town; on busy road. $ *Rooms from: $303* ✉ *1800 8th St., Cody* ☎ *307/587–2572* ⊕ *www.bestwestern.com* ⇥ *70 rooms* ⊗ *No Meals.*

★ **Bill Cody Ranch**
$$$ | **B&B/INN** | **FAMILY** | A classic Wyoming dude ranch that retains its rugged and historic 1925 ambience, this sprawling property in the high country west of Cody offers inclusive packages that include meals in the Western-theme saloon and restaurant as well as daily four-hour horseback rides or less expensive lodging-only rates. **Pros:** stunning surroundings; guided horseback rides for guests of all ages; tasty food (with dining-inclusive packages available). **Cons:** no cell service; no laundry facilities; a half-hour drive from Cody. $ *Rooms from: $215* ✉ *2604 North Fork Hwy., Cody* ☎ *307/587–2097* ⊕ *billcodyranch.com* ⇥ *16 rooms* ⊗ *No Meals.*

★ **Chamberlin Inn**
$$$$ | **B&B/INN** | Named for Agnes Chamberlin, who opened a boardinghouse on this spot in 1904, this artfully restored redbrick inn a block off Cody's main street counts Ernest Hemingway and Marshall Field among its many past guests. **Pros:** filled with historic accents and furnishings; welcoming service; short walk to downtown dining. **Cons:** no elevator; summer rates are quite steep; breakfast is a bit meager. $ *Rooms from: $329* ✉ *1032 12th St., Cody* ☎ *307/587–0202* ⊕ *www.chamberlininn.com* ⇥ *22 rooms* ⊗ *Free Breakfast.*

Cody Cowboy Village
$$$ | **HOTEL** | The simple but attractive single and duplex log cabins here are pure Western, right down to the pitched-roof

The Chief Joseph Scenic Byway is one of the best drives in Wyoming, which roughly follows the route the Nez Perce used to evade the U.S. Army in 1877.

beam ceilings, iron bedsteads with horseshoe designs, and bathroom wallpaper printed with boots and cowboy hats. **Pros:** large outdoor hot tub; cabin porches have nice mountain views; close to Cody Nite Rodeo and Old Trail Town. **Cons:** not within walking distance of town; breakfast is a bit meager; closed fall through spring. ⑤ *Rooms from: $239 ✉ 203 W. Yellowstone Ave., Cody* ☎ *307/587-7555* ⊕ *www.codycowboyvillage.com* ⊘ *Closed Nov.–early May* ⇴ *50 rooms* ⑩ *Free Breakfast.*

The Cody Hotel
$$$$ | **HOTEL** | This upscale low-rise hotel on the west side of town abounds with comfy perks, including an indoor pool and hot tub, a well-equipped gym, a patio with a fire pit, and an inviting lobby and library with a fireplace. **Pros:** attractive common spaces; very good breakfast included; close to rodeo and Old Trail Town. **Cons:** on a busy road; rooms feel a bit cookie-cutter; a couple of miles west of downtown. ⑤ *Rooms from: $309 ✉ 232 W. Yellowstone Ave., Cody* ☎ *855/746-3431* ⊕ *www.thecody.com* ⇴ *75 rooms* ⑩ *Free Breakfast.*

Irma Hotel
$$$ | **HOTEL** | Built in 1902 by Buffalo Bill and named for his daughter, this striking downtown property retains both its frontier charm and rough edges, with period furniture and pull-chain commodes in many rooms, a large restaurant open all day, and an elaborate cherry-wood bar said to have been a gift from Queen Victoria to Buffalo Bill. **Pros:** tons of character, history, and charm; on-site restaurant serving breakfast, lunch, and dinner; in the heart of downtown historic district. **Cons:** in a busy area; a bit dated; restaurant is just so-so. ⑤ *Rooms from: $220 ✉ 1192 Sheridan Ave., Cody* ☎ *307/587-4221* ⊕ *www.irmahotel.com* ⇴ *40 rooms* ⑩ *No Meals.*

★ K3 Guest Ranch Bed and Breakfast
$$$ | **B&B/INN** | **FAMILY** | Here you have the chance to stay at an authentic, upscale 33-acre Western ranch, just a 15-minute drive from downtown Cody, without

spending a mint or having to contend with a minimum-stay requirement. **Pros:** truly one-of-a-kind accommodations; a variety of tours around the region can be arranged; campfire breakfasts included in the rates. **Cons:** remote setting down well-posted gravel road; 15-minute drive into town; sheepherder's wagons have baths in separate location (though still private). ⑤ *Rooms from: $249* ✉ *30 Nielsen Tr., Cody* ☎ *307/587–2080* ⊕ *www. k3guestranch.com* ⤴ *7 rooms* ❍❙ *Free Breakfast.*

★ Rimrock Dude Ranch

$$$$ | **RESORT** | **FAMILY** | One of the oldest ranches on the North Fork of the Shoshone River, Rimrock offers horseback-riding adventures into Shoshone National Forest's surrounding mountains, excursions to Cody Nite Rodeo and nearby Yellowstone National Park, fishing in a trout-stocked pond, rafting trips, and more—all for one set weekly price. **Pros:** cabins have exceptional views; lots of fun adventures and activities for families; friendly, gracious owners. **Cons:** half-hour drive from nearest town (Cody); one-week minimum stay; credit cards accepted for initial deposit only (not final balance). ⑤ *Rooms from: $396* ✉ *2728 N. Fork Hwy., Cody* ☎ *307/587–3970* ⊕ *www.rimrockranch.com* ☽ *Closed Oct.–May* ⤴ *9 cabins* ❍❙ *All-Inclusive* ⤳ *7-night min.*

Yellowstone Valley Inn & RV

$$$ | **HOTEL** | About 15 miles west of Cody and 30 miles east of Yellowstone National Park's east entrance, this sprawling property offers basic accommodations in a mountain setting on the Shoshone River. **Pros:** rustic but clean rooms; beautiful location between Cody and Yellowstone; pet-friendly. **Cons:** bar crowd can be noisy; same for live music in dance hall several nights a week; a half-hour drive to downtown Cody. ⑤ *Rooms from: $195* ✉ *3324 N. Fork Hwy., Cody* ☎ *877/587–3961* ⊕ *www.yellowstonevalleyinn.com* ⤴ *35 rooms* ❍❙ *No Meals.*

Nightlife

Cassie's

LIVE MUSIC | A trip to Cody isn't complete without a chance to scoot your boots to live music at this rollicking supper club festooned with Western memorabilia and mounted taxidermy. The tunes are a mix of classic country, the live band's Western originals, and today's hits. Opened in 1922 by a local "sportin' lady," Cassie's today has three levels with a steak house restaurant, a dance floor, and three bars. ✉ *214 Yellowstone Ave., Cody* ☎ *307/527–5500* ⊕ *www.cassiessteakhousecody.com.*

★ Silver Dollar Bar

BARS | Offering one of the region's largest selections of draft and bottled beer, a large patio, and live music on weekend evenings, this festive downtown bar is a fun place to shoot pool and meet the locals. The pub fare is pretty tasty, too. ✉ *1313 Sheridan Ave., Cody* ☎ *307/527–7666* ⊕ *www.facebook.com/ silverdollarcody.*

Performing Arts

On Thursday evenings from early July through late August, free jazz, country, and pop concerts and ice cream socials are held at **City Park on Sheridan Avenue.**

Cody Cattle Company Dinner Show

CONCERTS | **FAMILY** | Feast on a chuck wagon dinner of barbecue brisket or chicken (and freshly baked brownies for dessert) during these hour-long country-western shows that end at 7:30 pm, just in time for you to make the five-minute stroll to the Cody Night Rodeo, just down the road. Shows take place late May through mid-September. ✉ *1910 Demaris St., Cody* ☎ *307/272–5770* ⊕ *www.thecodycattlecompany.com.*

Dan Miller's Cowboy Music Revue

CONCERTS | From June through September, head to this redbrick performance space behind the Irma Hotel to watch the popular country-cowboy variety shows led by Dan Miller, a popular radio and TV host, singer, and actor. ⊠ *1601 Stampede Ave., Cody* ☎ *307/899–2799* ⊕ *www. cowboymusicrevue.com.*

★ Wild West Spectacular
THEATER | FAMILY | Held in downtown's historic 1937 Cody Theater, this colorful western revue—held five nights weekly from late June through early August— uses comedy, dance, and music to tell the tale of Buffalo Bill Cody. ⊠ *1171 Sheridan Ave., Cody* ☎ *307/527–9973* ⊕ *www. codywildwestshow.com.*

⬤ Shopping

Sheridan Avenue, Cody's main drag, is a great place to browse and shop among its many Native American and Western-theme shops. Most carry high-quality goods, but if ever in doubt, confirm that the item you're interested in is made from natural rather than artificial materials.

ART GALLERIES
★ Big Horn Galleries
ART GALLERY | At one of Wyoming's most respected galleries of Western and wildlife art, you'll find sculptures and paintings by more than 75 artists, including James Bama, Chris Navarro, and Vic Payne. ⊠ *1167 Sheridan Ave., Cody* ☎ *307/527–7587* ⊕ *www.bighorngalleries.com.*

Cody Country Art League
ART GALLERY | Adjacent to the Cody Country Chamber of Commerce visitor center, this expansive and eclectic gallery displays paintings, wood carvings, bronzes, and pottery by both established and emerging regional artists, and at a wide range of prices. ⊠ *836 Sheridan Ave., Cody* ☎ *307/587–3597* ⊕ *www. codycountryartleague.com.*

Open Range Images
ART GALLERY | This gallery in a handsome historic downtown building carries the work of some of the area's top photographers. Wyoming's wildlife, flora, and landscapes provide the primary scenes, but less traditional themes also are presented. ⊠ *1201 Sheridan Ave., Cody* ☎ *307/587–8870* ⊕ *www.openrangeimages.com.*

★ Simpson Gallagher Gallery
ART GALLERY | Stop by this respected gallery to browse contemporary representational art by Harry Jackson, Kathy Wipfler, T.D. Kelsey, Kang Cho, and Greg Scheibel, as well as works for 19th- and early-20th-century luminaries like Carl Rungius. ⊠ *1161 Sheridan Ave., Cody* ☎ *307/587–4022* ⊕ *www.simpsongallaghergallery.com.*

BOOKS
Legends Bookstore
BOOKS | In addition to stocking a wide selection of travel books, histories, and outdoor guides to Wyoming and the Rockies, this friendly independent bookshop is a good bet for distinctive local gifts. ⊠ *1350 Sheridan Ave., Cody* ☎ *307/586–2320* ⊕ *www.legendsbooks. com.*

CLOTHING
★ Custom Cowboy Shop
CLOTHING | Stock up on top-quality western apparel, ranging from felt hats and bolo ties for men to women's paisley Western shirts and wool jackets; and there's a huge selection of custom gear for horses. You'll also find an impressive array of Western books and household and kitchen goods. ⊠ *1286 Sheridan Ave., Cody* ☎ *800/487–2692* ⊕ *www. customcowboyshop.com.*

Wayne's Boot Shop
SHOES | The Lundvall family has operated this beloved purveyor and repairer of traditional cowboy as well as hiking and work boots, plus many other brands

of casual shoes. You'll find top boot brands like Nocona, Allen's, Justin, and Tony Lama. ✉ *1250 Sheridan Ave., Cody* ☎ *307/587–5234* ⊕ *www.waynesbootshop.com.*

FOOD
Wyoming Buffalo Company

FOOD | Stop by for buffalo-meat products, such as sausage and jerky, in addition to specialty foods such as huckleberry honey, barbecue sauces, candy, and other products made in the Cowboy State. ✉ *1270 Sheridan Ave., Cody* ☎ *307/587–8708* ⊕ *www.wyobuffalo.com.*

SPORTING GOODS
★ Sunlight Sports

SPORTING GOODS | Whether you're prepping for a spring rafting trip or a summer hike at Yellowstone, or it's winter snowshoeing and skiing you're planning, this exceptionally well-stocked shop is an excellent place to pick up gear and advice on where to pursue your adventures. You'll find a terrific selection of camping supplies, outerwear, and backpacks by top brands like Osprey, Burton, Mountain Hardware, and Smartwool. ✉ *1131 Sheridan Ave., Cody* ☎ *307/587–9517* ⊕ *www.sunlightsports.com.*

 Activities

CAMPING
Buffalo Bill State Park–Lakeshore Campground.

Located on the shores of the Buffalo Bill Reservoir, nine miles west of Cody, the Lakeshore Campground is open year-round and offers RV and tent sites. Many guests enjoy boating on the reservoir and exploring nearby Yellowstone National Park. ✉ *4192 Northfork Hwy, Cody* ☎ *307/587–9227* ⊕ *wyoparks.wyo.gov/index.php/places-to-go/buffalo-bill.*

Cody KOA. At breakfast, this campground 3 miles southeast downtown, serves free pancakes. With water jets

at the pool, a giant checkers set, bike rentals, basketball courts, horseshoe pits, and a playground, this venue with RV and tent sites as well as cabins caters to families. ✉ *5561 Greybull Hwy., Cody* ☎ *307/587–2369, 800/562–8507* ⊕ *www.codykoa.com.*

Ponderosa Campground. This centrally located Cody campground offers 20 acres of cabins, tent sites, full hook-up RV sites, and even teepees to stay in. There is free Wi-Fi, cable TV, and a large gift shop and convenience store on site. ✉ *1815 8th St., Cody* ☎ *307/587–9203* ⊕ *www.codyponderosa.com.*

CANOEING, KAYAKING, AND RAFTING
Gradient Mountain Sports

CANOEING & ROWING | This outfitter provides kayaking excursions, as well as instruction, sales, and rentals of single and tandem kayaks, stand-up paddleboards, and canoes. ✉ *1390 Sheridan Ave., Cody* ☎ *307/587–4659* ⊕ *www.gradientmountainsports.net* 🛶 *Guided trips from $50.*

River Runners

WHITE-WATER RAFTING | Book two-hour and half-day whitewater rafting adventures on the Shoshone River with this popular outfitter. Excursions are offered from late May through August. ✉ *730 Yellowstone Ave., Cody* ☎ *307/527–7238* ⊕ *www.riverrunnersofwyoming.com* 🛶 *Guided trips from $47.*

Wyoming River Trips

WHITE-WATER RAFTING | FAMILY | The folks at Wyoming River Trips arrange several family-friendly rafting and float excursions along the Shoshone River, lasting from one hour to a full day. ✉ *233 Yellowstone Ave., Cody* ☎ *307/587–6661* ⊕ *www.wyomingrivertrips.com* 🛶 *Guided trips from $75.*

FISHING

Casting into a clear stream or placid blue lake is a popular pastime all over Wyoming, with good reason: the waters of the entire state teem with trout, pike, whitefish, catfish, and bass of all kinds. Most fishing enthusiasts stick to the land near Yellowstone, leaving the blue-ribbon streams of northern Wyoming relatively underutilized. The Bighorn River, Powder River, Crazy Woman Creek, Keyhole Reservoir, and Buffalo Bill Reservoir are all excellent angling venues.

Fly-fishing is especially big here, and there's no shortage of outfitters to equip you, both in the towns and in the wilderness. Anyone with a pole—be it an experienced fly-fisher or novice worm dangler—is respected out here. All the same, if you're a beginner, you'd do well to hire a guide. Tackle-shop staff can direct you to some good fishing spots, but you're more likely to find the choicest locations if you have an experienced local at your side.

Wyoming Trout Guides

FISHING | Shop for fishing tackle and gear, gain insights into some of the best local fishing locations, or book a guided half-day or full-day fishing trip with Wyoming Trout Guides, Cody's only fully permitted fishing outfitter and guide service. All equipment is provided for guided fishing trips; you just need to get your fishing license. ⊠ 1210 Sheridan Ave., Cody 📞 307/578–8217 ⊕ wyomingtroutguides. com ⌛ Half-day trips from $500; full-day trips from $650.

HORSEBACK RIDING
Cedar Mountain Trail Rides

HORSEBACK RIDING | FAMILY | From mid-May through mid-September, book trail rides of an hour to a full day through this company that also offers pack trips themed around fishing and photography. ⊠ W. Yellowstone Ave., Cody ⊹ 1 mile west of rodeo grounds 📞 307/527–4966 ⌛ One-hour rides from $40 (cash only).

Cody Country Outfitters and Guides Association

HORSEBACK RIDING | This local organization of Cody-area outfitters is a useful resource for planning horseback, hunting, fishing, and ranching adventures. ⊠ Cody ⊕ www.codycountryoutfitters.com.

RODEOS
★ Cody Nite Rodeo

RODEO | FAMILY | Begun in 1938 and billing itself the world's longest-running nightly rodeo, this festive, family-friendly summer spectacle at Stampede Park is less flashy and more endearingly intimate than bigger rodeos around the region, such as Cheyenne Frontier Days. Kicking off at 8 pm each evening from June through August, the Cody Nite Rodeo offers kids' competitions, such as goat roping and junior barrel racing, in addition to the regular adult events. Over early July's Independence Day weekend, the annual Cody Stampede features a full long weekend of events at the same venue. ⊠ Stampede Park, 519 W. Yellowstone Ave., Cody 📞 307/587–5155 ⊕ www.codystampederodeo.com ⌛ From $23.

SKIING
Wood River Ski Touring Park

SKIING & SNOWBOARDING | In Shoshone National Forest's peaceful and secluded Wood River valley near Meeteetse, southeast of Cody, this Nordic ski area has 25 kilometers of groomed trails, a warming hut, rentals, and a basic cabin for overnight rentals. Use of the trails is free, but donations are appreciated. Check in with the town recreation office in downtown Meeteetse; the ski area is another 22 miles southwest. ⊠ Meeteetse Recreation District Office, 1010 Park Ave., Meeteetse 📞 307/868–2603 ⊕ www.meetrec.org.

Sheridan

147 miles north of Casper via I–25 and I–90.

Proximity to the Big Horn Mountains and Bighorn National Forest makes Sheridan (population 19,095) a good base for hiking, mountain biking, skiing, snowmobiling, and fly-fishing, and the small city's European-flavored cowboy heritage makes it an interesting stop for history buffs. Soon after trappers built a simple cabin along Little Goose Creek in 1873, the spot became a regional railroad center. Cattle barons, many of them English and Scottish noblemen, established ranches that remain the mainstay of the economy. Sheridan still has ties to Britain's aristocracy; in fact, Queen Elizabeth II herself has paid the town a visit. Recently, coal mines and oil wells to the east have brought much-needed jobs and tax income to this community of fewer than 20,000 residents.

The biggest annual draw remains the **Sheridan WYO Rodeo,** held each July since 1931. It's more than the nightly rodeo exhibitions of calf-roping and bronc busting. The whole town opens up for events and amusements, including a giant carnival. Besides the high professional standards of the riders and ropers who come, what distinguishes this rodeo is that it's also an important Native American event. There's always a Native American Pow Wow and Dance as well as the World Championship Indian Relay Race. For rodeo aficionados, this is one of the year's highlights.

GETTING HERE AND AROUND

Whether you're arriving from the northwest or east via Interstate 90 or the south via Interstate 25, the Big Horn Mountains provide an impressive backdrop to this decidedly Western town. Take the East 5th Street or East Brundage Lane exits to Big Horn Avenue and the downtown core, and then park and walk to a host of art galleries, Western stores, restaurants, and outfitters. You'll also discover more than 90 pieces of artwork on permanent display throughout downtown.

VISITOR INFORMATION

Located right off Exit 23 of I–90, this visitor center, which also houses a small museum, is the perfect first stop on your visit to Sheridan. The free museum offers exhibits on Wyoming wildlife, Native American battlefields, historic sites, and a diorama of the Big Horn Mountains. The visitor center has a plethora of free maps, brochures, and information about the area.

CONTACTS Sheridan Visitor Center. ✉ *1517 E. 5th St, Sheridan* ☎ *307/673–7120* ⊕ *www.sheridanwyoming.org.*

 Sights

King's Saddlery

STORE/MALL | Although local cowboy legend Don King died in 2007, his sons still operate King's Saddlery and King's Ropes, where they've been hand-tooling saddles since the 1940s. They also make high-quality equipment for area ranchers and professional rodeo performers. King's has crafted gear for many celebrities, including Queen Elizabeth II. Unless you're in the market for an expensive saddle, what makes this a worthy stop (and a real treat) is found across a small alley directly behind the store, where a small museum is chock-full of Western memorabilia, ranging from more than 400 vintage firearms and handcrafted spurs to historical photographs, wildlife mounts, and arguably the largest collection of Western saddles anywhere. ✉ *184 N. Main St., Sheridan* ☎ *307/672–2702* ⊕ *www.kingssaddlery.com* ⊗ *Closed Sun.*

★ Sheridan Inn

HOTEL | FAMILY | Evidence of the area's old-world ties can be found at the Sheridan Inn, just a few blocks from downtown near the old railroad depot. Modeled after a hunting lodge in Scotland, the 1893 building sports 69 gables in a show of architectural splendor not often seen around these parts. On the National Register of Historic Places, the inn once lured the likes of Herbert Hoover, Will Rogers, and Ernest Hemingway, and Buffalo Bill auditioned performers here for his Wild West Show. The Inn underwent a $4.8 million restoration from 2006 to 2009, employing "green" technologies, and an additional $2.8 million was spent in 2010 to refurbish the 22 guest rooms. The original oak-and-mahogany Buffalo Bill Bar on the main floor is purported to be a gift sent from England by Queen Victoria. ⊠ *856 Broadway St., Sheridan* ☎ *307/674–2178* ⊕ *www.sheridaninn. com.*

Trail End State Historic Site

HISTORIC HOME | A Flemish Revival mansion built in 1913 for John B. Kendrick, cattleman and one of Wyoming's first governors and senators, is now the Trail End State Historic Site. The furnishings and exhibits in the home are designed to depict early-20th-century ranching on the Plains. Highlights include elegant hand-carved woodwork and a third-floor ballroom. ⊠ *400 Clarendon Ave., Sheridan* ☎ *307/674–4589* ⊕ *www.trailend. org* 🎟 *$8.*

🍴 Restaurants

★ Olive

$$$ | ITALIAN | This Italian and Mediterranean restaurant is a delightful surprise, distinguishing itself in a town renowned for its Western cuisine. The intimate and cozy atmosphere beckons you to indulge in the delightful flavors of dishes like spicy shrimp pappardelle and freshly baked Italian cannoli. **Known for:** all

pasta made in-house; an extensive wine collection; hand-rolled black gnocchi. ⑤ *Average main: $28* ⊠ *342 Whitney La., Sheridan* ☎ *307/620–9471* ⊕ *www. facebook.com/OliveWYO* ⊗ *Closed Sun. and Wed.*

P.O. News & Flagstaff Cafe

$$ | AMERICAN | FAMILY | A tobacco store in the front and a casual restaurant in the back, the historic Flagstaff Cafe is one of the longest-running, continually operating businesses in Wyoming. This classic family-style menu offers hearty breakfast and lunch to weary travelers and locals alike. **Known for:** locally sourced Legerski sausage; all hamburgers ground fresh every day by the nearby Sacketts Market; convenient location in the heart of downtown Sheridan. ⑤ *Average main: $19* ⊠ *1 N. Main St., Sheridan* ☎ *307/673–5333* ⊕ *www.facebook.com/FlagstaffCafe* ⊗ *Closed Sun. No dinner.*

Uptown Shabby Eatery & Catering

$$ | FRENCH FUSION | FAMILY | With a farmhouse feel and an eclectic menu, this local favorite serves up iconic classics like skillet mac and cheese, flatbreads, and burgers, each with its own twists. You won't be leaving hungry here with meals like the blackened crab cake eggs bennie or jalapeño popper mac and cheese. **Known for:** the famous blueberry cheesecake burger; weekend breakfast tacos; unique and extensive French toast menu. ⑤ *Average main: $15* ⊠ *330 N. Main St., Sheridan* ☎ *307/763-4133* ⊕ *www.uptownshabbyshack.com.*

☕ Coffee and Quick Bites

Sackett's Market

$$ | SANDWICHES | With a back-to-basics approach to food, Sackett's sells freshly butchered meats and fresh-picked vegetables free from all chemicals, additives, and preservatives. But the market has become equally popular for its delicious sandwiches, salads, and a fresh soup

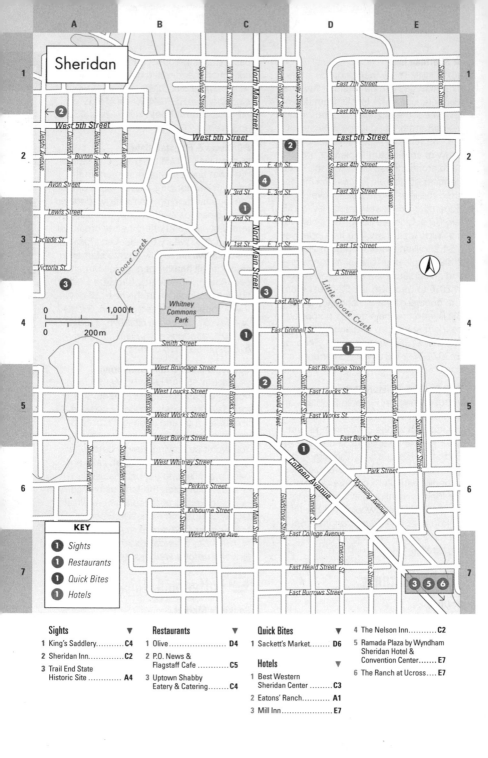

Sheridan

KEY
- ① Sights
- ① Restaurants
- ① Quick Bites
- ① Hotels

Sights ▼
1 King's Saddlery...........**C4**
2 Sheridan Inn.............**C2**
3 Trail End State
  Historic Site **A4**

Restaurants ▼
1 Olive.....................**D4**
2 P.O. News &
  Flagstaff Cafe **C5**
3 Uptown Shabby
  Eatery & Catering.......**C4**

Quick Bites ▼
1 Sackett's Market........**D6**

Hotels ▼
1 Best Western
  Sheridan Center **C3**
2 Eatons' Ranch...........**A1**
3 Mill Inn....................**E7**

4 The Nelson Inn...........**C2**
5 Ramada Plaza by Wyndham
  Sheridan Hotel &
  Convention Center.......**E7**
6 The Ranch at Ucross....**E7**

of the day, all made for take-out. **Known for:** smoked meats made in-house; deli counter modeled after the original in Big Horn Mercantile; all products sourced from the mountain states. ⓢ *Average main: $12* ✉ *184 E. Burkitt St., Sheridan* ☎ *307/672–3663* ⊕ *www.sackettsmarket. com* ☯ *Closed Sun.*

Hotels

Best Western Sheridan Center
$$$ | HOTEL | The rooms at this hotel are popular with tour groups to the region and are typical of chain motels, but some have lodgepole-pine furniture and earth and green tones. **Pros:** good restaurant on premises; friendly and helpful hospitality staff; nice pool area. **Cons:** travelers have complained about a lack of security; unimaginative, albeit free, breakfast options; conventioneers have felt ignored by hotel management. ⓢ *Rooms from: $200* ✉ *612 N. Main St., Sheridan* ☎ *307/674–7421* ⊕ *www.bestwestern. com* ⇆ *139 rooms* ⦿ *Free Breakfast.*

Eatons' Ranch
$$$$ | RESORT | This spread is credited with inventing the dude ranch, back in the late 19th century, and it's still going strong, as well as being a working cattle ranch. **Pros:** a pleasantly rustic experience; plenty of chances to get in the saddle; attentive and friendly staff. **Cons:** with the minimum stay, if you find you don't like ranch life you're stuck for a few days; far from the amenities of downtown; cabins are basic. ⓢ *Rooms from: $325* ✉ *270 Eatons' Ranch Rd., Wolf* ☎ *307/655–9285* ⊕ *www.eatonsranch.com* ☯ *Closed Oct.– May* ⇆ *51 rooms* ⦿ *All-Inclusive.*

Mill Inn
$ | HOTEL | A former flour mill near a bridge has been converted into this inviting small hotel, which is listed on the National Register of Historic Places. **Pros:** near downtown; complimentary breakfast; historic accents with great photography by L.A. Huffman. **Cons:**

some think the inn is overpriced; bathrooms unaccommodating to those with disabilities; all rooms open directly to the outdoors, and those facing the street can be noisy. ⓢ *Rooms from: $95* ✉ *2161 Coffeen Ave., Sheridan* ☎ *307/672–6401, 888/357–6455* ⊕ *www.sheridanmillinn. com* ⇆ *42 rooms* ⦿ *Free Breakfast.*

★ The Nelson Inn
$$$ | HOTEL | FAMILY | Experience the industrial Wild West while based in these spacious suites (almost all over 1,000 square feet) featuring high ceilings, natural light, bold style, and all the modern comforts of home. **Pros:** plenty of room to spread out; attention to detail, with beautiful modern touches in every room; walking distance to downtown, with plenty of shops and dining opportunities. **Cons:** no free breakfast, though each suite has a full kitchen; small and tends to book up quickly in the summer months; no pool or hot tub. ⓢ *Rooms from: $230* ✉ *723 N. Main St., Sheridan* ☎ *307/763–4414* ⊕ *www.thenelsoninn.com* ⇆ *9 suites* ⦿ *No Meals.*

Ramada Plaza by Wyndham Sheridan Hotel & Convention Center
$$ | HOTEL | The soaring atrium of this five-story hotel, which is five minutes from downtown by car, has a waterfall and is filled with overstuffed chairs and couches, as well as Scooter's Sports Bar. With white-and-blue accents and tan walls, the rooms are typical of chain hotels, but most have some Western-style touches, and some look out on the Big Horn Mountains. **Pros:** large and modern; good dining options; a fun and friendly staff. **Cons:** this is a big hotel with a business feel, even though it's not right downtown; breakfast is not included; rooms and ambience have a dated, 1970s feel. ⓢ *Rooms from: $160* ✉ *1809 Sugarland Dr., Sheridan* ☎ *307/218–2076* ⊕ *www.wyndhamhotels.com* ⇆ *212 rooms* ⦿ *No Meals.*

The Ranch at Ucross

$$$ | RESORT | If you're looking to get in touch with yourself—or your traveling companion—this Old West–style ranch on the banks of Piney Creek in the foothills of the Big Horns may well be the place. **Pros:** stay one night, and you'll wish you owned the place; quiet and relaxing; great activities, like horseback riding, on-site. **Cons:** a long way from anywhere; some guests have noted the rooms have a dated appearance; not all rooms have Wi-Fi or TVs. $ *Rooms from: $200 ⊠ 2673 U.S. Hwy. 14, 30 miles southwest of Sheridan, Clearmont ☎ 307/737–2281 ⊕ www.theranchatucross.com ↪ 31 rooms ❀ All-Inclusive.*

 ## Nightlife

Luminous Brewhouse

BREWPUBS | FAMILY | With a focus on being curious with brewing techniques, Luminous Brewhouse has made a name for itself with a solid lineup of staple beers along with fun rotating seasonal beers. Along with beer, there's a stage for live music, including an open mike night every Thursday. Luminous Brewhouse also prides itself on being family-friendly with house-made root beer and more. ⊠ *504 Broadway St., Sheridan ☎ 307/655–5658 ⊕ www.luminousbrewhouse.com.*

Performing Arts

WYO Performing Arts and Education Center

THEATER | Built in 1923 as a vaudeville theater called the Lotus, the WYO Theater was closed and nearly demolished in the early 1980s. A strong show of support from the community saved the building, and now the refurbished art deco structure hosts everything from orchestras and ballets to lectures and Broadway revivals, especially in the summer. ⊠ *42 N. Main St., Sheridan ☎ 307/672–9084 ⊕ www.wyotheater.com.*

 ## Shopping

The suburban malls that have drained so many downtowns are absent in Sheridan; instead, Main Street is lined with mostly homegrown—and sometimes quirky—shops.

Best Out West Antiques

SPECIALTY STORE | In a break from typical gift stores stocked with rubber tomahawks, the Best Out West Mall is a two-story bazaar of Western paraphernalia, with booths hawking everything from spurs to rare books. Some items are new, but most are antiques. ⊠ *109 N. Main St., Sheridan ☎ 307/674–5003.*

Bozeman Trail Gallery

ART GALLERY | A stronghold of frontier culture, the Bozeman Trail Gallery has a varied collection of 19th- and 20th-century art and artifacts from the American West, ranging from vintage Colt revolvers and leather saddles to Cheyenne Sioux moccasins and Navajo rugs. The gallery also maintains a collection of significant Western paintings from artists such as E.W. Gollings and Edward Borein. ⊠ *190 N. Main St., Sheridan ☎ 307/672–3928 ⊕ www.bozemantrailgallery.com.*

Crazy Woman Trading Company

ANTIQUES & COLLECTIBLES | The Crazy Woman Trading Company sells unique gifts and antiques, including deluxe coffees and T-shirts picturing a black bear doing yoga. Lulu McDougal, the store's CEO (and the owners' golden retriever), is usually sleeping near the front door. The store is closed on Sunday. ⊠ *134 N. Main St., Sheridan ☎ 307/672–3939 ⊕ www.crazywomantrading.com.*

Activities

Like every other community on the edge of the Bighorn National Forest, Sheridan abounds with opportunities for outdoor recreation. A love of sports seems to be a common thread among people here, whether they're visitors or locals, winter enthusiasts or sunseekers, thrill hunters or quiet naturalists. Because of Sheridan's proximity to U.S. 14, a mountain highway near hundreds of miles of snowmobile trails and alpine streams, the town is especially popular among sledders in the winter and fly-fishers in the summer and autumn.

CAMPING
Big Horn Mountains KOA Journey. On the banks of Big Goose Creek minutes away from downtown Sheridan is this KOA, a well-developed campground with 45 campsites, a pool, horseshoe pits, and a miniature golf course. ⊠ *63 Decker Rd.* ☎ *307/674–8766.*

FLY-FISHING
Angling Destinations
FISHING | More of a custom adventure company than an outfitter, Angling Destinations arranges multiday fishing trips to some of the most remote locations of Wyoming, Montana, and Idaho, as well as international destinations. ⊠ *7 E. Grinnell Plaza, Sheridan* ☎ *800/211–8530* ⊕ *www.anglingdestinations.com.*

Fly Shop of the Big Horns
FISHING | The full-service store offers rentals, fishing apparel and gear, guided trips on private and public waters, and a fly-fishing school, as well as the largest fly selection in the region. ⊠ *201 N. Main St., Sheridan* ☎ *307/672–5866.*

Big Horn

9 miles south of Sheridan via Hwy. 335.

Now a gateway to Bighorn National Forest, this tree-lined town with mountain views was originally a rest stop for emigrants heading west. An outpost on the Bozeman Trail, which crossed Bozeman Pass, Big Horn City in the mid-19th century was a lawless frontier town of saloons and roadhouses. After pioneers brought their families to the area in the late 1870s, the rowdy community

quieted down. It never officially incorporated, so although it has a post office, fire department, and school, there is no bona-fide city government.

GETTING HERE AND AROUND
Located between the vast Bighorn National Forest and Interstate 90 south of Sheridan, the town of Big Horn can be reached via State Highway 335 south to County Road 28 East. It's a town of just 382 residents; you won't have trouble finding your way around.

 Sights

Bighorn National Forest
FOREST | Big Horn is an access point to the 1.1-million-acre area, which has lush grasslands, alpine meadows, rugged mountaintops, canyons, and deserts. There are numerous hiking trails and camping spots for use in the summer, and it's a popular snowmobiling area in the winter. ⊠ *Ranger station, 2013 Eastside 2nd St., Big Horn* ☎ *307/674–2600* ⊕ *www.fs.usda.gov/bighorn.*

Bozeman Trail Museum
SPECIALTY MUSEUM | **FAMILY** | A hand-hewn-log blacksmith shop, built in 1879 to serve pioneers on their way to the goldfields of Montana, houses the Bozeman Trail Museum, the town's historical repository and interpretive center. The jewel of its collection is the Cloud Peak Boulder, a stone with names and dates apparently carved by military scouts just two days before the Battle of the Little Bighorn, which was fought less than 100 miles to the north in 1876. The staff is very friendly to children, and there are some old pipe organs that kids are encouraged to play. ⊠ *335 Johnson St., Big Horn* ☎ *307/751–4908, 307/751–5741* ⊕ *bhm-mc.org/bozeman-trail-museum* ⛁ *Free* ☉ *Closed weekdays and Sept.–May.*

The Brinton Museum
SPECIALTY MUSEUM | If you're not staying at a ranch and you want to get a look at one of the West's finest, visit the south

Did You Know?

The Cloud Peak Wilderness is one of the most majestic and unspoiled areas in the Bighorn National Forest known for its picturesque lakes and towering peaks. It's fairly easily accessible from U.S. Highway 16, called the "Cloud Peak Skyway" between Ten Sleep and Buffalo.

of Big Horn on the old Quarter Circle A Ranch. The Brinton family didn't exactly rough it in this 20-room clapboard home, complete with libraries, fine furniture, and silver and china services. A reception gallery displays changing exhibits from the Brinton art collection, which includes such Western artists as Charles M. Russell and Frederic Remington. ⊠ *239 Brinton Rd., Big Horn* ☎ *307/672–3173* ⊕ *www.thebrintonmuseum.org* ⊠ *Free* ⊘ *Closed late Dec.–mid-Feb.*

Restaurants

Just LeDoux It Saloon & Steak Out
$$ | AMERICAN | Originally called The Bozeman Stable, the wood-slat building with a false front and tin roof is the oldest operating bar in Wyoming, established in 1882. It was rechristened "Just Ledoux It" in 2021 (after singer and rodeo star the late Chris Ledoux). **Known for:** Ernest Hemingway was a patron; small-town friendliness; options for everyone. ⑤ *Average main: $18* ⊠ *158 Johnson St., Big Horn* ☎ *307/655–5176* ⊕ *www.ledouxsaloon.com.*

Activities

POLO
Big Horn Equestian Center
POLO | Perhaps the most unexpected sport to be found in the outdoor playground of the Bighorn National Forest is polo. The game has been played at the Big Horn Equestrian Center ever since upper-class English and Scottish families settled the area in the 1890s, making these the oldest polo grounds in the United States. You can watch people at play for free on Sunday in the summer. The 65 acres here are also used for other events, including youth soccer and bronc riding. ⊠ *352 Bird Farm Rd., Big Horn* ✛ *Near state bird farm, on Hwy. 28, west of Big Horn* ☎ *307/673–0454* ⊕ *www. bighornequestriancenter.org.*

Buffalo

34 miles south of Big Horn via I–90, U.S. 87, and Hwy. 335.

Buffalo is a trove of history and a hospitable little town in the foothills below Big Horn Pass. Here cattle barons who wanted free grazing and homesteaders who wanted to build fences fought it out in the Johnson County War of 1892. Nearby are the sites of several skirmishes between the U.S. military and Native Americans along the Bozeman Trail. Buffalo is 182 miles due west on I–90 of Sturgis, South Dakota. The first week of every August, Sturgis hosts a very popular and legendary bikers' conclave. So, if you're passing through at this time of year, don't be surprised to hear the occasional roar of "hogs."

Buffalo's Occidental Hotel may be the best place to begin your visit to the Big Horn region, particularly on a Thursday night. That's when you'll find bluegrass music flowing through the doors of its Western-style saloon, and virtually the entire town assembled there. It's a good chance to meet the locals, enjoy some great music and refreshments, and contribute to local charities, for which the gathering has raised thousands of dollars. This is as friendly as the West gets.

GETTING HERE AND AROUND
Arriving in the region via Interstate 25, take the U.S. 87 or East Hart Street exit west to South Main Street and the downtown business district. Then park and explore area parks, shops, museums, and the famed Occidental Hotel. For a quiet, shaded picnic, check out City Park and Prosinski Park a block southwest of the Occidental.

VISITOR INFORMATION
CONTACTS Buffalo Chamber of Commerce. ⊠ *55 N. Main St., Buffalo* ☎ *307/684–5544* ⊕ *www.buffalowyo.com.*

◉ Sights

Fetterman Massacre Monument

MILITARY SIGHT | The Fetterman Massacre Monument is a rock monolith dedicated to the memory of Lieutenant William J. Fetterman and his 80 men, who died in a December 21, 1866, battle against Lakota-Sioux warriors. Today, an interpretive trail with 21 signs spans the entire length of the battlefield, explaining the combatants, leaders, weapons, tactics, positions, and theories of a battle that lasted all of 30 minutes. This was the worst defeat for the U.S military on the Northern Plains until the Little Big Horn battle a decade later. Five miles west of the Fetterman site is the site of the Wagon Box Fight, which also has a short interpretive trail. Fort Phil Kearny is the starting point for both battle sites, providing brochures, guides, and an overview of the history of Red Cloud's War. ⊠ *Buffalo ⊹ 18 miles north of Buffalo, off I–90; obtain directions at Fort Phil Kearny.*

Fort Phil Kearny State Historic Site

MILITARY SIGHT | Fort Phil Kearny State Historic Site was the focal point of Red Cloud's War, and Phil Kearny was probably the most fought-over fort in the West. This is the largest 8-foot stockaded fort ever built by the U.S. military, covering 17 acres; it experienced almost daily skirmishing against Cheyenne or Lakota warriors. Its location eventually led to major battles, including the December 21, 1866, Fetterman Fight, in which 81 soldiers were killed (the first time in American military history that a whole command was defeated to the last man), and the August 2, 1867, Wagon Box Fight, in which 32 men held their position in a daylong fight against more than 800 Lakota. This battle was considered a victory by both sides.

The fort's mission was to protect travelers on the Bozeman Trail going to the goldfields in southern Montana. However, there are theories that it may have been placed in what were the last and best hunting grounds of the Northern Plains tribes in order to draw them away from the railroad construction across southern Wyoming that was occurring at the same time. In the fall of 1868, the U.S. government signed the Fort Laramie Treaty, ending Red Cloud's War—the only war Native Americans won against the United States. The treaty closed the Bozeman Trail, making all the land between the Black Hill and Big Horn Mountains, and the land between the Yellowstone and North Platte rivers, unceded First Nations land where white people could not go. However, it also for the first time established Indian Agencies along the Missouri River for the different Lakota tribes. So, although the Indigenous people won the war, they lost the peace. As part of the treaty, Fort Phil Kearny was abandoned in August 1868. Within two weeks, it is believed, Cheyenne, under Two Moon, occupied and then burned the fort to the ground. No original buildings remain at the site, but fort building locations are marked, and the visitor center has good details. The stockade around the fort was re-created after archaeological digs in 1999. ⊠ *528 Wagon Box Rd., Banner ⊹ 15 miles north of Buffalo on I–90* ☎ *307/684–7629* ⊕ *fortphilkearny.com* ✉ *$8* ⊙ *By appointment only Nov.–Apr.*

★ Jim Gatchell Memorial Museum

SPECIALTY MUSEUM | The Jim Gatchell Memorial Museum is the kind of small-town museum that's worth stopping for if you're interested in the frontier history of the region, including the Johnson County Cattle War. It contains Native American, military, outlaw, and ranching artifacts collected by a local pharmacist who was a close friend of area Native Americans. The museum completed a $300,000 renovation project in 2011. Visitors will discover new exhibits and interpretive opportunities. ⊠ *100 Fort St., Buffalo* ☎ *307/684–9331* ⊕ *www.*

jimgatchell.com 🍴 *$10* ⏱ *Closed weekends Sept.–May.*

 **Restaurants**

Bozeman Trail Steakhouse
$$ | AMERICAN | This eatery, which is literally on the Bozeman Trail, serves decent food, from chicken, taco, and Cobb salads to local favorites such as prime-rib melts and club sandwiches or bison steak, burgers, and king-cut prime-rib plates amid Western memorabilia. You can also dine outdoors on the deck and sip from the large selection of microbrews. **Known for:** best place in town to try a bison steak; 19 beers on tap from around Wyoming and the country; diverse menu with something to please everyone. $ *Average main: $20* ✉ *675 E. Hart St., Buffalo* ☎ *307/684–5555, 888/351–6732* ⊕ *www.thebozemantrailsteakhouse.com.*

★ The Cookhouse at the TA Ranch
$$$ | AMERICAN | This culinary gem is a 15-minute drive south of downtown Buffalo, an historic 1882 ranch that, while still a working ranch, also offers guests meals, accommodations, and activities. It's where the essence of hearty, home-cooked meals comes to life with farm-to-table cuisine and rotating seasonal menus. **Known for:** locally sourced Wyoming beef; creative and delicious custom cocktails; "Reef and Beef," a massive portion of ribeye, lobster, sea scallops, charred greens, and crunchy potatoes. $ *Average main: $30* ✉ *28623 Old Hwy. 87* ☎ *307/684–5833* ⊕ *www.taranch.com* ⏱ *Closed Tues. No lunch.*

Pie Zanos
$$ | ITALIAN | This charming wood-fired pizza and pasta restaurant is situated within a historic building in the heart of downtown Buffalo. Patrons have the delightful opportunity to witness their pizzas as they cook in the expansive wood-fired pizza oven, the focal point of the kitchen. **Known for:** impressive list of craft cocktails; hand-tossed artisan pizza dough; large portion sizes for reasonable prices. $ *Average main: $18* ✉ *17 N. Main St., Buffalo* ☎ *307/278–0161* ⊕ *www.piezanoswy.com* ⏱ *Closed Mon.–Wed. No lunch Sun.*

 Hotels

Hampton Inn Buffalo
$$$ | HOTEL | FAMILY | Enjoy the comfort of a solid chain hotel with a fitness room and a pool. **Pros:** big patio area to enjoy on summer mornings; hot breakfast bar with great offerings; 24-hour pool and fitness room. **Cons:** not walkable from downtown Buffalo; typical chain hotel; no hotel bar or restaurant. $ *Rooms from: $194* ✉ *85 U.S. Hwy. 16 E, Buffalo* ☎ *855/605–0317* ⊕ *www.hilton.com* ⮐ *75 rooms* ❂ *Free Breakfast.*

★ The Occidental Hotel
$$$ | B&B/INN | This enchanting, fully restored grand hotel, founded in 1880, served emigrants on the Bozeman Trail, two U.S. presidents, and some of Wyoming's most colorful characters, and it remains in top form. **Pros:** well-stocked library; owners on premises offering gracious service; well-appointed rooms. **Cons:** no pool; old plumbing (but it doesn't leak); breakfast is not included. $ *Rooms from: $195* ✉ *10 N. Main St., Buffalo* ☎ *307/684–0451* ⊕ *occidentalwyoming.com* ⮐ *19 rooms* ❂ *No Meals.*

★ Paradise Guest Ranch
$$$$ | RESORT | FAMILY | Not only does this dude ranch have a stunning location at the base of some of the tallest mountains in the range, but it's also one of the oldest (circa 1907) and most progressive, as evidenced by its adults-only month (September) and two ladies' weeks. **Pros:** clean cabins with rustic, beautiful views; hospitable staff; good children's programs. **Cons:** minimum 1-week stays; not so close to Buffalo; no cell phone service at ranch. $ *Rooms from: $799* ✉ *282 Hunter Creek Rd., Buffalo* ✛ *Off U.S. 16,*

13 miles west of Buffalo ☎ *307/684–7876* ⊕ *www.paradiseranch.com* ⊗ *Closed Oct.–Apr.* ⇥ *18 rooms* ⊙ *All-Inclusive* ⌒ *One-week min.*

SureStay Plus by Best Western Buffalo
$ | HOTEL | Several blocks from downtown, this motel is close to Clear Creek Trail, the city's bike and walking path. **Pros:** clean and contemporary; good breakfast; walking distance from shopping and dining options. **Cons:** standard chain hotel with no frills; some guests complained that the rooms were musty; hotel could use an update. ⑤ *Rooms from: $105* ⊠ *65 U.S. Hwy. 16 E, Buffalo* ☎ *307/684–9564, 800/424–6423* ⊕ *www. bestwestern.com* ⇥ *63 rooms* ⊙ *Free Breakfast.*

Activities

The forested canyons and pristine alpine meadows of the Big Horn Mountains teem with animal and plant life, making this an excellent area for hiking and pack trips by horseback. The quality and concentration of locals willing to outfit adventurers are high in Buffalo, making it a suitable base camp from which to launch an expedition.

ADVENTURE OUTFITTERS
South Fork Mountain Lodge & Outfitters
LOCAL SPORTS | The folks at South Fork Mountain Lodge & Outfitters can customize about any sort of adventure you'd like to undertake in the Big Horns, whether it's hiking, hunting, fishing, horseback riding, snowmobiling, or cross-country skiing. The company can arrange for all of your food and supplies and provide a guide, or render drop-camp services for more experienced thrill seekers. ⊠ *7558 Hwy. 16 W, Buffalo* ⊹ *16 miles west of Buffalo on U.S. 16* ☎ *307/267–2609* ⊕ *www.lodgesofthe-bighorns.com* ⌸ *3-day hunting trips from $3400.*

CAMPING
Deer Park Campground. Although one section of this campground is quiet and relaxed, reserved for campers over 55, the main campsites are busy. In addition to a heated pool and a hot tub, Deer Park offers ice-cream socials at night for $1. ⊠ *146 U.S. 16, Buffalo* ☎ *307/684–5722, 800/222–9960* ⇥ *33 full hookups, 33 partial hookups, 34 tent sites, 3 cabins.*

Buffalo KOA Journey. Ideally located along the beautiful Clear Creek and a short drive to downtown Buffalo, this campground is open year-round and offers streaming capable wifi, a seasonal pool, a volleyball court, and more. ⊠ *87 US-16, Buffalo* ☎ *307/684–5423* ⇥ *80 full hookups, 4 tent sites, 7 cabins.*

Gillette

70 miles east of Buffalo on I–90.

With a population that's boomed from 17,000 in 1981 to over 31,000 in 2023, Gillette, the metropolis of the Powder River Basin, has many relatively new properties, restaurants, and shopping opportunities. Thanks to the region's huge coal mines, it's one of Wyoming's wealthiest cities, and as a result, it has an excellent community infrastructure that includes the Cam-Plex, a multi-use events center that hosts everything from crafts bazaars and indoor rodeos to concerts and fine-arts exhibits. Gillette is also a gateway town for Devils Tower National Monument, the volcanic plug that is one of the nation's most distinctive geological features and a hot spot for rock climbers.

Gillette has worked hard to make itself presentable, but you don't have to look very hard to find a shovel bigger than a house at one of its giant strip mines. Once a major livestock center, from which ranchers shipped cattle and sheep to eastern markets, the city now mines millions of tons of coal each year and ships it out to coal-fired power plants. In fact, if Gillette (and surrounding Campbell County) were its own nation, it would be the world's sixth-greatest producer of coal. Currently, the county turns out nearly a third of all American-mined coal. Gillette, however, is a big fish in a small pond, one of only two incorporated towns in the county (the other is Wright, population 1,619).

GETTING HERE AND AROUND

Gillette may well serve as the heartbeat of eastern Wyoming, with a new college, an elaborate recreation center, new I-90 overpasses, and miles of new roadways built in the town since 2008. Travelers will find hotels, restaurants, shopping malls, and residential areas south of Interstate 90 on State Highway 59/South Douglas Highway. Heading north on the same route takes motorists directly downtown.

VISITOR INFORMATION

CONTACT Gillette Visitor Center. ✉ *314 S. Gillette Ave., Gillette* ☎ *307/686–0040* ⊕ *visitgillettewright.com.*

 Sights

Keyhole State Park

STATE/PROVINCIAL PARK | You can fish, boat, swim, and camp at Keyhole State Park. Bird-watching is a favorite activity here, as up to 225 species can be seen on the grounds. The park is 45 miles east of Gillette and 20 miles south of Devils Tower. ✉ *22 Marina Rd., Moorcroft* ☎ *307/756–3596* ⊕ *wyoparks.wyo.gov* ✄ *$12.*

Rockpile Museum

SPECIALTY MUSEUM | Local artifacts, including mining tools, cattle brands, and rifles, make up the collection at the Campbell County–run Rockpile Museum. The museum's name comes from its location next to a natural rock-pile formation that served as a landmark for pioneers and cattle drives. ✉ *900 W. 2nd St., Gillette* ☎ *307/682–5723* ⊕ *www.*

campbellcountywy.gov/2169/Rockpile-Museum ✄ *Free* ⊙ *Closed Sun.*

Thunder Basin National Grassland

NATURE PRESERVE | A vast area that stretches from the edge of the Black Hills almost to the center of Wyoming, Thunder Basin truly is the outback of America. Except for a handful of tiny towns, deserted highways, and coal mines, it is entirely undeveloped. Farmers from the east settled this area at the end of the 19th century, hoping to raise crops in the semiarid soil. Experienced only with the more humid conditions east of the Rockies, the farmers failed, and the region deteriorated into a dust bowl. Most of the land has reverted to its natural state, creating millions of acres of grasslands filled with wildlife. Among the many species is one of the largest herds of pronghorn in the world (numbering approximately 26,000), prairie dogs, and burrowing owls that live in abandoned prairie-dog holes. Highway 116, Highway 59, and Highway 450 provide the best access; a few interior dirt roads are navigable only in dry weather. The grasslands, though, are most impressive away from the highways. Take a hike to get a real sense of the vast emptiness of this land. Stop by the District Forest Service Office in Douglas for maps, directions, and tips. ✉ *2250 E. Richards St., Douglas* ☎ *307/745–2300* ⊕ *www.fs.usda.gov* ✄ *Free.*

 Restaurants

Hong Kong

$ | CHINESE | Lunches here are served fast and cheap (between $7 and $8) and include more than 30 different dishes, such as Mongolian beef and cashew chicken. They're popular with the business crowd, so you might want to avoid the noon lunch rush. **Known for:** extensive menu; large portions; friendly service. ⑤ *Average main: $8* ✉ *1612 W. 2nd St., Gillette* ☎ *307/682–5829.*

🛏 Hotels

Best Western Tower West Lodge

$ | **HOTEL** | A range of earth tones decorates the comfortable rooms of this hotel on the west side of town. **Pros:** easy interstate access; restaurant on-site and several close by; cheap rates. **Cons:** located a fair distance from the downtown area; poor setting next to an industrial area; neighboring interstate is busy and noisy. ⑤ *Rooms from: $110* ⌧ *109 N. U.S. 14/16, Gillette* ☎ *307/686–2210* ⊕ *www.bestwestern.com* ⮑ *190 rooms* ⍾ *No Meals.*

🎭 Performing Arts

Cam-Plex

CONCERTS | Anything from a rodeo or crafts show to a concert or melodrama could be going on at the Cam-Plex, Gillette's multi-use facility. There's something scheduled almost every day; call or check the website for details. ⌧ *1635 Reata Dr., Gillette* ☎ *307/682–0552, 307/682–8802 for tickets* ⊕ *www.cam-plex.com.*

Powder River Symphony

MUSIC | Founded in 1986, the Powder River Symphony continues to perform on a regular basis at the Cam-Plex Heritage Center, a 960-seat auditorium within the Cam-Plex. The orchestra is composed of area musicians of all ages, and they play everything from Beethoven to Andrew Lloyd Webber. ⌧ *1635 Reata Dr., Gillette* ☎ *307/660–9800* ⊕ *www.prsymphony. org.*

🏃 Activities

Gillette is especially fitness conscious, and as a result, the town has invested in many new recreational facilities—including a massive $52 million city-schools recreation center and two health clubs—that cities of a similar size lack. There are also more than 49 miles of developed trails within the city limits, including

paths on the north end of town, off West Warlow Drive, in McManamen Park, a prime bird-watching spot.

Devils Tower National Monument

65 miles northeast of Gillette via I–90 and U.S. 14; 32 miles northeast of Sundance via U.S. 14. 60 miles west of Spearfish, SD via U.S. 14 and I–90.

Devils Tower is a rocky, grooved butte that juts upward 1,280 feet above the plain of the Belle Fourche River. Native American legend has it that the tower was corrugated by the claws of a bear trying to reach some children on top, and some tribes still revere the site, which they call Bear Lodge.

GETTING HERE AND AROUND

Located in extreme northeast Wyoming, America's first national monument can be accessed from several routes. Traveling from the west on Interstate 90, motorists may take U.S. 14 E at Moorcroft 25 miles, then Route 24 6 miles north to Devils Tower. After visiting the monument, travelers may then head south on Route 24, returning to U.S. 14 E to Sundance and I–90. Alternatively, after leaving the monument, stay on Route 24 for a scenic drive through Hulett to the small town of Aladdin and its quirky General Store, and then return south to I–90 via Route 111.

👁 Sights

★ Devils Tower National Monument

NATURE SIGHT | As you drive east from Gillette, the highways begin to rise into the forested slopes of the Black Hills. A detour north will take you to Devils Tower. Geologists attribute the butte's strange existence to ancient volcanic activity. Rock climbers say it's one of the best crack-climbing areas on the continent.

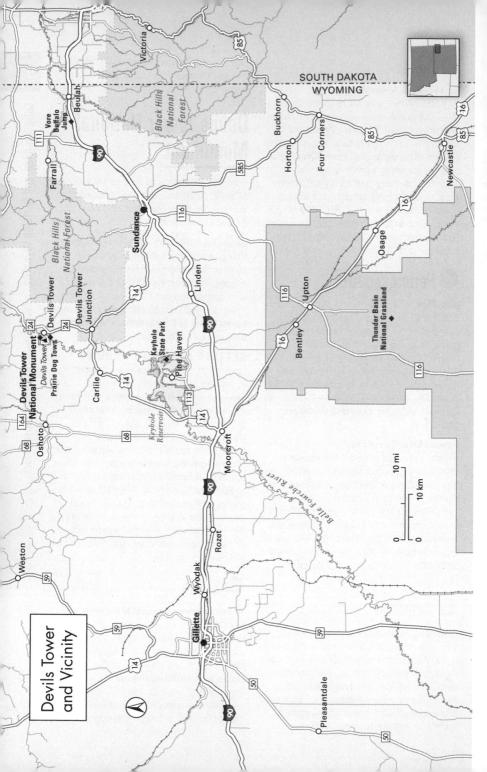

The tower was a tourist magnet long before a spaceship landed here in the movie *Close Encounters of the Third Kind*. Teddy Roosevelt made it the nation's first national monument in 1906, and it has attracted a steadily increasing throng of visitors ever since—up to nearly half a million people a year. When you visit, take some time to stop at the visitor center. Exhibits here explain the geology, history, and cultural significance of the monument, and a bookstore carries a wide selection of materials relating to the park. Park rangers can provide updated information on hiking and climbing conditions. A short and easy walking path circles the tower. ⊠ *Hwy. 110, Devils Tower* ☎ *307/467–5283* ⊕ *www.nps.gov/ deto* ⊠ *$25 per vehicle.*

Prairie Dog Town

OTHER ATTRACTION | At the Prairie Dog Town on the monument grounds between Devils Tower and the Belle Fourche River, you can observe the burrowing, chirping rodents in their natural habitat. Prairie dogs were once plentiful on the Great Plains, but ranching and development have taken their toll; today, most sizeable populations of the animal are found on protected federal lands. ⊠ *Hwy. 110, Devils Tower* ☎ *307/467– 5283* ⊕ *www.nps.gov/deto* ⊠ *$25 per vehicle entrance to the monument.*

🛍 Shopping

Devils Tower Trading Post

SOUVENIRS | At the entrance to Devils Tower National Monument, you can purchase informative books, Western art, buffalo hides, clothing, knickknacks, and souvenirs. A giant Harley-Davidson flag (supposedly the world's largest) flies over the store, so it's no wonder that bikers overrun the place during the massive Sturgis Motorcycle Rally in August. The old-fashioned ice-cream parlor, which also serves a mean sarsaparilla, is a treat in the heat of summer. ⊠ *57 Hwy. 110,*

Devils Tower ☎ *307/467–5295* ⊕ *www. devilstowertradingpost.com.*

Activities

CAMPING

Belle Fourche River Campground. Tucked away in a bend of the Belle Fourche River, this campground is small and spartan, but it is the only place in the park where camping is allowed. ⊠ *Hwy. 110* ☎ *307/467–5283, 307/467– 5350* ⊠ *47 sites.*

Devils Tower KOA. Less than a mile from Devils Tower, this campground lies in the literal shadow of the famous stone monolith for part of the day. The view of the sheer granite walls above red river bluffs is one of the property's greatest assets. Another is the bordering Belle Fourche River, which nurtures several stalwart cottonwood and ash trees that provide at least some areas with shade. Weather permitting, the campground stages a nightly outdoor showing of *Close Encounters of the Third Kind*. ⊠ *60 Hwy. 110* ☎ *307/467–5395, 800/562–5785* ⊠ *80 sites.*

HIKING

Aside from affording excellent views of Devils Tower and the surrounding countryside, the hiking trails here are a good way to view some of the geology and wildlife of the Black Hills region. The terrain that surrounds the butte is relatively flat, so the popular **Tower Trail,** a paved 1.3-mile path that circles the monument, is far from strenuous. It's the most popular trail in the park, though, so if you're looking for more isolation, try the 1.5-mile **Joyner Ridge Trail** or the 3-mile **Red Beds Trail.** They're a bit more demanding, but the views from the top of Joyner Ridge and the banks of the Belle Fourche River are more than adequate rewards. Both the Tower and Red Beds trails start at the visitor center; Joyner Ridge Trail begins about a mile's drive north from there.

President Thedore Roosevelt named Devils Tower the first U.S. national monument in 1906.

ROCK CLIMBING

Climbing is the premier sporting activity at Devils Tower. Acclaimed as one of the best crack-climbing areas in North America, the monument has attracted both beginners and experts for more than a century. There are few restrictions when it comes to ascending the granite cone. Although climbing is technically allowed all year, there is generally a voluntary moratorium in June to allow for peaceful religious rites performed by local Native American tribes. Additionally, the west face of the formation is closed intermittently in the summer to protect the prairie falcons that nest there. Before ascending Devils Tower you should sign in at the visitor center and discuss conditions with park officials. You can obtain a list of park-licensed guides here; courses are offered at all skill levels and sometimes include excursions into the Rockies or South Dakota. Some tour operators continue to guide climbs during the voluntary ban in June.

Devils Tower Lodge. Offering guided climbs for over 20 years, the instructors at Devils Tower Lodge are some of the best in the area. Each climbing trip is personalized to the experience and wants of the climber so that beginner to advanced climbers have an enjoyable experience. ⊠ 37 W Rd. ☎ 307/467–5267 ⊕ www.devilstowerlodge.com.

Wyoming Mountain Guides. Knowledgeable guides will take climbers up a variety of climbing routes on 1-, 2-, or 3-day custom rock climbing tours at Devils Tower. ☎ 307/431–1741 ⊕ www.wyomingmountainguides.com.

Sundance

31 miles southeast of Devils Tower National Monument via U.S. 14.

A combination of traditional reverence and an infamous outlaw's date with destiny put Sundance on Wyoming's map, and continues to draw visitors today. Native American tribes such as the

Crow, Cheyenne, and Lakota consider Sundance Mountain and the Bear Lodge Mountains to be sacred. Before European settlers arrived in the 1870s, the Native Americans congregated nearby each June for their Sun Dance, an important ceremonial gathering. The event gave its name to this small town, which in turn gave its name to the outlaw Harry Longabaugh, the Sundance Kid, who spent time in the local jail for stealing a horse. Ranch country and the western Black Hills surround the town. The Crook County Fair and Rodeo, held during the last week in July, offers live music shows, cook-offs, a ranch-style rodeo, and many other events; it's a popular draw for area residents.

GETTING HERE AND AROUND

This is a classic small Western town where you'll be tabbed as an outsider if you don't return a "hello" from a passerby on the street. To reach the downtown area, exit Interstate 90 on U.S. 14/E Cleveland Street or Route 585.

Sights

Vore Buffalo Jump

INDIGENOUS SIGHT | Thousands of buffalo bones are piled atop each other at the Vore Buffalo Jump, where Native Americans herded bison over a cliff between the years 1500 and 1800, when hunting was done on foot rather than on horses imported from Europe. The site is open to visitors even as it continues to be excavated by archaeologists. ⊠ *369 Old U.S. 14, Sundance* ✛ *15 miles east of Sundance via I–90 or Old U.S. 14* ☎ *307/266–9530* ⊕ *www.vorebuffalojump.org* ⊠ *$11* ⊙ *Closed Oct.–May.*

Hotels

Bear Lodge Motel

$ | HOTEL | A cozy lobby, a stone fireplace, and wildlife mounts on the walls distinguish this downtown motel. **Pros:** downtown location; close to restaurant, bars,

lounges; short walk to a city park. **Cons:** slightly outdated appearance; no elevator for second-story rooms; long drive to most area attractions. ⑤ *Rooms from: $120* ⊠ *218 E. Cleveland St., Sundance* ☎ *307/283–1611* ⊕ *www.bearlodgemotel.com* ⇨ *34 rooms* ⍥ *Free Breakfast.*

Serena Inn & Suites

$$ | HOTEL | Brown carpeting and red drapes decorate the spacious rooms of this hotel. **Pros:** contemporary furnishings; easy access just off Interstate 90; gas and convenience store next door. **Cons:** just outside of town, not a walkable area; interstate noise; very basic rooms. ⑤ *Rooms from: $150* ⊠ *2719 Cleveland St., Sundance* ☎ *307/283–2800* ⇨ *44 rooms* ⍥ *Free Breakfast.*

Activities

CAMPING

Mountain View RV Park. Clean and new, this contemporary RV park offers large pull-through sites ideal for the big rigs. ⊠ *117 Government Valley Rd.* ☎ *307/283–2270*

Lusk

140 miles northeast of Cheyenne via I–25 and U.S. 18.

Proudly rural, the 1,500 townspeople of Lusk often poke gentle fun at themselves, emblazoning T-shirts with phrases such as "End of the world, 12 miles. Lusk, 15 miles." You'll see what they mean if you visit this seat of Niobrara County, whose population density averages 524 acres of prairie per person. If you find yourself traveling the main route between the Black Hills and the Colorado Rockies, a stop in this tiny burg is worth the time for a quick lesson in frontier—particularly stagecoach—history. You can also find gasoline and food, rare commodities on the open plain.

Lusk owes its existence to rancher Frank S. Lusk, who cut a deal with the Wyoming Central Railroad in 1886. The railroad originally planned to build its route through central Wyoming along the Cheyenne–Deadwood Stage Line, which ran between the territorial capital and the Black Hills gold-rush town. Officials selected Silver Cliff, where Ellis Johnson ran a store, saloon, and hotel, as the area's station. When Johnson tried to raise the price for his land, the railroad changed its plans and bought from Lusk. The rail line bypassed Silver Cliff for the station named Lusk.

The stagecoach line that passed through Lusk played a role in the development of the Black Hills, but Lusk became a different sort of pioneering town in the 1990s. Town leaders installed fiber-optic cable lines and obtained computers for schools, public facilities, and homes, placing Lusk on the frontier of technology when other small Wyoming towns had barely even heard of the Internet. The media spotlight shone briefly on the town that led the state of Wyoming into the 21st century.

GETTING HERE AND AROUND
A vehicle is your only option for getting around.in this part of the state, and Lusk is at the crossroads for U.S. 20 and U.S. 85.

Sights

Spanish Diggings
INDIGENOUS SIGHT | FAMILY | A few miles east of Glendo State Park lies a vast stone quarry initially mistaken for the work of early Spanish explorers. Archaeologists later determined the site, known as the Spanish Diggings, to be the work of various indigenous tribes on and off for the past several thousand years. Tools and arrowheads carved from the stone quarried here, including quartzite, jasper, and agate, have been found as far away as the Ohio River valley. To see

the diggings you'll have to drive through Glendo State Park. ⊠ *397 Glendo Park Rd., Lusk* ☎ *307/777–6323* ⊕ *wyoparks. state.wy.us* ⊠ *$7 for residents, $12 for nonresidents.*

Stagecoach Museum
HISTORY MUSEUM | FAMILY | Artifacts from early settlement days and the period when the Cheyenne–Deadwood Stage Line was in full swing are some of the displays at the Stagecoach Museum. You also can get information about the Texas Cattle Trail. ⊠ *322 S. Main St., Lusk* ☎ *307/334–3444* ⊕ *dooperca.wixsite. com/stagecoachmuseum* ⊠ *Free (donations encouraged)* ⊗ *Closed weekends. Closed Nov.–Apr.*

Restaurants

Pizza Place
$ | PIZZA | FAMILY | A casual atmosphere and good food come together at this downtown eatery. Pizza, calzones, and sub sandwiches made with homemade bread are on the menu, and there's also a salad bar. **Known for:** from-scratch dinner rolls, and they'll even sell you a batch to take home; dough made fresh every day; sausage that's ground and seasoned in-house daily. ⑤ *Average main: $10* ⊠ *214 S. Main St., Lusk* ☎ *307/334–3000* ⊗ *Closed Sun. and Mon.*

Hotels

Best Western Pioneer Lusk
$$ | HOTEL | FAMILY | Although the exterior of this motel near downtown and the Stagecoach Museum is unremarkable, the lobby is attractive, with a ceramic-tile floor, hardwood trim, and wrought-iron tables and lamps. **Pros:** nice furnishings; omelet bar from an authentic 1890 chuck wagon from Memorial Day to Labor Day; pet friendly. **Cons:** outdoor pool open only part of the year; some guests complain about the rooms being smaller than average hotel rooms; more expensive than hotels in nearby towns. ⑤ *Rooms*

from: $135 ✉ 731 S. Main St., Lusk
☎ 307/334–2640 ⊕ www.bestwestern.
com ⮬ 30 rooms ⦿❙ Free Breakfast.

Covered Wagon Motel
$ | **MOTEL** | **FAMILY** | With a covered wagon
on the front portico, an indoor pool, and
an outdoor playground, this U-shaped
motel is an inviting place for families with
kids. **Pros:** newly installed playground
for the kids; indoor headed pool and
sauna; free breakfast. **Cons:** books up
quickly in the summer, so plan ahead;
dated furnishings in rooms; some guests
complained of noise in rooms facing the
street. ⑤ Rooms from: $100 ✉ 730 S.
Main St., Lusk ☎ 307/334–2836 ⊕ www.
coveredwagonmotel.com ⮬ 51 rooms
⦿❙ Free Breakfast.

Douglas

_55 miles west of Lusk via U.S. 18 and
I–25._

Douglas is best known for two things:
the Wyoming State Fair, which has been
held here annually in early August since
1905, and the jackalope. A local taxider-
mist assembled the first example of the
mythical cross between a jackrabbit and
an antelope for display in a local hotel.
There's an 8-foot-tall concrete jackalope
statue in Jackalope Square in downtown
Douglas, and many businesses sell jackalope figures and merchandise.

Surveyors plotted the town of Douglas
(named for Stephen A. Douglas, the
presidential candidate who lost to Abe
Lincoln) in 1886, in preparation for the
construction of the Fremont, Elkhorn,
and Missouri Valley Railroad. The railroad,
which owned the townsite, prohibited
settlement before the rails arrived. Eager
to take up residence, a few enterprising
souls built shelters on Antelope Creek,
outside the official boundaries. When the
railroad arrived on August 22, they put
their structures on wheels and moved
them into town.

GETTING HERE AND AROUND
A car is required for transportation
here. Douglas is right off I–25, about
three-quarters of the way between Cheyenne and Casper.

◉ Sights

Ayres Natural Bridge
NATURE SIGHT | Overland immigrants
sometimes visited a rock outcrop that
spans LaPrele Creek. It's now a small but
popular picnic area and campsite where
you can wade in the creek or simply
enjoy the quiet. No pets are allowed
at the campsite. ✉ Douglas ✛ Off I–25
☎ 307/358–3532.

Fort Fetterman State Historic Site
MILITARY SIGHT | Built in 1867 to protect
travelers headed west, the army post
here is preserved today as the Fort Fetterman State Historic Site. Although the
fort was never very large and had difficulty keeping its soldiers from deserting, its
location on the fringes of the Great Sioux
Indian Reservation made it an important
outpost of civilization on the Western
frontier. After white settlers overran the
Black Hills and the government did away
with the reservation, soldiers from here
helped end armed Plains Indian resistance—and thus put an end to the fort's
usefulness. Two buildings, the ordnance
warehouse and officers' quarters, survived decades of abandonment and today
house interpretive exhibits and artifacts
related to the area's history and the fort's
role in settling the West. The remains of
other fort buildings can still be seen, as
can the ruins of Fetterman City, which
died out when Douglas was founded several miles to the south. ✉ 752 Hwy. 93,
Douglas ☎ 307/358–2864 ⊕ wyoparks.
wyo.gov ✉ Free ⊙ Closed Sun. and Mon.
Closed Labor Day–Memorial Day.

Medicine Bow National Forest, Douglas District
FOREST | The Medicine Bow National
Forest, Douglas District, southwest

of Douglas in the Laramie Peak area, includes four campgrounds ($5–$10 for camping; campground closed in winter) and areas where you can fish and hike. ✉ *2250 E. Richards St., Douglas ✛ Douglas Ranger District* ☎ *307/358–4690* ⊕ *fs. usda.gov/mbr.*

Wyoming Pioneer Memorial Museum
HISTORY MUSEUM | FAMILY | At the Wyoming Pioneer Memorial Museum, the emphasis is on the Wyoming pioneer settlers and overland immigrants, but this small state-operated museum on the state fairgrounds also has displays on Native Americans and the frontier military. ✉ *400 W. Center St., Douglas* ☎ *307/358–9288* ⊕ *wyoparks.wyo.gov* ▢ *Free* ⊙ *Closed Sun. and Mon., May–Oct. Closed Sun.–Thurs., Nov.–Apr.*

Restaurants

Plains Trading Post
$$ | AMERICAN | FAMILY | Antique furnishings and portions of old bank buildings set the scene at this restaurant, where the menu is diverse but basic—chicken, burgers, steaks—and the portions are large. It's open 24 hours a day, a rarity even in the larger cities. **Known for:** pie by the slice; open 24 hours a day; the Plains Burger. ⑤ *Average main: $15* ✉ *628 Richards St., Douglas* ☎ *307/358–4489.*

🛏 Hotels

Hampton Inn & Suites Douglas
$$$ | HOTEL | The modern rooms are spacious and comfortable at this hotel located right off I–25 on the outskirts of town. **Pros:** nice indoor pool and fitness center; pet-friendly; good breakfast. **Cons:** typical chain hotel; some guests think the rooms were overpriced; highway noise can be heard from some of the rooms. ⑤ *Rooms from: $200* ✉ *1730 Muirfield Ct., Douglas* ☎ *307/358–0707* ⊕ *www.hilton.com* ⇆ *100 rooms* ⑪ *Free Breakfast.*

Activities

CAMPING
Esterbrook Campground. Nestled among pine trees near Laramie Peak, 30 miles south of Douglas, Esterbrook is only a few miles from Black Mountain Lookout, one of the few staffed fire lookouts remaining in the country. During fire season (generally mid-June through September) be sure to ask the ranger-in-residence before exploring his or her home. ✉ *Forest Rd. 633* ☎ *307/745–2300* ⇆ *12 sites.*

Casper

115 miles south of Buffalo via I–25; 180 miles north of Cheyenne via I–25.

Several excellent museums in Casper illuminate central Wyoming's pioneer and natural history. The state's second-largest city, it's also one of the oldest. Some of the first white people to venture across Wyoming spent the winter here in 1811, on their way east from Fort Astoria in Oregon. Although they didn't stay, they helped to forge several pioneer trails that crossed the North Platte River near present-day Casper. A permanent settlement eventually arose, and was named for Lieutenant Caspar Collins; the spelling error occurred early on, and it stuck. The town has grown largely as a result of oil and gas exploration, and sheep and cattle ranchers run their stock on lands all around the city.

GETTING HERE AND AROUND
Natrona County does have an airport, about 7 miles northwest of Casper, but you'll need a car to explore this sparsely populated area.

VISITOR INFORMATION
CONTACTS Casper Convention and Visitors Bureau. ✉ *139 W. 2nd St., Suite 1B, Casper* ☎ *307/234–5362, 800/852–1889* ⊕ *www.visitcasper.com.*

◉ Sights

Casper Planetarium
OBSERVATORY | FAMILY | The Casper Planetarium has multimedia programs on astronomy. There are also interactive exhibits in the lobby and a gift shop. Public programs, which last an hour, are scheduled regularly year-round. ✉ *904 N. Poplar St., Casper* ☎ *307/577–0310* ⊕ *www.sites.google.com/myncsd.org/ casperplanetarium* 🖃 *$3* ⊗ *Closed Sun. and Mon.*

Edness Kimball Wilkins State Park
STATE/PROVINCIAL PARK | FAMILY | Edness Kimball Wilkins State Park is a day-use area with picnicking, swimming, fishing, and a 3-mile walking path. This park is along a migratory flyway, with more than 100 different species of birds frequenting the area. For this reason, Edness Kimball State Park has been designated one of Audubon Wyoming's important bird areas. ✉ *8700 E. Hwy. 20/26, Evansville, Casper* ✛ *6 miles east of Casper* ☎ *307/577–5150* ⊕ *wyoparks.wyo.gov* 🖃 *$12 per vehicle for non-Wyoming residents, $7 per vehicle for Wyoming residents.*

Fort Caspar Historic Site
HISTORIC SIGHT | FAMILY | The Fort Caspar Historic Site re-creates the post at Platte Bridge, which became Fort Caspar after the July 1865 battle that claimed the lives of several soldiers, including Lieutenant Caspar Collins. A post depicts life at a frontier station in the 1860s, and sometimes soldier reenactors go about their tasks. Museum exhibits show the migration trails. ✉ *4001 Fort Caspar Rd., Casper* ☎ *307/235–8462* ⊕ *www. fortcasparwyoming.com* 🖃 *$4.*

★ National Historic Trails Interpretive Center
OTHER ATTRACTION | FAMILY | Five major emigrant trails passed near or through Casper between 1843 and 1870. The best-known are the Oregon Trail and the Mormon Trail, both of which crossed the North Platte River in the vicinity of today's Casper. The National Historic Trails Interpretive Center examines the early history of the trails and the military's role in central Wyoming. Projected onto a series of screens 11 feet high and 55 feet wide, a film shows Wyoming trail sites and scenes of wagon travelers. You can climb into a wagon to see what it was like to cross the river or learn about Mormon pioneers who traveled west with handcarts in 1856. ✉ *1501 N. Poplar St., Casper* ☎ *307/261–7700* ⊕ *www. nhtcf.org* 🖃 *Free.*

Nicolaysen Art Museum
ART MUSEUM | FAMILY | A showcase for regional artists and mostly modern artwork, the Nicolaysen Art Museum also exhibits works by national artists. The building's early-20th-century redbrick exterior and contemporary interior are an odd combination, but this makes the museum all the more interesting. There are hands-on activities, classes, and children's programs, plus a research library and a Discovery Center. ✉ *400 E. Collins St., Casper* ☎ *307/235–5247* ⊕ *www. thenic.org* 🖃 *$5* ⊗ *Closed Sun. and Mon.*

★ Tate Geological Museum
SPECIALTY MUSEUM | FAMILY | Casper College's Tate Geological Museum in the Tate Earth Science Center displays fossils, rocks, jade, and the fossilized remains of a brontosaurus, plus other dinosaur bones. The centerpiece for the Tate is Dee, an 11,600-year-old Columbian Mammoth. Dee is one of the largest complete Columbian Mammoths ever discovered. ✉ *125 College Dr., Casper* ☎ *307/268–2447* ⊕ *www.caspercollege. edu* 🖃 *Free* ⊗ *Closed Sun.*

Werner Wildlife Museum
SPECIALTY MUSEUM | FAMILY | The Werner Wildlife Museum, near the Casper College campus, has displays of birds and animals from Wyoming and around the world. There are more than 400 birds, fish, and animal species on display across 36 different exhibits. ✉ *405*

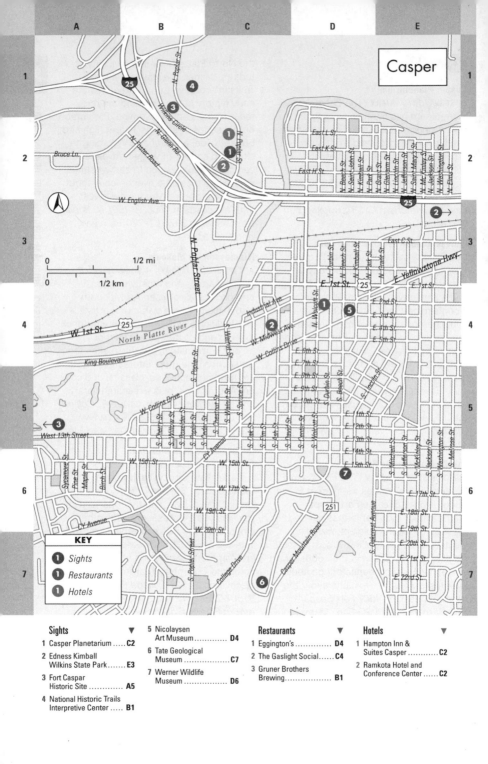

Casper

KEY
- 1 Sights
- 1 Restaurants
- 1 Hotels

Sights ▼

1 Casper Planetarium **C2**
2 Edness Kimball
  Wilkins State Park **E3**
3 Fort Caspar
  Historic Site **A5**
4 National Historic Trails
  Interpretive Center **B1**
5 Nicolaysen
  Art Museum **D4**
6 Tate Geological
  Museum **C7**
7 Werner Wildlife
  Museum **D6**

Restaurants ▼

1 Eggington's **D4**
2 The Gaslight Social **C4**
3 Gruner Brothers
  Brewing **B1**

Hotels ▼

1 Hampton Inn &
  Suites Casper **C2**
2 Ramkota Hotel and
  Conference Center **C2**

E. 15th St., Casper ☎ 307/235–2108 ⊕ www.caspercollege.edu 🎫 Free ⊘ Closed weekends.

 Restaurants

Eggingtons

$ | **AMERICAN | FAMILY** | It's not uncommon to see a line out the door here on weekend mornings. With a wide selection of breakfast and lunch options, there's something for everyone. **Known for:** 6 am opening time for the early birds; build-your-own omelets; nine staple burgers to choose from. $ *Average main: $11* ⊠ *229 E. 2nd St., Casper* ☎ *307/265–8700* ⊕ *www.eggingtons.com* ⊘ *No dinner.*

The Gaslight Social

$ | **MEXICAN FUSION | FAMILY** | This fun, open bar and grill has a build-your-own burrito among flavorful appetizers and a full drinks menu. Gaslight Social also functions as a concert venue and event complex. **Known for:** 37 beers on draft from around Wyoming and the country; big outdoor space with cornhole and other yard games; arcade games and golf simulator to bring out the kid in you. $ *Average main: $10* ⊠ *314 W. Midwest Ave., Casper* ☎ *307/337–1396* ⊕ *www. thegaslightsocial.com* ⊘ *Closed Sun.*

★ Gruner Brothers Brewing

$$ | **AMERICAN | FAMILY** | Come for the beer, stay for the views. This brewpub is run by two actual brothers who love making good beer to enjoy after a long day of work or play. **Known for:** incredible views of downtown, the North Platte River, and Casper Mountain; flatbread made with local, fresh ingredients; happy hour everyday from 3–6 pm. $ *Average main: $19* ⊠ *1301 Wilkins Circle, Casper* ☎ *307/370–7293* ⊕ *grunerbrewing.com* ⊘ *Closed Sun. and Mon.*

Hotels

Hampton Inn & Suites Casper

$$ | **HOTEL** | The rooms in this clean and very quiet lodging have coffeemakers, large cable TVs, white fluffy comforters, and easy chairs with ottomans. **Pros:** still feels relatively new; Cloud Nine beds give rooms a cozy feel; great pool and fitness center. **Cons:** some guests said the rooms weren't soundproof enough; typical chain hotel; no restaurant in hotel and limited options nearby. $ *Rooms from: $145* ⊠ *1100 N. Poplar Rd., Casper* ☎ *307/235–6668* ⊕ *www.hamptoninn. com* 🛏 *120 rooms* ⦿ *Free Breakfast.*

Ramkota Hotel and Conference Center

$$ | **HOTEL** | This full-service hotel, off I-25, has everything under one roof, from dining options to business services. **Pros:** staff are friendly and helpful; complimentary hot breakfast buffet; top-rated restaurant, the Remington, located within the hotel. **Cons:** typical chain hotel; thin walls; some guests noted the hotel design feels dated. $ *Rooms from: $148* ⊠ *800 N. Poplar St., Casper* ☎ *307/266–6000, 307/473–1010* ⊕ *ramkotacasper. com* 🛏 *229 rooms* ⦿ *Free Breakfast.*

Nightlife

Backwards Distilling Company

COCKTAIL BARS | Backwards is the go-to spot for cocktails and bottles to go of their colorful cast of characters: Ringleader Vodka, Sword Swallower Rum, Contortionist Gin, Strongman Gin, and Milk Can Moonshine. A vibrant interior with plush couches and chairs, Edison bulbs, and a wall of mirrors give off a fun-house type environment. Along with refined spirits, Backwards has a rotating list of inventive cocktails that change with the season. ⊠ *214 S. Wolcott St., Casper* ☎ *307/337–1255* ⊕ *www.backwardsdistilling.com.*

 Performing Arts

★ David Street Station

CULTURAL FESTIVALS | FAMILY | An adaptive open-air gathering place in the heart of downtown Casper, David Street Station hosts everything from farmer's markets and concerts in the summer, to ice skating in the winter months. Make sure to check out their website for an events calendar as there is always something going on. ✉ *200 S. David St., Casper* ☎ *307/235–6710* ⊕ *www.davidstreetstation.com.*

Gertrude Krampert Theater

PERFORMANCE VENUES | Both the Casper Symphony Orchestra and the Casper College Theater Department perform at the 465-seat Gertrude Krampert Theater. ✉ *Casper College, 125 College Dr., Casper* ☎ *307/268–2365* ⊕ *www.caspercollegearts.cc.*

Stage III Community Theater

THEATER | FAMILY | Stage III Community Theater presents plays and other dramatic performances at various times. ✉ *904 N. Center St., Casper* ☎ *307/234–0946* ⊕ *www.stageiiitheatre.org.*

Shopping

Eastridge Mall

MALL | The largest shopping center in a 175-mile radius, the Eastridge Mall, anchored by such standbys as Best Buy, JCPenney, Target, and Ross Dress for Less, is popular and important to locals. ✉ *601 S.E. Wyoming Blvd., Casper* ☎ *307/265–9394* ⊕ *www.shopeastridge.com.*

Activities

With thousands of acres of empty grassland and towering mountains only miles away, the landscape around Casper is full of possibilities for enjoying the outdoors. Casper Mountain rises up 8,000 feet no more than 20 minutes from downtown, providing prime skiing and hiking trails.

HIKING

★ Casper Mountain

HIKING & WALKING | Casper Mountain is an iconic landmark for residents and tourists alike. There are a number of hiking and mountain biking trails, camping spots, an archery range and even a small ski resort on the mountain. ✉ *139 W. 2nd St., Casper* ☎ *307/234–5362* ⊕ *www.visitcasper.com.*

Platte River Parkway

HIKING & WALKING | FAMILY | The hiking trail runs adjacent to the North Platte River in downtown Casper. Access points are at Amoco Park at 1st and Poplar streets, or at Crosswinds Park, on North Poplar Street near the Casper Events Center. Also at the Amoco Park is Casper's own white water park, with a man-made rock structure to simulate rapids for kayakers and boaters. ✉ *Casper.*

SKIING

Hogadon Ski Area

SKIING & SNOWBOARDING | FAMILY | Perched on Casper Mountain a few miles outside of town, this small ski resort has a vertical drop of 600 feet. Less than a quarter of the runs are rated for beginners; the rest are evenly divided between intermediate and expert trails. Also here are a separate snowboard terrain park and a modest lodge. ✉ *2500 Hogadon Rd., Casper* ⊹ *Casper Mountain Rd.* ☎ *307/235–8499* ⊕ *hogadon.net* ▣ *Day lift tickets $60 per day.*

Mountain Sports

SNOW SPORTS | The locally popular sporting goods store provides more than just ski and snowboard sales. It also runs Wyomaps, which sells personal Global Positioning System products and provides custom mapping services. In the summer it's a great resource for mountain bikers. ✉ *543 S. Center, Casper* ☎ *307/266–1136* ⊕ *www.facebook.com/mountainsportscasper.*

Index

Photo Credits

Front Cover: John M. Chase/Getty Images [Descr.: View of U.S. Presidents George Washington, Thomas Jefferson (partially obscured), Theodore Roosevelt (obscured), and Abraham Lincoln (partially obscured) sculptures at Mount Rushmore National Monument.] **Back cover, from left to right:** Jim Parkin/iStockphoto. Rinusbaak/Dreamstime. HTurner/Shutterstock. **Spine:** Wick Smith/Shutterstock. Interior, from left to right: Jason Patrick Ross/Shutterstock (1). Turtix/Shutterstock (2-3). **Chapter 1: Experience The Black Hills of South Dakota:** Vivian Fung/Shutterstock (6-7). Chrissieracki/Dreamstime (8-9). Travel South Dakota (9). Jess Kraft/Shutterstock (9). Courtesy of South Dakota Department of Tourism (10). Refocus/Dreamstime (10). City of Sturgis (10). Crazy Horse Memorial Foundation (10). Courtesy of South Dakota Department of Tourism (11). Jason Stitt/Shutterstock (11). Travel South Dakota (12). South Dakota School of Mines and Technology (12). Reptile Gardens (12). Black Hills Playhouse (12). Travel South Dakota (13). Courtesy of Travel South Dakota (18). Courtesy of Travel South Dakota (18). Courtesy of Travel South Dakota (18). Courtesy of Travel South Dakota (19). Mike Bartoszek (19). Travel South Dakota (20). HelloRF Zcool/Shutterstock (20). Rido/Shutterstock (20). Travel South Dakota (22). Travel South Dakota (22). Raisa Nastukova/Shutterstock (21). Garry Chow/iStockphoto (22). Travel South Dakota (22). Travel South Dakota (22). Travel South Dakota (23). Travel South Dakota (23). Travel South Dakota (23). Travel South Dakota (23). **Chapter 3: Rapid City and the Central Black Hills:** Lavin Photography/iStockphoto (43). Ashmephotography/Dreamstime (46). Travel South Dakota (47). Checubus/Shutterstock (47). NPS Photo (48). StelsOne/Shutterstock (53). Exploring and Living/Shutterstock (57). Paul R. Jones/Shutterstock (58). Paul R Jones/Shutterstock (61). Megan Johnson/ Firehouse Brewing Company (63). Jbatt/Dreamstime (70). Travel South Dakota (74). James Dalrymple/Shutterstock (76-77). Patti McConville/Alamy (80). Checubus/Dreamstime (82). **Chapter 4: The Northern Black Hills:** Kubi Trek/Shutterstock (85). RaksyBH/Shutterstock (91). Nagel Photography/ Shutterstock (95). NatalieMaynor/Flickr (97). JCsullivan24/Flickr (101). Lavin Photography/iStockphoto (103). Doubleclick7Dreamstime (104). CheriAlguire/Dreamstime (109). Fiskness/Dreamstime (112). Sjcummings1776/Dreamstime (116). Mitgirl/Dreamstime (118). **Chapter 5: The Southern Black Hills:** Cimbala9/Dreamstime (125). Danita Delimont/Alamy (131). Cimbala9/Dreamstime (138). Wheels/Shutterstock (142-143). HTurner/Shutterstock (146). Jacob Boomsma/Shutterstock (148). Dj1234514/Dreamstime (152). **Chapter 6: The Badlands:** Loren Kerns (155). Steve Cukrov/Shutterstock (161). Mauritius Images GmbH/Alamy (162). Jon Lyle/Shutterstock (164). Virrage Images/Shutterstock (168-169). **Chapter 7: Badlands National Park:** Joecho-16/iStockphoto (171). Virrage Images/Shutterstock (179). Evan Sloyka/Shutterstock (182-183). Travel South Dakota (186). Bdingman/Dreamstime (188). **Chapter 8: Wind Cave National Park:** Zack Frank/Shutterstock (191). Zack Frank/Shutterstock (199). HTurner/Shutterstock (201). Zack Frank/Shutterstock (205). Courtesy of Travel South Dakota (206). Cheri Alguire/iStockphoto (208-209). **Chapter 9: Cody, Sheridan, and Northern Wyoming:** Jason Koperski (211). Melissamn/Shutterstock (219). DC_Colombia/iStockphoto (222). Courtesy of Buffalo Bill Center of the West (224). Milosk50/Dreamstime (229). Jimsphotos/Dreamstime (231). Clint Farlinger/Alamy Stock Photo (242-243). Anthony Heflin/Shutterstock (252). LaMccray/Shutterstock (256-257). **About Our Writers:** All photos are courtesy of the writers except for the following: Tanya Manus, courtesy of April Lutheran Hill.

Every effort has been made to trace the copyright holders, and we apologize in advance for any accidental errors. We would be happy to apply the corrections in the following edition of this publication.

Notes

Fodor's THE BLACK HILLS OF SOUTH DAKOTA

Publisher: Stephen Horowitz, *General Manager*

Editorial: Douglas Stallings, *Editorial Director;* Jill Fergus, Amanda Sadlowski, *Senior Editors;* Brian Eschrich, Alexis Kelly, *Editors;* Angelique Kennedy-Chavannes, Yoojin Shin, *Associate Editors*

Design: Tina Malaney, *Director of Design and Production;* Jessica Gonzalez, *Senior Designer;* Jaimee Shaye, *Graphic Design Associate*

Production: Jennifer DePrima, *Editorial Production Manager;* Elyse Rozelle, *Senior Production Editor;* Monica White, *Production Editor*

Maps: Rebecca Baer, *Map Director;* Mark Stroud (Moon Street Cartography), *Cartographer*

Photography: Viviane Teles, *Director of Photography;* Namrata Aggarwal, Neha Gupta, Payal Gupta, Ashok Kumar, *Photo Editors;* Jade Rodgers, Shanelle Jacobs, *Photo Production Intern*

Business and Operations: Chuck Hoover, *Chief Marketing Officer;* Robert Ames, *Group General Manager*

Public Relations and Marketing: Joe Ewaskiw, *Senior Director of Communications and Public Relations*

Fodors.com: Jeremy Tarr, *Editorial Director;* Rachael Levitt, *Managing Editor*

Technology: Jon Atkinson, *Executive Director of Technology;* Rudresh Teotia, *Associate Director of Technology;* Alison Lieu, *Project Manager*

Writers: Jim Holland, Tanya Manus, Kelsey Olsen

Editor: Jill Fergus

Production Editor: Elyse Rozelle

2nd Edition

ISBN 978-1-64097-696-2

ISSN 2767-6579

All details in this book are based on information supplied to us at press time. Always confirm information when it matters, especially if you're making a detour to visit a specific place. Fodor's expressly disclaims any liability, loss, or risk, personal or otherwise, that is incurred as a consequence of the use of any of the contents of this book.

SPECIAL SALES
This book is available at special discounts for bulk purchases for sales promotions or premiums. For more information, e-mail SpecialMarkets@fodors.com.

PRINTED IN CANADA

10 9 8 7 6 5 4 3 2 1

About Our Writers

 Jim Holland calls the Black Hills his home. He was raised in ands still lives in Sturgis. He recently retired from a 42-year career as a journalist for newspapers in South Dakota and Nebraska. He also worked as a photographer for the Associated Press State Capitol Bureau in Pierre. For this book Jim worked on the Experience, Travel Smart, Rapid City and the Central Black Hills, Northern Black Hills, Badlands, and Badlands National Park chapters. You can find him on Facebook.

 Tanya Manus is an award-winning journalist who lives in western South Dakota. She is a reporter for the *Rapid City Journal*. Tanya is also a freelance writer whose work appears in such regional magazines as *Black Hills Lifestyle, Empire,* and *Home Ideas,* and in trade publications including *Convention South* magazine. Tanya updated the Southern Black Hills and Wind Cave National Park chapters. Follow her at ⊕ *linkedin.com/in/tanyamanus.*

 Kelsey Olsen is a Canadian-based freelance writer and an avid adventurer. She has hiked many trails in Montana, Wyoming, and other destinations and has summited several mountain peaks. She loves art, running, fine food, and exploring new places. Follow her adventures at ⊕ *www.wanderwoman.ca* or on Instagram @kelseyrolsen. Kelsey updated the Cody, Sheridan, and Northern Wyoming chapter.